Living
Water

Living *Water*

a creative resource for the Liturgy

Complete Resource Book
YEAR B

Susan Sayers

with Father Andrew Moore

Kevin Mayhew

First published in 1999 by
KEVIN MAYHEW LTD
Buxhall
Stowmarket
Suffolk IP14 3BW

0 1 2 3 4 5 6 7 8 9

ISBN 1 84003 405 X
Catalogue No. 1500295

The other titles in the *Living Water* series are

Prayer of the Faithful	ISBN 1 84003 404 1	Cat. No. 1500299
Treasure Seekers	ISBN 1 84003 408 4	Cat. No. 1500296
Pearl Divers	ISBN 1 84003 407 6	Cat. No. 1500297
Gold Panners	ISBN 1 84003 406 8	Cat. No. 1500298

Cover photographs:
Family group – courtesy of Comstock Photo Library
Background – courtesy of Images Colour Library Limited, London
Cover design by Jaquetta Sergeant
Edited by Katherine Laidler
Typesetting by Kevin Whomes
Illustrations by Arthur Baker
Printed in Great Britain

FOREWORD

Living Water is designed to help you make the most of the possibilities of the three-year lectionary, particularly in parishes which are concerned to meet the needs of all ages and stages.

My aim is to spark ideas and start you off. The demands on those leading worship and preparing teaching are enormous, and I hope you will find here materials and suggestions which help take the strain and free you to enjoy the work of enabling people's faith to grow and of deepening their relationship with the living God.

As I was writing, I tried to keep these principles in mind:

- All-age worship needs to be just that, and not children's worship at which adults happen to be present.

- Different age groups need some teaching suited to their particular stage of development, but all benefit from studying the same passages of scripture on the same day. The whole parish is then able to grow together and share insights and discoveries.

- Separate children's ministry for part of the service is there to develop the children's faith now, and also to prepare them for taking a full part in your church's Sunday worship when they are older. Their age-appropriate worship and activities should aim to ease them gradually into full participation with the adults in church, rather than creating a completely separate culture which makes the transition difficult.

- We sell our children and young people short if we only teach them facts about our faith; what they need is to be introduced to a real relationship with God, in which the foundations are laid for life-long habits of prayer, study of the Bible and an openness to God's Spirit.

- We journey into faith, so all our worship and teaching must respect the diversity of stages reached, and the emotional and cultural luggage brought along. Any resource material should therefore be flexible, easily adapted, and accessible at a number of different levels.

- The cerebral and the academic approaches cherished by many in positions of leadership are not the only, nor necessarily the most effective ways to explore and express our faith! Unless we also make use of the senses and the emotions, we shall be shutting doors through which our God could reach the people he loves.

Let us worship the Lord in the beauty of holiness.

SUSAN SAYERS
with Father Andrew Moore

This book is dedicated to my family and friends,
whose encouraging support has been wonderful,
and to all those whose good ideas are included here for others to share.

ACKNOWLEDGEMENTS

The publishers wish to express their gratitude to the following for permission to reproduce their copyright material in this publication:

H. Aschenhoug & Co, Sehestedsgate 3, PO Box 363 Sentrum, N0102, Oslo 1, Norway, for the extract from *The Solitaire Mystery* by Jostein Gaarder.

CopyCare, PO Box 77, Hailsham, E. Sussex, BN27 3EF, for *Spirit of the Living God* (1963 Birdwing Music/Universal Songs), *Purify my heart* (chorus) (1990 Mercy/Vineyard Publishing/Music Services), *Jesus is Lord!* (verse 1) (1982 Springtide/Word Music), and *You are the King of glory* (1978 Springtide). Used by permission.

The Rt. Rev'd Timothy Dudley-Smith, 9 Ashlands, Ford, Salisbury, Wilts., SP4 6DY, for *Lord, for the years* (verse 5).

Iona Community, Pearce Institute, 840 Govan Road, Glasgow, G51 3UU, for *Jesus Christ is waiting* (verse 2). Taken from *Enemy of Apathy* (1988 Wild Goose Publications).

Kingsway's Thankyou Music, PO Box 75, Eastbourne, East Sussex, BN23 6NW, UK, for *5000+ hungry folk* (1985), *Be still for the presence of the Lord* (verse 3) (1986), *I'm accepted, I'm forgiven* (1985), *Meekness and majesty* (verse 2 and chorus) (1986) and *The King is among us* (verse 1) (1981). Used by permission.

Make Way Music, PO Box 263, Croydon, CR9 5AP, UK, for *My Lord, what love is this* (verse 1 and chorus). All rights reserved. International copyright secured. Used by permission.

OCP Publications, 5536 NE Hassalo, Portland, OR 97213, USA, for *Make me a channel of your peace* (dedicated to Mrs Francis Tracy) and *All that I am* by Sebastian Temple, (1967 OCP Publications). All rights reserved. Used by permission.

Oxford University Press, Great Clarendon Street, Oxford, OX2 6DP, for *Over the earth is a mat of green*. Used by permission.

Scripture Union, 207-209 Queensway, Bletchley, Milton Keynes, Buckinghamshire, MK2 2EB, for *Jesus' love is very wonderful*. Used by permission.

Josef Weinberger Ltd, 12-14 Mortimer Street, London, W1N 7RD, for *Lord Jesus Christ* (last verse) and *O Lord, all the world* (verse 4). Used by permission.

All other material contained in this publication is © Kevin Mayhew Ltd.

CONTENTS

Complete programmes for the following special feasts, covering Years A, B and C, may be found in the *Living Water* Complete Resource Book for Year A. (Worksheets for the children and young people are included in the Treasure Seekers, Pearl Divers and Gold Panners books for Year A.)

Mary, Mother of God – 1 January
The Presentation of the Lord (Candlemas) – 2 February
Saint John the Baptist – 24 June
Saints Peter and Paul – 29 June
The Transfiguration of the Lord – 6 August
The Assumption – 15 August
The Triumph of the Holy Cross – 14 September
All Saints – 1 November
Feasts of the Dedication of a Church

HOW TO USE THIS BOOK

PLANNING

You can select from the week's material as much as you find useful for your particular needs on any one week, as all the ideas are independent of one another, although they are all linked to the weekly readings.

All-age worship is not about the entertainment business, nor is it child-centred worship, or 'watered-down' worship. Neither need it be noisy and extra-hassle worship. There are usually many other age groups represented in our churches as well as children and our aim must be to provide for the middle-aged and elderly as well as for the young, for the stranger as well as the regulars.

Since God is in a far better position to know the needs of your congregation than anyone, it is naturally essential to prepare for Sunday worship in prayer. I don't mean asking God to bless what we have already planned, but to spend time discerning God's priorities and listening as he tunes in to the needs of those who will be there. Think about gathering a group of all ages to commit themselves to this each week, either together in church or separately at an agreed time. All the ideas in this book and other resource books are only secondary to this prayerful preparation.

Each week is set out as follows:

Thought for the day

Use this on the weekly handout, or as an initial focus when starting your planning.

Reflection on the readings

There are ideas here for getting your mind going when sermon preparation jams. Or the reflection can be used for individual and group Bible study.

Discussion starters

These are provided for adult group work and could sometimes be used for adults in the sermon slot while toddlers, children and young people follow their own programmes. Small group work within a service is rarely contemplated, but it can be a valuable way of involving everyone, avoiding the automatic pilot syndrome, and bringing the readings to life.

Some churches have parents present during the children's liturgy; consider providing a parents' class within that programme for a short time as a way of reaching those who are wary of actually 'going to church'.

All-stage talk

In my experience the difference in faith stages is more important than the age differences, so these talks aim to present the teaching in ways that people of all ages and stages can relate to. There are so many ordinary experiences which are common to all of us and these can be used and enjoyed without anyone being excluded. Abstract thinking and reading skills are not necessarily common to all, but deep and abstract concepts can often be grasped if explained through concrete images, like three-dimensional parables.

In all these talks I want to encourage adaptation, so that the talks come across as fresh and owned by you, rather than another person's jacket, stiffly worn. Get the ideas, and then enjoy yourself!

All-age ideas

I have suggested particular worship ideas for each week, but here are some more general guidelines to use to get your own ideas flowing.

Dramatised readings

Having read and prayed the readings, I find it helps to imagine myself sitting in the congregation, seeing and hearing the readings creatively expressed. If I imagine I am a child, a young adult, an elderly person and so on, I am more likely to pick up on what *won't* be helpful, and what *will* really make me think.

- Have a narrator to read, and simply mime what is read. Anyone not involved in the action at any one time freezes in his/her last position, like 'statues'.

- Give individuals their words to say. During the narration the characters act their parts and speak their own words.

- Have one or two instruments (guitar and flute, for instance, or organ) to play quietly as a background to the reading.

- Use a few materials as props and costumes. They need not be elaborate, just enough to aid imagination.

- Use live or taped music and depict not only the actions, but also the atmosphere, through mime or dance. Keep it natural, simple and controlled, and do make sure all types and ages are involved.

- There may be times, not just Palm Sunday, for involving the whole congregation in the telling of a story, either by writing their words on the weekly sheet, or by displaying their words, noises and actions at appropriate places in the narration.

Acts of worship

Sometimes something very simple will speak deeply to people. As you prepare try to give the cerebral a break for a while, and listen to what the readings make you feel. Then translate this into some music, communal action (or stillness), which will help people respond to God with their hearts as well as their minds.

Church decoration

The church building speaks. Our churches are visited and admired by many, and it is important that visitors see evidence of the living church of today as well as the beauty of the past. During services the mind and heart can be steered quietly towards the message of the day by means of a particular flower arrangement, exhibition of pictures, display or banner.

If those who arrange the flowers so faithfully, week by week, have access to the *Thought for the day* and the *Reflection on the readings*, they will be able to express these themes in an arrangement.

Prayer of the Faithful

The main aim of those who lead the people's intercessions is to provide a climate for prayer, so that the congregation are not just listening passively, but are actively involved in the work of prayer. I suggest times of silence at each section, rather than pauses, so as to allow for this, and you could have music playing quietly during these times, open prayer or prayer clusters as well as individuals praying fervently together in the stillness of their Father's company.

During this time the young children can be praying through pictures, following a prayer trail, praying in pairs with an adult, or singing some quiet worship songs.

Music

Music, played or sung well, drawn from a range of traditions, always sensitive to the liturgy of the day or season and appropriate to the resources available, can provide a 'landscape for worship' in which people are helped to focus their attention on God, and lift their hearts to him.

Both recorded and live music can be used in worship to help people settle to an inner stillness, give them space for reflection, and provide the environment for spiritual attentiveness. Use whatever gifts your congregation offers; organ music is lovely but need not be used exclusively. Consider a small ensemble of string and wind instruments with piano; a single instrument such as recorder, flute or trumpet; or a selection of percussion instruments such as shakers, triangles and bells. Many churches develop a music group of voices and instruments to provide a different sound for certain services each month. Welcome and involve young people and children, not necessarily as a separate group.

Choose recorded music from a wide range of traditions and styles, bearing in mind the people who are likely to be present. Keep a notebook handy to record titles of suitable pieces that you hear, and ask members of the congregation for their ideas.

There is now such a richness of material available that an attempt at an exhaustive list would be foolish and impractical. Whatever books you use at your parish, make the most of the choice they provide.

Treasure Seekers
3-5 year olds

I have included suggestions for a programme which picks up on some of the important truths of the weekly readings which form a foundation to build on. For the youngest children this teaching can slot into a general play session, where the care, good humour and friendliness of those in charge of the children will continue to help them realise how much God loves them, and enable them to develop trust – the beginning of faith.

Parents are encouraged to pray with their children during the week, using the worksheet prayers.

Pearl Divers
6-10 year olds

When planning for children's work it is advisable to read through the Bible passages prayerfully. You are then in a better position to see how the programme relates to the readings, and also to enable you to supplement and vary the programme as a result of your own insights and the specific needs of your group.

You may prefer to split your Pearl Divers group into two age groups, adapting the suggestions and worksheets accordingly.

The children are encouraged to pray during the week, using the suggestions on their worksheet. These can be built into a collection of prayers and made into a personal prayer book.

A few general ideas about story-telling:

- Tell the story from the viewpoint of a character in the situation. To create the time-machine effect, avoid eye contact as you slowly put on the appropriate cloth or cloak, and then make eye contact as you greet the children in character.

- Have an object with you which leads into the story – a water jug, or a lunch box, for instance.

- Walk the whole group through the story, so that they are physically moving from one place to another; and use all kinds of places, such as broom cupboards, under the stairs, outside under the trees, and so on.

- Collect some carpet tiles – blue and green – so that at story time the children can sit round the edge of this and help you place on the cut-outs for the story.

Gold Panners
11 years and over

Many churches are concerned about this age group feeling too old for children's liturgy but not able to relate to what the adults are doing in church. We have a wonderful resource here which we tend to ignore; many young people are happy to be involved with a music or drama group, and are excellent at preparing role-play material with a wit and challenge that is good for everyone.

As they move towards owned faith, it is vital that the church provides plenty of opportunity for questions and discussion, in an atmosphere which is accepting and willing to listen. Although many will be very valuable on the children's liturgy teams, I am convinced that they need feeding at their own level as well.

The factfiles on each week's worksheet can be collected into a book so that the course becomes a reference manual.

The Gold Panners material provides a transitional course from separate ministry for children to full participation in the service with adults.

RECOMMENDED BIBLES

It is often a good idea to look at a passage in several different versions before deciding which to use for a particular occasion, especially if you plan to involve several people in the reading. As far as children are concerned, separate Bible stories, such as those published by Palm Tree Press and Lion, are a good introduction for the very young. Once children are reading, a very helpful version is the *International Children's Bible* (New Century version) published by Word Publishing. Here children have a translation based on experienced scholarship, using language structure suitable for young readers, with short sentences and appropriate vocabulary. There is a helpful dictionary, and clear maps and pictures are provided.

For young people the New Century version is called *The Youth Bible*, and the layout includes various anecdotes and Bible studies which are inviting and challenging. A vivid version of the New Testament and parts of the Old Testament in contemporary language is Eugene Peterson's *The Message*. This catches the imagination and aids understanding. It is particularly good for reading aloud.

ADVENT

FIRST SUNDAY OF ADVENT

Thought for the day

Be alert and watchful; keep yourselves ready.

Reflection on the readings

Isaiah 63:16-17, 64:1, 3-8
Psalm 79
1 Corinthians 1:3-9
Mark 13:33-37

There is a sense, in the reading from Isaiah, that, but for God's mercy, we are in a hopeless situation. Even as we beg for God's help, recognising that he has proved himself to be the one and only real God, we know that our behaviour has been a rejection of all God is and values. So what point can there be in asking for help from the One we spend so much time ignoring, rejecting and dismissing?

Yet there is hope; the prophet clings on to the fact that we are of God's making. Perhaps his love and affection for us will, even now, move God to show mercy to his wayward creation of humankind. Psalm 79 echoes this pleading for rescue and restoration, undeserved as it is. Both these readings from the Old Testament give us a flavour of the generations of longing and yearning for a saviour, often from the pit of human experience and in a very candid recognition of the human condition.

In contrast, the reading from Paul's letter to the Christians in Corinth is written after the coming of Jesus, the promised Saviour. It is full of the confidence which comes from knowing that, though we cannot save ourselves and our weaknesses are as weak as ever, the life of Jesus in us has power to keep us strong to the end and uphold us in what is right and good. God has indeed acted with an outpouring of unearned and undeserved love and generosity, simply because it is God's nature to act with grace and mercy. Since God is utterly faithful, we can trust him even with the worst of ourselves; his power in us is always going to be sufficient.

Today's Gospel is Jesus speaking to us of real and serious things. Never does Jesus pretend to us; never does he gloss over costs or dangers. Treating us with respect, he warns us so as to prepare us, and we need to take notice of what he is saying. Although he is speaking of great cosmic turmoil, even Jesus is not in possession of the exact times and dates, but he is concerned to pass on to his followers, with considerable urgency, the need to be alert and watchful, so that whatever time the end comes we will be ready and prepared.

Discussion starters

1. Why does Jesus advise us to be alert and watchful?

2. How does the expectation of Jesus coming again with great power and glory affect the way we think and speak and act and spend in the meantime?

All-stage talk

Beforehand prepare a large sun shape from yellow paper and a large cloud from grey paper. First show everyone the sun. If this is showing in the sky during the summer, what can we tell about the best clothes to wear? Now slide the large grey cloud over the sun, so that the sun is hidden. What might it be wise to take with us if we are going out in this weather? We are very good at reading the signs in the weather to help us keep comfortable.

We read lots of other signs as well. At traffic lights, or at the top of scary water chutes, we know that red means stop and green means go. We know by the special music when *The Simpsons* or the news is about to come on. We know by the smell of cooking that dinner is nearly ready.

In today's Gospel, Jesus tells us to keep alert and check the signs which will tell us when he is going to come to earth again. This time he won't be coming as a tiny baby, but full of God's glory and in great power, riding on the clouds of heaven. It will be such an amazing event that it will rock the whole cosmos – the whole of nature will be shaken. Jesus told his disciples that the sun will be darkened, and the moon will lose its light, and stars will fall from heaven. This is something that every being will notice, both those who are alive on earth at the time and those who will have already died. Jesus tells us that even he doesn't know exactly when it will happen, but it certainly will take place, and we will all need to be ready for it, whether we are still alive here or already dead.

So how can we make sure we are ready? How can we read the signs?

The best way of making sure we stay ready is by keeping our eyes open – our spiritual eyes. That means keeping in touch with God on a daily basis. We need to get into a habit of praying, not just once a week on Sundays, but all times of every day. A good way of remembering, and getting ourselves into such a habit, is to get in touch with God every time we check our watches, or every time we put something to eat in our mouths.

Sensible sailors or hill walkers will check the weather forecast every time before they set out, so they are prepared. We need to check with God his will and guidance every time before we make decisions or spend money. Then our faith will be living and active, growing as we grow, and keeping us alert and available, so that whenever Jesus comes again in glory we shall be ready to welcome him with joy.

All-age ideas

- This response can be used at the Penitential Rite:
  Lord, we are sorry for the days we hardly speak with you at all.
  Lord have mercy.
  Lord have mercy.
  Lord, we are sorry for the times we refuse to follow in your way.
  Christ have mercy.
  Christ have mercy.
  Lord, we are sorry for the opportunities we miss for serving you in others.
  Lord have mercy.
  Lord have mercy.

- Direct people to look at the cross as a sign of God's generous, self-giving love, and think about a spiritual 'new year' resolution at this beginning of the Church's year. This can be done either in a time of silence or accompanied by quiet music.

Prayer of the Faithful

Celebrant
As we begin a new year in the life of the Church, we pray to the God who made us.

Reader
We come to the Lord just as we are
and ask that his kingdom may come
to be within us and in this place.
We pray for an increase in faith
that we may become the lights in darkness
that we are called to be.

Silence

O God, keep us awake to you:
and alive to your call.

The signs in our world of hate, distrust and greed
are shown to us clearly every day.
May our eyes see the signs of hope and victory;
the opportunities for loving service,
for encouragement, reassurance and thanksgiving.

Silence

O God, keep us awake to you:
and alive to your call.

May the parenting and befriending
in all our relationships be blessed,
and may our love for one another be increased.
We pray for the humility
to accept guidance and warnings, lovingly given,
and the courage to uphold one another in the faith.

Silence

O God, keep us awake to you:
and alive to your call.

In love, we bring to our prayers
those who are weary
with ongoing pain and weakness,
those who are frail with age
and all who are vulnerable;
May the Lord pour his living strength into their lives
and protect them from all that is harmful.

Silence

O God, keep us awake to you:
and alive to your call.

We pray for all who have come
to the end of their earthly life,
and for those whose lives
feel empty without them.
May the Lord give comfort to the bereaved,
and everlasting peace to all who rest in his love.

Silence

O God, keep us awake to you:
and alive to your call.

With Mary, the Mother of Jesus,
let us pray:
Hail, Mary . . .

In silence, now,
we bring to God our Father
any needs and concerns
known to us personally.

Silence

Celebrant
Lord, our Creator,
we thank you for the wonder of our being,
and ask you to hear our prayers,
through Jesus Christ.
Amen.

TREASURE SEEKERS

Aim: To think about getting ready for Jesus.

Starter

Have three different types of music available, such as a drum, some bells, and a children's praise tape. Whenever they hear the drum they stomp about, whenever they hear the bells they run about silently on tiptoes, and whenever they hear the praise tape they dance. They will need to be ready and alert.

Teaching

Explain that today we are starting Advent which is 'getting ready' time because it means 'coming'. What's coming? Christmas! Who came to us as a baby at Christmas? Jesus!

Tell the children this rescue story.

Jake was a fisherman. When the tide came in he set off from the slipway and started the engine on his boat. Then he chugged out between the green and red buoys which showed him where the deep water was, until he reached the open sea. And there he fished and ate his sandwiches and drank his hot tea from a flask and fished some more. Jake enjoyed fishing. So did his dog, Sprat.

One day, when Jake was just halfway down his mug of hot tea, the sky got darker and darker and the wind blew stronger and stronger. The boat rocked up and down, up and down, this way and that way, and the hot tea slopped over the side of the mug, even though Jake had drunk it halfway down. Sprat made growling noises at the wind, but the wind wasn't frightened. It blew even harder.

'Dear me,' said Jake. 'This isn't a good time to be sitting out here fishing. We'd better make for home.'

He tried to start the engine but the engine just went splutter, splutter, clunk. Sprat barked at it with one ear up, to encourage it, but the engine could only go splutter, splutter, clunk.

'This is serious, Sprat,' said Jake. 'We can't stay here and we can't go home. What we need is someone to come and rescue us.'

They waited. Jake ate his other sandwich (it was tuna and salad) and Sprat had a dog biscuit, noisily. The boat went up and down, and the wind blew and blew.

Suddenly Sprat pricked up both ears and his nose twitched. He could hear something which made his tail wag. That made Jake look up. A smile began to spread over his face and he stood up, waving both arms.

'It's Bert! Hello, Bert! Ahoy there, Bert!' yelled Jake across the wind and waves.

Bert was a fisherman too, and here he was, chugging over in his boat towards Jake and Sprat. 'Bert to the rescue,' he grinned.

It wasn't long before Jake had thrown a rope across from his boat to Bert's and Bert had made it fast. Jake hauled up the anchor and there they were, being towed home by Bert. It felt so good to be rescued!

When they got back to the slipway Sprat gave Bert one of his half-chewed biscuits to say thank you, and Jake treated Bert to a drink at the pub.

'We couldn't have made it home on our own, you know,' said Jake into his pint of bitter.

Bert nodded. 'Good job I came to the rescue then,' he said.

Sprat thumped his tail on the pub carpet, happy to be a rescued dog.

Talk with the children about Jake and Sprat waiting to be rescued. Long before Jesus came, the people knew they were in a mess and needed God to come to the rescue. For years and years they waited and hoped for rescue, and then Jesus came into the world. Jesus was the rescuer!

Praying

Thank you, Jesus, Son of God,
you have come to save us all.
Thank you, Jesus, Son of God,
you came because you love us all. Amen.

Activities

During Advent the children will be making a Christmas landscape, adding to it week by week, so that it is ready to take home after the Fourth Sunday of Advent. This is how it might look eventually.

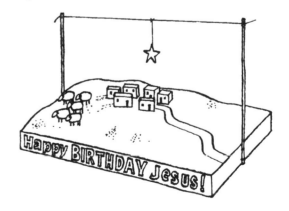

This week the children are forming the base from crumpled paper on a shoe box lid which is covered with green paper (or painted green). There are instructions on the worksheet, together with pictures of situations in which they can be the rescuer, drawing in the badly needed help.

PEARL DIVERS

Aim: To know that Jesus will be coming back in glory.

Starter

Get ready to . . . Each time the children crouch in the 'get ready' position, and when you show a symbol of a particular activity, they have to mime it until the whistle blows for the 'stop and get ready' stage again. (Possible items might be a football, tennis racket, swimwear and goggles, a horse shoe and a paintbox.)

Teaching

Prepare the signs and symbols below to be placed on the floor during the teaching.

Explain that Advent means 'coming' and the person we're waiting and preparing for is Jesus. Now place down the '1st' rosette as you tell them about the first time Jesus came to earth. (Involve them and use what they already know.) As you discuss that first coming, place down the picture of the Nativity.

As you display the '2nd' rosette, tell them that the manger at Bethlehem wasn't the only time for Jesus to come to our earth. We are told in the Bible, by the prophets and by Jesus himself, that he will be coming again one day. Place down the 'When?', 'Where?', and 'How?' cards, and read excerpts from today's Gospel to find out the clues we have been given. Go over these in discussion, displaying the big question mark as you draw the clues together and establish that there is still lots we don't know (and even Jesus didn't know) about exact times and dates. What we do know is that it will happen, and we need to make sure we keep ourselves alert, so that we'll be ready for Jesus when he comes in glory.

Praying

Jesus, get us ready to meet you
when you come again in glory,
so that we can welcome you
when we see you face to face.

Activities

During Advent the children will be making a four-stage pop-up model which can eventually be a table centrepiece or a crib at home. Instructions and outlines are given for stage one on this week's worksheet. You may like them to mount the sheet on thin card to make it all stronger. They will need scissors that really work, and colouring materials. Try paints with thin brushes for a change. For younger children you could enlarge the sheets during Advent to A3.

GOLD PANNERS

Aim: To sense the longing for the Messiah and the need for rescue.

Starter

Try this short sketch about 'waiting'.

Mark What's up?

Dawn Uh? Oh, nothing.

Mark But there's a Fuse bar here that you haven't eaten.

Dawn Uh? Oh, so there is.

Mark And I haven't had any e-mail from you for over a week.

Dawn Uh? Oh . . . no, I haven't written any.

Mark Well, what's the matter for heaven's sake?

Dawn *(sighs)* Well, it's no use.

Mark What's no use?

Dawn Everything's no use. Only one person has the key to my freedom and peace of mind, and I'm trapped in this prison.

Mark Well, ask the person with the key to open it!

Dawn That's just it – I can't.

Mark Why ever not?

Dawn Because I've completely ignored the person with the key for ages, and before that I messed up their life big time. So there's no reason in the world why they should even be friendly ever again – let alone get me out of my mess now.

Mark You could ask them.

Dawn No, it's too late for that. I'll just have to recognise that I've blown it for ever.

Mark Well, you could still ask. Maybe he's super-human in the mercy line. Maybe he still cares for you enough to come and rescue you.

Dawn Do you think so?

Mark No harm in trying, is there? After all, he did create you.

Dawn Yes, that's true. OK. Let's ask him.

Both O Lord God, I know you've got no reason to hear this prayer after the way we've treated you, but, well, you did make us, remember? Could you find it in your heart to come and rescue us? Sort us out? We need that so badly, and we can't do it ourselves . . .

(A paper dart comes flying in, and they read what is written on it)

Both 'For God so loved the world that he gave his one and only Son, that whoever believes in him shall not perish but have eternal life.'

(They look at one another in excitement, and throw the paper dart up into the air as both shout: YES!)

Teaching

Start by reading the passage from Isaiah, drawing out the way it moves in mood from 'If only' through 'But heck!' to 'Still, maybe?' Then look at 1 Corinthians 1. What has happened in the meantime to make for the hope and confidence expressed in Paul's letter? It is the life, death and resurrection of Jesus the Christ which has turned everything around.

Remind them that not only did Jesus come as our Saviour two thousand years ago; he is also going to come again, but this time in the full glory of God. Read the Gospel from Mark 13 and pick up on the clues and the unknowns, and the need to be watchful and ready.

Praying

O Lord, you are our Father.
We are the clay, you are the potter;
we are all the work of your hand.
Oh look upon us as we pray,
for we are all your people
in need of your mercy.

Activities

On the worksheet there is a bus queue of prophets with Bible references in their speech bubbles, so that the growing sense of need and longing for rescue is explored. There is also a selection of disaster pictures which link with the human condition spiritually and our need for rescue.

SECOND SUNDAY OF ADVENT

Thought for the day

John the Baptist prepares the way for the coming of the Messiah by helping the people to realign their lives.

Reflection on the readings

Isaiah 40:1-5, 9-11
Psalm 84
2 Peter 3:8-14
Mark 1:1-8

Mark's Gospel bursts straight in with the dynamic claim that we are hearing about nothing less than the Messiah, the Son of God, entering into the realm of ordinary human life. Just as the prophet Isaiah had foretold, this event would require some drastic preparation work, and here is John (we are given no other introductory details about him) suddenly fulfilling the old prophecy and urging people to get their lives and attitudes sorted out and cleaned up. He is using the effective symbolism of baptismal washing as a sign of washed lives.

If you are willing to step into the river, publicly, confess your sins and be pushed down under the water as a sign of your repentance, you are quite likely to mean what you say, and emerge from the experience full of new, fresh enthusiasm for walking God's way.

This is exactly the thorough kind of repentance we all need regularly. Perhaps we should remember this every time we have a shower or a bath – and experience daily the fresh start and openness provided by God's forgiveness of acknowledged and confessed sin.

Along with John's call to thorough repentance and baptismal washing was the message he preached, directing his followers to look for the powerful person of great honour who would be coming shortly and whose baptism would be not with water but the Holy Spirit of God. Just imagine standing dripping and cleansed by the Jordan as you hear about someone who will drench and immerse you in the holiness of the Spirit of God. It must have triggered in many the deep longing and expectant thirsting for God which allows lives to be shaken, hearts to be softened and the kingdom to come.

The same is true now. It is as an expectant people, thirsty for God and longing for a total immersing in his life, that we prepare during the season of Advent for the festival of Christmas. The extent to which we respond to John's call across the centuries will determine how open and receptive we are to welcoming Jesus and allowing him into our lives. The life which Peter describes – of harmony, repaying even evil with blessing, and doing good regardless of the consequences – is a direct result of living immersed in the Holy Spirit of God.

Discussion starters

1. Why is a repentant people more likely to be able to receive Jesus the Christ?

2. Forget, for a moment, the traditions of our Church, and imagine yourself on the shore of the river Jordan, having been totally immersed in cold water. In the light of this experience, how would you imagine being 'baptised with the Holy Spirit'? How did (and does) Jesus do this?

All-stage talk

Bring in a washing-up bowl with some water in it and a mop. Produce a mug or two which you were using earlier and explain how these are dirty and need washing up. You hope the mugs won't be too embarrassed by being shown dirty like this in full view of everyone. They are very particular mugs and prefer people to see them clean.

We are often a bit like that. We like people to see us when we're proud of what we are like and what we are doing. We don't like it much if someone catches us screaming at the dog, telling or living a lie, or being lazy or greedy. Usually we try to cover up the things we do which we aren't proud of. Perhaps we'll make out it's someone else's fault that we're late or grumpy; perhaps we'll think up good excuses for wrong behaviour. We get so good at this that often we believe our cover-up stories and stop noticing that instead of pretending we're clean-living Christians, what we actually need is a good, thorough wash.

The people who came to hear John the Baptist were just like us. There were things in their lives which were wrong and selfish, and they had become used to making excuses for themselves till they were quite content to live with their bad habits and carefully groomed images. But John got them thinking. And as they thought about their real selves and what they were really like, they suddenly started to realise that they were like dirty mugs which needed a good wash. If they were washed clean, they could be free from all the pretending and cover-ups, and just be themselves again.

John told them it was quite easy to do – they just needed to name all those big and little sins aloud to God without hiding them, and choose to turn their back on that way of living. He said he would dip them right under the water in the river as a sign that their lives were being washed clean.

(Ask for a volunteer to come and wash up the mugs.) For some of them it must have felt very humiliating to do that in public, especially if they had groomed their images so well that they had kept their sins well hidden. And it must have been such a relief for others, who had worried about their sin for years and years, to have it washed away at last.

When they were all washed clean, like our mugs, without any need to hide from God or each other any more, John told them something very important. This washing was just the beginning; soon someone was coming who would be able to plunge them deep into the depths of the Holy Spirit, so they would be completely surrounded and filled with the loving God. And the person who would make that possible was coming very soon.

During Advent we can get ourselves ready for Jesus' coming to us, just as they did. We can look at what we are really like; how we really behave with others; recognise the parts of us that are real enough but we hope others won't see. Anything we find which needs washing away we need to confess to God, tell him how sorry we are about it, and the way we have made excuses, and choose to turn our backs on that way of living. You can talk to God on your own or go to your priest for the Sacrament of Reconciliation, especially if you feel you need some help with changing. We all need to come to God regularly for thorough washing, and he is the only one who can make us clean and free.

All-age ideas

• Use the Rite of Blessing and Sprinkling Holy Water in place of the Penitential Rite.

• Use today as an opportunity for everyone to renew their baptismal promises.

Prayer of the Faithful

Celebrant
As we gather expectantly in God's presence,
let us pray.

Reader
We pray that God's cleansing and liberating power
may give us the courage and perception
to see ourselves as we really are,
and lead us to true repentance.

Silence

Come, O come, Emmanuel:
come and live in us.

We pray for the world's leaders and all in authority,
that they may lead and govern wisely and honestly,
without corruption and for the common good.

Silence

Come, O come, Emmanuel:
come and live in us.

We pray that every family
may be surrounded and upheld
by God's loving presence,
that conflicts may be healed and needs provided for,
and every act of kindness blessed.

Silence

Come, O come, Emmanuel:
come and live in us.

We pray for reassurance and healing,
hope and patience
for all who are suffering in any way;
for freedom to all imprisoned by hate or guilt,
and for a change of heart to all who need to forgive.

Silence

Come, O come, Emmanuel:
come and live in us.

We pray for those
who have completed their time on earth.
May they know the freedom, joy and fullness
of unending life in heaven.

Silence

Come, O come, Emmanuel:
come and live in us.

We make our prayer with Mary,
who prepared a way for the Lord:
Hail, Mary . . .

As God's stillness fills our hearts,
we make our private petitions and thanksgivings.

Silence

Celebrant
In great thankfulness
for your compassionate love,
dear Father,
we ask you to accept our prayers,
through Jesus Christ our Lord.
Amen.

TREASURE SEEKERS

Aim: To continue getting ready for Jesus at the Christmas festival.

Starter

Involve the children in preparing a road for the game. Give each of them a longish piece of string, and help them add their piece to make a continuous winding road on the floor. Now give them a second piece of string to mark out the other side of the road in the same way. When the road is ready, choose different children to walk, hop or skip along the road.

Teaching

Point out how we all had to get the road ready before we could use it for walking, hopping and skipping along. Some of them might have seen a road being made or mended, and you can talk with them about how this has to be done very carefully so that everyone can drive and cycle on it safely.

Getting ourselves ready for Jesus is a bit like building a good road. If there are bumpy, rocky places of grumpiness and bad temper, we can start clearing them away. If there are holes in our road where we are unkind, or unfair to other people, we can fill those places up with God's love. (If you draw all this on a blackboard, then you can rub out and re-draw as you speak.)

In Advent, when we are opening the windows in our Advent calendars every day, we can get our own roads sorted out so that Jesus can walk straight into our lives without falling down holes made of our unkindness, or tripping over rocks made of our grumpiness and bad temper.

Put all kinds of boxes and 'holes' on their string road and let everyone help to clear it again. As they are clearing, comment on what they are doing: for example, 'Here's a great lump of selfishness – let's get rid of that; oh, and here's a few clumps of wanting our own way all the time – let's clear those away, too, so the road is better to walk along. That's much better, now; well done!'

Praying

Dear Jesus,
I am learning how to be kind and helpful,
I am building a good strong road of love.
Help me to build my good strong road
of kindness, goodness and truth.
Amen.

Activities

Today we are making the next stage of our Christmas landscape. We are adding the town of Bethlehem, and the road. Instructions are on the sheet, together with a picture of road building to colour.

PEARL DIVERS

Aim: To hear about John the Baptist and his teaching about watching closely.

Starter

What's different? Get into pairs. Take it in turns for one to hide their eyes while the other changes something about the way they are standing or what they are wearing. See if the difference is recognised, then swap roles. Ideas for differences: cross arms in different way, hair tucked behind other ear, shoelace undone/done up, ring on different finger.

Teaching

Sometimes we don't notice things that we are used to seeing. Today we are going to look at someone who got people noticing things they had stopped looking at. (Have two people in conversation for this.)

What was his name?

His name was John. One day no one had heard of him and the next, there he was out in the wild desert outside Jerusalem, drawing huge crowds of people because of what he was saying. They felt he was telling them what they knew they needed to hear. They didn't come because what he said was easy – in fact, it was very challenging – but he made them feel they wanted to go for it with everything they had.

Go for what?

Sorting their lives out. They started to look closely at how they were really thinking and behaving – John helped them notice their own bad habits and the unloving, discontented way they were living. They suddenly wanted to put those things right. John told them it was like road-building.

Road-building?

Yes. He said they needed to build their lives like a good road ready for God to come to them, a road that was straight and true with no mountains of greed or empty pits of cruelty and grumbling. And they needed to start building it straightaway.

Why?

Because John said it wouldn't be very long before God's Messiah was coming to live among them, and they all wanted to be ready for that.

So what did they do about their road-building?

Well, like I said, they had a good look at themselves, saw what needed to be changed, told God about it and then John washed them.

Washed them?

Yes, they waded into the local Jordan river, and when they confessed their sins John dipped them right under the water as a sign that their lives were being washed clean.

That's a good idea. You'd really feel you were making a fresh clean start if you were dipped right under water in a flowing river. Now they would feel they'd done what they could to be ready for the Messiah.

Yes, that's right. And we can do the same, you know.

We can?

Oh, yes. If we take a look at how we speak to people, and what we do for them, and what we don't do for them, we'll soon see which bits of our road need changing. Then we can tell God we've noticed them and are sorry.

What will God do?

He'll forgive us and give us a fresh start.

Perhaps we could do that in the bath or shower?

Good idea.

Praying

Loving God, open my eyes to see
what needs changing and putting right
in my thinking, speaking and doing,
because I want to turn away from sin
and turn towards you.
Amen.

Activities

The children will be making Stage Two of the Christmas pop-up model. There are instructions and outlines for this on the sheet. You may like them to mount it all on thin card for extra strength. As with all the Advent sheets, younger children in PEARL DIVERS may find it easier if it is enlarged to A3 size.

GOLD PANNERS

Aim: To look at Mark's treatment of John the Baptist's ministry, and the fulfilment of Isaiah's prophecy.

Starter

Have one of those frog toys with a suction pad which you press down and wait until it suddenly hops. (Or a rubber thimble for separating sheets of paper works just as well.) Take it in turns to start the thing off and everyone shouts, 'Now!' when they think it will pop up or hop.

Teaching

Read the beginning of Mark's Gospel, noticing how we are suddenly in the centre of all the action, and John seems to appear as if from nowhere. (Compare this with the first reference we get to the prophet Elijah's sudden appearance in 1 Kings 17:1.) Mark starts his account of Jesus with his public ministry, rather than the birth events, and John the Baptist is clearly the 'Elijah', the voice in the desert which the prophets had foretold.

Have a look at that prophecy in Isaiah 40, and look at how John was fulfilling it. See how the prophet is foretelling both the coming of Jesus in his ministry on earth and his second coming in all God's glory at the end of time.

Go back to the Gospel reading and discuss whether John seems to be calling individuals to repentance or the nation as a whole (or both). Why would baptism with water be a helpful symbol of what the people were doing spiritually?

Praying

Show us your unfailing love, O Lord,
and grant us your salvation.
I will listen to what God the Lord will say:
he promises peace to his people, his saints –
but let them not return to folly.
Surely his salvation is near those who fear him,
that his glory may dwell in our land.

(From Psalm 84)

Activities

There are various 'watery' experiences on the sheet to help pick up on the symbolism of water, and they are encouraged to look at different areas of their life which may need sorting out or cleaning up.

THIRD SUNDAY OF ADVENT

Thought for the day

In Jesus, God will be fulfilling the Messianic prophecies about the promised Saviour.

Reflection on the readings

Isaiah 61:1-2, 10-11
Magnificat: Luke 1:46-50, 53-54
1 Thessalonians 5:16-24
John 1:6-8, 19-28

Advent almost engulfs us with its spirit of urgent preparation. Everyone writes lists and tries to organise food, apt presents and thematic decorations; the store cupboard fills with things no one is allowed to touch yet, and tops of wardrobes become hiding places for bulky secrets. The Church's season of Advent is a kind of spiritual equivalent of all this, not just because we are rehearsing Christmas carols and Nativity plays, but because we are standing alongside the people of Israel in their period of waiting and preparation for the coming of the promised Saviour. In these four weeks we can sense something of their generations of waiting and longing.

It is the Messiah's Advent that we journey through at this time of year, and here too we find checklists and plans, secrets and mysteries, half-seen puzzles, and truths which have yet to be unpacked and savoured. The Isaiah reading for today is a case in point. We are given a kind of checklist of pointers to look out for in the promised Saviour, which will ensure that we recognise him when he comes. It is a wonderful checklist, full of hope and freshness, the overturning of negatives and the victory of good over evil.

Hearing the Magnificat (the Responsorial Psalm for today) from the standpoint of the Isaiah passage is like having a peep into the wrapped future, and sensing that on Christmas morning we shall not be disappointed. And, of course, the Incarnation of Christmas morning is indeed the unwrapping of that promised secret. Even as John the Baptist was teaching by the river Jordan, he knew that the Christ was already there among them, though still hidden, since his public ministry had not yet begun. It would not be long before those qualities on Isaiah's list could be checked out and validated by the people, provided they had eyes open to recognise in Jesus all that the prophets had foretold.

But at the moment we are still in the waiting place, and all that is in the future. For now, we sense the expectancy of the faithful people of Israel, and also recognise our own place of waiting for that final coming of total accomplishment at the end of time. We live with our hopes and our questions, our puzzles and our trust in the faithful God. We know that in God's way all the checklists of qualities and characteristics both for the first and the second coming will hold good.

John the Baptist finds the authorities trying to do a full story on him, mistakenly homing in on the messenger instead of the coming King. He describes himself, in the words of the prophet, as simply a voice – not to be curiously interviewed, but heard, with the heart as well as the ears. We can make this Advent such a time of listening to the real message, rather than being sidetracked by all the less important things. The reading from Thessalonians gives us sound, practical ideas for this.

Discussion starters

1. Why did the authorities want to check out John's identity and authority?

2. Examine the advice of the Thessalonians passage and look at how our lives, individually and as the Church, measure up.

All-stage talk

Talk about the buying of Christmas presents and take out a list you've been making of all the Christmas jobs and how far you have all got with them. At this stage of Advent some people have probably got all their presents bought, wrapped and hidden, while others have hardly begun.

Before Jesus had been born, the people of Israel had been waiting ages and ages for God's Saviour to come and save them. Every young woman would pray that her baby might be the Messiah, just as her grandmother had done before her. Through all the terrible crises of national life, the prophets had kept alive in the people of Israel their calling to be God's people. One day, the prophets all said, God would actually come in some way to be really 'with them' personally. They were to keep themselves ready and watchful for when that happened.

(Take out another 'list', and unroll it. On this are written the checkpoints from today's Isaiah reading.) The prophets even gave them a kind of 'Christmas' or 'Messiah' list of things to look out for in God's chosen one, the Messiah, or Christ. They would be able to recognise the Messiah when he came because these are the things he would do:

- tell the good news to the poor
- comfort the broken-hearted
- set free those feeling imprisoned
- announce the time when God would show his merciful judgement
- give people clothes of praise and joy to replace their sadness
- be fair to everyone
- make what is right grow strong
- put wrong things right

Now who do we know who did come and do those things, and is still doing them now? Jesus! And when was it that Jesus came into our world? At Christmas. So all their waiting and hoping was worth it. And anyone who wasn't sure could check with the Christmas (or 'Messiahmas') list and see for themselves. And so can we.

All-age ideas

- Have the Isaiah passage read with a group of voices, people of different voice tones speaking different sections. Work the best way out for your group by gathering to read through the whole passage and talking about it first, so their understanding will be reflected in the reading. Try out suggestions and be prepared to adjust them if they don't sound right. Each person can mark their parts on a copy of the passage.

- Mime the Gospel reading, but have the conversation section learnt so the actors say their own words.

Prayer of the Faithful

Celebrant
Let us pray now to the living God,
who always keeps his promises,
and who knows us so well.

Reader
May the Church always be faithful
in telling the good news, comforting the desolate,
actively loving justice
and drawing many to freedom
through the joy of the Father's loving forgiveness.

Silence

Keep us faithful, Lord:
to your calling.

As the Church, we pray for the world,
that there may be integrity in leadership;
mercy and justice for rich and poor,
strong and weak;
that there may be peace among nations
and respect for all.

Silence

Keep us faithful, Lord:
to your calling.

As the family of believers, we pray
for those around us now and their needs;
and for the families we represent, and their needs.
May the love of Christ be shown in what we do
and how we speak and how we spend.

Silence

Keep us faithful, Lord:
to your calling.

In compassion we call to mind
all who are locked in physical or emotional pain,
all who are weighed down with worry,
guilt or despair.
Restore and refresh them, comfort and free them.

Silence

Keep us faithful, Lord:
to your calling.

As resurrection people,
we commend to the Father's love
those who have died to this earthly life.
May they, and we in our turn, experience for ever
the joy of eternal life.

Silence

Keep us faithful, Lord:
to your calling.

With Mary,
who mothered the Son of God,
we make our prayer:
Hail, Mary . . .

In the knowledge
that God wants our spiritual happiness,
let us pray our private petitions.

Silence

Celebrant
As part of your generous creation, Father,
we give you thanks and praise,
and ask you to accept these prayers,
through Christ Jesus.
Amen.

TREASURE SEEKERS

Aim: To get ready for Christmas, and for Jesus.

Starter

Play some taped music which the children dance
around to. Whenever the music stops, call out
something for them to mime getting ready for, such
as eating dinner (wash hands), driving a car (turn
the ignition key), climbing a mountain (pull on
boots), being a film star (put on make-up), and
having a swim (changing clothes).

Teaching

Tell the children this story about waiting for someone and recognising them when they arrive.

One day the postman delivered a letter to the
house where Hari and Meera lived. The envelope
was pale blue, and it had a red and blue pattern all
round the edge. (Hold an airmail letter as you
speak.) 'That's an airmail letter,' said Hari. 'It's
come from far away.'

Mum opened the letter, and read it. 'Who's it
from?' asked Meera.

'It's from my brother, your uncle,' said Mum,
'and he says that he's coming to visit us. He'll be
flying into Heathrow airport next month.' She was
smiling and very excited.

Hari and Meera were excited too. They had never
met Uncle Satich, but they had heard lots of stories
about him. He sounded good fun and very kind. He
never forgot their birthdays or Christmas, either.

A month seemed ages to wait for him to come.
Meera kept counting the days left on the calendar
until Uncle Satich was due to arrive. They all
helped get Hari's room changed round, as Uncle
Satich would be sleeping there as well for a few
weeks. Dad borrowed a put-you-up bed from the
next-door neighbours, and carried it up to the bedroom. The children picked some flowers and put
them on the bookcase next to the bed. They did
want him to feel welcome and happy in their home.

At last it was time to drive to the airport to meet
him. The airport was full of people. 'How shall we

know which is Uncle Satich?' asked Hari. 'We might miss him,' said Meera.

'Well, I shall know him, because he's my brother!' laughed Mum. 'But you will know him because he will look just like the photo he sent us at Christmas, and if I know Satich, he'll be smiling. Oh, and he'll probably tell me how much like Mother I look!'

They all stood around waiting for the passengers to come in from India. Everyone was pushing trolleys with luggage on, or carrying bags and parcels. There were families with tired children, old men, young men, old women and young women. The children looked at each person to see if they were anything like the Christmas photo, and if they were smiling.

Suddenly, there was a man coming with a big smile on his face, looking quite like that photo, but wearing different clothes. He came straight up to Mum and Dad, dumped his cases down and gave them a big hug. 'Oh, you look so much like Mother!' he said to Mum. So then Hari and Meera knew for certain that this was Uncle Satich.

Uncle Satich had stopped hugging Mum and Dad, and now he turned to the children, and knelt down so he was the same height as them. 'Hello, you must be Hari, and you Meera! I am very, very happy to meet you both!' he said. And they all hugged.

Talk about how the children were looking forward to their uncle coming even though they had never met him in person, because they knew their mum and dad loved him, and that he was kind. Talk about how they knew which person was their uncle. They knew what to look out for.

Before the first Christmas no one knew exactly what Jesus would be like, but they were looking forward to him coming because they knew he would be loving and fair and good. They knew they would be able to recognise him because he would be comforting those who were sad and setting people free to live good lives.

Praying

Lord Jesus,
as we get ready for Christmas
help us to know who you are
so we can welcome you
into our lives.
Amen.

Activities

The Christmas landscape continues. Today we are making the star, and fixing it above the house they choose in Bethlehem. Instructions and outlines are on the sheet. The children will need glue and glitter, two lengths of stick and some cotton each.

PEARL DIVERS

Aim: To know that the prophets foretold the coming of Jesus, and Jesus fulfilled these prophecies.

Starter

The next object is . . . Have a number of objects hidden from view. Give out a short description of an item, such as: 'This object is black and white and re(a)d.' The children raise their hand when the item matching the description is shown. Show several other items before showing a newspaper, which fits the description, even though it may be slightly different from what was expected. Here are some other ideas:

- The next object has a face all the time (a clock)
- The next object is for the heads of li(e)rs (a pillow)
- The next object is to play with when you get round to it (a ball)
- The next object is put up at the down times (an umbrella)

Teaching

Talk about how we knew what to look out for in that game, so we could recognise the object when it appeared. And sometimes we understood the description better after we'd seen the object.

Today we are looking at some of the things the prophets said to describe the coming Messiah, long before Jesus was born. When Jesus did appear on earth, those things came true, and people found they understood them better than they had before.

On a large sheet of coloured paper, draw an outline of Jesus, his arms stretched out in welcome, based on the picture below, and lay this on the floor. On top of it have a sheet of the same size but different colour, which has been cut into sections. On each section have written out the different sections of Isaiah's prophecy. Across all these lay a title on white paper which says 'Messiah' on one side and 'Christ' on the reverse. It should all look like the pictures opposite.

Explain how the prophets were sent by God to prepare the people for the coming of his chosen one. The Hebrew word for this anointed, chosen person was 'Messiah'. The Greek word was 'Christ'. (Turn the title over and back as you say this. Leave it on the Messiah side.) As the Old Testament is written in Hebrew, we'll stick with their word, Messiah, while they are waiting for him to come.

In order to help the people get ready, God spoke through the prophets to tell them what the Messiah would be like when he came. That way they could recognise him, and be ready for him. Let's look at

Tell the good news to the poor	Comfort the broken-hearted
Set free those feeling imprisoned	Announce the time when God would show his merciful judgement
Give people clothes of praise and joy to replace their sadness	Be fair to everyone
Make what is right grow strong	Put wrong things right

MESSIAH

some of the things they said about this Messiah. Lay the Messiah title at the side, and look at the sections, one by one, with all the readers reading them out. In turn take each section off and lay them all around the emerging picture. Gradually we can see that all these descriptions fit the Jesus we know from the Gospels. And as the New Testament was written in Greek, we'll use the Greek word for him: the Christ. (Reverse the title.)

Praying

Jesus, Jesus, we have come to see
that you must really be
the Son of God our Father.
We've been with you and we all agree
that only in your service
can the world be truly free!

Activities

On the sheet the preparations continue for the third stage of the Christmas pop-up model. Instructions and outlines are provided, but you may wish to strengthen the models with thin card. Also, if time permits, look at how the Bible is split into Old and New Testaments, and look at the names of the prophets, flicking through the Old Testament to find the books of Isaiah, Jeremiah and the others.

GOLD PANNERS

Aim: To see how the coming of the Messiah was God visiting and redeeming his people.

Starter

Each person in turn adds a word to a gradually developing sentence, so that some kind of story starts to take shape, which no one person has planned.

Teaching

All through the history of the people of Israel words were spoken by the prophets to reveal a bit more about what God meant and what God was like. Gradually the people started to grasp that one day God would be among his people to save them, in a new and very personal way. They started to think in terms of a Messiah, one anointed by God, who would come to them.

Look at the reading from Isaiah 61 to discover what the Messiah would be like. Pick out the characteristics in discussion and make a note of them. Then look at today's Gospel, stopping at verse 22, where they ask, 'Who are you?' Why might they have thought that John was the Messiah or Elijah? (You can refer to the notes made.) Then read on to find out how John describes himself. Link this with the passage from Isaiah which you've just read. Why did John talk about the Messiah being already among them, though not yet known? (Think back to when John and Jesus had been born.)

Read through the Magnificat, which takes the place of the Psalm today, to see Mary praising God for what an amazing thing he has done. How does her excitement fit in with the Messiah promises, and the people's hopes?

Praying

With all my heart I praise the Lord
and I am glad because of God my Saviour.
He helps his servant Israel
and is always merciful to his people.
The Lord made this promise to our ancestors;
to Abraham and his family for ever.

(From the Magnificat)

Activities

On the sheet there is space to record some of the prophecies foretold about the Messiah, together with other references to look up which fill out the picture of a promised Saviour, given to the people of Israel through their history. They are also encouraged to look at what signs we should be expecting to see in a Christian church claiming to be followers of the way of the Messiah (or Christ).

FOURTH SUNDAY OF ADVENT

Thought for the day

God's promised kingdom, announced both to King David in ancient times and to Mary by the angel Gabriel, will go on for ever.

Reflection on the readings

2 Samuel 7, 1-5, 8-11, 16
Psalm 88
Romans 16:25-27
Luke 1:26-38

When King David is filled with enthusiasm for building a great and holy temple to house the ark of the covenant, his offer is turned down, but the graciousness of his attitude very much accepted by God. Through the prophet Nathan, God points out to David that the seeming permanence of a grand building is nothing to be compared with the real permanence of the eternally present God. With such a nature there is no problem with flexibility; eternal Presence can move wherever the people go, untied by structural foundations.

Having assured King David that the building idea will be taken up by his son, God reveals his own blueprint for an everlasting kingdom, and the coming of a reign within the royal House of David which will eventually spread throughout the whole world. It was out of this promise that the hope of God's Messiah was born, particularly in the dark years following the collapse of the monarchy. Gradually the understanding of this Messiah became less tied in people's minds with temporal ruling power and more with a priestly kind of kingship which would bring worldwide blessing and hope.

So when we find Gabriel visiting Mary with a message that her son will reign on the throne of his ancestor, David, and his kingdom will never end, we are listening in on a gathering together of all the hopes and longings of generations, right back to King David himself. By this time, the overtones of a Messianic, priestly kingship will be there, and through Mary those hopes and plans can be accomplished for the saving of the whole world.

The passage from Romans gives us a glorious sense of a crescendo as the full spread of God's kingdom builds to completion. John Ellerton's well-loved hymn *The day thou gavest, Lord, is ended* puts it like this:

So be it, Lord; thy throne shall never,
like earth's proud empires, pass away;
thy kingdom stands and grows for ever
till all thy creatures own thy sway.

Our amazing privilege is to be part of the building.

Discussion starters

1. In the light of today's readings, why do you think Jesus put in so much teaching about the nature of the kingdom of God during his earthly ministry?

2. How can we further the kingdom and hasten its full coming?

All-stage talk

Bring in something to show which you thought would last you a long time, but hasn't (like a pair of shoes or a felt-tip pen), and something else which you didn't think would last at all and it has (like a paper bookmark or a jar of Marmite). Talk about these and the way some things, like great cathedrals, are built to last for hundreds and hundreds of years, while other things, like newspapers or toilet paper, are not designed to last very long at all.

King David was wanting to build a temple for the glory of God which was a strong, permanent structure, rather than a temporary tent. And God told David that his ideas for the kingdom were far more long-lasting even than a strong building;

God's idea was for a kingdom of love and peace that lasts not just for a long time but for ever and ever and ever. And Jesus would be the king. The angel Gabriel was sent to Mary to tell her all about it.

'You are going to have a child, Mary,' said Gabriel, 'and he's going to be the king of a kingdom that will last for ever.' The angel even told Mary what to call her child when he was born. (Show a large notice with the word 'Jesus' on one side of it.) He was to be called Jesus.

Names are important, and they often have a special meaning. Pick out some of the names in the congregation and look up what they mean in one of those 'your baby's name' books. The name Jesus has a meaning as well. It means 'Saviour: the one who saves' (show this written on the other side of the Jesus sign). Through King Jesus, God was coming to save his people.

When Jesus, the Saviour King, was born at the first Christmas, that was just the beginning! God's kingdom is still here today, and it's still growing.

All-age ideas

- Set out the passage from Romans on a sheet for everyone to read, like this:

Men/boys	Now to him who is able to establish you, by my Gospel and the proclamation of Jesus Christ,
Women/girls	according to the revelation of the mystery hidden for long ages past,
Men/boys	but now revealed and made known
Women/girls	through the prophetic writings by the command of the eternal God,
Men/boys	so that all nations might believe and obey him –
All	to the only wise God be glory for ever through Jesus Christ! Amen.

- Place a globe or a world map near the Advent candle wreath.

Prayer of the Faithful

Celebrant
Gathered as the Church of God in this place,
let us pray together for the coming of the kingdom.

Reader
We pray that the Church
may be quiet enough to hear God's voice,
humble enough to move in God's way,
and excited enough to spread the good news.

Silence

Living God:
let your kingdom come.

We pray that all who lead
may do so with integrity and respect for others;
that those in positions of authority
may be blessed with humility and a sense of right;
that unjust practices may be changed for good
and conflicts of great tension be peacefully resolved.

Silence

Living God:
let your kingdom come.

May our homes be places
of loving acceptance and developing faith;
in all our friendships may we learn
to grow in generosity of spirit.

Silence

Living God:
let your kingdom come.

When the waiting is long and painful,
may all who have to wait
be given patience and courage;
may those who are wounded,
whether physically or emotionally,
be granted healing
and the assurance of God's presence.

Silence

Living God:
let your kingdom come.

May those who have died to this life,
and whose hope is in the Lord,
be welcomed into eternity.
May those who mourn them be comforted,
and their pain be touched by the divine love.

Silence

Living God:
let your kingdom come.

Remembering Mary's humble acceptance
of God's will,
we join our prayers with hers:
Hail, Mary . . .

The God of Peace is listening;
in this silence we name those we know
who are in any particular need.

Silence

Celebrant
Heavenly Father, accept our prayers,
and make us channels of your peace,
through the power of Jesus Christ.
Amen.

TREASURE SEEKERS

Aim: To prepare for King Jesus coming into the world.

Starter

Have a cardboard crown and put it on one of the children who then leads the others to do whatever they do (follow my leader). Swap the crown over till everyone who wants to has a turn at being king or queen.

Teaching

Put the crown on one child's head, and a kingly robe round their shoulders. Once there was a famous king of Israel called King David. He loved God and was a very good king. King David had been born in a city you might have heard of. It was the city of Bethlehem! King David was not brought up in a palace. (Take out a toy sheep and hold it.) He was brought up as a shepherd boy on the hills near Bethlehem, where he helped to look after the sheep. He grew up strong and good, and looking after the people as their king.

(Get out a shiny star, and take the crown from King David. Place the star, the crown and the sheep on the floor together.) Many years later another baby was born in the city of Bethlehem who would grow up to be a king and a shepherd. Do you know what his name was? It was Jesus! (Place a Christmas card or picture showing the Nativity on the floor with the other things.) And as we get ready for Christmas we are getting ready to welcome Jesus, the baby king, who was born into our world at King David's city of Bethlehem.

Praying

Lord Jesus, my King,
 (bow head)
to you I will bring
 (kneel down)
my living, my loving,
 (arms out, palms up, then hands on heart)
and every good thing!
 (arms stretched up, hands open)

Activities

Today we complete the Christmas landscape, putting sheep on the hill and a title round the edge: 'Happy Birthday, Jesus!' Instructions are on the sheet. There is also a picture of King David on which to stick a crown and a robe.

PEARL DIVERS

Aim: To see how Gabriel's news to Mary fitted in with God's promise to King David.

Starter

Pass the ring. Thread a ring on a length of string. Everyone holds the string, passing it through their hands. One person stands in the middle of the circle. The ring gets passed secretly along the string from hand to hand. The person in the middle has to try and guess where it has got to. When they are right someone else takes over in the centre. Finish by giving a pack of sweets to whoever is holding the ring, and asking them to hand the sweets round to everyone, so that as the ring is revealed, everyone is given a gift.

Teaching

Explain that all through the hundreds of years before Jesus was born, God's promise had been passed on, from one generation to the next, sometimes seen and sometimes hidden from public view, until at the first Christmas, when Jesus the Christ was born, that message was seen clearly, and has been bringing blessing to everyone ever since.

But what was the message? Let's first go back in time to about 1000 BC – that's about three thousand years ago. We are in the city of Jerusalem, and this is King David. (Dress a child appropriately.) He is thinking deeply. (King David thinks deeply.) Then he has a good idea. (Turn on torch above his head.) He talks it over with Nathan the prophet. (Choose someone to be Nathan and give them both this script.)

King David Hello, Nathan. I've been thinking.

Nathan Not too hard, I hope, your majesty.

King David I would like to build a fantastic temple for God to live in. The best temple ever for the best and only God. We all have nice houses to live in, but the ark of the Covenant is still in a tent.

Nathan Well, it sounds a very good idea, your

majesty. Let me go and sleep on it and pray about it. See you tomorrow. Goodbye.

Narrator So Nathan went away and next day he was back.

King David Good morning, Nathan! What did God think of my idea?

Nathan Well, it's a good idea and God is happy that you love him and worship him. But he is quite happy living in a tent and moving around with all of you. The temple can be built later on.

King David Who will build it then?

Nathan The temple will be built by your son, when he is king. But God has an important message for you.

King David Really? What does he say?

Nathan God wants you to know that he has planned a kingdom which will last for ever and ever. The king who will reign for ever will be from your own family. Long after your days are over, this King will bring joy to the whole world.

King David Goodness, that's amazing. Excuse me, Nathan, I must go and say thank you to God for this.

Narrator Hundreds of years later a woman was visited by an angel. The angel, whose name was Gabriel, told her she would have a rather special baby, and must call him Jesus, which means someone who saves or rescues.

(Choose two children to be Mary and Gabriel and give them the following script to read.)

Gabriel You are to call the child Jesus. He will be great and will be called the Son of the Most High. The Lord God will give him the throne of his father David, and he will reign over the house of Jacob for ever; his kingdom will never end.

(King David walks into the scene and says to the children sitting watching . . .)

King David Hey, did you hear that? This woman is going to have the king that God promised would come! And this woman is engaged to Joseph, and he's from my family. So God was right. As usual. He's never lets you down, you know!

Gabriel (To King David) Excuse me, but could I get on with my message to Mary, please?

King David Oh, sure! Sorry to push into another time zone. I just got excited, that's all!

Mary I am the Lord's servant. May it be to me as you have said.

Praying

Once in royal David's city
stood a lowly cattle shed,
where a mother laid her baby
in a manger for a bed.
Mary was that mother mild,
Jesus Christ her little child.

Activities

Today the pop-up model will be completed, using the drawings and instructions on the sheet, strengthened with thin card. Also discuss with the children how God's promise to King David was fulfilled when Mary said yes to God. Jesus' kingdom is still growing today.

GOLD PANNERS

Aim: To see how the hope of a Messiah took shape through the years and was fulfilled in the birth of Jesus.

Starter

Provide crayons or heelball sticks to try some 'brass rubbing' on any effective surfaces (for example, coins, relief metal trays, shoe soles or manhole covers).

Teaching

Today we are looking at a gradually revealed picture of God's plan to save the world. Begin by reading the passage from 2 Samuel 7, noting the details of God's promise about the coming kingdom on a sheet of paper. Explain how, when the monarchy of Israel had crumbled, people started to think of this promised Saviour as a spiritual leader, rather than an ordinary worldly king. He became known as God's anointed, or chosen, One – the Messiah.

Then go on to read today's Gospel, with different people reading the parts of Mary and Gabriel. Go through the points noted already and tick those which match up. What about the coming king being of the house of David? (See verse 27.) Recap on King David's background (2 Samuel 7:8) and link his position with Mary's in Luke 1:46-55. Draw them to see how the ancient promise is being worked out through good people who make themselves available to God.

Praying

O come, O come, Emmanuel,
and ransom captive Israel,
that mourns in lonely exile here,
until the Son of God appear.
Rejoice, rejoice!
Emmanuel shall come to thee, O Israel.

Activities

On the sheet they can explore the nature of the Messiah, both as a priestly and a kingly figure, and there is the script of a conversation between two rocks on a hill near Bethlehem, remembering events there through the years and drawing attention to the historical and spiritual links of today's teaching.

CHRISTMAS

CHRISTMAS DAY

Thought for the day

Jesus Christ, the world's Saviour, is here with us, born as a human baby.

Reflection on the readings

Note: These readings are from the Mass at Dawn. Reflections on the readings for the Day Mass are to be found in Living Water Year A, and for Midnight Mass in Living Water Year C.

Isaiah 62:11-12
Psalm 97
Titus 3:4-7
Luke 2:15-20

Dogs and cats will never let you forget that it's feeding time. They go on and on reminding you loudly until you do something about that empty bowl. At the same time they are voicing (and wagging) their excitement that you will definitely be feeding them because you always do. Today's reading from the book of Isaiah has a lovely sense of God's watchmen being posted where they can see what is going on, and given clear instructions to keep shouting both their need for God to send the promised Saviour, and their faith that he will, until he acts. Christmas is the great celebration of that action – of God breaking into his creation in a new and extraordinary way in order to save us.

Like the shepherds, we have been getting on with our daily and nightly lives, and on this night we remember the splash of God's glory across the sky, and the cry of a newborn child on a heap of straw. The ordinary and the extraordinary are shaken together, the hopes and promises become fused in practical reality, and the whole world is closer to salvation than ever before.

The Incarnation – with all its risk, its glory laid aside, its daring love – speaks as clearly to us, two thousand years on, as it did to those shepherds marvelling at the angels' message as they discovered the baby in the stable. Marvelling is filled with questions as well as wonder, and most of us find that God's presence in our world as a human baby raises many questions. Such questions are to be valued, as they can lead us forward into deeper understanding.

We are told that Mary kept all these questions and pondered them in her heart. Christmas is a time for such pondering, as well as the more usual feasting and celebrating. Wrapped up in those swaddling bands is God's answer to our longing for inner peace, our need for healing and wholeness, and our recognition that we cannot save ourselves no matter what effort we put into it. The baby in Mary's arms is God hearing our hidden fears and tears, and coming in person to save us and set us free.

Discussion starters

1. A new baby always speaks of new life and a fresh beginning. How is that particularly true in the case of Jesus?

2. What line or image from the Christmas carols, cards or readings has been specially meaningful for you this year, and helped you understand the Christmas message, or challenged you in a new way?

All-stage talk

Ask a few volunteers to take the microphone (or shout) and wish everyone a happy Christmas. We've all spent the last month preparing everything – the food and drink, the surprises, the gifts, the decorations – so that we can make a good job of wishing our loved ones a really happy Christmas.

What are we wishing them when we say 'Happy Christmas!' to them? Collect some ideas of what we want for them. They will probably include lots of good wishes directly linked with partying and family celebration. We choose this particular day to wish people those good things we might want for them every day of the year.

Why is the festival of Christmas such a good time to wish people wonderful things in their life? (Arrange for someone to be given a lighted candle at the back of the church at this point, which they carry up to you.) All those things we wish those we love are to do with wanting their lives to be bright and shining, well lit and beautiful in every way. And today, Christmas Day, we are celebrating a life shining with God's glory, which has come right among us. Jesus, the promised Christ, has been born.

So we are right to wish everyone a happy Christmas. What better way to celebrate God's great love for us all than by wishing everyone we meet the light of loving in their lives! Don't let it stop at the ones in your family or circle of friends. Wish it (and mean it) even to those you don't always get on with; wish it to those you hardly know, like the bus conductor, the toll collector at the road tunnel, the other people walking their dogs this afternoon and anyone else you should meet. Pray for them and wish them the light of God's blessing in their lives as you spread the message – Happy Christmas!

All-age ideas

- Have lots of candles around the church today, ensuring that they are really safe. Try nightlights on window ledges and/or along the front edge of the altar. Have some of the children holding candles around the altar at the Eucharistic Prayer. Or give every family a candle, which has been alight during worship, to burn at home each day of the twelve days of Christmas.

- Dress the children up to mime the Gospel, in a series of 'stills'.

- Give out bells, shakers and streamers to be shaken and waved all over the church during the Gloria.

Prayer of the Faithful

Celebrant
As we gather to celebrate Christmas,
let us pray to the living God.

Reader
With gratitude for our Church and its people,
for our deacons, priests and bishops,
and all who pray,
may we all be blessed and strengthened
in our service,
so we can touch the world with your love.

Silence

Holy God:
be born in us today.

We are thankful for the blessings of creation,
for our world and all its beauty.
May we learn God's ways of love and truth,
that his kingdom may grow and flourish.

Silence

Holy God:
be born in us today.

We pray for God's blessing on all those we love –
our families, neighbours and friends,
whether present with us today or far away.
May we all grow closer
in the happiness of human loving and sharing.

Silence

Holy God:
be born in us today.

With gratitude for our own health and strength,
we pray now for help and healing
wherever people ache with pain and sorrow,
loneliness or fear.

May they be blessed in their need
and surrounded with love.

Silence

Holy God:
be born in us today.

We pray for those who have died
and all for whom Christmas
sharpens the loss of loved ones.

Silence

Holy God:
be born in us today.

We make our prayer with Mary,
in whom the Word was made flesh:
Hail, Mary . . .

We name in this silence
any known to us
with particular needs or burdens.

Silence

Celebrant
Father, we can never thank you enough
for coming to rescue us;
please hear our prayers which we offer
through Jesus, your Son.
Amen.

TREASURE SEEKERS, PEARL DIVERS AND GOLD PANNERS

It is important that children, young people and adults worship together for a festival such as Christmas. Involve all age groups in the singing and playing of carols, and in the other ministries of welcoming, serving, collection of gifts and so on. Have nativity toys for the very young to play with, such as knitted Mary, Joseph and Jesus, sheep and shepherds. There are pictures to complete and colour on the Treasure Seekers and Pearl Divers worksheets, but there is no worksheet for Gold Panners. Instead involve the young people in some of the planning of the service and in decorating the church.

First Sunday of Christmas: The Holy Family

Thought for the day

The Saviour of the world is born as a fully human baby into a real human family.

Reflection on the readings

Ecclesiasticus 3:2-6, 12-14
Psalm 127
Colossians 3:12-21
Luke 2:22-40

Whatever the current trends in marriage and family life, and however the models of good parenting shift and change from one culture and age to another, it remains true that a baby is helpless to survive and thrive without the support structures in place involving either the child's parents or substitute parenting. The Son of God, entering our world in order to save us, shared that same vulnerability and complete dependence on caring parents.

Families are remarkably resilient. They are a bit like birds' nests, swayed about alarmingly sometimes, but still a safe haven and a base for fledglings to fly from. Much of what Jesus became must have been influenced by the years he spent growing up in his family, fed physically with food prepared and cooked by Mary, and also fed spiritually and emotionally through the hugs and conversations, the jokes and scolds, the affectionate teasing and the expected appropriate behaviour. Whatever attitudes Mary and Joseph held would have been picked up by the growing Jesus; what they valued would have become etched into his own values.

It may seem obvious that Jesus would be born into a Jewish family, but it is significant that the parenting God chose for his Son was firmly within the traditional teaching. We can tell from the Magnificat that Mary was passionate about her faith in God, with a gift of prophecy. Her love and excitement about the scriptures would have been communicated to Jesus right from the start.

In today's Gospel we find the Holy Family taking part in the ancient tradition of purification, making the considerable journey to Jerusalem to present their firstborn son to the Lord, all in accordance with the Law of the Lord. Both Mary and Joseph could be counted on to do things properly and raise this child as an upright and devout Jewish boy.

It is the duty of all Christian communities to support parents in this work of raising their children in the faith. As the Africans say, it takes a whole village to raise a child. We need to look at any gaps in our support systems and address them, so that as a church we become a holy family, nurturing our young in the love and practical care of God.

Discussion starters

1. What do you value most about being a member of a family or a member of the Church family?
2. What can we learn about Christian parenting, both in the nuclear family and in our church community, from looking at the Holy Family?

All-stage talk

If possible play a snatch of the music from one of the 'pet rescue' type of programmes currently showing. One of the popular sections of such programmes is when various creatures are shown who need a good home, and people can phone in to offer that 'home' care which the animals so badly need. So many people phone in that they have to limit the response to those living in the area, and remind all the generous, loving children that they must check with their parents before the family home is offered!

Produce a realistic-looking toy dog or rabbit, and invite everyone to choose an ideal home for such an animal. Work out a short history of the animal, such as its age and background, expected full-grown size and eating requirements, together with any particular problem it may have (such as being scared of cats, or needing lots of company). Gather ideas about a suitable home for this animal.

When Jesus was born into our world as a human baby, it was very important that he was born into a suitable home to grow up in. Let's forget what we know about Jesus' family for a minute and imagine that we are in God the Father's place – looking for a good home for Jesus to be born into. What sort of home might God have thought it had to be? Collect ideas of a good home for Jesus, the Saviour of the world, and write these up, either on an OHP or on large sheets of paper which volunteers can hold up and show everyone.

Now look at how these can be seen to fit in with the home that Mary and Joseph provided. It wasn't a rich home with lots of money to spend on Jesus, but there was lots of love in it, both for God and for one another. In many ways it was very ordinary, so that Jesus grew up knowing what ordinary family life was like for everyone else. It was a home where the parents really believed in God and lived that out in their everyday lives.

If we invite Jesus to live with us in our homes, then every home we represent can become a holy family, where Jesus shares our ordinary living, our tears of laughter and of sadness, and our dependence on God for everything.

All-age ideas

- This week's Gospel could be mimed, using nativity play costumes if available.
- Consider having a collection today, either of money or basic toiletries, to be taken to a local organisation which provides practical help for families in need or in crisis.
- Involve extended families (including singles and 'adopted' grandparents, aunts and uncles) in readings, prayers and welcoming ministries.

Prayer of the Faithful

Celebrant
We are all members of God's family.
Let us pray to him now.

Reader
We pray that our church communities
may reflect the love and mutual care
shown to us in the example of the Holy Family;
that we may recognise our responsibility
to provide spiritual nurture for our young.

Silence

Come, Lord:
and live among us.

We pray for all parents and children,
that our laws and structures of society
may uphold and support them.
We pray for the very poor
and those who struggle to survive.

Silence

Come, Lord:
and live among us.

We pray for the families we know well,
especially those with conflicts or pressures;
may the Holy Spirit protect them
so that each family member
may know they are loved
and grow in love themselves.

Silence

Come, Lord:
and live among us.

We pray for all refugees and war-torn families;
for all children at risk of abuse,
and all families where there is violence.
We pray that the Spirit may bring hope,
healing and transformation.

Silence

Come, Lord:
and live among us.

We pray for those who have died
and for their families who mourn them.
May they receive a merciful judgement
and experience the unending peace of heaven.

Silence

Come, Lord:
and live among us.

We make our prayer with Mary,
Mother of the Church:
Hail, Mary . . .

As members of Christ's family,
we pray to our loving Lord,
who considers each one of us special.

Silence

Celebrant
Heavenly Father, dwell in our hearts and homes,
and accept these prayers through Jesus Christ,
our brother and Redeemer.
Amen.

TREASURE SEEKERS

Aim: To know that Jesus was born into a family.

Starter

Set out some simple Nazareth 'wendy houses' for the children to play in. Mark out the walls with chairs, have blankets rolled up for beds, bread-boards and playdough for bread-making, a broom, cooking pot and fire (red crepe paper in a box) and water bucket. In another part of the room have the village 'well' where they can come to collect water. Let the children play houses.

Teaching

Gather in one of the homes, or around the village well for the teaching. Talk together about what it was like living in homes like this, unrolling the beds to sleep on each evening and rolling them up in the morning, collecting water, making bread and cooking on the fire. There are lots of people in the world who still live in homes like this, and collect their water each day.

When Jesus was their age he would have walked with his mum to the well and played with the other children while their mums drew up the water from the well. He would have helped his mum make the bread.

Show the children some off-cuts of wood, and either hammer some nails in, or saw a piece off, or sand some wood down so they can watch, listen and smell it. Joseph was a carpenter, so Jesus would have heard him sawing and seen the saw-dust. Perhaps he used it to play with, and made patterns in it, or roads. There is lots of sunshine in the country where Jesus lived, so they could often play outside. Instead of cars people had donkeys to carry their loads, and there were sheep and lambs in the fields nearby. Hens and chickens walked about pecking in the dust.

Help the children to imagine what it was like and point out the things that are quite like the way we live as well – we have places to sleep, jobs to do, we cook food and eat it and clean up afterwards. It was at home with his family that Jesus would have first learnt to pray, and to know about God, who loved them all. He was a real child, living in a real family.

Praying

Gather some objects to help the children pray. As they look at a few baby clothes or nappies they can pray for all babies and their families. Coins remind them to pray for those who are too poor to have a good meal every day. A broom reminds them to pray for those who have lots of work to do looking after their family.

Our heavenly Father,
bless my home and family
and fill it with your love.
Amen.

Activities

The children may like to have a bit longer playing in the Nazareth homes, and they can make their own model house using a box, a bed-shaped piece of cloth, and so on, as instructed on the sheet.

PEARL DIVERS

Aim: To look at Jesus' family, and our own.

Starter

Family album. Whenever the music stops call out a typical family photo situation. They have to get into groups and freeze in position as if they are in the photograph. Ideas for 'pictures': Mum and Dad watching baby walk properly for the first time; two children in the family playing ball in the garden; family of four pulling crackers at Christmas time; Dad asleep on the beach as three children pour sea water on his tummy; two children fast asleep in the car.

Teaching

Bring along a family album and show the children one or two pictures from it. Talk over all the things that are important about being part of a family, and why we need each other in this way. Talk over the things they particularly enjoy and the things they can see are useful, even if they don't always enjoy them – like sharing the jobs at home.

If God's Son was going to live among us on earth he needed a family to be part of as well. What kind of family did God choose for Jesus to be born into?

(Place down a crown.) Joseph was part of King David's family, so the family Jesus was born into was one which was linked with the memory of the good King David.

(Place down a scroll.) The family were Jewish, worshipping God and doing their best to live God's way. They read the Bible and prayed together, went to the temple for festivals and to the local synagogue each Sabbath.

(Place down a speech bubble with the word 'Yes' written in it.) Both Mary and Joseph were the kind of people who were ready to say 'Yes' to God. They were both happy to work with God.

(Place down a heart shape.) It was a family with lots of love in it.

Now see if the children can tell you what the family was like – prompt them by pointing to each of the objects in turn.

Praying

Thank you, Father God, for my family,
and all the people who love and care for me.
Bless . . .
Fill them with your love
and guard them from evil.
Amen.

Activities

Each child will need a box on which to stick the walls of the prayer house, pictured on the sheet. The children draw all the members of their house-hold on separate pieces of paper and keep these in the prayer house. At their prayer time each day they take out the drawings, one by one, and pray for the people they represent.

GOLD PANNERS

Aim: To look at the Holy Family and learn from it.

Starter

Wedding photos. Give everyone a slip of paper providing them with an identity at a family wedding – bride, bridegroom, bride's mother, best man, chief bridesmaid, page boy, and so on. One slip is labelled 'official photographer', and this person has to be bossy, calling out for a list of wedding shots, with the appropriate people coming in role to pose for the group photos.

Teaching

Read the passage from Colossians, looking out for the benefits of this kind of attitude and behaviour in family life. Talk over the tensions and conflicts of family life which are caused by us living without this clothing of compassion, kindness and humility, gentleness and patience, forbearance and forgiveness. Then take a look at the words from Ecclesiasticus, which, though written so long ago, ring true with us just as much today. Talk over our treatment of elderly members of our families, their needs and their wealth of time and experience.

The Holy Family had enormous pressures and hardships to face together, and the responsibility of raising God's Son, so it can't have been without its difficulties. Look back over the Colossians reading to see what would have helped and strengthened Mary, Joseph and Jesus during the years of Jesus' upbringing.

Read the Gospel for today, noticing the support they also relied on from the faith community, and talk about how our church community supports families, and any ways they feel it could develop such support.

Praying

Lord of all kindliness, Lord of all grace,
your hands swift to welcome,
your arms to embrace;
be there at our homing and give us, we pray,
your love in our hearts, Lord,
at the eve of the day.

Activities

On the sheet they can fill in the factfiles of Mary and Joseph and their domestic circumstances, so they see that this was not a family who had it all easy, but a family who prayed together, united in their love of God. There is also a jelly person chart to help them think over where they feel the different members of their family are in relation to one another.

SECOND SUNDAY OF CHRISTMAS

Thought for the day

The Word made flesh at Christmas was always with God, always expressing his creative love.

Reflection on the readings

Ecclesiasticus (Sirach) 24:1-4, 12-16
Psalm 147
Ephesians 1:3-6, 15-18
John 1:1-18

Sympathy cards will often bear messages like 'A word of comfort . . .', and the whole idea of sending cards of sympathy to those who are distressed or grieving is the knowledge that the expressed sympathy of another human, sharing the anguish, can be so supportive and comforting.

The supreme Word of comfort and hope to all of us in any age and every circumstance is the Word of God's loving wisdom, lying here among us as a human baby in the hay. All the nakedness, vulnerability and self-giving, which assure us of real, trustworthy love, are here, spelt out to us in the Christmas season as we marvel at the intimacy of God with his people, the Creator with the created.

All through the process of creation, this expressive Word of love has drawn life and hope into tangible form. All through the developing discernment of spiritual things, the expressive Word has spoken eternal truth and mystery, Godliness and the way of love.

So Christmas does not spring on to our consciousness a raw, untried and untested phenomenon, out of nowhere. The Incarnation tenderly affirms and shows in person all that the human spirit had sensed through the ages, and the created world from the first calling of light into darkness and order into chaos.

Discussion starters

1. Why do you think the eternal Word came into our world as a human baby, born as vulnerable and dependent as the rest of us?

2. How does our faith in Jesus affect the way we look at the books of the Old Testament?

All-stage talk

Start by giving everyone one minute to find out from and share with someone else something that went really well, or was really funny, or was a complete disaster over this Christmas. One thing all humans have always loved doing is talking together! Toddlers, children, young people, middle-aged and old people all love a chat. Even babies talk, in their own way. What would we do without the telephone, especially if we can't get out like we used to. With e-mail we can chat to people all over the world, and with television, radio, magazines and newspapers people can chat to us about anything and everything. Ground control can direct astronauts in space, pilots can be talked down to a safe landing, and surgeons can talk their students through complicated heart operations. Politicians can shout their ideas to crowds of people, and friends can whisper their secrets. All of this is the magic of words.

Why do we talk about Jesus as the Word of God?

Whenever we use words we express ourselves. Jesus expresses God, not in a speech bubble but as a human being like us, so that we can understand God in a better way than ever. God has always expressed himself, of course, so the Word of God has been there as long as God has – for ever. God *said*, 'Let there be light!' God *said*, 'Let there be stars and plants and animals, fish and birds.' God *said*, 'Let there be people in our likeness to look after the earth.' So it was the Word of God which spoke those things into being through love.

Then, at Christmas, the Word of God actually took shape itself – human shape. And his name was Jesus, which means 'the one who saves us'.

All-age ideas

- For the Penitential Rite:

  The shape of God's Word is a loving Saviour;
  how loving are the words we speak?
  Lord, have mercy.
  Lord, have mercy.
  The Word of God is willing to be vulnerable and
      accessible;
  how high are the walls we build?
  Christ, have mercy.
  Christ, have mercy.
  In humility, the Word of God lays aside his glory;
  what importance have we given to the things we
      possess and desire?
  Lord, have mercy.
  Lord, have mercy.

- On the walls or pillars, have speech bubbles with the following sentences in:

  Let there be light.
  Let the earth produce growing things.
  Let us make human beings in our image.

In one speech bubble have a picture of the infant Jesus.

Prayer of the Faithful

Celebrant
Let us pray to the God
who loves us enough to come and save us.

Reader
We pray for the areas of the Church
which are weak in faith,
despondent or complacent;
that we may be recharged
with the power of God's love,
reawakened to the good news,
and revitalised with the breath of the Spirit.

Silence

Living Word of God:
be spoken in our lives.

We pray for all areas of misunderstanding
between peoples and nations,
between needs and offers of help;
make us more ready to listen than instruct,
more ready to encourage than crush.

Silence

Living Word of God:
be spoken in our lives.

We pray for family feuds and difficulties
to be resolved and learnt from;
for the words we speak
to express love and respect,
with true charity and forgiveness.

Silence

Living Word of God:
be spoken in our lives.

We pray for all who have difficulty
hearing and speaking,
reading and writing;
for the oppressed and persecuted
whose voices are silenced,
and for all who have yet to hear
the good news of God's love.

Silence

Living Word of God:
be spoken in our lives.

We pray for those who have died
and those who are dying now;
may the Word of life
encourage them on their journey
and bring them safely to the eternal kingdom.

Silence

Living Word of God:
be spoken in our lives.

We join our prayers with those of Mary,
whose Son has brought us salvation:
Hail, Mary . . .

In a time of silence
we share with God our Father
any needs and burdens
known to us personally.

Silence

Celebrant
Almighty Father, hear our prayers
and make us alert to your response,
through Christ our Lord.
Amen.

TREASURE SEEKERS

Aim: To know that Jesus is God saying, 'I love you!'

Starter

Collect some model cars and trucks (sized to suit the children in your group) and sit everyone down, spread out. Let them whizz the cars from one to another across the spaces.

Teaching

Talk about how we can send a car off to reach a friend (demonstrate with one car to a child on the other side of the circle) and they can send it back to us. We do the same thing with messages. I can think to myself, 'Mmm, I'd like to thank the children for putting the cars away so nicely', and all I have to do is say the words out loud (say them out loud) and the message races across to your ears! Hands up if you caught the message. Clever, isn't it?

(You could have one or two children sending out a message, and the rest of you catching the spoken message with your ears.)

You can't see those messages, can you? But you can hear them. Some messages you *can* see. What's this one? (Show the road sign for a school.) And this? (Show a green man sign.) That time you caught the message with your eyes.

At Christmas God sent us a very important message. The message looked like this. (Show a picture of the Nativity.) And it meant this. (Show a red heart with the words 'I love you' on it, and read them out.)

Jesus is God's message of love. Jesus is God saying, 'I love you!' (All join in.)

Praying

Dear God, I am glad
that you love us so much.
It makes me happy!
Amen.

Activities

On the sheet they can match the messages and send a loving one to someone. Provide envelopes for the messages.

PEARL DIVERS

Aim: To know that Jesus is sometimes called 'the Word of God'.

Starter

Play a simplified game of Pictionary, using a blackboard or sheets of lining paper fixed to the wall. Whisper the word to the first drawer and everyone shouts what they think it is. First to guess gets to draw next.

Teaching

As we saw, it's sometimes quite hard to know what someone is thinking if you can't use words. Words make it much easier for us to understand one another. That's what they're for. Ask them to give instructions for getting to somewhere close by – their school, for instance, or a well-known shop – and to give a description of a familiar object.

God wanted all the people he had made to understand that he really loved them. He wanted them to understand what God was really like. If we were to look at the world God made, what could we tell about him? (Collect their ideas.) So we can tell that God is generous and loving, careful and thorough, clever and organised, gentle and powerful, just by looking at the world, because it expresses what God is like, just as words do. It was through God's Word that all this came to exist.

Now show some Christmas cards with Jesus as a baby on them. Eventually, God's Word was not just spoken but actually lived. Jesus is sometimes known as the Word of God, because his life expressed exactly what God is like – a living Word for us to understand in our human language!

Praying

Word of the Father,
now in flesh appearing!
O come, let us adore him,
Christ the Lord.

Activities

There is an activity to look at the words we speak, and what message they give, and there are speech bubbles in which to draw God's Word, not just as a baby but also at other times of his life.

GOLD PANNERS

Aim: To see how the Word can be seen present from the beginning.

Starter

Play hangman, where the word is there already and just needs them to uncover it.

Teaching

First read the Gospel for today, noticing the capital W in Word and discussing who John is talking about. In what way is Jesus God's Word? Was God's Word there at the beginning, as John says? (Look at Genesis to check.)

Now look at the Old Testament reading, picking up on the Word (sometimes thought of as the wisdom of God) being there all the time and not suddenly arriving on the hay in Bethlehem from nowhere. (Look at the picture on the sheet.)

Explain how John was writing for the Greek philosophers who would find it helpful to think of God in this way. Link it, too, with what God called himself when talking to Moses (Exodus 3:13-15) and with Jesus' 'I AM' teaching (John 8:58, for example).

Praying

Jesus, living Word of God,
you show us what loving means
and what it costs.

Activities

On the sheet they are encouraged to see God's Word in terms of the Trinity, and to explore the beginning of John's Gospel more deeply, expressing their ideas in drawing.

THE EPIPHANY OF THE LORD

Thought for the day

Jesus, the promised Messiah, is shown to the Gentile world.

Reflection on the readings

Isaiah 60:1-6
Psalm 71
Ephesians 3:2-3a, 5-6
Matthew 2:1-12

We are well used to thinking of the Church's call as outreach. Partly this is because of falling Mass attendance figures. Partly it is a growing awareness of the deep spiritual hunger of many who have not been brought up to go to church and do not see it as a viable answer to their need. So there is almost a daydream quality for us, as well as the dispirited people of Israel, when we are asked to imagine crowds and crowds of people from all walks of life, actively seeking us out, in order to find God and spiritual fulfilment.

I wonder how the Church would cope with such a situation? Would we be able to help them with their search? Would we understand their questions? Would we be overjoyed to see them pouring through the doors, or would they pose a threat to our traditional way of doing things?

When we recognise that being 'a light to lighten the Gentiles' can actually be quite disturbing, we can start to understand something of the hesitation the Jewish people had about welcoming the early Christians, many of them totally 'unsynagogued'. We can also thrill to the hope of a new direction – of a Church on the grow at last. The signs are there, and the tide is turning.

Epiphany has therefore particular significance for us at the moment. The light of the world is for everyone – all groups and nations, all cultures and ages, not just those we are familiar with or approve of, or who know 'how we do it' in our own church. Since most of us are Gentiles ourselves, the significance of Christ being shown to the Gentile 'outsiders' tends to pass us by unnoticed, unless we ask ourselves another question. Which 'outsiders' might those wise men represent today? To enter into the spirit of Epiphany we need to alter our vision until we understand that God has no outsiders, and no person or group is excluded. It was God's delight to reveal his baby Son to searching pagan foreigners.

As we hear once again the story of these outsiders, travelling many miles over difficult terrain in order to find for themselves the world's enlightenment, we could do well to bear in mind all those in our own times who are spiritually awake and searching, many travelling over difficult terrain, and make sure that we light the lamps, ready to welcome them.

Discussion starters

1. Why do you think Matthew, writing for the Hebrew people, considered this event of the wise men's visit so important to include?

2. What can we, both as Gentiles and as members of the established Church, learn from the Magi visit about our own attitudes and calling?

All-stage talk

Consider using the suggested sketch in the All-age Ideas just before the talk. Have a number of masks, based on the pictures below, to put on some volunteers, which alter the way we see them and act towards them.

Vicky

Sidney

With the first volunteer, explain that Vicky is feeling really fed up because her Christmas tokens were stolen before she got round to spending them. (Aah!) Have everyone making a 'ding dong' doorbell noise. It's the football squad coach! Quick, Vicky chooses to put on the bright, happy mask! (Help her on with it.)

With the second volunteer, explain that Sidney's feeling really fed up because his Christmas tokens went through the wash by mistake and are now a

hard crusty blob. (Aah!) The doorbell rings again. (Ding dong.) It's someone Sidney doesn't know, and they're wearing the colours of a team Sidney doesn't support! Quick, where's that angry 'What on earth do you think you're doing here?' mask? (Help him on with it.)

We all have lots of masks which we keep by the door. Sometimes it's right to wear them, and helps us get out of a bad mood faster. But sometimes we forget what is mask and what is real, and that's not so good.

For some people we are always on our best behaviour, showing them how kind and friendly we are, how ready to help and forgive them. With others we want to show them that although we're doing our grudging best to be polite, it's a real effort and we'd far rather we didn't have to have anything to do with them. Some people we're happy to welcome to church, some we hope will never come, at least to the same church as us! Sometimes we're not very good at welcoming people who look different, wear different clothes or speak with a different accent from ours. We make it quite clear to them that they are outsiders.

But today we hear that God led these strangers all the way to Bethlehem, specially to show them his baby Son! We hear that King Herod pretended to make them welcome. And we hear that at Jesus' home they really were made welcome. God wanted these 'outsiders' to be among the first to meet his Son because Jesus had come into the world for everybody, and not just for the Jewish people.

As Christians, we need to remember that the good news of the Gospel is for everyone, and not just those like us. So today we ask God to turn us into people who are happy to welcome outsiders, without needing any masks to pretend.

All-age ideas

* This short sketch explores the idea of Jesus coming for the whole world.

    (Joseph, Mary and the baby Jesus are at the front of the church. The wise men walk up the aisle towards them and knock on a 'door'.)

1st wise man   Excuse me, is anyone there?

(Joseph comes to the door)

Joseph   Bit late for visiting, isn't it? What do you want?

2nd wise man   Our navigation lights only work at night, I'm afraid. *(Points up to the star)* Is there a baby king here at all?

Joseph   You must be joking – does this look like a palace? Go and annoy some of your own lot – we're a respectable Jewish household here. *(Slams door. Wise men shrug, look at their presents and turn away.)*

3rd wise man I thought it was too good to be true – a Saviour for the whole world. It's not for us, then. We're not included, obviously. *(They walk away)*

Mary What was all that, Joseph?

Joseph Oh, a bunch of star-gazing weirdos. You should have seen their ridiculous clothes! I didn't let on about our little Jesus, though. Got to protect him from all those prying Gentiles, haven't we!

Producer CUT! What's happening? That's not the script! It didn't happen like that at all! *(Turns to wise men)* Come on, you lot! God wouldn't have got you seeking just to have you turned away!

(The wise men turn and walk back up the aisle. As a narrator reads Matthew 2:10-11, they mime the actions, and Joseph and Mary embrace them.)

• Have gifts of burning frankincense, gold and myrrh brought at the offertory, while the appropriate verses of *We three kings* are sung.

Prayer of the Faithful

Celebrant
Let us pray to the God who loves us
and knows the terrain we travel.

Reader
We thank God for all those who brought
the good news of Jesus to us,
and all who nourish our faith today.
We pray that the whole people of God
may work in unity and openness
for the coming of God's kingdom.

Silence

Lord God:
we offer you ourselves.

We thank God that salvation is for all people,
and pray for a just and accepting world
where none is rejected, despised
or treated with contempt.

Silence

Lord God:
we offer you ourselves.

We thank God for the privilege of parenting
and of living in communities;
we pray that our homes and churches
may be welcoming and generous-hearted.

Silence

Lord God:
we offer you ourselves.

We thank God for all who care
with such thoughtfulness and practical loving
for those who are vulnerable,
and especially for the very young.
We pray for healing and wholeness,
peace of mind, protection and hope.

Silence

Lord God:
we offer you ourselves.

We thank God for all who have reached
the end of their earthly journey in faith,
that they may be welcomed into your eternity.
May we use the time left to us here
as good stewards of God's gifts.

Silence

Lord God:
we offer you ourselves.

We make our prayer with Mary,
who showed her Son to the Wise Men:
Hail, Mary . . .

Knowing that our loving Father is listening,
we bring our personal petitions to him now.

Silence

Celebrant
In thankfulness, Father,
we offer you our lives
and our prayers,
through Jesus Christ.
Amen.

TREASURE SEEKERS

Aim: To know that the wise men brought presents to Jesus.

Starter

Fix a star on to a stick and give it to one of the children. Wherever this child goes with the star, the others follow. If the star stops, everyone stops. Swap the star around until everyone who wants to lead has had a go.

Teaching

On a long strip of lining paper or wallpaper draw some hills and a starry sky, based on the picture below. Lay the sheet out in front of the children, and have at the ready a shiny star and a cut-out picture of the wise men. The smaller you make these the longer the journey will look.

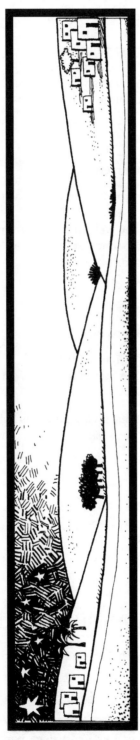

Who do we know who followed a star? Yes, it was the wise men from many miles away. They followed a great bright star in the sky which was moving,

night by night. (Move the star as you speak, and then make the wise men walk after it to catch it up.) The star went on like this for nights and nights, until at last it stopped. (Stop the star over the city of Bethlehem.) And the wise men followed it all the way to a city called Bethlehem. Who did they find at Bethlehem? They found Jesus there. (Place a Christmas card of Joseph, Mary and Jesus on the city of Bethlehem.)

What did they do when they found Jesus? (Swap the Christmas card for one showing the wise men giving their presents.) They treated Jesus as if he was a little king. They bowed and knelt in front of him, and gave him the presents they had brought.

What were the presents? There was gold (lay down something gold – preferably real gold if practical! If you are wearing a gold ring you can take it off and place it down, which says a lot about real giving without a word spoken) . . . frankincense (again the real thing is ideal, so they can smell what it's like) . . . and myrrh (the Body Shop sells it, or use any spicy ointment and let them rub a bit into their skin if they want to).

Praying

Jesus, can you guess
   (pretend to hide a present behind your back)
what I have brought
to give you?
It's ME!
   (bring hands out and hold them up and out, as you jump forward)

Activities

There is an activity to match objects with their silhouettes, and a picture to colour of the wise men giving their presents.

PEARL DIVERS

Aim: To understand that Jesus was being shown to the Gentiles as well as the Jewish people.

Starter

Sit in a circle, passing a locked box round to each in turn. As each one holds the box they say, 'One day I would love to go to . . . and see . . .' This can be a place or a person, a thing or an event, anywhere in the world or the universe. (Start it off yourself so they get the idea.)

Teaching

Share something or somewhere you had always hoped to see and which was different but even better than you had expected when you actually got to visit it. Today we are learning about some people who found what they were hoping to find, but it was all a bit different from what they expected.

Have everyone kneeling back on their heels, as in 'Do you want to go on a lion hunt', slapping their thighs with their hands to make the walking noise.

The children just repeat what you say.

Chorus
We're going on a journey . . .
a very long journey . . .
far away from home . . .
We're looking for a king.

We've noticed a star . . . *(point up)*
a very big star . . . *(look up, screwing up eyes)*
and we know it means a king!
Hold on! . . . We've come to a river . . .
Let's wade across . . . Swish, swish, swish.

Chorus

Hold on! . . . We've come to a mountain . . .
Let's climb over it . . .
  (do slow slaps up it and fast down the other side)

Chorus

We stopped at a palace . . . *(stop the 'walking')*
a very fine palace . . . *(bow to the ground)*
but there was no new king. *(shake head)*
Herod didn't know anything! *(shrug shoulders)*

Chorus

The star led us to Bethlehem . . . *(stop the walking)*
it led us to a house . . . *(point forward)*
a very ordinary house . . .
  (a 'can this be the right place' look!)
and we knocked at the door . . . *(clap three times)*

Chorus (changed to 'We've been on a journey')

And he's here!
We gave him our presents
  (carefully place gift on floor in front of you)
We bowed in worship *(bow to the ground)*
He wasn't in a palace . . .
  (resume the thigh slapping and shake head)
He isn't rich at all . . . *(shake head again)*
But he's king of the mountains and rivers . . .
  (speed up the thigh slapping)
and king of us all!
  (fast drumming on thighs, finishing with applause)

Praying

We bring you the GOLD
of our obedience.
Help us to live as you want us to.

We bring you the FRANKINCENSE
of our worship.
You are God and we worship you.

We bring you the MYRRH
of our world's sadness.
Help us look after one another better.

Amen.

Activities

On the sheet the children learn about the word 'Gentiles' and see the wise men's visit as Jesus being shown to the Gentile world.

GOLD PANNERS

Aim: To look at how people 'journey' to faith.

Starter

In a circle, pass a bus or train ticket around, and each person in turn says how they got here today. Then pass a cross around. Each person says how they're a Christian, or where they feel they are, how they got here and who has helped them on the way. (As with all circle time, those who don't wish to speak can pass the cross on, and it's fine to say the same as someone else has said if their situation is the same.)

Teaching

Start with today's Gospel reading, establishing what we know from the account about where they came from, how many and who they were. Draw attention to their not being Jewish, but pagan foreigners. Imagine together some of the dangers they may have faced on their journey. Why were they wanting to bother with it? How was the king they found different from what they were expecting?

Now look at Ephesians 3 to see how Paul's calling was carrying on the mission to spread the good news to all the non-Jewish people, including us, if we are Gentiles. Finally look at Isaiah 60 to see how this had been prophesied generations before.

Praying

O Lord, our King,
let your kingdom come
in every nation

and every person,
starting with me.
Amen.

Activities

Make a banner or poster which expresses our many different journeys to Christ, who welcomes us wherever we have come from. On the sheet there are some examples of such journeys, and space to think about their own journey.

THE BAPTISM OF THE LORD

Thought for the day

Through the Holy Spirit, Jesus is affirmed at his Baptism as God's beloved Son, and we too are given the Spirit of God which affirms us as God's adopted daughters and sons.

Reflection on the readings

Isaiah 42:1-4, 6-7
Psalm 28
Acts 10:34-38
Mark 1:7-11

There are still many people today who value Jesus' ethical teaching, and use his guidelines as ideals to strive for, but have not taken on board as a real possibility that God's life can live in them, changing them from the inside out. The affirmation of Jesus as God's beloved Son at his Baptism opens up this possibility for all of us.

We have to acknowledge that it is indeed an odd concept. All the time we are making decisions of the will – about which potatoes to buy for baking, which make of car to go for, whether to stop smoking or carry on, whether to give money to an appeal or not. We also make decisions about life direction – we decide to marry, or to complete the tax return honestly, to campaign for justice or to eat no meat. All this reinforces that we are in control of our own lives, as mature, independent people.

The Holy Spirit can sound like a takeover bid, and many are suspicious of this, and find it all rather far-fetched. Yes, we can choose to live God's way, as rational human beings, but aren't we kidding ourselves to talk about God's life and Spirit actually taking up residence?

All today's readings give us evidence of the real living Spirit of God at work. The Spirit is given to the Lord's chosen servant. As Jesus is baptised, God's Spirit settles on him, affirming his identity and his mission, an even told not only in the Gospel but repeated by St Peter in Acts. God breaks into our human confines with his divine nature, and that opens up possibilities of full life which could never otherwise happen. Rather than a takeover bid, it is a setting free; rather than kidding ourselves, it is truth in all its fullness.

Discussion starters

1. Why do you think Jesus was baptised by John when he didn't need to repent?

2. Is the thought of God's Spirit dwelling in us a little frightening; would we prefer God to keep his distance?

All-stage talk

Bring along a pair of wellington boots which fit you, or arrange beforehand for a volunteer to bring their boots and do the actions as you talk.

Stand the boots together where they can be seen, and explain that these boots (being very keen, conscientious boots) want to walk wherever you go. (Walk about and watch the boots, still sitting there and not moving.) They are trying very hard, but they don't seem to be getting anywhere, do they? Perhaps they need a bit of encouragement. (Some of the children can encourage the boots from a distance!)

Poor old boots – they'd love to be walking where you walk, but they just can't manage it. Why not? Because they haven't got you inside them!

Climb into the boots and see the difference. Suddenly they are able to walk around wherever you walk. They can even jump with you, run with you and dance with you! And all because they have you in them.

Now what has a keen pair of boots got to do with our readings for today? Well, we can know lots about Jesus and what he did on earth and what he said, and that can make us very keen to live like him – in a loving, generous, honest way. But unless we ask God to be in us, getting to know him as a person, rather than a set of facts, or a bit of a history lesson, we'll be like the boots on their own, wanting to move with God, but not able to do it on their own. (As you say this, take off the boots and put them on their own while you move around.)

As soon as we ask God into our life, his Spirit comes and moves in us (put the boots on again), and that makes it possible for us to go wherever God wants us to go, and act as God wants us to act. The Spirit of God which was seen settling on Jesus when John baptised him in the river Jordan, settles on all of God's children as they put their faith and trust in him.

So let's not waste our time trying hard to do good things *for* God like a pair of boots without any living feet in them. Instead, let's invite the Spirit of God every day to come and fill us, so God's life is *in* us, and can let us dance through life with praise, walk beside those who need our help, and stick to the right path all the way to heaven.

All-age ideas

- Decorate the font with blue and white flowers, shells and stones, and have posters or banners nearby expressing the Spirit of God, with the words: 'Come, Holy Spirit, fill my life!'
- Renew baptismal vows, and recall our own baptism, with everyone marking a cross on their foreheads with their thumb as they say, 'I turn to Christ'.
- Invite everyone to pray silently and fervently for the Holy Spirit to come and fill them and the whole Church with God's life. Encourage everyone to continue that prayer wherever they are each day at midday. If every person did that in every parish using this book, that's a huge crowd of praying people, all focused on asking for more of God in our lives!

Prayer of the Faithful

Celebrant
Let the Spirit of God in our hearts plead
for the Church and for the world.

Reader
We pray that the Spirit
may fill the Church with such joy in believing
that all Christians overflow with love,
compassion, generosity and humility.

Silence

May the Spirit of God:
fill us to overflowing.

May God's power and justice
fill the arenas of leadership and conflict
with sharpened consciences and with courage,
so that wise decisions are made,
needs met and wrongs righted.

Silence

May the Spirit of God:
fill us to overflowing.

May God's gentleness and truth
fill every home with new insight
and greater understanding.
Break down the divisive barriers
and build up our capacity to love.

Silence

May the Spirit of God:
fill us to overflowing.

May God's attentive caring
fill us with practical compassion;
may all who suffer be heard,
comforted and cared for.
May there be healing for both their situation
and our hardness of heart.

Silence

May the Spirit of God:
fill us to overflowing.

May God's unending being
fill death with life and the dying with hope.
May we all be prepared
for life which lasts for ever.

Silence

May the Spirit of God:
fill us to overflowing.

Mary opened her life
to the loving power of God;
we now make our prayer with her:
Hail, Mary . . .

Conscious of the Holy Spirit among us,
we share with God our Father
our personal burdens, joys and sorrows.

Silence

Celebrant
Father, we rejoice
in your uncompromising love for us,
and ask you to hear our prayers,
through Jesus Christ.
Amen.

TREASURE SEEKERS

Aim: To know what baptism is.

Starter

Have a time of water play. To cut down on mess, protect the floor with plastic sheeting (plastic table-cloths are good for this job) and have several washing-up bowls with a lowish level of water in them. Gather an assortment of containers, tea strainers and funnels to play with.

Teaching

Talk about playing in the water at a swimming pool, on the beach or by a river, and what the water looks, sounds and feels like. What is it like under the water? What happens to dirty things when they're washed in water?

When people promise to spend their life following Jesus, they are washed in water in church, and given their name. It's called being baptised, or Christened. (Talk about the font in your church, and any baptisms they remember, and show some pictures of people being baptised.)

Today we remember when Jesus was baptised in the river Jordan. He waded into the water and John the Baptist (who was Jesus' cousin) dipped him right under the water. When he came up, all wet, he heard God, his Father, saying to him, 'You are my Son and I love you. I am very pleased with you.'

Praying

Lord God,
I am one of your children.
I belong to you!
Amen.

Activities

Have some strips of blue and silver wool, paper or cloth which the children can stick on to the picture of Jesus' baptism for the water in the river Jordan. A reminder of their own baptism can be made using the outline provided, and more water-coloured wool or string.

PEARL DIVERS

Aim: To become familiar with Mark's account of Jesus' Baptism and the significance of the dove.

Starter

Give out long strips of crepe paper, or several sheets between a group, or use a parachute as the whole group. These things are waved in a way that expresses different moods, for example: angry, happy, gentle, excited, peaceful, wild, controlled, hopeful.

Teaching

Share this poem:
It's funny,
my puppy knows just how I feel.
When I'm happy he's yappy
and squirms like an eel.
When I'm grumpy he's slumpy
and stays at my heel.

It's funny,
my puppy knows just how I feel.

(Anon)

As humans we can feel all sorts of different things, and as God made us like him, and as Jesus showed us, we can tell that God also feels sad and happy, he's both peaceful and powerful, both gentle and strong. So the Spirit of God will show that too. Sometimes, like at the beginning of creation, we are told the Spirit of God was 'brooding over the face of the deep', full of love and hope for all that was going to be brought to life. (They can move their streamers like this, starting still, moving gently and then more powerfully.)

Today we are hearing about the time when Jesus was baptised. As they listen to the way Mark tells it, suggest they listen out for what mood the Spirit of God was in at this particular time. Use a clear translation to read today's Gospel; you may find it helps the children to have it projected on an OHP with a picture of water on an acetate behind it. Or have it written clearly on a blackboard with coloured chalks or on a length of wallpaper, with a 'watery' border drawn round it. Talk about the Spirit of God resting gently on Jesus, like a gentle white bird, and let them move the streamers to express this.

Everyone can read out together the words of God which Jesus heard as the Spirit rested on him.

Remind everyone of how the Spirit of God came at Pentecost, powerful and sounding like a great rushing wind and like fire. (Move the streamers or sheets like this.) The Spirit can come on all of us gently and powerfully, quietly or noisily. Sometimes the Spirit makes us feel suddenly very full of peace and calm, and other times it makes us feel full of excitement about Jesus and enthusiasm for following him no matter what.

Praying

Spirit of the living God,
I believe and trust in you,
and want to follow you all my life.
Come into my life and live there,
so that each day I may know you better
and love you more.
Amen.

Activities

On the sheet there are instructions for making a Holy Spirit mobile, with the Spirit of God expressed in the power of flame and the gentleness of a dove. Either copy the sheet on to thin card or mount it on thin card before tying on to cotton for hanging up.

GOLD PANNERS

Aim: To explore the presence of the Holy Spirit, particularly at Baptism.

Starter

Play some gentle music and give out paper and paints for them to express in colour and form what they hear as the passage from Isaiah is read.

Teaching

Where is the Spirit of God in this passage? Point out the effects it has on the servant and how this looks forward to Jesus.

Now read Mark's account of Jesus' Baptism, noticing how the Spirit of God is portrayed here, and exploring why it might have seemed like a dove. Link this with the words God speaks to affirm Jesus in his identity and his mission.

What are the effects of the Holy Spirit in their own lives? When they sense God's presence, is it like this or different again? Help them to see that God's Spirit comes to fill us only when we genuinely seek God and long to be filled with his life. How the Spirit comes varies, but always there is a sense of inner peace and joy, a deepening of love for God and a deepening realisation that God is real, alive and active.

Praying

Spirit of the living God, fall afresh on me!
Spirit of the living God, fall afresh on me!
Melt me, mould me, fill me, use me,
Spirit of the living God, fall afresh on me!

(Daniel Iverson
© 1963 Birdwing Music/Universal Songs/CopyCare)

Activities

The activities on the sheet help them to see how gentle, dynamic and creative the Holy Spirit is revealed to be in creation, in Baptism and in us.

LENT

First Sunday of Lent

Thought for the day

After his Baptism Jesus is led by the Spirit into the wilderness before returning to proclaim God's kingdom.

Reflection on the readings

Genesis 9:8-15
Psalm 24
1 Peter 3:18-22
Mark 1:12-15

Today we begin the season of Lent, committing the next six weeks to preparing ourselves for the festival of Resurrection by looking seriously at the implications of turning to God at our baptism. So it is appropriate to start at the point immediately following Jesus' Baptism when he was filled with God's Spirit and promptly driven into a six-week ordeal of vocational testing and spiritual battling.

Jesus' ministry did not begin with warm glowing feelings but rigorous self-discipline, painful soul-searching and cost-counting. When he later spoke about our need to count the cost of discipleship he was talking from personal experience. Committing ourselves wholeheartedly to God's service is indeed a costly business, and one it is quite natural to back away from as we start to realise the full implications. Are we really willing to say to God, 'Thy will be done; thy kingdom come'? Wouldn't we far prefer it to be our will and kingdom with God's blessing! Most of us feel fine about obedience until it differs from what we want in life; at which point we start jumping up and down complaining about the unfairness of it all.

One of the precious, valuable things we can learn from Jesus' example is to recognise the conflicts as a valid part of the process. Jesus knew he had some difficult things to face, and he knew he would not be ready for his ministry until he had taken time out to face them squarely, however unpleasant that might be. All too often our reaction is to deny our fears and questions, or edit them before approaching God with them, as we consider them inappropriate prayer material.

But the truth is that God wants our real, honest selves, and can't start working in earnest with us until we are willing to share with him everything – and that includes misgivings, things which embarrass us to mention to anyone, recognition of things we had hoped for and dreamed about and which we dislike the idea of giving up. If there is anything we feel ashamed to mention to God, then that's probably the most important thing he wants us to say.

Of course, we are not going to come to any of this lightly or easily. We are wonderfully inventive when it comes to rewriting agendas we find threatening to us or prefer to ignore. That is why we all need a wilderness, and time to be alone with God, without distraction. The wilderness is honesty, and we need to get used to its bare and uncompromising landscape, where conflicts are bound to confront us, but from which we will emerge stronger and more integrated as people, ready to go out in God's power.

Noah and his family are at that point as the rainbow of God's saving promise marks the end of the storms and floods, and they can walk as new people into a new landscape.

Discussion starters

1. Why can God only work with us in earnest when we are totally honest with him?

2. What is it that makes us decide whether or not discipleship is too costly?

All-stage talk

Bring with you a compass, and a chart showing that there are six weeks before Easter Day.

Explain that in six weeks' time it will be Good Friday and Easter Day, when we will all be celebrating Jesus rising to new life that lasts for ever, after being put to death on the cross. That's such a very special, important thing to celebrate that the Church decided we all need a few weeks to get ourselves ready for it. Time to think carefully about what it means to be a follower of Jesus. Time to sort our lives out a bit. Draw attention to the change of colour in church – purple is quite a serious, thoughtful colour, to match our serious, thoughtful mood in these next six weeks, which are called Lent.

Why *six* weeks? We are told that when Jesus had gone to the river Jordan and been baptised by John, he went straight off into the desert hills, to spend forty days, getting ready to tell everyone the good news of God's kingdom. He didn't get ready by reading lots of books and doing lots of homework, or talking to lots of people. He got ready by living very simply, even going without food, and letting God lead him into the areas he needed to think about. He wanted to spend time finding out what God really wanted him to do with his life.

So, as the Church, we're going to do the same.

Today is the day we all set off into the desert for six weeks. What do you think we'll need to take with us? Produce various items of combat gear, and mountain-walking clothing and equipment. Then kick it all away. We're not going to need any of this. All we need is one thing – a compass. What does a compass do? It helps you walk in the right direction. We need a special compass that always points us in God's direction.

Explain that you happen to have just the compass we need, and produce a cross – a wall-hanging one is about the right size so that people can see it easily. This is a special compass for us to take into the desert of Lent with us. Hold the cross flat. It points us always towards God's love, and at the same time it points back at ourselves. We can't pretend in this desert. We've got to be honest to God about who we are and how we are thinking and feeling. That's the only way the compass will point us in the right direction. Are we ready for the desert of Lent?

The first step on our journey is to agree to live more simply for a while, and go wherever God takes us. We can spend this week doing that, remembering to use our compass every day.

All-age ideas

- Invite everyone to close their fists and think of all the things they would hate to have to give up. Thank God for them all, recognising that we are not owners of anything, but stewards. As they feel ready to, invite everyone to open their hands slowly to God, with all that is in there open to be used in his service of love. As they do so they can say, silently, 'Here I am, Lord. I offer you my life.'

- In place of the Creed consider using the baptismal promises, to remind everyone of their baptism.

- Construct a rainbow of God's promise for people to walk under as they come into church. This might be a paper archway fixed with blutack above the doorway and painted by the children.

Prayer of the Faithful

Celebrant
As we begin this season of Lent,
let us move off into the desert
to communicate with our God.

Reader
As we come before God
with all our muddled priorities
and conflicting agendas,
we pray that we may be made whole
as the Body of Christ;
that we may have the strength to renounce evil,
and the courage to announce the kingdom of peace.

Silence

With our God:
all things are possible.

With the world's clamour ringing in our ears,
with comfort zones beckoning us,
but the pain of injustice refusing to be shut out,
we pray for the world's healing,
and for an end to all lying and deceit.

Silence

With our God:
all things are possible.

We come with the demands of home, family, work,
and expectations warring in us
for space and attention.
We pray on behalf of those
too busy or too exhausted to pray;
that our daily lives may be washed in peace,
ordered in holiness and lit up with joy.

Silence

With our God:
all things are possible.

We come with the needs and sorrows,
pain and suffering of our brothers and sisters
all over the world, who are aching –
physically, emotionally or spiritually;
we pray that they may be touched
by God's comforting and healing love.

Silence

With our God:
all things are possible.

In this Lenten season,
we come to realign our lives
in the context of eternity,
and to commend to God's love
our own loved ones
who have passed through earthly death
to the life which has no ending.

Silence

With our God:
all things are possible.

Remembering Mary's dedication and love,
we pray with her:
Hail, Mary . . .

We make our private petitions
and thanksgivings
together now in silence.

Silence

Celebrant
Father, we thank you
for showing us the way to abundant life,
and ask you to hear our prayers
through Jesus Christ.
Amen.

TREASURE SEEKERS

Aim: To know the story of Noah, the flood and the rainbow.

Starter

Put stickers of different colours on the children and stand in a circle, holding hands to make archways. When you hold up a colour, the child wearing that colour sticker runs in and out of the archways, round the circle and back to their place. Whenever you hold up a picture of a rainbow, the whole circle joins hands and comes in to the middle and out again, shouting, 'God loves us!'

Teaching

Spread out carpet tiles or a large sheet on the ground and sit around it. Use cut-outs, based on the pictures below to tell the story of Noah and the flood. Animals can be models if you prefer. The children can help move the characters around. Bring out the way God rescued Noah and his family and kept them safe, and how the rainbow is a sign of God's love that will never let us down.

Praying

(This can be sung to the tune of *One, two, three four five, once I caught a fish alive*)

Violet, indigo and blue –
God loves me, that's always true.
Green, yellow, orange, red –
that is what the rainbow said!

Activities

The sheet can be turned into a rainbow mobile. The children will need lengths of different coloured wool, glue sticks and cotton, and you may prefer to copy the sheet on to thicker paper than usual.

PEARL DIVERS

Aim: To think about the value of Jesus going into the desert after his Baptism.

Starter

Getting your bearings. Draw a large compass, showing the different directions clearly, and fix it to the middle of the floor. Everyone stands in a space and the leader calls out instructions – go two paces north, one pace south-east, two paces west, and so on.

Teaching

Mix up the separate letters of these words on the floor and get the children to help sort them into order: Who? What? How? Explain that Lent is a time for thinking about some big questions, and here are three big questions to start us off. Talk together with the children about plans for their lives. What kind of person do they want to be? (Who) What do they think they would like to do with their lives? (What) How are they hoping to do it? (How)

Then spread a large desert-coloured sheet or towel on the floor in the centre of the circle, keeping the words visible, and explain that as soon as Jesus had been baptised and filled with the Spirit of God, he felt led to go off on his own into the desert. (Place a small picture of Jesus somewhere on the desert, so that the emptiness and aloneness is emphasised to them.) And he lived there for forty days – about six weeks. While he was there he didn't eat. He wanted to clear his life completely for a while so he could give his whole attention to God.

Why did he want to do that? Because he wanted to listen to God very carefully, and find out *who* he was, *what* God wanted him to do in his life on earth, and *how* he should set about doing it. He knew they were hard questions, and wouldn't be easy to tackle, but he knew it had to be done so his life wouldn't be wasted or go off in the wrong direction.

As you look at Jesus, remembering him taking time to find out how his life could best be lived, pray for each other's lives, that God will make it clear to us how they can best be lived, and what he would like us to do in them.

At the end of Jesus' forty days in the desert, he had travelled a very long way, not just on foot over the sand and scrub land, but also in his mind and his heart. And now he was ready to go back into the towns and villages to start his work – God's work – of loving and caring for people, teaching them and helping them get to know God and themselves better.

Praying

Heavenly Father,
my life stretches ahead of me,
full of hopes and ideas and dreams.
Please help me to understand myself,
show me how you would like me to live,
and what you would like me to do. Amen.

Activities

On the sheet there is a map of a desert for the children to work out the safe way to cross it, based on compass directions, and there are instructions for making a special compass that will keep them in God's direction through their lives.

GOLD PANNERS

Aim: To look at the value of Jesus' time in the desert and our season of Lent.

Starter

Set up a short orienteering course, with something to collect from each point as they reach it. You will need to make a chart of the area on squared paper, marking the squares with numbers and letters (as shown below) so that they can find their way by map co-ordinates.

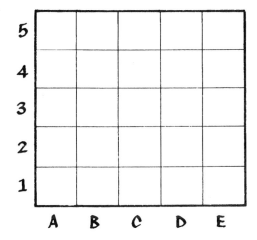

Teaching

Going through life is rather like finding our way through a landscape, and we need maps and a compass to guide us. Jesus referred to himself as the Way, which we can follow and trust. But, before he was able to start on that ministry, he had some working out to do himself.

Read the Gospel for today. What happened straight after Jesus had been baptised? Did he start his work immediately? No, he went out into the loneliness and discipline of the desert for forty days to search out what his role was, and how he needed to be spending the rest of his life on earth. It was a time of severe and difficult testing, which he had to go through, keeping to the right direction by keeping close to God and his word in scripture, as the doubts and temptations battled in him.

Only then could he come back into circulation and start his life's work. What are we told his work was? Proclaiming that God's kingdom is very near.

Now look at Noah and his family, setting out into the new, post-flood world. What do they receive from God to set them up for the rebuilding work ahead? God's promise of faithful, sustaining love, in the sign of the rainbow.

Lent gives us a chance to spend the same amount of time as Jesus spent in the desert, facing ourselves and our commitment to living God's way; to live more simply and rigorously while we allow God to prepare us for our own ministry as baptised Christians, proclaiming the risen Christ. It's all carefully thought out that Easter, the festival celebrating Christ's Resurrection, follows straight on from this 'desert season' of Lent.

Praying

Lead us, heavenly Father, lead us
o'er the world's tempestuous sea;
guard us, guide us, keep us, feed us,
for we have no help but thee;
yet possessing every blessing
if our God our Father be.

Activities

On the sheet there are some desert questions to reflect on, and some more teaching about Lent, with suggestions for using it profitably. Encourage the young people to take part in the parish Lent course, or lay one on specifically for them.

SECOND SUNDAY OF LENT

Thought for the day

Christ's willingness to face suffering and death, in order to save us, proclaims the total sacrificial love of God.

Reflection on the readings

Genesis 22:1-2, 9-13, 15-18
Psalm 115
Romans 8:31-34
Mark 9:2-10

We are in the landscape of mountains today. God leads Abraham to a mountain by what must have been one of the severest routes ever – a father leading the son he loves in order to offer him as a sacrifice to the God he loves and is ready to obey, whatever the instructions. We can only guess at the terrible pain, as each step takes him closer to destroying his beloved child; an act which would appear to fly in the face of God's gift, and his promise. Yet something assures Abraham, at the very depth of his being,

that God is in control here, and all shall be well, even though in human terms it seems impossible.

And, true to his name, God redeems the situation, requiring not the sacrifice of the child at all, but of Abraham's heart. In taking Isaac with him and building that altar on the mountain, Abraham was relinquishing all his past, present and future, his hopes and dreams to a great act of faith in God – 'Let *your* will be done!'

The disciples are led by Jesus up another mountain to witness another sacrifice by a Father of his Son, and the sheer glory of it terrifies them. They hear Jesus affirmed as God's beloved Son and are urged to listen to him. This comes moments after Jesus has been discussing (so Matthew tells us) his sacrificial suffering and death.

Paul makes the point clear in his letter to the Romans: God's complete offering of love involves refusing to hold anything back at all.

This might be read as sounding appallingly callous, rather than loving. What was a loving God doing allowing his own beloved Son to undergo insult, torture and a cursed death? But, of course, the Father is in the Son and the Son in the Father. Whatever torture was inflicted on the person of Jesus was experienced completely by God the Father as well. The sense of separation felt so sharply by Jesus, as he hung on the cross with the weight of the world's sin choking his life, pierced the heart of his Father just as keenly.

It was unthinkably terrible and yet it was allowed to happen, simply because love in all its glory was the only way of setting us free.

Discussion starters

1. Think through your own areas of possessions and control which you enjoy and value. Imagine the prospect of relinquishing them, one by one. Where do you find yourself feeling instinctively possessive or protective?

2. What arguments might have been used to justify Jesus avoiding suffering and death – and why won't they hold water?

All-stage talk

Gather ideas about how to listen well. This may include such things as stopping our own noise, being very still, wanting to find out what's going on, concentrating our minds, and engaging ears, brain and heart all at once. Having talked about it, try it out, by listening to every sound around us (and even inside us!).

Now show a mountain picture on an OHP, or in a few calendar pictures which children walk around the church, while you describe how mountains have long been thought of as very special, holy places. Jesus took three of his disciples up a mountain where they watched Jesus lit up with the glory of God's brightness as he prayed. Part of that amazing experience was hearing the voice of God speaking into their hearts and minds. They heard it and didn't miss it because they were really concentrating and wanting to know what all this was about. They were still and their ears were engaged with their brains and their hearts.

So what did they hear?

Have the words written large (in lower case) for everyone to read in a stage whisper: 'This is my beloved Son – listen to him.'

Out of all the listening we do every day, and out of all the listening we'll do over our whole lifetime, there's one thing which God himself has told us to listen to. And that isn't a particular programme or CD, it isn't a particular political leader or even our best friend. It's Jesus. And God has given us a personal recommendation to listen to Jesus with all our very best listening skills, because God knows that if we really listen to Jesus we shall start to understand the meaning of life, who we are, and how to live this life we've been given.

All-age ideas

- Fill the church with light from candles – in clusters, or held by the congregation.

- For the Penitential Rite:
  We have been possessive
  over what is freely given by you.

  Lord, have mercy.
  Lord, have mercy.

  We have avoided standing up
  for what we know to be right,
  in case it brings suffering.

  Christ, have mercy.
  Christ, have mercy.

  We seek our personal comfort
  more than we seek your kingdom.

  Lord, have mercy.
  Lord, have mercy.

Prayer of the Faithful

Celebrant
Let us pray to our God
whose glory fills heaven and earth.

Reader
That in focusing our lives and our worship on God

we may increasingly reflect his love and brightness
so that others are drawn to worship him.

Silence

Lord, open our eyes:
to see your glory.

That the world's leaders may be committed
to alleviating unnecessary suffering
and working co-operatively
for the good of all who inhabit this planet.

Silence

Lord, open our eyes:
to see your glory.

That every word we speak
and every meeting we arrange
may further the building of God's kingdom.

Silence

Lord, open our eyes:
to see your glory.

That all who suffer, whether physically,
spiritually, mentally or emotionally,
may know the comfort, healing
and transforming of God's love.

Silence

Lord, open our eyes:
to see your glory.

That those who have died to this earthly life
may share in the glory of heaven.

Silence

Lord, open our eyes:
to see your glory.

With Mary,
who shared her Son's sorrows,
we make our prayer:
Hail, Mary . . .

We pray in silence, now,
for our individual needs and concerns.

Silence

Celebrant
Father, whose character is always full of mercy,
hear our prayers
through the pleading of your Son, Jesus Christ.
Amen.

TREASURE SEEKERS

Aim: To sense God's glory and holiness.

Starter

Use a set of Christmas tree lights, strung across a notice board or round a door frame. If you haven't access to any fairy lights, bring a couple of bedside lamps and a multisocket, so you can turn them all on and off from one switch. Everyone jumps and dances around the room, but whenever the lights go on they stop and face them, standing completely still.

Teaching

When everyone is sitting in a circle, turn on the fairy lights, make the room as dark as possible and light some candles, standing them on a mirror or some foil so that the lights are reflected. As you light the candles have some quiet music playing, and talk about how good light is, and how beautiful. Draw the children's attention to the colour of the flames, and the bright reflections. Remind everyone that God is here with us, and he loves us and our families very much. For a short while, encourage everyone to sit here very still in the candlelight with the music playing, in God's company. Then explain how we often think of God as being like light, because he is so full of goodness and loveliness. The prayer can be sung (to the tune of *See-saw, Marjorie Daw*) as you sit around the candles.

Praying

Jesus, Jesus,
Lord of earth and heaven,
Jesus, Jesus,
Lord of earth and heaven!

Activities

The sheet can be turned into a stained glass window by colouring the outline with wax crayons, and then sponging a little cooking oil over it. Leave to dry out, and the paper will have become translucent.

PEARL DIVERS

Aim: To become familiar with the story of the Transfiguration.

Starter

Climb a mountain on the spot. Everyone finds a space, and we all set off walking (on the spot) towards the high mountain. We stop and shade our eyes from the sun as we look up at the top in the distance; *that's* where we're going! As we go on it gets steeper . . . and steeper . . . and steeper . . . till we're struggling to walk upright. Soon we have to use our hands as well as our feet. Now we come to a high cliff face. We look up at it towering over us, and feel the cold rock with our hands. We'll have to be very careful, and find a hold for our right hand . . . then our left . . . then pull up on our feet and quickly find a new handhold . . . and another . . . as we make our way up the cliff face. When we climb over on to the top we've got to walk along a really narrow ledge. We flatten our hands against the rock to steady us, and move slowly along the narrow ledge. At last it starts to broaden out, and we're nearly at the top. It's not too steep, here, and we run the last bit to reach the very top of the mountain. Now we can stand on top of the world and look right down to the tiny path where we started off, far, far below. We can see far into the distance every way we look. (They can stay at the top, do the journey down again, or abseil down, and look back at what they've achieved.)

Teaching

Everyone lies face in arms on the floor, as we imagine a rather different kind of mountain experience. Play some quiet music and lead the children in imagination on that walk up the mountain with Jesus, Peter, James and John, imagining it yourself as you speak, so that it rings true. Think of what you might see and hear and feel.

Praying

Holy, most holy, all holy the Lord,
in power and wisdom for ever adored!
The earth and the heavens are full of your love;
our joyful hosannas re-echo above!

(From the 'Slane Sanctus' by Michael Forster
© 1995 Kevin Mayhew Ltd.)

(Music for this may be found on page 235.)

Activities

Using the outlined drawing on the sheet, the children make string pictures which they can then paint with colours and print on black paper. They will need string, glue, thick paint, card for mounting, and black paper.

GOLD PANNERS

Aim: To see that Jesus is glorified both on the mountain and on the cross.

Starter

Beforehand prepare a message which they can communally discover by making a rubbing of it. (Cut out each letter of the message from cardboard and stick the letters on a card or paper base. Cover the whole thing with lining paper, secured with sticky tape.) Give everyone wax crayons to rub over the lining paper in order to see the message:

NOW YOU HAVE SEEN THE HIDDEN MESSAGE!

Teaching

Point out that the message was just as much there before they saw it; it was simply hidden from view. Today we are going to look at a time when God's glory became very obvious in Jesus. Read Mark's account of the Transfiguration on the mountain top. Think over what it revealed about Jesus, what it made clear and plain. (That Jesus was God's Son; he was filled with God's glory; he had God's authority; he was fulfilling the Law and the prophets; suffering and death had to be part of the rescue plan.)

How else in his life did Jesus show God's glory, but not by literally 'shining' with it? (In the way he spoke and taught; the way he healed and comforted; and, above all, in being willing to die a cursed death on the cross.)

Look at what John says about this in his Gospel (John 1:14).

Also read the Psalm for today, verse 3, and Exodus 3:2, Exodus 13:21, Deuteronomy 4:24, 2 Kings 2:11 and Daniel 7:9-10. Notice how the image of shining brightness and fire is seen as a sign of God's presence.

Praying

Shine, Jesus, shine,
fill this land with the Father's glory;
blaze, Spirit, blaze,
set our hearts on fire!

(From the song by Graham Kendrick
© 1987 Make Way Music)

Activities

There is space on the sheet to explore the references in more detail, and look at the crucifixion in terms of 'the Son of Man being glorified'. They can also try expressing this shining glory in a collage of words suggested on the sheet, using glowing, shining paper and foil. Have a variety of materials available.

THIRD SUNDAY OF LENT

Thought for the day

God's wisdom may shock us. Jesus, obedient to God's Law and fulfilling it, dies a death which, according to the Law, makes him cursed.

Reflection on the readings

Exodus 20:1-17
Psalm 18
1 Corinthians 1:22-25
John 2:13-25

Probably no one was more surprised at Jesus' behaviour in the temple than those sitting buying and selling there. It had become normal practice – a tradition even – for the marketing side of worship to flourish, and the petty corruption involved was something everyone had come to expect and live with. We all get used to our own dirt and scruffiness and stop noticing it after a while. But Jesus finds it highly offensive. Why?

One of the hallmarks of Jesus' life is obedience, born of attentive listening to his heavenly Father. Understanding the Father's longing and will urges him to work for its accomplishment on earth. Lack of obedience, on the other hand, is closely linked with the desire to act independently of God. Throughout the desert time of testing, Jesus drew great strength for resistance from his mature obedience to the words of God in scripture. He found, like the writer of Psalm 18, that 'the Law of the Lord is perfect, reviving the soul'. Jesus knew that he had come to fulfil the scriptures, and that full obedience, even when severely challenging, was the only way for this to happen.

In our own society there is very little of an obedience ethic, and a rather distorted image of obedience as being something mature people can grow out of as they achieve rational independence. So we find the whole idea of commandments rather heavy, and might even feel that the rights of those temple sellers need to be upheld against Jesus' action.

Jesus knows that our holiness will only develop in line with our obedience to God, and, if we casually break God's Law as if it doesn't matter, we will find ourselves weak and unable to withstand temptations when they come. For our own survival spiritually we have to be rigorous with ourselves. One of the benefits of this desert time of discipline in Lent is that we are strengthened.

What Jesus finds offensive is that God's temple,

set apart to be a place of holiness and prayer, is filled instead with buying and selling, profit-making and cheating. Our bodies are temples of the Holy Spirit. Are they also filled with buying and selling, profit-making and cheating? And, if so, do we care that we are therefore being disobedient to God's Law? Does it occur to us that we would be stronger and better enabled to resist temptation if we were rather 'houses of prayer'?

Discussion starters

1. In what way is the 'Law of the Lord' refreshing to us, reviving the spirit?

2. What was it about the temple that made Jesus so angry? Might he find anything in our churches to anger him?

All-stage talk

Begin by asking for some volunteers to read the following conversations.

1. **Mum:** David, it's time to stop playing and go to bed now.
   David: Oh, but Mum, I'm much too busy!

2. **Dad:** Turn that music down, Gary!!
   Gary: But I like it, and it needs to be loud!!

3. **Hilda:** George, it's time you gave up smoking.
   George: But, Hilda, it's my decision, and none of your business.

4. **Fred:** Now, Mother, you need to wear a hearing aid.
   Mother: What's that, Fred?
   Fred: A HEARING AID! YOU NEED TO WEAR ONE, MOTHER.
   Mother: No, I don't – I can hear perfectly when people bother to speak up properly!

All through our lives we're supposed to be obedient, and all through our lives we prefer to do as we like!

Today we're on the third week of our desert journey together through Lent. And we're going to look at what it means to be obedient, and why it's a good thing to work at, even though we all find it so very difficult to do what we're told.

Scatter the ten commandments, written on pieces of card, over the aisle, or stick them with blutack on to pillars.

In our first reading we heard the ten commandments – ten useful rules to help us live God's way. These rules were given to the people through Moses, the great leader who had led the people out of slavery in Egypt. They've all been in the desert for quite a long time, learning to be God's people,

like we are through Lent. And then God gives them the Law, which they are told to obey. They are still good rules, and when Jesus came he didn't say, 'Listen, everyone, now I've come you don't need to bother with all those commandments any more!' Jesus insisted that he had come not to destroy the Law but to fulfil it, to fill it full of God's love.

So Jesus summed all the rules up in two parcels. Produce one bag labelled 'Love God' and another one labelled 'Love one another', and sort out the first four commandments into the first bag and the second six into the second bag. That makes them easier for us to carry around in our heads (hold a bag in each hand), but we need to remember what's inside each bag, and take them out to look at from time to time, like we've done today.

So Jesus thought it was good to be obedient. He was obedient to his heavenly Father, even when that turned out to mean he had to die on the cross! The reason he was obedient was because he really understood why it was important.

If we understand the reason for being obedient, we're much more likely to try and do what we're told. If Fred's mother really understood how difficult it was becoming for the family to talk to her without her hearing aid, she'd *want* to wear it. If Gary really understood how hard it was for his Dad to concentrate on his work with the music so loud, he'd *want* to turn it down a bit.

In other words, obedience is all to do with acting out of love. As we get to understand and love God better, we shall find we are more and more keen to do what he wants us to.

All-age ideas

• Use the first reading as an extended form of penitence, encouraging everyone to get to know the commandments by adding visual clues. (These might be a large number one; a blank piece of paper; a cardboard speech bubble with 'Keep it clean' written on it; a calendar page with Sunday circled in red; a bunch of flowers with a label reading, 'To Mum and Dad'; a gun; a wedding congratulations card; a swag bag; a file clearly labelled 'Lies'; and a thought bubble with 'If only . . .' written on it.)

• Have two voices to read the commandments alternately, with someone holding up a finger as each is read, till all ten fingers are held up. In their places, everyone can follow this counting off process as a focus. After each commandment, pause for reflection before everyone says, 'Lord, have mercy on us'.

• The commandments could be written up and displayed on walls and pillars for today.

Prayer of the Faithful

Celebrant
As God has called us,
so we have come to pray.

Reader
We pray for the Church, the Body of Christ,
with all its collected gifts and weaknesses;
may we receive the grace to recognise
that in the Spirit we are one,
and curb in us all tendency to division.

Silence

May we hear you, Lord:
and want to obey.

We pray for the world
in all its beauty and richness;
may we have the desire
and the generosity of spirit
to share our planet's food and resources,
to care for its people's well-being,
and to foster peace and justice for all.

Silence

May we hear you, Lord:
and want to obey.

We pray for those we love –
those we see each day and those we miss;
may we cherish one another
as we live the loving way of your commands.

Silence

May we hear you, Lord:
and want to obey.

We pray for all victims of selfish or violent acts,
and for those whose lives are trapped in sin.
We pray for all whose bodies and minds
have difficulty functioning.
May we be more sensitive to their needs.

Silence

May we hear you, Lord:
and want to obey.

We pray for those who have died
and for those who miss their physical presence.
May the Lord have mercy on them;
may they, and we in our turn,
rest in the peace of God's enfolding love.

Silence

May we hear you, Lord:
and want to obey.

We pray with Mary,
our spiritual Mother:
Hail, Mary . . .

As God's stillness fills our hearts,
we name any we know
who especially need our prayer.

Silence

Celebrant
Father, we thank you
for giving us this opportunity to pray,
and ask you to hear us,
through Jesus Christ.
Amen.

TREASURE SEEKERS

Aim: To know Jesus' summary of the Law.

Starter

Traffic lights. Prepare three coloured circles – red, amber and green. Explain that to play this game we have to obey the rules. When the green is shown, everyone jumps and dances around the room. When amber (or yellow) is shown, everyone gets ready to stop. When red is shown, everyone stops quite still. When red and amber are shown together, everyone gets ready to move again.

Teaching

Praise them for obeying the rules so well. That meant we could all enjoy playing the game together. It's very useful to have rules. Some rules are there to keep us safe (like not playing in the road), and some are to make sure that things are done fairly (like queuing up for rides at a theme park).

Jesus gave us two good rules to help us live our lives really well, and we're going to learn them today. As we've got two hands each we can use our hands to help us learn the rules.

Demonstrate raising one hand to heaven as you say, 'Love God', and then stretching the other hand out, palm up, as you say, 'Love one another'. Then everyone can try it a couple of times. The rules can also be written on two balloons with an OHP pen, and the balloons inflated. Any of the children who now think they can say the two rules on their own can do that in front of the others. (Everyone will benefit from the reinforcement, and the children enjoy being able to do it well.)

Now we've learnt God's two rules, all we have to do is live by them! Each day we can think over what we've done and ask ourselves, 'How have we been loving God today? And how have we been loving one another today?' And the next day we can try and do it even better!

Praying

(Say the prayer with actions.)

Love God, love one another,
that's the way to live.
Love God, love one another,
happy to forgive.

Activities

There is a picture on the sheet with children and adults of all ages. The children can pick out all the loving God and loving one another that is going on. Part of the sheet can be made into wrist bands with the two rules on, which the children can decorate and wear.

PEARL DIVERS

Aim: To know the story of Jesus in the temple, and understand some of the reasons for it.

Starter

An emptying and filling activity. Give each two or three children a small pot full of dried peas, a jug of water and two straws. To prevent spillage, put these on trays, fixing the pot of peas to the tray with a piece of blutack. The aim is to fill the pot with water, but to do this they first have to empty it of peas, using the straw-sucking method to pick up one pea at a time and drop it on the tray.

Teaching

Point out that we couldn't fill the pots with water at first because they were full up with peas; we had to empty the pot before we could fill it as we wanted. Today we are going to hear about a whole building which needed to be emptied before it could be filled!

Find Isaiah 56 verse 7 in the Bible, and also have it written out clearly so everyone can read it together: 'My temple will be called a house of prayer.' Explain that what God wanted was that the whole temple would be filled with prayer, so that people could go to it and feel close to God there. The temple, at Jerusalem, was to be a very special place.

But when Jesus came to the temple at Jerusalem, he found that instead of being filled with prayer it was filled with a whole lot of other things. People were bustling about buying and selling; money was clattering at the money-changing desks, tradesmen called out their bargains; there were sheep bleating, pigeons cooing, and cattle mooing. What a racket! Give different children different noises to make (coins can be shaken in a pot) and orchestrate all the noise of the temple.

Jesus knew that this was the last thing the temple was meant to be like, because God had said (everyone joins in), 'My temple will be called a house of prayer.' There was only one thing to do; the temple had to be emptied of all this cheating and buying and selling so it could be filled with prayer as it was meant to be.

As God's Son, Jesus strode into all the noise and started upending the tables so all the coins went flying (do this with a couple of tables as you speak), and overturning the boxes and baskets, driving out all the people who were using the temple of God as a market place. And as he walked about, he shouted to the people, 'It is written, "My temple will be called a house of prayer", but you have made it a den of thieves!'

All the people were shocked and a bit scared. They knew Jesus was right. They knew they had filled the temple up with wrong things. But now it was empty, and ready to be filled with prayer, as God intended it to be.

Praying

Jesus, my life is filled with lots of thoughts,
lots of words and lots of activities.
Please show me which of them are good
and which are not,
so I can be like God's temple,
empty of anything wrong
and filled with your love.

Activities

There is a picture on the sheet of all the buying and selling going on in the temple court. On the other side the same outline is filled with nothing, and they can fill that with the prayer suggested. The ten commandments are also taught.

GOLD PANNERS

Aim: To explore the implications of obeying God's Law.

Starter

They invent a simple ball game with clear rules, which gives everyone a chance to be involved.

Teaching

Point out the value of the rules, which make it possible for the game to be played and uphold fair play. Before you read the ten commandments from Exodus, check that they remember who is being given these rules and when. (The people of Israel, through their leader, Moses, after they had escaped from slavery in Egypt and were wandering in the wilderness.)

As each of the commandments is read (reading around the group), place cards of individual commandments on the table, together with memory joggers as described in the All-age Ideas.

Draw attention to the first commandment, and discuss what they might expect God's temple to be like, in the light of this rule. You could also refer to Isaiah 56:7. Bearing those ideas in mind, read the Gospel for today, so they can see how far the people had wandered from God's will as expressed in that first commandment.

How was Jesus being obedient to God's Law? When might obedience to God mean getting into trouble with the Law?

Praying

Jesus Christ is raging, raging in the streets
where injustice spirals and all hope retreats.
Listen, Lord Jesus, I am angry too;
in the kingdom's causes let me rage with you.

(Taken from the song *Jesus Christ is waiting*
by John L. Bell and Graham Maule
© 1988 WGRG, Iona Community)

Activities

On the sheet there is an obedience quiz and some headline situations to get them thinking about what makes them angry 'in the kingdom's causes', and what might be done about such things. The discussion may lead on to wanting active involvement in working for justice, peace and reconciliation. Useful resources for this are:

- Pax Christi – 9 Henry Road, Manor House, London N4 2LH
- CARE – 53 Romney Street, London SW1P 3RF
- CAFOD – Romero Close, Stockwell Road, London SW9 9TY
- Young Christian Workers – St Joseph's, Watford Way, London NW4 4TY
- CAYA (Catholic Association of Young Adults) – 6 Brownsville Road, Heaton Moor, Stockport SK4 4PE

FOURTH SUNDAY OF LENT

Thought for the day

God loves us so much that he is generous with his mercy.

Reflection on the readings

2 Chronicles 36:14-16, 19-23
Psalm 136
Ephesians 2:4-10
John 3:14-21

Condemnation is crushing and destructive. That is why it is used to express society's verdict on offenders in courts of law. To be condemned slams the shutters down on hope and gives us the bleak prospect of a landscape where nothing grows except despair. Yet throughout human history, and in every family network of relationships, there are those who experience condemnation. Children growing up in its influence develop the very survival strategies which ensure it is continued on into the next generation.

Today's readings break into that cycle and proclaim new possibilities of life without condemnation, pouring out from the loving nature of God which is its antithesis. Everything in God's nature is to do with saving, enabling, encouraging and redeeming. Jesus' life, death and resurrection is the living visual aid which celebrates the truth of God's love for his people and his passionate desire to save us, that nothing be lost.

In the Old Testament passage the patient mercy of God is carefully chronicled. Over and over again the people act in ways which justify condemnation, yet God sends messenger after messenger to lead them back to repentance. Repeatedly the messengers receive condemnation until the course of history measures out national catastrophes which the people have brought upon themselves. In our own time, too, people rail at God for allowing evil to happen, without recognising the rejected efforts of God to lead us in right directions which would have enabled many such evils to be avoided.

But God never gives up on us. As Paul writes in his letter to the Christians in Ephesus, we are God's work of art, and it is only through his grace that we can be saved. The coming of Jesus proves that God is not out to condemn us. Any image of God as fierce, judgemental and condemning is a false one set up by those with unhealed condemnation in their own hearts. The one, true, living God loved us so much that the ultimate rescue operation was put into action. Rather than being condemned, we can, through believing in Jesus, catch hold of the saving love of God and live without the crushing weight or fear of condemnation hanging over us or distorting our behaviour.

Discussion starters

1. Have we allowed Jesus to deal with any areas of condemnation in our own lives? Do we really believe he can?

2. Why doesn't God give up on us?

All-stage talk

Ask if anyone has ever tried to rescue a bird or worm, dog, cat or snail, and invite one of two of these stories to be told. Children, particularly, are ready to rescue small creatures, even if the hope of recovery seems slight. Adults are good at doing such rescues as well. We think it's worth having paramedics to race to where someone has had an accident or a heart attack and try their best to keep them alive and make them better.

Whenever we do this we are behaving like God our Father. It is God's character to want to rescue and save.

We know it feels wrong and sub-human to walk past someone who's suddenly fallen down and hurt themselves. We know it feels right and human to do whatever we can to help them.

In our Gospel today we're listening in on a conversation Jesus is having. He is teaching Nicodemus about how much God loves us. In some ways we are all like people who have collapsed on the pavement and badly need a paramedic to give us the kiss of life. We may be physically fit and healthy, but when we look at the state of our souls, at the secrets we guard and the ways we think, it doesn't look quite such a healthy picture. By the unloving things we think, speak and do, and the loving things we fail to do, we are in dire need of a spiritual kiss of life.

And that's what God gives us, through Jesus coming to live among us, dying for us and rising to new life. He is the one who can give us that spiritual kiss of life we need, breathing his life into us and saving us from being condemned to everlasting death. That's why he came – not to condemn us, but so that we may be saved.

All-age ideas

- Have a group of people to help read the Gospel. All the way through from 'Yes, God loved the world . . .' there are alternating phrases – 'not to . . . but so that . . .' – so that it can almost be read antiphonally, with the main reader reading the introductory verses.

- This mime can be done in silence or while people sit and sing either *Only by grace can we enter* or *Make me a channel of your peace*. Prepare large signs in the shape of arrows, with one of the words on one side and one on the other: Hate/Love; Conflict/Peace; Death/Eternal life; Doubt/Faith; Despair/Joy; Injury/Pardon. All the negatives point the same way. People walk to the centre or front with their arrows clearly showing on the negative side. Someone carrying a processional cross walks slowly along the line of people. As the cross comes close to them each turns direction so that the arrows are all pointing the way the cross is going, and the positives are displayed.

Prayer of the Faithful

Celebrant
Trusting not in our own worthiness,
but in God's mercy,
let us pray.

Reader
We pray for all who lead worship
and teach the faith to others;
that hearts may be open to receive
the message of spiritual health and life.

Silence

Day by day, O Lord:
may we remember your love.

We pray for all world leaders,
both in their public office
and in their private lives.
We pray for a collective desire for peace
and the courage to uphold right values.

Silence

Day by day, O Lord:
may we remember your love.

We pray for those we live and work with,
that none may be taken for granted
or live in a climate of condemnation;
but that we may all encourage one another in love.

Silence

Day by day, O Lord:
may we remember your love.

We pray for all condemned to death
or long prison sentences;
for those with long-term and debilitating illness;
for all who have been damaged.

Silence

Day by day, O Lord:
may we remember your love.

We pray for those who have died
and those who miss their physical presence;
May they see the fullness of eternal life.

Silence

Day by day, O Lord:
may we remember your love.

Remembering Mary's hopefulness and love,
we make our prayer with her:
Hail, Mary . . .

We pray in silence, now,
for any who especially need our prayer.

Silence

Celebrant
Merciful Father,
you know our deepest needs;
let your will be done in our lives
and in the lives of those for whom we pray,
through Jesus Christ.
Amen.

TREASURE SEEKERS

Aim: To know that God helps us try and try and try
again, without giving up on us.

Starter

Have some bean bags (or rolled socks) and some
buckets. The children try to throw the bean bags
into the buckets.

Teaching

Some things are hard to manage and we have to keep
trying at them until we get better. Share together
things you have all found hard, but trying and trying
has worked in the end. (Talking and walking, feeding
ourselves, drawing, throwing a ball, riding a bike,
for example.)

All of us here have been given a life to live –
perhaps seventy or eighty years of it. It was God
who gave us all this gift of a lifetime to spend, and
he gave us a good planet to live on, and people to
look after us and play and work with. What we
have to learn while we are alive is how to love God
and love one another. Is it always easy to be loving?
It's easy when we feel like it but it's hard when we
don't feel like it and would much rather please
ourselves.

So we need to practise. We need to try and try and
try again. Will we always get it right? No, sometimes
we know we are not at all loving – sometimes
we can be mean and selfish and a real pain!

When that happens, don't give up. Talk to God
about it and tell him you are sorry. He will forgive
you and help you try again. God loves us all so much
that he *always* helps us try again, and never thinks
we're useless or no good. God believes in us and is
always close by, helping us.

Praying

Jesus' love is very wonderful,
Jesus' love is very wonderful,
Jesus' love is very wonderful,
O wonderful love!
So high you can't get over it,
so low you can't get under it,
so wide you can't get round it,
O wonderful love!

(H. W. Rattle. © Scripture Union)

Activities

There is space on the sheet for the children to make
a picture of God's wonderful love, using paints,
crayons or sticking on all kinds of beautiful things.
Have a selection of shiny shapes, pieces of bright
wool, and any small-scale junk which they might
enjoy using. Or have some natural objects, such as
petals, feathers and leaves.

PEARL DIVERS

Aim: To look at condemnation and God's mercy.

Starter

Musical chairs or any similar game, where once you
are out you are out.

Teaching

Give the children this short script to read.

Set up a table and chair where a judge sits. The
prisoner has his hands tied together and is led by a
policeman. The rest of the children are the jury, sitting
in a row near the judge.

Judge   Bring in the prisoner!

*(The prisoner is brought in and stands in front of the
judge and jury.)*

Judge   People of the jury, you have had time to
hear the evidence and think about it carefully. How do you find this person – guilty
or not guilty?

Jury   We find him guilty, my lord.

Judge Very well. Matthew Bishop, you have been found guilty. You are condemned to live in a poky cell with a nasty toilet for years and years and years. You will have only dry crusts of bread to eat and watery orange squash to drink. It is what you deserve. No mercy will be given to you. Take the prisoner away!

(The prisoner is led off as the jury hiss and boo.)

Give each other a round of applause for the acting, and especially the prisoner, so that everyone is de-roled positively.

Talk about what it means to be condemned. The prisoner was condemned to spend years and years in a poky cell with a nasty toilet. Sometimes, in some countries, people are condemned to death.

In the Gospel today Jesus has some very comforting words for us. Read John 3:16-17. God loves us so much that, even though we deserve to be condemned, he is full of mercy, and forgives us when we turn to him.

Teach the children John 3:16 with actions, so that they are helped to memorise it:

For God
(arm points upwards)

so loved the world
(hands on heart, then trace a big circle with both hands)

that he gave his only Son
(gesture of giving with both hands)

so that everyone who believes in him
(point to yourself and other people, then raise arm to heaven)

may not be lost
(cower down, hands over head)

but have eternal life.
(both arms raised)

Praying

Thank you, Father,
for loving us so much
that you sent your Son
into the world
not to condemn us
but to set us free.

Activities

There are instructions on the sheet for making a prison. The children will need a box to make the prison and eight drinking straws each to make the prison bars. They are looking at the way God's love sets us free.

GOLD PANNERS

Aim: To look at God's mercy and the way he sets us free, rather than condemning us.

Starter

One by one competitors sit in the hot seat and try to keep a perfectly straight face, while everyone else (from a short distance away) endeavours to make them smile. Have ready a whoopee cushion or some other sound effect to use for announcing that a player is out of the game.

Teaching

As soon as we broke the 'no smiling' rule we were out, with no mercy shown and no second chance in that round. When people break the rules in society the whoopee cushion for them is the charge brought against them and the sentence they are given. If they are condemned, is mercy shown to them? Our legal system was founded on Christian principles. We do have the possibility of mercy, in such things as being granted bail, remission for good behaviour and the right to appeal.

What about when we break God's law of love? Read together the passage from Chronicles, noticing God's mercy and patience as his people continue to break the law of love, in spite of the help they are sent again and again. Their law-breaking is bound to end them in national disaster; by insisting on following evil they bring it on themselves. Talk about the way it seems to be human nature to do this – we aren't able to do the good we know we should, and all too often we end up doing the opposite. That means that we all break the law of love, and deserve God's condemnation.

Now read today's Gospel. What does Jesus say? Was he sent into the world to condemn us in a massive clean-up operation? No, he wasn't sent to condemn but so that through him the world might be saved.

Finally read the passage from Ephesians. Paul realises that we can't sort it out for ourselves. That's doomed and condemned to failure. But grace is a different matter. Grace is God's freely given love which we can't earn, but we *can* accept. In accepting, we are showing that we put our trust in Jesus.

Praying

O most merciful Redeemer, friend and brother,
may we know you more clearly
love you more dearly
and follow you more nearly
day by day. Amen.

(From St Richard of Chichester's prayer)

Activities

On the sheet there is a mixture of condemning and mercy vocabulary to sort and read out, so that the contrast alerts us to the true nature of God. They also look at what we mean by 'grace' in relation to God's mercy.

FIFTH SUNDAY OF LENT

Thought for the day

Through Christ's death, full life would come to people of all nations and generations.

Reflection on the readings

Jeremiah 31:31-34
Psalm 50
Hebrews 5:7-9
John 12:20-33

The people of Israel had been advised to strap the Law to their foreheads and around their doorposts in order to try and keep God's rules always in mind, but Jeremiah looks forward to a time when people will have God's Law deep within them in a new and dynamic way. And it is with the coming of Jesus that the prophecy can be fulfilled. With Jesus Christ there in person, people can see and understand what God is like, and with God's Spirit poured into their hearts, after Jesus' Ascension, the new and intimate relationship with God becomes a reality for those in every age and place.

In today's Gospel we are told by John that some Gentile Greeks are actually seeking Jesus out. He had just finished cleansing the temple so that it could be restored as a house of prayer for all nations, and now here are representatives of those other nations asking for him. With their coming, it is as if Jesus suddenly catches sight of that future, rolling out into the distance of time and space, with people of all nations giving God glory and worshipping him in Spirit and in truth. At the same time he recognises that his own finger is poised on the button that will make it possible. He is acutely aware of the necessary agony he must suffer for it to happen, and, in his humanness, shrinks from that. He battles with what we all know so well – the powerful human instinct to preserve ourselves and avoid pain and conflict. Being the Son of God did not immunise Jesus against the struggle of sacrifice. Gloriously,

love triumphs, and Jesus relinquishes everything to the will and glory of God; it must be done, and willingly done.

Immediately and powerfully the Father's love affirms what he has chosen, and all in the crowd who have ears to hear, whether Jew or Gentile, hear that unity of loving will for the good of the whole world.

Discussion starters

1. How does it help that even Jesus shrank from the thought of the suffering ahead?

2. How is it that Jesus being lifted up (both when crucified and ascended) can draw all humanity to himself?

All-stage talk

Bring with you a box of assorted sweets or chocolates, and invite a couple of volunteers to choose one. Ask them why they chose it (there may be no reason at all) and whether they are happy with the choice they made.

All our life long we are faced with making choices. Sometimes the choice isn't that important; if you make a mistake and choose a chocolate which isn't a favourite, you haven't lost out much. But sometimes the choices are more important. Invite a couple of car owners to talk about their choice of car and whether they are happy with their decision. Ask a student which A levels they have chosen to take, or which degree course, and a child what they have chosen to do for a birthday treat.

Sometimes we have to choose even more important things than that! Let's look at a very hard choice Jesus had to make, which we heard about in today's Gospel. Jesus knew that he was alive on earth for a very important mission – he was here to save the world, and he really wanted to do that, because he loved the people. But there was a problem. He also knew that saving the world was bound to land him in terrible pain and danger, more pain and agony than anyone has ever faced before or since. It would involve taking on himself all the sin and evil of the world, and going on loving right through it.

So he had the choice – to go ahead with saving the world, taking on the suffering as part of the deal, or to avoid all that appalling suffering by opting out, in which case the world would have no hope of being saved.

And it wasn't an easy thing to choose. Everything human in him screamed out against going through the pain of it all; but everything divine in him pleaded for love and compassion, and selfless giving whatever the cost.

We know what Jesus chose. Love won, and he

chose to go through hell, giving up everything, including his life, just so that we could be set free to live.

All-age ideas

- As a form of preparation for the Pentitential Rite, provide everyone with the words of Psalm 50 and play a recording of it (*Miserere* by Allegri) so they can have a time of meditation and sorrow for sin. For children use a larger print and this simplified version:

  O God, have mercy on me
  because you are loving.
  I know about the things I have done wrong
  and cannot forget them.
  Please wipe out all my wrong doing.
  Wash away my guilt
  and make me clean again.
  Give me back the joy that comes
  when you save me.
  Keep me strong by giving me a willing spirit.

- Use music as a background to the reading from Jeremiah – such as the slow movement from Mozart's *Clarinet Concerto*, or *The Swan* by Saint-Saëns.

Prayer of the Faithful

Celebrant
Let us pray to the God who loves us
and understands our needs.

Reader
We pray for all Church leaders,
teachers and pastors,
and all who are being called
into particular ministries, both lay and ordained.
We pray especially for any who are wrestling
with the demands of such a calling,
that they may be given courage
to offer themselves in the Lord's service.

Silence

Let your name be glorified:
let your will be done.

We pray for the nations of the world,
that, in all their plans and actions,
conflicts and disasters;
the Lord may guard the children,
guide the leaders
and give us all his peace.

Silence

Let your name be glorified:
let your will be done.

We pray for those
who are weighed down with suffering,
or imprisoned by their fears.
May their burdens be eased
and may they be given the strength
to bear what cannot be avoided.

Silence

Let your name be glorified:
let your will be done.

We pray that those whose earthly lives have ended
may have mercy and everlasting peace.

Silence

Let your name be glorified:
let your will be done.

With Mary,
whose heart was pierced with sorrow,
we make our prayer:
Hail, Mary . . .

We pray to our heavenly Father
about our own particular concerns.

Silence

Celebrant
Father, with thankful hearts
we offer these concerns
for the Church and for the world,
through Jesus, our Saviour.
Amen.

TREASURE SEEKERS

Aim: To know that Jesus loves us enough to help us even when it hurts.

Starter

Play shops, with cartons, fruit and vegetables for sale and toy money, so that they get the idea of there being cost and payment.

Teaching

Talk about their shopping, and bring out a carrier bag from a local supermarket, with some cheap and expensive items in it. Talk together about which don't cost very much, and which cost a lot. Mention other things which cost lots and lots of money, like houses and holidays. We have to save up for things like that. Sometimes we see a toy or a game we would like, but we don't think it's worth all the money, so we choose not to get it. (Or Mum and Dad say that!)

There was something that Jesus wanted very, very much. It wasn't a toy, and it wasn't something to eat or wear. What Jesus really wanted was to save the world. He wanted us all to be happy and free. But how much would it cost? It couldn't be bought with money. It could only be bought with his life.

Jesus thought about it. He wondered if it was really worth giving up his life so we could be happy and free. He knew that giving up his life would hurt. A lot.

But remember, Jesus loves us very much. He loves us so much that he decided he was even willing to give up his life so we could be free and happy. He thought it was worth the cost of all that hurt. So he did it, and that's why we can be happy and free!

Praying

(Sing this to the tune of *Frère Jacques*, with the children echoing the leader's words and actions.)

I am dancing, **I am dancing,**
(*dance*)
'Thank you, God!' **'Thank you, God!'**
(*clap hands*)
I am singing, **I am singing,**
(*sway*)
'Thank you, God!' **'Thank you, God!'**
(*clap hands*)

Activities

On the sheet there is a purse full of pictures, and some other things which 'cost' the items in the purse. The children choose what they would be willing to give up for the experiences 'on offer'. There is also a 'thank you, Jesus!' hat to make and wear. Have a selection of sparkly and shiny things to decorate it with.

PEARL DIVERS

Aim: To recognise that Jesus' willingness to give his life is proof of his love for us.

Starter

Forfeits. Sit in a circle and spin a tray in the middle, calling out someone's name. That person tries to catch the tray before it clatters to the ground. If they fail, they have to pay a forfeit. Ideas for forfeits: count from ten (or twenty) back to zero; hop round the outside of the circle; give one of your hairs; blow up a balloon; wear a hat for the rest of the game.

Teaching

One of the helpers (or a primed child) produces a tube of Rolos which has only one sweet left in it. You notice it and beg to have it as you love Rolos. The Rolo owner lays it on thick that this is their pack of Rolos, and they saved up all their pocket money to buy them. It's an awful lot to expect them to give up. Go on begging, reminding them of how nice you are and how much you mean to them. Eventually they say, 'Oh, OK – I suppose you're worth it!' and give you their last Rolo. Everyone else can say, 'Aah!'

Explain that today, the Fifth Sunday in Lent, we're starting to look at what it cost Jesus to do his work as our Saviour. (Place a cross down on the floor in the middle of the circle.) It's one thing to dedicate your life to teaching and healing, wandering around the country with no definite place to stay, and working long hours without pay. Jesus had been doing that for the last two or three years.

But now things were taking a new turn. He knew that it wouldn't be long before his work of loving people to freedom led him straight into trouble, trouble that would be bound to end in giving up his life in a tortured, shaming death on the Roman gallows. (Raise the cross to standing and hold it there.)

Not surprisingly, Jesus shuddered at the thought of having to go through all that. It wouldn't just be the physical pain, either. It would mean taking on himself the whole terrible load of the world's sin and evil, and going on loving and forgiving to the very end. (Cover the cross with a purple cloth.) Everything human in Jesus cried out against having to do that. The cost was so great and so demanding.

But then he remembered that the whole point of him being on earth was that he had come to save the people he loved. And to Jesus we are worth all the suffering. (Uncover the cross.) So today we remember that Jesus was prepared to say, 'Yes!' because he loves us that much.

Praying

My Lord, what love is this,
that pays so dearly,
that I, the guilty one, may go free!
Amazing love, O what sacrifice,
the Son of God given for me.
My debt he pays and my death he dies,
that I might live.

(Taken from the song *Amazing love* by Graham Kendrick © 1989 Make Way Music)

Activities

The sheet can be made into a prayer corner for the next two weeks, to help them think about the cross and begin to understand at a deeper level what it meant for Jesus to give his life to set us free. Encourage them to look up the Bible references for each day and set aside a short time each day to pray the prayer.

GOLD PANNERS

Aim: To look at the significance of the Gentiles coming to Jesus and hearing his teaching at this point.

Starter

Have some blotting paper and dampen it so they can watch a blob of colour from various dark-coloured felt-tip pens spreading out in all directions and revealing lots of hidden colours.

Teaching

Have the spreading blots displayed as you read the passage from Jeremiah, focusing on the opening-up of people's knowledge of God – '. . . all of them will know me, says the Lord.' Go on to look at John 12:20-22. As this Gospel is very condensed, it's best to take it in sections.

Explain that the Greeks were Gentiles, and John wants us to know that here are representatives from the 'other nations' seeking Jesus out. Take them briefly back to the wedding at Cana (John 2:3-5) where Jesus had said his hour had not yet come, and then read what Jesus says when he finds these Gentiles looking for him (John 12:23). Everyone can read this verse aloud together. This is the point in Jesus' ministry when the 'stand by for action' lights start flashing. The big act of total self-giving has moved from the long-term planning stage to red alert, and, humanly speaking, Jesus' adrenaline starts pumping.

As he starts teaching them about what to expect (John 12:24-26) all the horror of what it will entail rushes into him, and John gives us a blow-by-blow account of Jesus, the Son of God, wrestling with the human temptation to scream, 'Stop! I can't go through with it!' (verse 27). What will happen? Wonderfully, Jesus manages to triumph in that battle, and chooses for God's name to be glorified, whatever the cost to himself (verse 28a).

We can imagine God the Father on the edge of his seat (so to speak) through Jesus' agonising, and now immediately he is there to affirm and comfort him, giving him a new surge of confidence, which we can hear in Jesus' voice in the last couple of verses (28b-33).

Praying

Father, may your name be glorified!
Whatever the cost,
may your will be done in me.

Activities

On the sheet they can trace the way Jesus has to go through this human temptation so that the self-giving is freely chosen, in full knowledge of the cost involved. This commitment is then related to their own lives and faith journey. They are also helped to see how the grain of wheat analogy works.

HOLY WEEK

PALM (PASSION) SUNDAY

Thought for the day

As the Messiah, Jesus enters Jerusalem, knowing that he rides towards rejection and death in order to save his people.

Reflection on the readings

Liturgy of the Palms:
Mark 11:1-10 or John 12:12-16
Psalm 118:1-2, 19-24

Liturgy of the Passion:
Isaiah 50:4-7
Psalm 21
Philippians 2:6-11
Mark 14:1-15:47 or Mark 15:1-39 (40-47)

Palm Sunday takes us through the great drama of what it means for Jesus to be the Messiah. This week, often named 'Holy Week', is the culmination and accomplishment of all the Law, prophets and history of the Bible. It's here that the promises make good, that the secrets of the kingdom are displayed, and that the truth of God's saving love is acted out. Just as at moments of crisis our brains click into a kind of slow motion where the events are crowded in, so the Gospels report this last week of Jesus' earthly life with all the detail and heightened perception of people witnessing to the most significant and important week ever.

As he comes into Jerusalem riding on a donkey, Jesus is choosing to act out, three dimensionally, what he is. He does what the prophecies had said the Messiah would do, spelling out to everyone both his authority and his style of leadership. Donkeys are humble beasts of burden, and Jesus, son of King David both as family and as the anointed One, is proclaiming that God's Messiah comes to his people as a servant King.

The only way we have any hope of grasping what this means is by going on to hear, as fully as possible, the extent to which the humility and obedience of this servanthood is taken. This enables us to see the waving palms and shouts of victory through the racking torture of the cross; and the seeming cursed failure of the cross through the waving palms and shouts of victory. Both are victory and both are sacrifice.

Mark's account of the Passion shows us a poignantly human Jesus, fully integrated with the frailty of human nature we are so familiar with ourselves. How he longs for it to be possible to avoid what he dreads, and how he needs support from his heavy-eyed and terrified disciples, who abandon him. Perhaps the most terrible part of the whole ordeal of the arrest, trial, torture and crucifixion, is that acute sense of utter abandonment, blocking him off even from his heavenly Father.

The liturgy of today shakes us and prepares us to travel with Jesus through this week of most costly loving.

Discussion starters

1. What do we discover about God's nature through the events of the Passion?

2. Why did the work of saving humanity have to end like this?

All-stage talk

Beforehand make two large, clear signs, one saying, 'Hosanna! Blessed is he who comes in the name of the Lord!' and the other, 'Crucify him!'

First remind everyone of the way the crowds had welcomed Jesus as he rode into Jerusalem on a donkey. They were all giving him the red carpet welcome, throwing down greenery and their coats for the donkey to walk on, and waving palm branches as flags, cheering and singing. One of the things they shouted was from one of their traditional songs, which we know as Psalms: 'Hosanna! Blessed is he who comes in the name of the Lord!' (Everyone can shout this as loudly as possible.) It meant they were welcoming Jesus as the new King David; they were really excited, expecting Jesus to become their king and throw out all the Romans so they would be free again. They thought they really wanted God's kingdom.

Sometimes we are like the people in this crowd. We get all excited by Jesus, and promise to work with him, and feel ready to do anything to help the kingdom come. 'Let your kingdom come! Let *your* will be done!' we pray, and we really mean it. We work hard at our praying, and do our best to be loving and honest in the way we live. We give God the worship we know he deserves, and we give of ourselves simply because we are filled with love for him.

In today's Gospel we heard what happened to Jesus on Good Friday. It makes us very sad to hear what happened to our friend, and we might find ourselves thinking that we wouldn't have left him alone like his friends did; we would have been there for him; we would at least have prayed with him and not fallen asleep in the garden.

But the crowd remind us of something rather nasty. They weren't singing 'Hosanna!' any more. They were shouting, 'Crucify him!' (All shout this.) And although we wish it wasn't true, we all know there are times when we do that as well. Those times when we know very well what is the right and loving thing to do or say, and we want Jesus out of the way so we can be as unkind and dishonest as we like. It's hard work having Jesus there when we don't want to be loving, or humble, or obedient. At those times we don't much like his kingdom. Every time that happens we are joining the crowd which shouted, 'Crucify him!'

Let's remember that, and pull ourselves together when it next happens so that, instead, we shout with our lives, 'Hosanna! Blessed is he who comes in the name of the Lord!'

All-age ideas

- Involve the whole congregation in the reading of the Passion, giving individuals and small groups their parts to read and having the words the crowds say held up on placards, or shown on a screen using an OHP.

- If you are having an outdoor procession, make it a festal one, with children shaking instruments and waving greenery or streamers, and everyone singing songs they know well and won't need words for. Consider inviting the local schools to take part, and possibly a real donkey.

Prayer of the Faithful

Celebrant
As we face up to the costly loving
shown by our God,
let us approach him in humility
and pray to him now.

Reader
We pray that as a Church
we may love God and one another,
and go on loving,
through insult and praise,
through acceptance and rejection,
in the sure knowledge that the Lord is our God.

Silence

Make us strong:
to do your will in all things.

May the kingdoms of this world
soak up the values of God's kingdom;
may their leaders and their peoples
uphold what is right and just,
and establish a social order
which is rooted in Godly love.

Silence

Make us strong:
to do your will in all things.

In all the heartaches and joys
of human relationships,
may we be governed by selfless love,
faithful and forgiving without limit.

Silence

Make us strong:
to do your will in all things.

May all who suffer come to know
the comforting presence and healing power
of God's forgiving love.

Silence

Make us strong:
to do your will in all things.

We pray for all
who are making that last journey of death,
that they may be surrounded with God's peace
and rest in his love for ever.

Silence

Make us strong:
to do your will in all things.

We join our prayers with those of Mary,
Mother of the King of love:
Hail, Mary . . .

Upheld by God's peace,
we pray now in silence
for any needs known to us personally.

Silence

Celebrant
Father, we rejoice
in your companionship and loyalty,
and ask you to hear our prayers,
for the sake of Jesus, our Saviour.
Amen.

TREASURE SEEKERS

Aim: To know that Jesus came into Jerusalem, welcomed and cheered by all the people.

Starter

If possible, let the children join in with the all-age procession, playing their instruments, dancing and singing as they go. Or gather all the age groups and take them on a Palm Sunday procession, preferably outside.

Teaching

Show a picture or a model of a donkey. There's a donkey in our story today. He was just an ordinary donkey, and a young one, but he was given a very important job to do.

Tell the children the story of Jesus' entry into Jerusalem from the donkey's point of view. Bring in what the donkey saw and heard and felt and smelt, and how pleased and proud he felt to have his friend Jesus riding on his back. If you prefer to have a 'script', Palm Tree Bible Stories have it written from the donkey's perspective in *Jesus on a donkey*, and Nan Goodall's classic, *Donkey's glory* (Mowbray, 1980), includes this special journey.

Praying

(Jingle some keys or bottle tops during this prayer.)

Donkey riding, donkey riding,
hear the children sing!
Donkey riding, donkey riding,
'JESUS IS OUR KING!'

Activities

Pin the tail on the donkey. Use the picture of a donkey and make a tail from some wool, with blutack on the top end. The children shut their eyes (or have them blindfolded) and fix the tail where they reckon it belongs. Using an old sock and some wool they can make a donkey puppet to remind them of today's teaching. (If you don't have any old socks, try the charity shops, or a jumble sale.)

PEARL DIVERS

Aim: To understand that Jesus is making a Messianic statement as he enters Jerusalem.

Starter

If possible, let the children join in with the all-age procession, playing their instruments, dancing and singing as they go. Or gather all the age groups and take them on a Palm Sunday procession, preferably outside.

Teaching

Bring along a little olive oil and a cloth, a crown, and this notice: 'Anointed as God's chosen one = Messiah (in Hebrew) = Christ (in Greek).'

Put the notice, the olive oil and the crown in the centre, and remind the children of when David was a shepherd boy and God chose him to be the future king. To show he was chosen (choose a volunteering child), David was anointed with olive oil. David was God's chosen king, and when he grew up, he became the king of Israel.

Long after King David had died, everyone looked back to those wonderful days when he had been their king, and they also looked forward to the time when God would send his anointed, chosen One to be King over all the world for ever. They knew this anointed one would be from King David's family. They called this anointed One the Hebrew for 'anointed' – which is 'Messiah'. We usually call it 'Christ' which is the same thing in Greek, the language the Gospels were written in.

Many, many years later, Jesus was born, of David's family. Gradually people began to realise that this was the Messiah, the son of King David who would reign for ever. When Jesus rode a donkey into Jerusalem, they all got really excited, and cheered and shouted and sang their hearts out. The prophets had even said the Messiah would enter Jerusalem riding on a donkey, and here Jesus was, doing it! 'Hosanna! Hosanna!' they all shouted. 'Hosanna to the Son of King David! Hosanna for the glorious kingdom he's going to bring us!' (One of the leaders can be a donkey and one of the children can ride the donkey while the others all shout their Hosannas and wave their streamers.)

What the people didn't quite understand was that Jesus' kingdom was not like a country on a map, but was a kingdom of love, joy and peace in people's hearts and lives. Jesus is the Christ, the Messiah, and reigns as King in our hearts now, just as he can reign in the hearts of anyone, living anywhere, at any time.

Praying

You are the King of Glory,
you are the Prince of Peace,
you are the Lord of heaven and earth,
you're the Son of righteousness.
Angels bow down before you,
worship and adore,
for you have the words of eternal life,
you are Jesus Christ the Lord.
Hosanna to the Son of David!
Hosanna to the King of kings!
Glory in the highest heaven,
for Jesus the Messiah reigns!

(Mavis Ford
© 1978 Springtide / CopyCare)

Activities

The different strips on the sheet can be mounted on card and fixed together to form the star of David, so that the children sense the drawing together of all the Law and the prophets in Jesus.

GOLD PANNERS

Aim: To look at why the Messiah had to suffer and die before he could rise in glory.

Starter

If possible, let the young people join in with the all-age procession, playing instruments, and carrying banners as they go. Or gather all the age groups and take them on a Palm Sunday procession, preferably outside. The banners read 'Jesus is the Christ' and 'Jesus is the Messiah'.

Teaching

Remind everyone of the way the prophets had known for many generations that God would one day send his chosen One, like a new King David, to save his people and reign for ever. The image they had of this Saviour was not all riding out to battle with the occupying army. Read from Isaiah 50, which is one of the passages about the suffering servant, noticing how the prophet senses the need for the Saviour to be despised and rejected as part of his saving work of love.

Notice the links with the story of the Passion, where we see Jesus in this suffering servant role. (Mark 14:1-15:47) Read the Passion with different voices for the different parts, with everyone reading the crowd parts. It is worthwhile to spend time on this.

Praying

Father's pure radiance, perfect in innocence,
yet learns obedience to death on a cross.
Suffering to give us life,
conquering through sacrifice,
and as they crucify prays: 'Father, forgive.'
O what a mystery, meekness and majesty.
Bow down and worship,
for this is your God.

(Taken from the song *Meekness and majesty* by Graham Kendrick © 1986 Kingsway's Thankyou Music)

Activities

There is space on the sheet this week to express the entry into Jerusalem with its welcome and praise, but with the shadow of the cross and its painful glory present.

GOOD FRIDAY

CHILDREN ON GOOD FRIDAY

Many churches organise separate worship and teaching for children on Good Friday. It is important that they are enabled to be part of this time, and Easter cannot really be celebrated with meaning unless we have also stood at the foot of the cross.

Whether you are planning to create a children's 'way of the cross' in and around the church, a prayer trail, craft activity, or dramatic presentation of the events, bear in mind that young children need to have the whole story, including the Resurrection, rather than being sent home with the pain and suffering of Jesus and no mention of Easter. We also need to be sensitive about dwelling on the horror of the Crucifixion, and it may be necessary to split the children into age groups for part of the time, even if you have very small numbers in each group. Hot cross buns with a drink can be part of the event, and they need to come away with some sense of the amazing love of God.

EASTER

EASTER DAY

Thought for the day

Jesus is alive; God's love has won the victory over sin and death.

Reflection on the readings

Acts 10:34, 37-43
Psalm 117
Colossians 3:1-4
John 20:1-9

So the unavoidable, total sacrifice was given, along with all its pain and suffering which Jesus had dreaded. Through rejection, brutal torture and utter abandonment, Love held strong and refused to be conquered by the worst that evil and sin could throw at it. It took the Lord of life deep into the darkness of death, so that even that journey, which we must all make alone, is graced for ever with his presence. Left behind, stunned and shaken, the followers and friends of Jesus don't know what to think about anything any more.

And now, on the third day after his death, the impossible happens, and Jesus returns to life. It isn't the same kind of life, of course – how could it be with that journey behind him? Death has taken him beyond ordinary human life. God's loving power has drawn him out of death into the 'entirety life' which is completely full and has no limits either of time or space.

In the Gospel accounts of the Resurrection we are constantly aware of the struggle people had with accepting that Jesus was really with them again. Whenever we are faced with amazing good news, we find it almost 'too good to be true', and these first fragmentary meetings with the risen Jesus are often as much filled with terror and confusion as joy.

Jesus lets them take their time to grasp the reality of what has happened. Patiently he explains the scriptures, eats with them and loves them, until it dawns on them that, although it is so extraordinary and so wonderful, they can believe it – because it's true.

Discussion starters

1. What did the disciples gain from seeing Jesus after the Resurrection?

2. Since the Resurrection, Jesus is alive for all time, including today. Do we still tend to think of him in history? What evidence have we that Jesus is with us now?

All-stage talk

Bring along a hot cross bun, a chocolate Easter egg, an ordinary hen's egg, and one of those fluffy Easter chickens.

Ask a volunteer to take the first object (the hot cross bun) around the church so everyone can see what it is. As they go, explain that these buns remind us that because God loves us so much he was prepared to live among us in person, and go on loving us even when he was arrested, tortured and killed on a cross. It's in Jesus' life, and in his experience on the cross, that we can 'taste and see that God is good'.

Now for the next object (another volunteer does the rounds) which is . . . a hen's egg. The egg looks as dead as a smooth oval stone, but we know better. We know that if the egg is fertilised, and kept warm by the mother hen, that hard shell will start to crack, and into the world will climb . . . (a volunteer takes the chick around) a fluffy yellow chick, full of life! So the egg reminds us that what looked dead and hopeless on Good Friday (when Jesus' dead body was taken down from the cross, and it seemed he had failed as a Saviour) was actually full of new life, because on the third day after that, Jesus broke out of death to be alive for ever!

And so our last object (a volunteer walks the chocolate Easter egg around) is what we all enjoy having on Easter Day – chocolate Easter eggs. They're always bright and colourful, fun and delicious, and that's because Easter Day is party time for Christians! Today we celebrate the fantastic truth that Jesus Christ is Lord – Love has won the victory over evil and death for ever!

All-age ideas

- Encourage people to make their own miniature Easter gardens and bring them to church on Easter Day.

- Fill the church with flowers and candles to celebrate – perhaps different groups and clubs could undertake an arrangement each, or work on an Easter banner. Ideas for banners: 'Love is stronger than death'; 'Jesus is alive!'; 'New life'; 'He is not here, he is risen'.

Prayer of the Faithful

Celebrant
As we celebrate the risen Christ,
let us pray to the God of life,
in whom we live.

Reader
That the Church of God
may be bursting with new life,

filled with the love
that takes even death in its stride;
that new and mature Christians together,
all in their various ministries,
may work in God's strength
for the coming kingdom.

Silence

You are our God:
who does all things well.

That the inhabitants of our planet
may recognise God's glory all around,
co-operate in the sharing of his gifts,
and cultivate the habit of caring love.

Silence

You are our God:
who does all things well.

That God will bless our homes and families,
our places of work and leisure,
with new life and the hope of new possibilities
touching the ordinary with beauty and joy.

Silence

You are our God:
who does all things well.

That all who feel trapped or imprisoned –
physically, mentally or spiritually –
may feel the stones rolled away
and new light pouring into their lives.

Silence

You are our God:
who does all things well.

That those who have died to this earthly life
may find the fullness of God's eternity,
flooded with the light of his love.

Silence

You are our God:
who does all things well.

With Mary in her Easter joy
we make our prayer:
Hail, Mary . . .

We pray for our own intentions now,
in silence filled with joy.

Silence

Celebrant
Father, in the name of the risen Jesus,
we ask you to bring the hope,
healing and joy of the Resurrection
to all these people for whom we pray.
Amen.

TREASURE SEEKERS, PEARL DIVERS AND GOLD PANNERS

If possible, it is recommended that the children and young people are in church with the other age groups today. Use and adapt some of the all-age ideas, and involve the young people in some of the music and in decorating the church.

TREASURE SEEKERS

Aim: To know that Jesus died and is alive again for ever.

Starter

Hide some Easter eggs (outside if possible) and have an Easter egg hunt before distributing them fairly among the children.

Teaching

Look together at some hens' eggs and pictures of chicks, birds and dinosaurs, all coming from eggs. Talk about the springtime and all the signs of new life around at the moment.

Today is Easter Day. It's very special because it's the day we remember Jesus coming to life for ever. Jesus went around doing good and loving people, making them better and helping them get to know what God is like. But some people wanted Jesus out of the way, and he was killed – they nailed him to a big cross. It was very sad, but Jesus went on loving and forgiving even then.

When some of his friends went to the grave on the Sunday morning, they couldn't find his dead body; it wasn't there. Why? Because Jesus wasn't dead any more – he was alive! He would never die again. Jesus is alive for ever! (You could all sing *Jesus' love is very wonderful* to celebrate.)

Praying

Did Jesus die? YES!
Is Jesus dead? NO!
Is he alive again? YES, YES, YES!
JESUS IS ALIVE!

Activities

On the sheet there are pictures of a chick being hatched to put in sequence, and a picture of the Easter garden to colour. This can be stuck on a folded piece of coloured paper and given as an Easter card to the family.

PEARL DIVERS

Aim: To sense the amazement, fear and joy of those meeting the risen Jesus.

Starter

As with the Treasure Seekers, a traditional egg hunt is good to have on Easter Day, preferably outside.

Teaching

Beforehand prepare an Easter garden on a tray, and use this as a focus for telling the story of the Resurrection. Follow either the Mark or the John version, according to what is being read in church; in a suitable version it can be read directly from the Bible. In your reading, think about pace and expression, allowing pauses and bringing out the different characters and responses in your voice. Make Jesus' words spacious and loving.

Praying

God of all life and power,
your love proved stronger than hate and evil,
stronger than death itself.
May the life of the risen Jesus
live in us today and for ever.

Activities

Prepare some hard-boiled eggs for the children to decorate, either with paints and felt-tip pens, or with sequins and beads stuck on. If there is a slope or some grass nearby, they can do some egg rolling. The egg which rolls furthest wins. Also on the sheet there is an explanation of the egg symbolism, and a look at the confused feelings of Jesus' followers on that first day of the Resurrection.

GOLD PANNERS

Aim: To look at the accounts of the Resurrection and weigh up the evidence.

Starter

Spread out a whole pack of cards and ask one person to choose a card, without giving away which one is chosen. The rest of you are going to detect the right card by a process of elimination. The card chooser can only answer everyone's questions with a 'Yes' or 'No'. As each question is answered, turn over all the cards now eliminated, until the correct card is there, plain to see.

Teaching

As we are used to celebrating Easter every year, the shock and impossibility of the event can get glossed over and taken for granted. As you read the Gospel account today, ask them to imagine they are particular characters (tell them which before you read) so that during the reading they are thinking through that person's head. Afterwards talk to everyone in character about how they felt, and how their feelings changed.

The reading from Acts will give extra insight into Peter's character, as this is his own later account of what happened, once he's had plenty of time to think things over. Has his conviction changed or is he still convinced that Jesus is alive?

Talk over the possibilities of what really happened. It's important that these are looked at and not assumed to be rubbish. Could Jesus have not really died, but just collapsed and later recovered? Could the disciples have stolen the body? Could the disciples and the women have wanted to see Jesus and so imagined they saw him?

Look at these questions in the light of the accounts they have read, so they can see that the strange truth is actually more likely. (*Who moved the stone?* by Frank Morison (Bromley, 1983) can be recommended for any wanting to read further.) The facts and circumstances point to Jesus dying and rising to new life. What does that say about who Jesus was? And is?

Praying

The dead One lives
and the power of death is broken
by the power of Love.
O my Lord, this is an amazing truth,
and you are an amazing God!

Activities

There is a role-play to explore the thinking and fears of the disciples, and some information about the Resurrection events. They are encouraged to think about the difference a crucified and risen Christ makes to the way we spend the rest of our own life.

SECOND SUNDAY OF EASTER

Thought for the day

Our faith in the risen Christ is bound to affect the way we live.

Reflection on the readings

Acts 4:32-35
Psalm 117
1 John 5:1-6
John 20:19-31

If we are travelling along dark roads at night and trust the road surface, we probably drive quite quickly and confidently, whereas driving along a road we know to be full of potholes is a matter of gingerly approaching and peering, so as to avoid damaging us or the car. What we believe affects the way we behave.

On this second Sunday of Easter the readings lead us to recognise that belief in a risen crucified Christ is bound to change things. With the Resurrection we know, more completely than ever before, that God is to be trusted, God is light without any darkness at all, and, what is more, we can share in that companionship of light and freedom with the living God.

In the reading from Acts we are shown a few snapshots of how this was worked out in practice for the early believers. We find them united in a common purpose, without in-house arguments, and free of possessiveness; individual belongings no longer seem important to them as their concern for one another's needs has taken over. Central to all this is the fact that they are still excited and amazed by the Resurrection; they are conscious of the risen Jesus living among them in person.

Do we, as a Christian community, live in that conviction, or has the Resurrection, over the years, turned into history for us? As we reflect on these Easter readings, they can light up our faith again; rather like turning up the thermostat on the heating, so that instead of just the quiet, steady pilot light burning away, the whole boiler flames into action. The risen Jesus walks into any gathering in any age, even those who have locked themselves in. And the meeting with Thomas, a week after the others have met with Jesus, shows us clearly that he is quite prepared to start with us where we are, addressing our particular fears, doubts and misgivings and leading us at a pace we can cope with, into the fullness of faith.

Discussion starters

1. Jesus breathes on his disciples the life which death cannot touch, the life of God's fullness. How does that change them?

2. What would you point to as evidence that Jesus is alive today, even though we cannot actually see him?

All-stage talk

Bring with you some items of clothing which alter the way you move when wearing them, such as a pair of flippers, a pair of very heavy boots, a pair of binoculars and a pair of very high-heeled shoes.

Invite volunteers to demonstrate that when they are wearing (or looking through) these, it changes the way they walk. The changed way of moving is all part of wearing them.

It isn't only clothes and footwear which change our way of going about; it's our thoughts and feelings as well. If we've just won a match, if the person we love has just realised they love us as well, if the mortgage rate has gone down, or if we've just been fed and changed, then the whole day looks rosy and happy, and we'll pass on our feel-good factor in the way we react to those we meet. On the other hand, if the cat's been sick on the new sofa, you've lost your spelling list and know you haven't learnt the words, if the 7:27 is half an hour late, or you're hungry and your bottom feels damp and sore, then those feelings will probably make you less friendly and forgiving, and far more grumpy!

When we look at today's picture of life in the early Church, we're struck by how much love there seems to be in the community. Something is making these people happy to look after one another instead of fighting and arguing, and happy to share everything instead of looking after number one all the time. So what is making them like this? It must be something very good and very powerful!

It's all to do with them knowing something. They *know* that Jesus is alive and among them, so they are living in Jesus' company all the time. Jesus being there changes the way they live.

Now for a big question we all need to ask ourselves. Would anyone guess, just from looking at how we think and speak and behave, that we *knew* Jesus was living here among us?

He is, so it should show!

All-age ideas

• As an introduction, or as an acted reflection, have someone knocking loudly on the outside of the church door. Then in the quietness, someone says:

If the risen Jesus knocked on the door of our church, would we be happy to let him in?

(Pause for reflection)

If he knocked on the door of our home, would we want to let him in?

(Pause)

What would he be glad to find?

(Pause)

What would he be sad to find?

(Pause)

(The door is knocked again)

Come, Lord Jesus, we welcome you among us!

- Cut out the letters of 'LIFE' from foil and stand lighted candles along them where people will see them.

Prayer of the Faithful

Celebrant
Knowing that the risen Christ is here among us,
let us pray in his name
for the Church and for the world.

Reader
We pray for God's blessing
on every group of Christians worshipping today
all over the world;
and we pray for all who doubt the truth.
We pray that our hearts may be set ablaze
with love,
and that we may walk as children of light.

Silence

My Lord and my God!
My Lord and my God!

We pray for all the areas of the world
which are torn apart by hatred and violence,
famine, disease, or religious differences;
we pray for an end to war
and a deeper commitment to peace.

Silence

My Lord and my God!
My Lord and my God!

We pray for those who face family rejection
if they become Christians,
and for all families divided by beliefs
or persecuted for their faith.
We pray for the children of our church
that they may grow up strong in the faith
with good role models to guide them.

Silence

My Lord and my God!
My Lord and my God!

We pray for those who wake up
to the prospect of another day filled with pain;
for those who long for someone
to spend time with them, enjoying their company;
and we pray for sight that notices needs.

Silence

My Lord and my God!
My Lord and my God!

We pray for those who mourn,
and we pray for those they love and miss,
commending all who have died
to the everlasting arms of the God of love,
in whom there is life in all its fullness.

Silence

My Lord and my God!
My Lord and my God!

We make our prayers with those of Mary,
whose trust made our salvation possible:
Hail, Mary . . .

In the silence of God's attentive love,
we name our particular petitions.

Silence

Celebrant
Trusting in your immense compassion, Father,
we offer you our prayers
and ask you to hear us,
through Jesus Christ.
Amen.

TREASURE SEEKERS

Aim: To know that Jesus is with us now.

Starter

Have four different sounds, such as a bell, a drum, a rattle and a whistle. When the children hear the sounds they do the appropriate actions. The bell means 'now clap', the drum 'now jump up and down', the rattle 'now sit', and the whistle 'now smile'.

Teaching

Talk about what we are all doing now. This might be sitting in a circle, listening, folding our arms, breathing, and thinking. Some things, like breathing, we do all the time, and hardly notice. Take a few breaths to notice what goes on day and night, when we're awake and when we're asleep, so that we stay alive. So there's lots going on *now* just in our own body.

What's going on now as well as us sitting in a circle in this church? Lots of other groups of Treasure Seekers are sitting in their circles in other churches! (Why not pray for them now – they will be praying for you!) What else is going on now? Think about what is happening at the moment on the roads and in hospitals, and in other countries, where some people are fast asleep and others are going to bed.

We only see our little bit of *now*, but God sees all of it! Jesus is here *now* for all the people and all the places!

Praying

(*Loudly*) Tick tock, tick tock,
Jesus you are with us NOW!
(*Softly*) Tick tock, tick tock,
(*Very softly*) Jesus . . . you are here.

Activities

On the sheet there are pictures of Jesus with us while we're playing, eating, travelling, working. It helps children to have it pictured for them, and then they have no problem in understanding that Jesus is with us even though we can't actually see him. They can colour the pictures and put them around the house at appropriate places to remind them. There is also a 'Jesus is my friend' badge to make.

PEARL DIVERS

Aim: To know the story of Jesus appearing to the disciples and helping Thomas.

Starter

Try again. Stand in a circle with one person in the centre. They throw a beanbag or soft ball to each person in turn. If someone misses a catch, they are given a second chance (or as many as it takes!).

Teaching

Sometimes we are given just one chance to get something right, and if we mess it up that time, there are no second chances. Share some examples, such as music exams, writing in ink rather than pencil, answering a question on a quiz show, converting a try, or entering a colouring competition. Sometimes we feel like kicking ourselves afterwards and would love to put the clock back, so we could do it again, but differently.

Today we're going to hear about someone who missed out, but was given a second chance.

Have everyone (apart from one who is going to be Thomas) sitting on chairs, and one extra chair left free. Have an unlit candle in the centre. Remind them about Jesus rising from death on the first Easter Day, and explain that he came to where the disciples were gathered on that Sunday evening. They had locked the door because they were scared. (Rattle a bunch of keys.) As they can see, one place is empty. That's Thomas's place, and for some reason, which we don't know, Thomas wasn't there that evening. Perhaps he was so upset about Jesus dying that he wanted to be by himself.

Suddenly (light the candle) there was Jesus in the room with them. Once they'd got over their fear and astonishment, they were all very happy to see him, real and alive! Then Jesus left them just as quietly as he had come. (Blow out the candle.) But what about Thomas?

Well, during the week the disciples told Thomas what had happened, and Thomas couldn't really believe it. It was just too good to be true. And he said, 'Unless I see him with my own eyes, and touch his wounds, I refuse to believe it.'

A week later, the disciples are all together again, and this time Thomas is there as well. Once again Jesus suddenly appeared among them, without a fuss – he was just there! (Light the candle.) And because Jesus understood what Thomas had been going through, he went straight to him. 'Here I am, Thomas,' he said. 'Here are the wounds in my hands and side and feet. It's really me! Do you want to touch my wounds to make sure?'

Thomas didn't need that kind of proof any more. The experience of Jesus' presence was good enough – now, he *knew* it was true, and Jesus really was risen from the dead.

Praying

Dear Jesus,
when Thomas had his questions and his doubts
you met him and helped him to see the truth.
We pray for all those who have questions and doubts.
May they soon discover how real you are. Amen.

Activities

On the sheet there is a dot-to-dot to discover a hidden picture, and various examples of camouflage, where something is there but we don't see it straightaway. The children will each need a piece of tracing paper or greaseproof paper and some plain paper to make the 'discovering truth' model.

GOLD PANNERS

Aim: To look at the stages of Thomas' journey to faith.

Starter

Give small groups clues to where the different components of a torch are. Each group races to be the first to assemble and light their torch. (Or you could have a tape player, lead, socket and tape to assemble.)

Teaching

Our torches only lit up once we had gathered all the pieces and fitted them together. That's also how Inspector Morse or any other detective works. Our questions and investigations help us put facts and experiences together to reach a conclusion. Today we watch this happening in Thomas, one of the disciples who very much wanted to believe Jesus was risen, but found it very difficult. Read today's Gospel. Faced with the impossibility of death turning into risen life, what makes Thomas believe?

Working with the text, go through the stages:

1. For some reason Thomas was not with the others – denial and avoidance strategy.

2. Thomas hears the stories of the others – witnesses heard.

3. Can it be true? – wavers but digs in to avoid being conned and insists on solid evidence.

4. Thomas joins the disciples same place, same time, a week later – takes a risk and puts himself in right place just in case.

5. Meets Jesus – finds that the meeting is more convincing than anything, solid proof no longer needed.

Finally read the passage from Acts to hear the faith in action.

Praying

Lord God, you hear my questions and my doubts –
they are all part of me seeking you;
lead me to a deeper understanding
of who you are and where we are going together.
Amen.

Activities

On the sheet there is a pictorial look at the early Church and how it showed Jesus' risen life. They are also helped to look at that breathing of 'beyond death' life, and how it still changes us now.

THIRD SUNDAY OF EASTER

Thought for the day

Having redeemed us by his death, Jesus can offer us the forgiveness of our sin, which sets us free to live.

Reflection on the readings

Acts 3:13-15, 17-19
Psalm 4
1 John 2:1-5
Luke 24:35-48

The Gospel for today recounts the events of that first Sunday evening after the crucifixion, when Jesus was suddenly there in person among his terrified disciples, putting their fears to rest, directing them to tell people they can be forgiven, and forgiving them in the name of the risen Christ. Of all the things Jesus might have said to his disciples on these brief encounters from life beyond death, why does he focus on repentance and forgiveness?

Surely because something had happened during those hours of agony on the cross, and at the moment of dying, which changed things for ever. We are told that the curtain of the temple ripped from top to bottom, a symbolic tearing down of the barrier of sin between God and his people; and now, from the perspective of the Resurrection, Jesus passes on to his disciples the urgent work of tearing down that barrier wherever it exists, in every person of all time.

In the reading from Acts we see Peter doing exactly what Jesus had said. Using every opportunity – in this case the people's amazement at the healing of the man unable to walk – he directs their attention to the real power and the powerful reality. It is through Jesus that the man is healed. This leads them straight on to the spiritual 'setting free' of repentance and forgiveness which is now available.

John, too, speaks from the viewpoint of one who knows what a difference it makes to be set free like this; the extent of God's love which makes such an enriched life possible still amazes him. It isn't a one-off operation, this forgiveness, though it often starts with a dramatic change of life direction. But we need to come regularly before the throne of God with humility to voice our sin, and our longing to be forgiven, and to experience that cleansing and refreshing which comes from God's acceptance and forgiveness.

In fact, as our relationship with the living Jesus deepens, we shall find it increasingly uncomfortable to carry on in a state of sin without going to God to have it lifted from us, so as to restore us once again to that marvellous freedom we have experienced before. It is God's longing that all his humanity should be able to share the liberating joy of repenting and being forgiven. Knowing what we are all missing out on by lugging our sin around, and living only the 'till death' kind of life, Jesus sees repentance and forgiveness as urgent priorities for us – the stuff of a new order; the stuff of God's kingdom.

Discussion starters

1. Do we pass over serious, regular repentance, thinking of it only being really necessary for a few 'heavyweight' sins which we haven't committed?

2. Does living the risen life feel different, as the apostles claim? If it doesn't, could it be we aren't living it yet?

All-stage talk

Bring along a dry stick and a growing plant with fresh shoots.

Easter is all about a different, richer sort of life which we can now have, thanks to Jesus going through death for us. It's a bit like the difference between this dry stick (show it) and this one which is full of life and growing (show it).

In today's Gospel we heard that Jesus comes into the locked room where his frightened disciples have met (display a number 1), and puts their minds at rest, so they aren't terrified, even though they are open-mouthed at God's power. Then (display a number 2) Jesus explains things to them so that they begin to understand that Jesus had to die and rise again, and lastly (display a number 3) he commissions them, sending them out to set everyone free to live this way (the shooting plant) instead of that (the dry stick).

We may not have noticed, but there are lots and lots of dry sticks like this walking around. Dry stick people are often disguised. Because they are only interested in money, possessions or following their own wants, they often look attractive, with the latest everything to wear, smear on their face, drive or play. But a look into their eyes will show you that they are hard and dry as people, without any real joy, and may well be full of worries and anxieties, guilt and fear. Many of these dry sticks really know that this way of living is 'second best' but don't know how to get fully alive, or are frightened that God would say they were beyond his help.

Today is great news for all dry sticks! In going through evil and death without love slipping, even for a split second, Jesus has won for us all the victory over the sin and evil which dries us up and stops us living God's full life. All any dry stick needs is God's forgiveness; as they admit to themselves and to God what they are really like, and how they are cut off from him, his forgiveness starts to work on them, turning them into vibrant, warm, joy-filled people, happy to be living God's full life, and no longer bullied and caged by things that don't matter.

All-age ideas

- Use a song such as *Purify my heart* as everyone calls to mind the areas in their lives and attitudes where repentance is needed, or *I'm accepted, I'm forgiven*.

- On a long piece of lining paper, have a dead-looking twig drawn. During the talk the younger children can stick on green leaves (pre-cut) so that this dead branch is given new life.

Prayer of the Faithful

Celebrant
May God be glorified now,
as we commit ourselves to the work of prayer,
interceding for those in all kinds of need.

Reader
In our worship,
and our openness to the Spirit of life,
in the Church's longing and outreach,
in the priests, the people,
in all seekers and honest doubters,
we pray that,

in all this:
God may be glorified.

Silence

In the welfare programmes
and peace-making missions,
in the struggle to uphold justice,
in the aid given to the hungry and homeless,
we pray that,

in all this:
God may be glorified.

Silence

In the loving and costly commitment
of mothers and fathers, brothers and sisters,
daughters and sons,
in the determination to forgive and forgive,
in all the lives shared and cherished,
we pray that,

in all this:
God may be glorified.

Silence

In the work of nursing, comforting and healing,
in the daily patient struggle
with pain and weakness,
and in the practical, good-humoured caring,
we pray that,

in all this:
God may be glorified.

Silence

In the twilight years and the facing of death,
in lives well lived and now breaking into eternity,
we pray that,

in all this:
God may be glorified.

Silence

With Mary, Mother of our Redeemer,
we make our prayer:
Hail, Mary . . .

We name in silence now,
any known to us
with particular needs or burdens.

Silence

Celebrant
Heavenly Father,
slow to anger and quick to forgive,
immerse us in your Spirit
and let your will be done in our lives,
through Jesus Christ.
Amen.

TREASURE SEEKERS

Aim: To know that Jesus calms our fears when
we're scared.

Starter

What's the time, Mr Wolf? The children creep up on
Mr Wolf, asking him the time, and he replies with
different times. If he says, 'Dinner time!' the children
turn and run as Mr Wolf tries to catch someone.

Teaching

Talk about how mums and dads make us feel safe
when we're scared or frightened. Sometimes they
make us laugh and show us that we don't need to
be frightened. (Like Dad pretending to wear a bib,
so the baby sees it as funny instead of scary.) Sometimes they explain so we aren't scared any more
because we understand it better. (Like barking being
a dog's way of saying hello.) And if something

really is frightening, mums and dads make us feel
safer just by holding us close to them, or just being
there. (You can use parent and baby soft toys to act
out these situations.)

Now explain that God is like that with us all.
When his disciples were all scared, on the first Easter
Day, Jesus came and comforted them. Jesus knows
when we're scared, and we can tell him all about it.
He will help us to be brave. He works through other
people to look after us, and he works through us to
look after other people who are scared. So whenever
we make someone feel better, or calm their fears,
we are working on God's team!

Praying

I will lie down in peace
and sleep;
it is you, Lord,
who keeps me safe.
Amen.

Activities

On the sheet there are some pictures of people who
need some help to stop them being frightened, and
the children can draw in the things or people they
need. The prayer can be hung up in the bedroom to
use as a night prayer.

PEARL DIVERS

Aim: To know today's Gospel, and the importance
of repentance and forgiveness.

Starter

Take the children on a scary 'lion hunt'.

Teaching

For the teaching today, write out the separate
speeches, and give them to different people to say
during the telling of the story. These are:

- Jesus: 'Peace be with you!'
- Various disciples: 'Help! It must be a ghost!' 'Aah!'
  'A g-g-ghost!'
- Jesus: 'Why are you so scared? I'm not a ghost!
  Look at my hands and my feet. It's me, Jesus!
  Touch me if you like. You can see I have a living
  body. A ghost does not have a body like this!'
- Various disciples: 'Oh Jesus, you're alive!' 'Yes, I
  can see you are real. That's incredible!' 'Yippee!
  Jesus is alive!'
- All together: 'Are you REALLY alive, Jesus? It
  seems too good to be true!'

- Jesus: 'Do you have any food here?'
- One disciple: 'Yes, there's some cooked fish. Here you are.'
- Jesus: 'Thanks!'
- Various disciples (whisper): 'Look, he's eating.' 'Ghosts don't eat normal food!' 'He MUST be alive!'

Give out the speeches and imagine you are all in the room where Jesus came. Narrate the events, with the characters reading their parts. Then go on to tell them how Jesus helped them understand what had been happening. Hold a Bible and flick through the Old Testament as you explain that he took them through all the things that had been written about him in the prophets and the Psalms.

- Jesus: 'It is written that the Christ would be killed and rise from death on the third day. You saw these things happen – you are witnesses.'
- Various disciples: 'Yes, that's true, we saw it all happen.' 'Yes, we did.' 'We know it's true.'
- Jesus: 'You must tell people to change their hearts and lives. If they do this, their sins will be forgiven.'
- One disciple: 'OK, Jesus, we'll tell them. Where do we start?'
- Jesus: 'You must start in Jerusalem and then preach these things in my name to all nations.'

Pray together for all the people who will only hear about Jesus' forgiveness because we tell them during our lifetimes.

Praying

Dear Jesus, when we are scared you make us brave,
when we are worried you calm us down,
and when we are listening you tell us what to do.
Help us to listen well and tell others about you,
so they can enjoy your friendship as well.

Activities

The sheet can be turned into a pop-up picture, where Jesus suddenly stands among his friends. They are helped to see that Jesus comes among us in person as we worship together.

GOLD PANNERS

Aim: To see the importance of spreading the news of forgiveness.

Starter

Cut out news headlines from their stories, and stick them around the room separately. Everyone goes round matching up the headline with the story.

Teaching

Begin with the Gospel – Luke's account of that Sunday evening encounter with the risen Jesus. Notice the similarities with last week's account, seeing how there is real fear registered at first, which Jesus carefully addresses. He doesn't even start telling them anything important until he is sure they are happy and at peace with him being there. It's the same now. We need to get used to spending quality time in Jesus' company if we are wanting him to help us understand things in life.

Now look at the passage from Acts, putting it briefly in context of the healing, and the crowd's enthusiasm to give Peter and John all the credit for it. Notice how they use the occasion to do what Jesus had told them to – telling people to change their lives, making them right with God and being set free by his forgiveness.

Finally look at the reading from 1 John, where the writer is still amazed and overjoyed by the way God's love changes lives. Again, the new life is tied up with whatever happens to us when we repent and are forgiven. It's something so good that it needs to be thoroughly investigated!

Praying

The King is among us, his Spirit is here,
let's draw near and worship, let songs fill the air.

(Taken from a song by Graham Kendrick,
© 1981 Kingsway's Thankyou Music)

Activities

On the sheet they unpack the steps Jesus goes through to sort out the disciples, and the steps Peter goes through to sort out the way the crowd is thinking. They are encouraged to look at situations where we can choose to pocket the glory ourselves rather than giving it to God. There is also a look at taking up Jesus' commission to tell others the good news of forgiveness.

FOURTH SUNDAY OF EASTER

Thought for the day

'I am the Good Shepherd and I lay down my life for the sheep.'

Reflection on the readings

Acts 4:8-12
Psalm 117
1 John 3:1-2
John 10:11-18

Having been imprisoned for the night may not look much like an opportunity, but in fact it provides the perfect opening for Peter to speak out about the power of Jesus who, though crucified, is now alive for ever. Just as Jesus had said would happen, he is given the words to say when asked to bear witness to the truth.

It is quite easy, of course, to make a point of not talking much to God about being given opportunities (in case he takes us up on it!) and to ignore or side-step such opportunities when they do happen. All too glibly do we persuade ourselves that we are not meant to force-feed people, or put them off by actually talking about God's involvement with lives and events. Certainly ramming God down people's throats is both unloving and counter-productive. But there is a great danger of using this as an excuse for avoiding the work we are commissioned to do, in many situations where people lose out on the blessings of forgiveness God longs for them to enjoy, simply because we chicken out of passing on the good news.

In today's Gospel, we hear the well-loved and treasured words of Jesus, describing himself as the Good Shepherd, the one who gathers the flock and tends the sheep, looking after their needs and leading them safely. In contrast to the hired worker, the authentic shepherd is even prepared to lay down his own life for the protection of the sheep. And that is good news worth passing on, at whatever cost to us.

Quite importantly, it makes clear that Jesus was not forced into dying; it would have been possible to avoid it, right up to the very last breath. There had been the temptation to do so at intervals throughout his ministry, and even as he hung dying he was goaded to 'show his power' by coming down from the cross. It was, then, at the moments of greatest weakness that Jesus actually showed his greatest strength of love.

And that is often true for us as well. Weakness feels just that; without glamour or nobility or anything other than the recognition that we have no strength of ourselves to do any more; yet it is in living through such times in God's strength that others turn out to be blessed and God's name to be glorified. If only we will trust God at such times, who knows what sheep will be rescued?

Discussion starters

1. Does our lack of trust in the Good Shepherd and our lack of expectation prevent his work being done?

2. How has God redeemed unpromising events in your life (as individuals and as a church) and turned them into good opportunities?

All-stage talk

Gather all the young children in the aisle and get them doing sheepy things like eating grass, drinking from a stream, sitting and chewing, and bleating. Place a few older children around the edges of the building to be wolves and bears, sheep-watching and hoping for a chance to eat one of the lambs. They can howl sadly as they wait, or growl. One person is a good shepherd, keeping an eye on the flock, and watching out for any signs of wolves and bears.

The wild animals are waiting for the shepherd to go for a break, or doze off, because that's when they might get a chance to grab a lamb or sheep. But this shepherd loves his sheep, and that means he isn't going to give the wild animals any opportunity to attack the flock. He's ready to defend them with his life, if necessary.

Now swap the shepherd for a hired hand. Here's a different flock, with a different shepherd, further up the valley. The wild animals have gathered here now, and they're still waiting. (Howls and growls.) A couple of wolves start to come closer, but this shepherd doesn't frighten them away – he just runs away! The wolves get more confident. They're getting dangerously close, and the sheep are all huddled together, when that good shepherd walks up, with stones in his catapult, and the wolves back off quick!

Thank the sheep and wild animals for their help, and explain that Jesus is like a good shepherd, who cares for us and looks after us, protecting us from evil. He loves us, so he isn't going to let us down, and is even ready to lay down his life for his sheep. In fact, as we know, Jesus did just that – he was ready to lay down his life to set us free.

All-age ideas

- Have a simple cut-out of a sheep on white paper for everyone and give these out as people come into church. Use them as a focus in a time of prayer, as an alternative form of Prayer of the Faithful. First people write their name on their sheep, and hold it as they pray for people in need of Jesus' shepherding in their own families, in this country and in the world. Then swap the sheep around by collecting them and distributing them again. Now everyone can pray for the person named on the sheep, knowing at the same time that they are being prayed for themselves.

- Incorporate a crook and sheep or lambs in one of the flower arrangements, using meadow flowers and grasses.

Prayer of the Faithful

Celebrant
The Lord is our Shepherd;
knowing his care for us, let us pray.

Reader
We pray for all who shepherd others
as bishops and pastors,
and for all in their care;
for Christians threatened and under attack;
and all whose ministry feels demanding.
For a greater affection and care, one for another, in the Church.

Silence

The Lord is our Good Shepherd:
there is nothing we shall lack.

We pray for all in positions of leadership
and influence in our world,
that they may use that power for good;
for an increase in our concern
for one another's well-being, across all barriers,
and for all who are working to build community.

Silence

The Lord is our Good Shepherd:
there is nothing we shall lack.

We pray for those who are wandering, lost and aimless,
with no idea that any Good Shepherd exists;
for those who die unaware that they are precious
and valued by the God who loved them into being.

Silence

The Lord is our Good Shepherd:
there is nothing we shall lack.

We pray for those who have died
to this earthly life,
that the Good Shepherd,
who understands what it is to die,
may bring them safely home.

Silence

The Lord is our Good Shepherd:
there is nothing we shall lack.

We pray with Mary,
Mother of the Good Shepherd:
Hail, Mary . . .

In the silence of God's accepting love,
we pray our individual petitions.

Silence

Celebrant
Loving Lord, we thank you
for this opportunity to pray,
and ask you to answer our prayers
in the way that is best for us.
In the name of Jesus we pray.
Amen.

TREASURE SEEKERS

Aim: To know that Jesus is our Good Shepherd.

Starter

Hunt the sheep. Use a soft toy sheep and take it in turns to hide it while everyone closes their eyes. Then everyone looks for it until it's found again.

Teaching

The children can help you make a landscape of hills, using a large towel draped over some upturned pots and basins, and arranging a few pot plants on it. Wind a long blue scarf between the hills as a stream of water. Place some sheep on the hills. These can either be model or toy ones, or they can be made from the pattern below.

Move the sheep around (the children can make all the sheep and lamb bleating noises) as you tell them how a good shepherd looks after the sheep, taking them to places where there is plenty of grass to eat, leading them to the water so they can drink, and making sure they are safe from howling wolves and growling bears. A good shepherd loves his sheep and knows each of them by name, and he'll never leave them in danger, even if it means getting hurt himself.

Explain that Jesus talks about himself as being like our Good Shepherd. (Move the sheep around as you talk about God's care of us.) He looks after us and loves us, and knows each of us by name. (Mention each of the children and leaders' names.)

Praying

The Lord is my Shepherd,
   (hold each finger in turn, so the ring finger is held on 'my')
there is nothing else I need.
   (keep holding ring finger and shake head)

Activities

Today's prayer, from Psalm 22, can be learnt by heart, using the actions as a memory aid. Encourage the children to pray this whenever they feel frightened, holding on to their ring finger to remember that Jesus, the Good Shepherd, knows and loves them by name, and they belong to him. This teaching is reinforced on the sheet and the children can make a sheep, with their own name on it.

PEARL DIVERS

Aim: To look at what it means for Jesus to be the Good Shepherd.

Starter

To the rescue! Firefighters, lifeboat crews and mountain rescue teams are all willing to drop what they're doing and race to the rescue. At one corner of the room have a hose pipe, at another have a length of rope (or a washing line), and at another a blow-up ring on a length of string. Everyone walks about in the space in the middle of the room until one of three alarms is sounded. If it's a bell they race to the sea rescue, and all line up holding the string, hauling the ring in. If it's a whistle they race to the mountain rescue, and all line up and walk along a pretend narrow ledge, holding the rope. If it's a 'nee-nor' siren (just voicing it is fine) they race to the fire rescue, and line up to hold the hose, directing it at the flames.

Teaching

It takes courage to join any of those rescue teams, and those who do it know that they may be putting themselves at risk, but they are willing to do it so that others will be saved.

It was a risky, dangerous business for Jesus to rescue the human race, using only the power of love. In today's Gospel Jesus talks about himself as the Good Shepherd, who is willing even to lay down his life for the sheep. We're going to look at what it means to be a good shepherd, so that we can better understand what Jesus meant.

Have most of the children as sheep, some as wolves and bears, one as a hired shepherd, who's only doing it for the money, and one as a good shepherd who loves the sheep. Talk the sheep through their life on the hillside, with the good shepherd watching that they don't get lost, finding them tasty pastures full of wet, juicy grass to munch, leading them to drink at the water, and getting them safely into a pen (made of chairs) for the night. The shepherd lies down in the doorway to sleep. Meanwhile the wolves and bears stand back, howling and waiting for a chance to catch a sheep. If they start to come near, the shepherd throws crumpled paper 'stones' at them and that frightens them off.

Stop the action and swap shepherds. This shepherd reads the newspaper instead of checking that the sheep have enough to eat and drink, and he's listening to his personal stereo so he can't hear the sheep bleating when they're frightened. If a wolf comes near, he might throw a stone or two, but the wolves know that it's worth waiting, as he'll soon lose interest. When he gets deep into his *Goosebumps* book, some of the wolves creep nearer and are just about to grab a sheep. The shepherd sees the wolves and runs away! That kind of shepherd is no good for the sheep. That kind of leader is no good for God's people.

So when Jesus says that he is the Good Shepherd, we know what he means – that he loves us and looks after us, even if it turns difficult and dangerous; even if it costs him his life.

Praying

Jesus, we thank you that you were willing
even to lay down your life for us.
May the love which saved us
live in us every day and for ever.
Amen.

Activities

There is a picture of the sheep about to be attacked by the wolves, with the hired shepherd running away. They draw in the good shepherd coming to the rescue. There is also a cost-counting activity and it includes Jesus going through with our rescue, even though he knew it would cost him his life.

GOLD PANNERS

Aim: To look at how Jesus takes on himself the role of the Good Shepherd.

Starter

Role-call. Give out identities to particular people, which they keep secret. Then provide a situation which they all act out in role. Onlookers have to guess the identities/characters from the way they are acting. (Example – travelling on a train: someone with chicken pox, a spy, a *Sun* reporter looking for a story, and the Queen travelling incognito.)

Teaching

Jesus knew the scriptures and what had been written about the Messiah in the books of the prophets, and the Psalms. There was quite a lot about God's shepherding (read Psalm 22) and the Messiah would be a kind of Shepherd King, like David. (Have a look at a few examples, such as 2 Samuel 5:2; Psalm 27:9; Ezekiel 34:16; Isaiah 40:11.) There was also a recurring theme of the false shepherding of God's people, who were left as sheep without a shepherd (Ezekiel 34:5). In Mark and Matthew, Jesus is said to have compassion on the people because of this (Matthew 9:36 and Mark 6:34).

Often the leaders of God's people are criticised for their unshepherdlike behaviour (Jeremiah 10:21; Ezekiel 34:2; Isaiah 56:11).

So now, with this background, look at today's Gospel, John 10:11-18. Jesus is not only showing his disciples the example of the real shepherds around on the hills where they were living. He is also directing them to see how he is fulfilling the prophets and the Psalms as the real, authentic leader of God's people, in contrast to those who are only out for themselves, and are not listening carefully to God.

Praying

The Lord is my shepherd; I shall not be in want.
He makes me lie down in green pastures
and leads me beside still waters.
He revives my soul
and guides me along right pathways
for his name's sake.
Though I walk through the valley
of the shadow of death,
I shall fear no evil;
for you are with me;

your rod and your staff comfort me.
You spread a table for me
in the sight of those who trouble me;
you have anointed my head with oil,
and my cup is running over.
Surely your goodness and mercy shall follow me
all the days of my life,
and I will dwell in the house of the Lord for ever.
(Psalm 22)

Activities

On the sheet there is a picture of a hired shepherd fleeing in danger, and they are helped to explore this symbol in terms of leadership of God's people, and our own Christian witness. They are also introduced to the full story in Acts (chapter 4, verses 2-12) of Peter and John putting themselves in danger for the sake of the Gospel, so that they can see how this links in with Jesus laying down his life for the sheep.

FIFTH SUNDAY OF EASTER

Thought for the day

To produce fruit we need to be joined on to the true vine.

Reflection on the readings

Acts 9:26-31
Psalm 21
1 John 3:18-24
John 15:1-8

This week's reading from Acts shows us some of the difficulties faced by the newly converted Saul. So fresh is his conversion that it will be some time before he becomes known as Paul. On seeing him, the disciples were not merely suspicious of their former persecutor but afraid, and Paul now had the tables turned on him when another group threatened his life. When any of us turn to the Lord we risk change, a change in our attitude, a change in the way we think or do things, and these changes may not easily be understood or accepted by those around us. But in the slow process that enriched and developed the life of the churches throughout Judea, Galilee and Samaria, it was the Spirit that gave consolation and strength, and worked for good. We need that same patience, shown by both Paul and the early churches, to allow the Spirit to bind us together to the vine that is Christ in order that this vine may produce good fruit.

The elderly John is still marvelling at the way God loves us, and is anxious to make it quite clear that double standards on our part will not do. Faced with the beauty of God's perfect love, it is no good claiming to love him unless we show it. Real and active love of God is bound to lead us on to love one another in the same tender, unselfish way that he loves us.

This is why the image of the vine and branches is such a vivid and useful one; being joined on to the vine makes all the difference, and we cannot expect to produce spiritual fruit unless we are well attached, with the life sap flowing through us. Jesus places himself in the role of vine and his Father as the gardener. Why does a gardener plant a vine and tend it? For the fruit! What a thought it is to imagine wine made from the fruit of our love, joy, peace, patience, kindness, goodness, faithfulness, gentleness and self-control, all possible because of the life of Jesus flowing through our living and growing. Wine of the kingdom of God.

Discussion starters

1. How can we check that we are still firmly attached to the true vine?

2. Does belonging to the true vine mean that we have to sacrifice our independence?

All-stage talk

Cut six long strips of green crepe paper, or lengths of green string. Also prepare ten cut-out bunches of grapes from coloured paper.

Begin by suggesting that if you came in and said you were a pair of curtains, everyone would probably tell you to pull yourself together. But in our Gospel today we find Jesus saying, 'I am a grape vine.' Obviously he wasn't really a grape vine, was he? So what on earth did he mean?

To help us understand, we're going to make a kind of grape vine. Ask one volunteer to hold a green string in each hand, and two others to tie the strings round their waists. They can now hold four strings between them, and four others can tie these round their waists. Now for the fruit. Each of the last four people can hold a bunch of grapes in each hand (eight altogether) and the other two bunches can be stuck with a loop of sticky tape to the fronts of the second two volunteers.

In just a short time, and with just a few people, we've grown quite a big vine and ten bunches of fruit! Just imagine how much fruit there would be if everyone here was joined on the vine.

Jesus said he was the true vine and his Father was the gardener, looking after the growing and helping the vine branches to produce as much fruit as possible. Obviously these branches are only able to produce their fruit if they're joined on to the vine, because all the life-giving sap feeds them and if they're cut off they don't get anything to keep them alive.

Jesus was really saying that if we want our lives to produce fruit like love, joy, peace, patience, kindness, goodness, faithfulness, gentleness and self-control (stick these labels on the grapes), then we have to make really sure that we're joined up to Jesus and in touch with him. We need his life in us all the time. We need to keep in touch with him every day!

All-age ideas

• Include some vine leaves, or vine-like plants, and grapes in one of the flower arrangements today.

• Pray particularly for church mission links today, including any updates and specific prayer concerns, photos and maps. Have an airmail open letter for people to add their encouragement and send it off today.

Prayer of the Faithful

Celebrant
Let us pray to the Lord God Almighty,
in whom we live and move and have our being.

Reader
We want to produce good fruit in abundance;
we pray that God may nurture us
as branches of the true vine,
train and prune us where necessary,
and that our spiritual harvest may make rich wine,
wine of the kingdom.

Silence

Your kingdom, let it come!
Your will, let it be done!

We see around our world
the tragic and expensive consequences
of branches cut off from the true vine.
We pray for a seeking after the truth
and a desire to act rightly and justly
in all areas of human society.

Silence

Your kingdom, let it come!
Your will, let it be done!

We pray for those to whom we are linked
by family, friendships or work;
especially we pray for those
separated from their loved ones or their home.

Silence

Your kingdom, let it come!
Your will, let it be done!

We long for healing and wholeness
in all who suffer
and in all dysfunctional communities;
may we be guided to understand
how we might be part of the healing.

Silence

Your kingdom, let it come!
Your will, let it be done!

We know that death cannot separate us
from God's love;
in that knowledge
we commend to God's loving keeping
those who have died and all who miss them.

Silence

Your kingdom, let it come!
Your will, let it be done!

With Mary, Mother of the true vine,
we make our prayer:
Hail, Mary . . .

Confident in God's welcoming love,
we pray in silence now
for our individual needs.

Silence

Celebrant
Merciful Father, fulfil our needs
according to your loving wisdom,
through Jesus Christ.
Amen.

TREASURE SEEKERS

Aim: To know they can be generous at passing on Jesus' love.

Starter

If you have access to a garden or patch of grass, give the children containers which you fill with water so they can go and water the plants. They can get a refill when their container is empty. Otherwise, play inside with water in washing-up bowls, funnels and containers.

Teaching

Talk about the way we were able to pour the water out on to the plants or into other pots because we had the water to use. What do we do at home if we need water to make a drink, or wash, or brush our teeth? We go and turn on the tap and out comes the water. If we get thirsty again, or need another bath after playing and being busy all day, we can go back to the tap and there's some more water waiting for us to use!

Have a bowl of water and a dry sponge. God's love goes on and on, and there's always plenty of it for us. Whenever we settle down with our friend Jesus (place the sponge in the water), we can't help soaking up some of his love, so we get more loving, just as this sponge is getting more wet by soaking up the water.

We can go back to soak ourselves in God's love every day, so that we are people filled with love. Then we can spread God's love around to other people and make the world a happy place.

Praying

Jesus, fill me up with your love
so I can spread love around
wherever it's needed!
Amen.

Activities

Each child will need an empty plastic pot. The children are going to decorate them with the picture and prayer which is on the sheet. There is also a picture to colour, of a gardener looking after a vine with grapes on it.

PEARL DIVERS

Aim: To look at the importance of our being joined on to the true vine, if we are hoping to produce fruit.

Starter

Grow a vine. As children come in, tie a length of green string or wool round their waist, so it hangs down the back like a tail. Leave one child (or a leader) with no string and sit that person on a chair. When everyone is ready, explain that they are going to make themselves into a grapevine, using all the children. It has to start from the person on the chair, who has two hands free, and they have to obey this rule: one string to one hand. (It's good training for children to practise organising themselves like this, sometimes. Don't interfere unless it's really necessary and let them work through the mistakes to the solution.) Give out grapes to everyone when they're ready.

Teaching

Bring along (or take them outside to see) a growing plant. Notice how its branches have grown, rather like we grew our 'grapevine', and notice any buds or flowers which are the first signs of fruit. Also look at an off-cut from the plant. Will this piece be able to flower and fruit like the other branches? No, it won't. Why not? Talk together about how the branches and stems carry all the goodness, and without being joined on to the living plant, with its strong roots, the cut-off branch dies.

Have a grapevine outline drawn on a large sheet of paper. Now, from a suitable translation of the Bible, read today's Gospel, where Jesus talks of himself as the true vine, and the importance of us being joined to him if we are going to produce fruit. Talk over what Jesus means, and what kind of fruit we are hoping to produce. As different ideas are given, stick clusters of grapes on to the drawn vine, labelling them.

Praying

Jesus, I know I can only produce good fruit
if I'm connected to you, the true vine.
Let your life flow into me and through me
so together we can make a huge harvest!
Amen.

Activities

Using the pictures and instructions on the sheet the children will be making a grapevine. Each child will also need pipe cleaners and green paint.

GOLD PANNERS

Aim: To understand the importance of us being 'joined on' to Jesus if we are to produce any fruit spiritually.

Starter

Have a small set of Christmas tree lights and arrange it so that it has one 'bad' bulb. Show how they are all linked together, and how they won't light up because of the one 'bad' bulb. Replace the bulb with a good one and show how they are all lit from the same source.

Teaching

We all enjoy being free to do the things we like doing and don't like it when anyone cramps our style or tries to restrict our freedom. Left entirely free, a vine plant will grow like any other creeper – all over the place; it may have a good free time but the grapes will scarcely be worth bothering with. If tied to some sort of frame and carefully pruned, the same vine will be much more productive and the grapes could be well on the way to becoming a famous vintage.

List some of the ways in which we are 'pruned' in ordinary activities, where our freedom to do what we like may be limited but for a good reason and with, hopefully, good results. (Things like sports training, music practice, getting a good night's sleep, even the rules of the games we play.)

Read the passage from John's Gospel. How can we make sure that we are part of the true vine? In what ways do other aspects of our lives need pruning?

Praying

Breathe on me, Breath of God,
fill me with life anew,
that I may love what thou dost love,
and do what thou wouldst do.

Activities

They are encouraged to check their own position on (or off) the true vine, reviewing how their practice matches up with where they want to be. They are also introduced to Barnabas and his distinctive ministry of encouragement.

SIXTH SUNDAY OF EASTER

Thought for the day

We are to love one another as Jesus loves us.

Reflection on the readings

Acts 10:25-26, 34-35, 44-48
Psalm 97
1 John 4:7-10
John 15:9-17

In the reading from Acts we witness an extraordinary outpouring of the Holy Spirit, which doesn't even wait for Peter to finish speaking. Not surprisingly, when you look back to what he had just been saying, you find once again that powerful truth about forgiveness, which Jesus had commissioned his disciples to tell everyone about. 'Tell them they can be forgiven,' he had said straight after the Resurrection. As Peter proclaims this, the little crowd of people in Cornelius' house, who are searching single-mindedly for God's truth, suddenly experience the rush of God's forgiving love, and the freedom it brings.

And this is the kind of love we are given as an example to follow – the kind of forgiving, accepting love that wants people to be free. So much of what we name as love is actually to do with self-gratification and possession. It is tied up with our own need for fulfilment. But the love that Jesus talks of in today's Gospel is about obedience, willing co-operation, and sacrifice which produces joy.

There is a danger of mishearing what Jesus means here. He is not saying that in order to be his beloved friends we have to obey his commands. That would be fine if we could earn God's love by clocking up the points, and many people conscientiously live like this. But it does not set them free. It was because we can't earn God's blessing that we needed a Saviour to give us freely the forgiveness which liberates us to live; and it is because God has treated us with such love and respect and generosity that, as his friends, we take delight in obeying his commands and living the loving way.

Jesus doesn't want to have us as servants, who obey because it's their job but know nothing of their employer's business. He has gone out of his way to involve us at every stage, pointing out the policies and plans, and the 'mission statement'. That makes us more like friends and colleagues with the God of creation, which is a heady prospect and also quite a responsibility.

Discussion starters

1. Jesus once observed that it is those who have been forgiven much who love much. Do we feel fully forgiven, with the rush of love that produces, or has the penny yet to drop?

2. Imagine walking through a normal day, meeting the usual people and problems, but in the knowledge of God's love and forgiveness, and literally loving as Jesus loves us. What would it be like, and how would it differ from how we usually live?

All-stage talk

Begin with the sketch in all-age ideas, which looks at the difference between servants and friends.

Invite everyone to spot the differences. Also ask those involved in the sketch what differences they felt. The kind of things which might come up are the sense of involvement and belonging which friendship gives, compared with the distance and lack of co-operation in servants; the difference in how they feel valued, and what response is acceptable.

Point out that Jesus said he was no longer thinking of us as servants but as friends. That means we are people he is happy to talk things over with, co-operate with and involve in the work. There is going to be companionship and perhaps some good-natured teasing. Above all is the sense that we are in this together, and enjoying one another's company.

Another thing Jesus said is that we are to love one another in the way he loves us. So how is that? How does Jesus love us? Collect people's ideas; here are some that occurred to me:

- as friends
- with affection
- treating us seriously
- understanding us
- with honesty
- with forgiveness
- ready to put himself out for us
- with faithfulness
- consistently

Is this how we are treating other people? Or is it how we treat the people we like? As Christians we don't have the option to choose certain people to treat with God's love, while behaving how we feel with all the rest. We can't claim to love God and then decide that some people aren't worth treating with respect or understanding.

Of course it isn't easy to love one another like this. Lots of people are difficult to love in God's way – perhaps we are, ourselves! But when we look at how amazingly God treats us, copying his way of loving is the very least we can do. And the often surprising thing is that putting ourselves out and making the effort to live God's way is very rewarding, and makes us feel much happier inside.

All-age ideas

- This sketch can be used to introduce the talk. Write two titles on sheets of paper or slate boards, which are walked around the church before each section, so everyone can see them: 'The Servant' and 'The Friends'.

The Servant
The employer is talking on his mobile phone, pacing up and down, with a file open. He's sorting out some complex problem. The office cleaner comes in with feather duster and starts cleaning.

Mr King (Into phone) Quite . . . Quite . . . But look at these figures on page 24 . . . (catches sight of Marg the cleaner) Marg, get me a strong coffee. And a doughnut or something. (Returns to phone) Yes, these figures should have warned us . . . Well, the point is what can we do about it now?

(Marg reappears with coffee and doughnut.)

Marg   Coffee, Mr King. It's strong. And a doughnut. *(Puts them on desk)*

Mr King   *(Still on phone, listening and making 'mm' noises. Motions with hand for Marg not to interrupt him as he's busy.)* Sorry, Steve, say that again . . . the schedules systematically reduced what? . . . Oh, I see. Yes, of course. So what are you going to do about it?

(Marg continues dusting.)

Mr King   *(Still on phone)* Marg, get me the February file – it's there on my desk. *(Talks into phone)* It seems to me we can possibly get ourselves out of this mess, Steve. I've just had an idea.

(Marg brings the February file to Mr King.)

Marg   The February file, Mr King.

Mr King   *(Takes it without thanking her and starts looking in it. Into phone he says)* Yes, here it is! I'm looking at these figures for the second week of February . . .

(Marg goes back to the dusting. The desk phone rings.)

Mr King   Answer that, Marg.

Marg   *(Picks up phone)* Hello, Mr King's office. Well, he's very busy at the moment, in an important meeting . . . Oh, I've no idea, I'm only the cleaner here. I just do what I'm told.

The Friends

Norman and Pete walk up to a bench and sit down. They put their rucksacks down.

Pete   Phew! That was quite a climb, wasn't it. What a view, though, eh?

Norman   Marvellous, isn't it. *(Pause)* Anyway, you were saying about your interview . . .

Pete   Oh yeah, that's right. So we've got to decide whether to move or not, basically. And that's a big decision to make.

Norman   How does Sheila feel about moving? She settled here, isn't she?

Pete   Yes, it would be quite a wrench for her, but you know Sheila, she's willing to give it a go if she feels it's what God wants for us.

Norman   Funny, isn't it. This time last year, there you were just made redundant, and no hopes for the future, and now this new door seems to be opening for you. I'm really happy for you, Pete.

Pete   Thanks, Norman. Well, you've been a good friend through all this – it's always good to talk things over with you. Shall we be on our way then? *(They get up and walk off.)*

All four characters   I no longer call you servants, because a servant doesn't know his master's business. Instead I have called you friends.

- As an alternative form of bidding prayers with a smaller group, try the following with a repeated response:

In our homes, at work and at school
help us to love one another.
In what we think and speak and do
help us to love one another.
When there are arguments
and when we disagree
help us to love one another.
When we are tired and not feeling our best
help us to love one another.
Every moment of every day,
whether it's easy or hard,
help us to love one another.

Prayer of the Faithful

Celebrant
Knowing God's love and affection for us,
let us pray to him now.

Reader
Wherever there is friction and conflict
in the Church,
and communities are divided and weakened;
may we have a greater longing for God's healing
and a deeper commitment to his forgiving love.

Silence

Help us, Lord:
to love one another.

Wherever tangled political situations
seem impossible to solve,
wherever conflicting interests threaten peace;
wherever the ears of the powerful
remain insulated against the cries of the oppressed;
may we have ears to hear the Spirit's guidance.

Silence

Help us, Lord:
to love one another.

Wherever families are dysfunctional
or children are in danger;
wherever the daily living conditions
are damaging to health and self-respect;
may God's kingdom come.

Silence

Help us, Lord:
to love one another.

Wherever the ill and injured
need comfort and assistance;
wherever the elderly and housebound
sit each day for hours alone;
may we bring love and help.

Silence

Help us, Lord:
to love one another.

Wherever people are travelling
that last journey of death,
may they be surrounded by God's love
and welcomed into heaven,
and may those who mourn be comforted.

Silence

Help us, Lord:
to love one another.

Mary's example teaches us
the power of loving response;
with her we make our prayer:
Hail, Mary . . .

Surrounded by God's love,
we pray in silence for our own needs.

Silence

Celebrant
Heavenly Father,
so unrestrictive in your mercy,
accept our prayers and fulfil our needs,
through Jesus Christ.
Amen.

TREASURE SEEKERS

Aim: To know that Jesus thinks of us as his friends.

Starter

Have an assortment of toys to play with, so that
everyone can enjoy playing together as friends.

Teaching

Talk together about friends. Friends play together,
giggle together and chat together. Friends stick up for
one another and share things. Friends like being with
each other. What do some of the children like about
their friends? (Pass a soft toy around. This is held
by the person who is talking, and the others listen.)

We are friends of Jesus. Jesus likes being with us
and chatting with us, listening to our news and all
the sad as well as the happy things. And he's always
there for us – he doesn't suddenly go off us and not
like us any more.

What do friends of Jesus do? They love one
another, just as Jesus loves them.

Praying

Jesus, you are our friend and we are yours.
In all we think and speak and do
    (point to head, mouth and then open hands)
help us to love one another.
    (spread arms wide)
Amen.

Activities

On the sheet there are some pictures of people
behaving like friends to tick, and some to cross out
where people are not behaving lovingly at all. They
can make a picture for Jesus to say 'thank you' for
something in their life.

PEARL DIVERS

Aim: To know that we are not servants but friends
of Jesus.

Starter

Do this, do that! The captain of the ship is given a
suitable hat to wear, and everyone else is the crew,
obeying the orders to make the ship sail well.
(Possible orders: scrub the decks; climb the rigging;
hoist the sail; lower the sail; drop anchor; weigh
anchor; coil the ropes; everyone to port; everyone
to starboard; all hands on deck.)

Teaching

Talk about jobs where it's very important that people
just do what they're told, and obey orders straightaway (such as soldiers and sailors, astronauts and
fire fighters, and those working in an operating
theatre). It doesn't matter whether they understand
why they're doing it – as long as the person in
charge knows.

When Jesus was talking to his disciples not long
before he died, he told them that he wasn't going
to call them servants any more, with him as their
master. Instead he was calling them friends. What's
the difference between being servants and being
friends?

Collect their ideas in two columns on a sheet of
paper, headed 'Servants' and 'Friends'.

Being friends of Jesus like this means that we'll be working with him on very important missions. There are things that Jesus needs done which only we can do! For instance, you may be the only friend of Jesus available to work with him in your classroom on your particular table, or in your playground. You are the only person who is right for a job of comforting someone in your family, or challenging the behaviour of someone who lives nearby.

Whatever jobs Jesus wants to work with us on, he will always give us the right training for it, the best opportunities and any special help we need. And we'll be working as a team, not with Jesus giving orders and us just doing it without understanding why.

So, if we want to be in God's team, we need to make sure we're keeping in touch with him all day long, asking his opinion and help, and not trying to go it alone. Jesus doesn't want us to work *for* him but *with* him.

Praying

Here I am, Jesus,
ready to work with you
for the coming of the kingdom.
What's our next mission together?

Activities

On the sheet is a cartoon version of how Peter worked with God on the Cornelius household mission. There are also instructions for making a model mobile phone, to which today's prayer is attached. Each child will need a suitably sized piece of thick card, or card box such as tablets come in, and a straw.

GOLD PANNERS

Aim: To look at what it means to be Jesus' friends.

Starter

Either use the sketch from All-age Ideas, or play a co-operative game such as making a circle of everyone sitting on the lap of the person in front, or telling a story in which each person in the circle adds a word.

Teaching

Begin by reading today's Gospel, which follows on from last week's picture of the vine and branches. Bear in mind when Jesus was saying these things – shortly before his arrest and death. Ask them to pick out particular phrases that seem specially important,

or which surprise them. Being Jesus' friends looks as if it brings both honour and responsibility. What are these? (That we have the privilege of working co-operatively with the living God; that we are to love one another as Jesus loves us.)

Now look at 1 John 4:7-10, particularly verses 7-8. Make it clear that we do not love God in order for him to like us. It's God's love for us which makes us love him and want to live like him.

Finally look at an example of co-operative friendship with Jesus – Peter going along with God's will even though it's not what he might have chosen to do on his own, with the result that all those people receive the Holy Spirit and the freedom that gives.

Praying

(To pray regularly throughout each day)

Here I am, Lord,
ready to work with you.
Show me how I can share your love
here . . . now.

Activities

On the sheet they are helped to explore how Jesus loves us, and what that is going to mean for us loving one another. They are also looking at the way we are chosen and appointed to go and bear fruit – both the honour and the responsibility.

THE ASCENSION OF THE LORD

Thought for the day

Having bought back our freedom with the giving of his life, Jesus enters into the full glory to which he is entitled.

Reflection on the readings

Acts 1:1-11
Psalm 46
Ephesians 1:17-23
Mark 16:15-20

The disciples have walked with Jesus on his journey to the cross, watched his suffering there and known the darkness of that time, then met him full of Resurrection life on various recorded occasions since Easter. During these encounters they have gradually begun to understand God's purposes and are getting used to knowing Jesus' constant presence, whether they can actually see him with them or not. And Jesus has accomplished all that he set out from heaven to do.

So the time has come for Jesus to move into the full glory of heaven, united with his Father and given his rightful place. In a sense the Ascension is like the completion of the Resurrection. Those post-Resurrection meetings were an essential part of the mission, preparation for the spread of the good news which could only be done after the victory over death.

When Jesus had met Mary of Magdala in the garden on that Sunday morning, he had told her not to hold him as he was not yet ascended to his Father. After his death, Jesus had preached to the dead, and now he was walking about among the living on earth. But this was not to be his per-manent home. With the Ascension, Jesus is finally 'resurrected' into the glory of heaven for ever. He is also fully available to touch every life in a way never possible before.

No one witnessed the Resurrection, but now, with the promise of power to be sent on the disciples, they see Jesus taken up into heaven. We are reminded of Elisha, promised Elijah's power only if he was allowed to witness his master's parting from earth. And from now on until the Day of Pentecost, they wait in expectant obedience for the empowering of the Holy Spirit.

Today is one of those festivals which look in both directions at once. We look back over all that led up to Christ's coming, and over that earthly human sharing from the manger to the empty tomb; and we look forward to the spreading of the kingdom far and wide through space and time, empowered by the Spirit. As Emmanuel, 'God-with-us', bridges earth and heaven at the Ascension, the human is caught up in the divine for ever.

Discussion starters

1. Compare the thoughts and feelings of the disciples after the Resurrection, and now after the Ascension as they go out to proclaim the Good News.

2. How does it affect the human condition, having the risen and ascended Jesus reigning in heaven?

All-stage talk

Prepare a large cardboard arrow pointer, and have the following things ready to use as signs: a Nativity play manger or a doll wrapped in swaddling clothes; a pair of sandals; a cross; a lit candle.

Explain that today is called Ascension Day (which means 'going up' day). Why is it called that? Because we are remembering the day when Jesus went out to a hill with his disciples this time after Easter, and they watched him returning to heaven. We are told that it looked as if Jesus was going upwards, not so much up into the sky as out of their sight. It was the last time Jesus was seen on the earth.

In a way, today is like being with the disciples on the top of a hill. If we look down one way (point the arrow backwards) we can look back to when Jesus first came to earth, as a newborn baby. (A volunteer takes the baby or crib to stand as far as possible behind the arrow, but where they are still visible.) We're not just looking back to last Christmas (which does seem quite a long time ago!) but right to when Jesus was actually born. From our Ascension hilltop we look back to Jesus' life, and all the travelling around he did. (The sandals are taken behind the arrow, but closer than the crib.) Jesus walked from town to village, healing the sick, teaching and loving the people. We can look back to the cross (the cross is brought behind the arrow, closer than the sandals) which Jesus' love brought him to, and we can remember what a great victory over evil was won there. And we can look back to that first Easter morning (the lit candle is brought close behind the arrow) when death couldn't hold the Lord of life any longer, and Jesus burst into fuller life than ever.

(Turn the arrow to point upwards.) So today marks the end of Jesus' time on earth, tied to a time and a place, and we are celebrating his triumphant return to heaven, having won the victory and defeated the power of evil for us.

(Turn the arrow to face forwards.) From today's Ascension hill we are also looking forward into the future. And what do we find in the future? Among other things, all of us, sitting in this church in this year, with our lives transformed and filled with joy because of our faith in the living Jesus!

All-age ideas

- Have some decorations with clouds cut from white paper and crowns cut from gold wrapping paper.

- After the narrative of the Ascension is read, have a group of people who walk forward as if following Jesus, while music plays. They kneel in worship and then all raise their eyes slowly upwards, till they are staring at the sky. They hold this position for a few moments, and then stand up, amazed and suddenly smiling at one another. As they turn to walk joyfully down the aisle, they shout above the music: 'Let the kingdom come! In every time, in every place, let the kingdom come!' (Suitable music: 'Morning' from Grieg's *Peer Gynt* Suite.)

Prayer of the Faithful

Celebrant
Rejoicing that Jesus has ascended into the heavens,
let us pray in confidence to God our Father.

Reader
We pray in thankfulness
for those who introduced us to Jesus
and who help us along our spiritual journey.
We pray for one another in this church
and for all Christians, young and old,
throughout the world.

Silence

Let the kingdom come:
let your kingdom come.

We pray with longing
for the world to be governed
in accordance with the law of love;
that all creation may be reverenced
and treated with respect.

Silence

Let the kingdom come:
let your kingdom come.

We pray with concern
for all the homes, schools and places of work
in this community;
rejoicing in all that is of God,
and asking for healing forgiveness
wherever there is discord or bitterness.

Silence

Let the kingdom come:
let your kingdom come.

We pray with hope
for the healing and restoration to wholeness
of all who are ill or troubled,
damaged or depressed.

Silence

Let the kingdom come:
let your kingdom come.

We pray with confidence
for those who have come to the end
of their earthly lives,
that they may be given merciful judgement
and welcomed into the glory of heaven.

Silence

Let the kingdom come:
let your kingdom come.

We pray with Mary,
sharing her joy at her Son's Ascension:
Hail, Mary . . .

In silence now,
we bring to our heavenly Father
our own particular concerns.

Silence

Celebrant
God of all mercy,
our hope and our joy,
we ask you to hear our prayers,
through Christ Jesus.
Amen.

TREASURE SEEKERS, PEARL DIVERS AND GOLD PANNERS

It is likely that Ascension Day services for schools
will not need a separate programme for children and
young people. However, in the books for TREASURE
SEEKERS and PEARL DIVERS I have included a
drawing and colouring activity for today.

SEVENTH SUNDAY OF EASTER

Thought for the day

Although now hidden from our sight, Jesus lives
for ever, and in him we can live the Resurrection life
even while we are on earth.

Reflection on the readings

Acts 1:15-17, 20-26
Psalm 102
1 John 4:11-16
John 17:11-19

With the Ascension, the earthly ministry of Jesus
drew to a close, with the prospect of God's Spirit
flooding into the believers, so that in that power they
would be enabled to spread the good news down the
generations and out to every far-flung community on
earth. In our reading from Acts we see the disciples
growing up and taking their responsibility seriously,
even before the empowering has taken place.

Already, we are told, there are about a hundred and fifty of them, and Peter is the leader. Their first job they see as choosing a Judas replacement, the main criterion being that the candidate should have been an eye-witness to the entire ministry of Jesus. Sensibly they pray for it to be God's choice – not 'help us to choose wisely' but 'show us who you have chosen'. That is an example well worth following.

The elderly John writes in his letter to remind his readers that the eternal life God gives us is invested in his Son, so it follows that those who accept Jesus as Lord will have that life, and those who reject him will not. We are into personal choices again.

Jesus, being human, well understands the kind of world we live in and the minefield of temptations we walk through. As he prayed for his disciples, knowing that he would soon be physically parted from them, Jesus prayed for our protection from evil, and for a realistic harmony and unity. Looking around at our sects and splits, it is easy to see why Jesus was so concerned. Our witness to the glorious, liberating truth is so weakened by our disunity.

Thankfully, we live in an age which is doing its best to refocus on Jesus, so that the great barriers erected through the centuries between Christians may in time crumble to rubble. All this is the work of God's Spirit; the more God's people open themselves to receive that empowering love, the more able we will be to love one another, respecting one another's differences but recognising that we are fellow workers, indwelt by the same Spirit.

Discussion starters

1. In what way are we 'one', in spite of the different labels and packaging?

2. How can we, who live two thousand years after Christ, be considered 'witnesses'?

All-stage talk

Prepare two short straws amongst a few full-length ones. Begin by asking for volunteers. Let all those who have offered come out but explain that as you only need two we'll choose by the fairest way – each pulling a straw from your hand. Those who pull the short straws will be the ones chosen.

Label these two Matthias and Joseph, and remind everyone of the problem the disciples had – there had been twelve of them and now there were eleven. Why wasn't Judas with them any more? Because he had helped get Jesus arrested, and afterwards gone and taken his own life.

So Peter organised the believers to choose a replacement for Judas. Who would they choose? If we were going to choose, what kind of person would we look at? What would that person have to have done?

(Collect the ideas, and re-read verses 21 and 22.)

Well, there were two possibilities, Matthias and Joseph, both good people, and both having been with Jesus all through his ministry. So how are they to choose? They did it in two stages:

1. They prayed, asking God to show them the one he wanted.

2. They used the straw method, like we used.

In effect, they had decided not to take on the choosing themselves, but felt it was so important that they should leave it entirely up to God's leading. And the one who drew the short straw was Matthias. That didn't mean that God liked Matthias better; it was just that God had another important job for Joseph, and knew that Matthias was going to be most useful for this one.

Although Jesus has ascended into heaven, and we can't see him here any more, he's very much with us *all* the time. When we have difficult decisions to make and important, scary things to organise, we don't have to do them alone. We can do what the disciples did, and keep in touch with God, wanting only what God wants and asking him to show us what that is. We can practise wanting what God wants at all kinds of times, just by saying in our hearts, 'Let your will be done!'

All-age ideas

- The mime suggested for Ascension Day (All-age Ideas, page 92) could be used today instead.

- Play some quiet, reflective music (either live or recorded) while everyone sits for a few minutes, opening themselves to God's possibilities for them and choosing to commit themselves to their calling as Christians.

Prayer of the Faithful

Celebrant
Let us pray together to our heavenly Father, knowing his love for us.

Reader
As the Church,
we are called to do God's will,
to live his way
and to serve one another in love.
We pray that we may be empowered
to do this.

Silence

Lord, we wait on you:
fill us, Holy Spirit of God.

We pray that our states and kingdoms
may display love, truth, justice and mercy,

that the walls of prejudice may be broken
and bridges of reconciliation and trust be built.

Silence

Lord, we wait on you:
fill us, Holy Spirit of God.

May our children be safely and lovingly nurtured,
our elderly valued,
our homes be places of welcome and warmth.

Silence

Lord, we wait on you:
fill us, Holy Spirit of God.

We pray for healing
for those whose lives are aching and weary;
for comfort and reassurance
for all who are imprisoned by fears and hate.

Silence

Lord, we wait on you:
fill us, Holy Spirit of God.

We commit our loved ones who have died
into God's safe keeping for ever.
May we all be worthy to enter eternal life.

Silence

Lord, we wait on you:
fill us, Holy Spirit of God.

We pray with Mary,
Mother of the Church:
Hail, Mary . . .

In the knowledge that God is listening,
we make our private petitions
and thanksgivings.

Silence

Celebrant
Trusting in your love for us, Father,
and full of hope in your promise to hear us,
we offer you these prayers,
in the name of Jesus Christ, your Son.
Amen.

TREASURE SEEKERS

Aim: To hear about Jesus going back to heaven.

Starter

Hello, goodbye. As the music plays, the children skip and jump about. When it stops, they find another person, shake hands and say, 'Hello'. As the music

starts again, they wave and say, 'Goodbye', before skipping and jumping off somewhere else.

Teaching

Our lives are full of hellos and goodbyes. Share some of the times we say hello and goodbye. Sometimes the goodbyes can be sad, if we've been with a special friend, or grandparents, and have to say goodbye to them. We know that means we won't be seeing them for a while.

Jesus' friends had got used to him being there to talk and laugh with. They loved being with Jesus. Even when Jesus had risen from the dead he would spend time with them sometimes. But now Jesus took his friends out to a hill and told them it was time to say goodbye. They wouldn't be seeing him any more as it was time for him to go back to heaven.

But Jesus wasn't going to leave his friends all alone. He loved them! He promised that in a few days he would send them a special present. When the present came they would be able to feel Jesus there with them all the time. That made the friends happy. They watched as a cloud took Jesus up out of their sight, and then they went back to Jerusalem to wait for the special present.

Praying

Be near me, Lord Jesus, I ask thee to stay
close by me for ever and love me, I pray.
Bless all the dear children in thy tender care,
and fit us for heaven to live with thee there.

Activities

The pictures of clouds and a crown can be coloured and hung together as a mobile. Or you can use the outlines as templates for white and gold thin card. The prayer can be stuck to one of the clouds.

PEARL DIVERS

Aim: To know what the disciples did about replacing Judas.

Starter

Tell everyone what the forfeit is for whoever draws the short straw. (For example, walk backwards to the window; hop around the circle; catch a ball thrown to you three times running.) Have as many straws as there are children in the group, and cut one of the straws short. Hold them so that only the ends show, and everyone takes one. Whoever has the short straw has to do the forfeit.

Teaching

If the children have missed out on Ascension Day, go over what happened in more detail. Otherwise refer them to the Ascension and explain what the disciples did when they got back to Jerusalem. They met up and prayed together, waiting as Jesus had told them to, so they would be ready for the coming of the Holy Spirit.

And they had a job to do, before that happened. How many apostles had Jesus chosen? Twelve. How many were there now? (Say the names of the apostles slowly, so they can count. The list is given in Acts 1:13.) Who was missing? Judas. Why? Because he was the one who had betrayed Jesus to the Roman guards, and had later killed himself.

What the disciples had to do was to replace the missing apostle, so that they would once again be twelve. Give the children cards with their own words on, written large and clearly.

Peter   Listen, everyone. Judas was one of us, and he is no longer with us. We must choose someone to take his place.

James   Must it be someone who was with Jesus all the time, like we were?

Peter   Yes, it must.

John   What about Justus? He is a good person.

Peter   Right. Any other ideas?

Andrew   What about Matthias? He is a good person, too.

Philip   And they have both been with Jesus all the time.

John   I wonder which person God thinks is best for this job?

Andrew   Let's pray, and ask him.

Peter   Yes, let's all pray. Lord, you know what everyone is like. Show us which of these two you have chosen. Thank you, Lord. Amen.

Explain that when they had prayed, they pulled straws, like we did in our game, and the one who drew the short straw was Matthias. So Matthias became the twelfth disciple.

Praying

Lord, please show me
the way you want me to live.
Train me to think like you think,
see as you see,
and love as you love. Amen.

Activities

On the sheet there is a pyramid to make up and use as a 3D checklist for making decisions God's way.

They are also told about Jesus praying for us to keep us safe while we are in the world doing God's work.

GOLD PANNERS

Aim: To look at what it means to live in Jesus and live the risen life.

Starter

Two teams (or more for larger numbers) sit facing each other, about a metre apart. The aim is to hit a balloon behind the other team's chairs.

Teaching

If no one has been involved in Ascension, include it now by starting the Acts reading from verse 9. Point out that Peter feels it is a matter of urgency to choose a replacement for Judas, and part of their preparation for receiving the gift of the Holy Spirit. They are putting everything in order, ready for the new life. Notice, too, how God's choice is what matters, not anyone else's. We can learn from this to get our lives facing the right direction in readiness for God to act in them, and actively to want God's will in all the choices and decisions we make each day.

Now read John 17:6-19. Jesus is praying for all of us who live as his followers in the world, knowing how difficult it will sometimes be for us, but not praying for us to be taken out of the dangers because the work we are doing is so vital; it needs doing. It is reassuring for us to know that whenever we are talking about our faith, or standing up for what is right, or helping someone else to think through their faith, Jesus is there praying for us and, through him, God's life is there in us, giving us the words to say, and the courage to do the work.

Praying

O come to my heart, Lord Jesus,
there is room in my heart for thee.

Activities

On the sheet they are encouraged to join the disciples in their waiting on God during this coming week, asking for a fresh outpouring of the Holy Spirit. And they are helped to look at any preparation in their own lives which needs to be done.

PENTECOST

Thought for the day

The Holy Spirit of God is poured out in power on the expectant disciples, just as Jesus promised.

Reflection on the readings

Acts 2:1-11
Psalm 103
1 Corinthians 12:3-7, 12-13
John 20:19-23

As humans we are quite a conservative bunch. Most of us like to hold on to what we are familiar with; to 'our' way of doing things. Since Easter, Jesus' disciples had been learning to let go of the familiar presence of their teacher and friend. He had assured them that he needed to leave them for a while, so that he would be able to send them the Spirit, but before the crucifixion this news had simply made them miserable and threatened, filled with grief. All they could see was a future without Jesus, a prospect that knocked the bottom out of their world.

Now, today, we are celebrating, because we join with the disciples as they are overwhelmed with joy. Whatever they had imagined it would be like to receive God's Holy Spirit, the actual experience hugely surpasses. Far from feeling destitute without Jesus' presence, they now sense him with them more deeply and closer than ever before.

All the things Jesus had patiently tried to explain to them they can understand with a new clarity, as if the light of God has suddenly been switched on in their thinking. All Jesus' urgency for telling people the good news now fills them with zeal they have never known before.

Suddenly the most important thing to do is communicate God's love to those who don't know it. The ability to speak in the different languages of the visitors to Jerusalem is all part of this newly given love for people which cannot wait to let them in on the secret of real freedom. The Holy Spirit, coming like flame, sets the disciples' hearts on fire with love for God and for other people.

Peter and the disciples will come to realise that they are experiencing the first wave of a new order, with God's Spirit flooding out into those of all nations; God living in his people in a dynamic, revolutionary way. The offer is available to anyone genuinely desiring more of the living God in their lives.

Discussion starters

1. Why isn't the Holy Spirit poured out more than it is in our own church? What can we learn from the disciples' expectant waiting?

2. Do we try to impose restrictions or guidelines for the Holy Spirit in case our lives are too much challenged by too much of God's presence?

All-stage talk

Cut flame shapes from red and orange paper (shiny paper is specially good), and have these given out to everyone as they come into church.

Remind everyone of how the Holy Spirit came, with the noise of a gale-force wind (the noise of which they can try making), and looking like fire, which split up into flames resting on each of those in the room. (Everyone holds up the flame they have been given, so there are flames all over the church.) That was how it seemed from the outside.

Inside each person, what was going on?

- (Display an exclamation mark.) The disciples were stunned by this display of the power of God. God meant business, and was clearly way outside their control. God was in charge.

- (Display a red rose or a red heart.) They suddenly knew, at first hand, what God's love really meant. They felt full of it, and it made them very happy and excited. They wanted to tell God all about it!

- (Display an empty speech bubble.) They wanted to tell other people all about it too. They wanted everyone to know God like this, because they knew how wonderful it was. And God's love in them made them want to share the good news, rather than keep it to themselves.

God is still pouring out his Holy Spirit on people, every day. Wherever anyone seriously wants to have the powerful love of God living in them, the Spirit will come and fill them.

Often we don't really want God that close. This may be because we are scared of God being really powerful; but we forget that with power which is full of love and goodness we don't need to be afraid. Mostly we just aren't bothered enough to take God seriously. The disciples were spending all day in God's company, waiting and hoping for the Holy Spirit to come. How much time do we focus our attention on God?

If we want something really badly, it fills our thinking all the time. Suppose we really want a computer, or to be a ballet dancer, or to drive a car. We'll be reading all the advertisements and the magazines, spending out on lessons and working hard at them, making sure we're in touch with the experts and so on.

So if each of us, and all of us as a church, are impressed by today's reading, and serious about wanting a fresh outpouring of the Holy Spirit, what can we do?

We can really want more of God in our lives. We can want that when we wake up, all through the day, and when we lay our heads down on the pillow at night. We can want it so much that we start listening to God and getting our lives ready to receive his gift. We can put God at the centre, instead of somewhere squeezed in at the edge.

And God will come to us, filling us with his Holy Spirit, and transforming our lives.

All-age ideas

- Give the children red, orange and yellow streamers to dance with in one or two of the hymns, or the Gloria.

- Make posters or banners with flame shapes of paper stuck on and words describing the life of the Spirit, such as love, joy and peace, power and gentleness.

- Arrange to have a parish party or picnic, so that the fellowship of the community is enriched. Suggest that everyone wears something flame-coloured.

Prayer of the Faithful

Celebrant
In the power of the Holy Spirit,
let us pray.

Reader
For a fresh in-breathing of life and power
in each church community,
which breaks down our barriers
and sets us on fire with God's love.

Silence

Come, Holy Spirit:
Holy Spirit, come!

For the grace to see this world
and its needs and problems
through the eyes of love, hope,
justice and mercy;
for the grace to abandon prejudice
and build bridges of reconciliation.

Silence

Come, Holy Spirit:
Holy Spirit, come!

For the Spirit of loving kindness
to fill our homes, schools and places of work;

for family rifts to be healed
and long-standing conflicts resolved.

Silence

Come, Holy Spirit:
Holy Spirit, come!

For the restoration of those who are sick
to wholeness and well-being;
for courage and patience in all suffering,
and for good to be distilled
from every painful, destructive experience.

Silence

Come, Holy Spirit:
Holy Spirit, come!

For God's merciful judgement
on those who have died,
and the opportunity for us all
to prepare carefully for meeting God
face to face.

Silence

Come, Holy Spirit:
Holy Spirit, come!

We join our prayers with those of Mary,
who joyfully received the Holy Spirit:
Hail, Mary . . .

Refreshed in the Holy Spirit,
we approach our loving Father
with our private petitions.

Silence

Celebrant
Loving Father,
rejoicing in your strength and fellowship,
we lay these prayers before you,
through Jesus Christ.
Amen.

TREASURE SEEKERS

Aim: To celebrate the Church's birthday.

Starter

Pass the parcel. Beforehand prepare an outline picture based on the one below.

Cut flame shapes from coloured paper to fit exactly over the flames in the picture. Pack the flames into the layers of the parcel and the silhouettes of the disciples' heads in the 'prize' place. You can add a sweet if you wish! As each flame is unwrapped the child sticks it on to the right space, until the group has collectively completed the whole picture.

Teaching

Today we are celebrating! It's rather like the birth-day of the Church, because today we remember how Jesus sent the Holy Spirit on his friends so they would be filled with God's love and power.

What did the Holy Spirit sound like? It sounded like a strong wind, blowing round the house. (All make the sound.)

What did the Holy Spirit look like? It looked like flames of fire. (Light twelve tea-light candles.)

What did the Holy Spirit feel like? It felt like being happy and excited and peaceful all at once, and wanting to tell everyone about how lovely it is to be loved by God.

Praying

Come, Holy Spirit,
and fill me up with God's love.
I may be small
and not very tall
but I can be BIG with God's love!
(Make yourself as big as possible)

Activities

The sheet can be made into a simple kite to fly. Each child will also need some cotton. Put reinforcers on the punched holes and staple the kites like this.

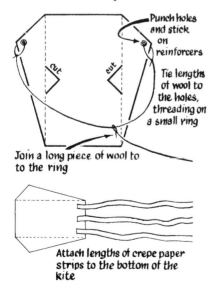

Punch holes and stick on reinforcers

cut

cut

Tie lengths of wool to the holes, threading on a small ring

Join a long piece of wool to to the ring

Attach lengths of crepe paper strips to the bottom of the kite

The kites should fly even in a very light breeze if the children run with them.

PEARL DIVERS

Aim: To know the events of Pentecost.

Starter

Give each child a different coloured bunch of wool lengths. (For larger numbers of children make several groups.) With the bunch of wool provide a written message, reading it out to the child as you give it, and checking they know what it says. Now they all go round giving their message, and one length of their wool, to every other child. Here are the messages:

1. The disciples were waiting and praying.
2. Pentecost means fifty days after Passover.
3. Jesus had promised to send the Holy Spirit.
4. The Spirit sounded like a rushing wind.
5. The Spirit looked like flames of fire.

(Add to these or prune them as necessary for your group.)

Teaching

Everyone should now have a bunch of different coloured wools. They lay these out in front of them. The children can now help you tell the story of Pentecost, by remembering the messages which went with each colour of wool.

Once everyone has added the bits of the story, pull it all together by reading the events as told direct from Acts, using a suitable translation. We have all been working together to tell the story today, and the Holy Spirit empowers us to work together with God and one another for good every day of our lives. What a lot of good can happen by seventy years' time if all of us, and all the children in all the other Pearl Divers groups, work in the power of the Holy Spirit every day for the rest of our lives!

Praying

Come, Holy Spirit of God,
come to me and fill my life.
Let me live in your strength from now on,
and work with you
so that great good gets done!

Activities

The children can make flame crowns from their sheets. Provide flame-size pieces of shiny red or orange paper to add to their coloured flames, and staple them to the rim. They are also encouraged to think of a quiet space during the day at home where they can get in touch with God each day, and pray the week's prayer.

GOLD PANNERS

Aim: To look at how the coming of the Holy Spirit affected the disciples and affects Jesus' followers now.

Starter

All change! Have a selection of scarves and hats, enough for everyone and as silly as you like. Use a CD player for music so that you can skip from track to track. When the music starts, each person dresses up. Whenever the track changes, they have to swap their hat and scarf with someone else.

Teaching

Explain that the disciples had seen a lot of changes in the last few years of their lives. Jesus had called them out of their normal jobs, they'd travelled around to different places, changed their way of thinking and their way of thinking about God. They'd lived through the crucifixion, Jesus being dead and Jesus being alive again. Now they were waiting for another change, not quite knowing what the Holy Spirit would do to them, but knowing it was important to be ready for it.

Now read from Acts. Consider having this reading prepared on tape, either from a professional recording, or using a couple of adults from the congregation, and adding the sound of the wind, or some music.

What has happened to the disciples with the coming of the Holy Spirit? How are they behaving? How are they different? Why are they so excited? What was it they wanted everyone to know?

Praying

Lord, that power the disciples were given –
I want it, too.
I've seen the way they were changed
and strengthened – and I want that, too.
Will you let your Holy Spirit
come to me and fill my life?

Activities

There is a short sketch to start them looking at the possibility of the Holy Spirit changing things still, today and here. And they are encouraged to learn how to wait on God, both privately and as a group, so that they grow in his Spirit.

FEASTS OF THE LORD

TRINITY SUNDAY

Thought for the day

The mysterious and holy nature of the one true God is beyond our understanding, but it is both communal harmony and individual personality, Father, Son and Holy Spirit.

Reflection on the readings

Deuteronomy 4:32-34, 39-40
Psalm 32
Romans 8:14-17
Matthew 28:16-20

The festival of Trinity allows us time in the Church year to contemplate the nature of God, and marvel at it. One thing we shall never be able to do, as humans, is to grasp it with full understanding, simply because God is not made in our likeness, but we in his. Often people shrug off the possibility of God because he does not behave according to the limitations of humankind, and they feel he ought to if he is real.

God's reality is of a nature we cannot quantify and contain, rather as our eyes can only perceive certain colours in the rainbow while others are beyond our powers of vision. Isaiah's glimpse of God's holiness and glory is more in the realm of sensing than understanding, and with us, too, the moments when we become fleetingly aware of the depths of God's nature are probably moments of sense and inner assurance, rather than quantifiable knowledge. This is not something to worry about but rejoice in; no matter how much we discover to love and worship in the living God, there will always be the joy of more to explore and other treasure to find, and we can delight in the discovering.

As soon as we try to nail God down mathematically, we are bound to run into trouble, and the concept of the Trinity reminds us that all our models and shapes are only rough guides to help us; the reality is always more and different.

What we do know is that there is more to this life than the seen. Even in the seen world there are invisible things like wind. How much more when we are in the realm of the Spirit. If we are open to the possibility of it being so, we shall start to notice it. It's actually the Spirit 'in line' with our spirit which makes the necessary connections.

One of the glorious things about people is their wholesome loathing of being fobbed off with lies

as the truth. The Spirit leads us into truth, and God is Truth, so we cannot seek Reality and Ultimate Truth without travelling deeper into the nature of the one true living God. The Son leads us to the Father and the Spirit; the Father leads us to listen to the Son and the Spirit; and the Spirit leads us to the Son and the Father.

Discussion starters

1. How does each Person of the Trinity testify to the others?

2. What would you like God to enable you to 'see'?

All-stage talk

Prepare either an OHP acetate or a very large cut-out triangle, as shown.

Also have three equal strips of card and three paper fasteners, or bring three equal strips of a large-scale construction toy, with the appropriate nuts and bolts – basically any three things which can construct a triangle.

Start by asking a volunteer to help by making a triangle from the separate strips. As they work, do a commentary on the progress, observing the sides move in all directions until that final join, at which point the triangle is a strong shape, with each two sides holding the other firm. It's such a strong shape that it is used in building – bridges, towers, pylons, roof rafters, for example.

Why on earth are we looking at triangles in church today? Explain that today we are exploring the nature of God. Will we be able to end up by bedtime knowing all about God, then? No! Human brains aren't big enough to cope with understanding our great God completely, any more than your hamster can understand completely what it is to be human.

But as your hamster gets to know you and become your friend, little by little he will understand more about you, as much as a hamster can.

So, back to the triangles. Perhaps they can help us understand a little bit more about the great and powerful God of love. (Show your triangle.)

We've seen how strong one three-sided shape can be. Suppose for a minute we look at the threeness and oneness of God as a bit like this triangle. We know that there is only one true God, and here we have one triangle. We know that God is our Father and Creator, Jesus our Saviour and the Holy Spirit. (Turn the triangle round as you refer to each side.) Whichever aspect of God we focus on, we are always looking at God in all his truth and fullness.

And there's another thing. The Son always directs us to see the Father and the Spirit; the Father always directs us to see the Son and the Spirit; and the Spirit always directs us to see the Father and the Son. (Turn the triangle round as you refer to each side.)

Of course, our God is far, far more than a mathematical shape – the God of love and glory is much more than a triangle! But the way a triangle works can help us understand a little more of how, for God, it's no problem to be one God, who is also Father, Son and Spirit. It's as natural for God to be like that as it is for us humans to be able to be in one place and think about being somewhere else, both at the same time.

All-age ideas

- Use the Baptismal promises in place of the Creed.

- The children can wave green streamers in one of the hymns today – not as a performance, or for anyone to see, but simply as part of their own worship offering.

Prayer of the Faithful

Celebrant
Let us pray to the Father
through the Son
and in the power of the Holy Spirit.

Reader
May the Church reflect the community and unity within the Trinity;
may there be Godly harmony, shared ministry, mutual support and encouragement in the faith.

Silence

May your will be done:
on earth as it is in heaven.

May the world's leaders
seek not personal power but the public good;
may conflicts be faced honestly
and needs recognised and met;
may all our communities be built up
on what is good, true, just and right.

Silence

May your will be done:
on earth as it is in heaven.

May there be love and respect
for one another in every household;
may there be mutual support
and thoughtfulness, consideration and trust.

Silence

May your will be done:
on earth as it is in heaven.

May the hearts' cries for help be heard;
the tears collected and the fears quieted;
may suffering be eased and guilt erased
through your healing love.

Silence

May your will be done:
on earth as it is in heaven.

May the dead rise to new and eternal life,
freed from their aching and restored for ever.

Silence

May your will be done:
on earth as it is in heaven.

Remembering Mary's special vocation,
we make our prayer with her:
Hail, Mary . . .

In silence filled with love,
we pray our individual petitions.

Silence

Celebrant
Heavenly Father,
eternal and always present,
we offer you these prayers
in the name of Jesus.
Amen.

TREASURE SEEKERS

Aim: To learn about God from the wind.

Starter

Go outside and feel the wind. Work out where it's coming from, and watch what it does to such things as a piece of thread, a balloon, our clothes, and blown bubbles.

Teaching

Come back inside and sit in a circle, talking about the wind. What did it feel like on our skin? What did it do? Was the wind real? Could we see it? No! The wind and air are invisible, but we know they are very real. How? Because we can feel the wind and see what it does.

The wind is very useful because it can teach us about God. Like the wind, God's love and closeness to us can't be seen, but it is very, very real. We can feel that God loves us. We can see all around us the beautiful world God has made. Like the wind, we can see the good things God does.

Praying

I can't see the wind
but I can feel it's there.
I can't see you, Lord God,
but I can feel your love!

Activities

Using the sheet they can make a prayer wheel to hang in the wind, and there is a windy day picture for them to look at and colour, spotting the things the invisible wind is doing.

PEARL DIVERS

Aim: To be introduced to God as Father, Son and Spirit.

Starter

Bring in a lot of tight rolls of newspaper, thick enough to be firm. Work together to make them into an Eiffel Tower, using sticky tape to join the rolls together. They should find that the strongest shape to use is a triangle. If they aren't getting beyond the bendy stage, you can subtly suggest the use of triangles!

Teaching

Draw their attention to the way triangles hold firm, and look at one to see why this is. All the way round, two hold the third in place.

Explain that today the whole Church is taking a look at what God is really like, and worshipping him. What do we know about God already? For a start, how many Gods are there? They may well mention lots of gods they have heard of. Agree that people through history have invented lots of gods, and anything we worship – including football stars and fashion – can be made into a kind of god by us. But we know that all these are pretend gods, which we make or think of ourselves.

There is only one true God and nobody invented God – God was already there; he always has been and always will be. That makes the one true God the only one worthy of our worship. And that's why we and our families make the effort to get up on a Sunday; we know that God is real and we come to worship him.

What is the only true God like? God is Father, the Creator (write 'Father' across the triangle), Son, our Saviour (write 'Jesus' in the same place), and Holy Spirit (write 'Holy Spirit' in the same place). We can't see the words clearly now because they are all one, and that's what God is like. If we also write the character of God round the edges (do this) we can see that the whole 'shape' of God is Father, Son and Holy Spirit all supporting and including each other.

That's why we call God a Trinity, or Tri-Unity – tri = 3 and unity = 1.

Praying

Glory be to the Father
and to the Son
and to the Holy Spirit,
as God WAS in the beginning
IS now
and SHALL BE for ever. Amen.

Activities

Using the sheet the children can make a hand-held creed. Each child will need a paper fastener for this. They can also build up a collage picture of God, using the qualities and characteristics named. For this the group will need a large sheet of coloured paper, and the words can be stuck all over it, together with pictures which match up with the descriptions. When planning, look at the words and bring pictures which you feel are appropriate, for the children to choose from.

GOLD PANNERS

Aim: To explore the nature of the Trinity.

Starter

Who are you? The group is going to discover as much as possible about you in five minutes. Before the timing starts, let them collectively establish what they do know about you already, so the question time isn't wasted. Explain that if you don't want to answer a particular question you will say so; but they can ask whatever they want to in order to get to know who you are and what you are like.

Teaching

Look back at how the group discovered more about you. They ran their minds over what they knew already and went on from there. Were there some things they thought they knew which turned out to be mistaken? Were they surprised by any of the new discoveries?

Today, on Trinity Sunday, we are focusing on who God is and what he is like. Collectively as a Church, over the years, some clear truths about God have been discovered:

• God is One Being

• God is Three Persons – Father, Son and Holy Spirit.

(Trinity means Tri-Unity, or Three in One and One in Three.)

Why does the Church describe God in this way? Look together at what they know of God as Father, Son and Spirit, to see how the concept of Trinity has developed, referring to these passages to help: Genesis 1:1-3; Isaiah 9:6; Luke 1:35; John 10:36-38; John 14:25-26; and John 3:1-17 where the invisible nature of the wind helps Nicodemus discover more about the nature of God.

Praying

Holy, holy, holy is the Lord Almighty;
the whole earth is full of his glory!

Activities

On the sheet there are aspects of the natural world which can help us understand more about the nature of God: the wind; infinity of space; simplicity/complexity of life structures; light; physical laws and order.

CORPUS CHRISTI

Thought for the day

In bread and wine at the Last Supper, Jesus offers himself, the Lamb of God who takes away the sins of the world.

Reflection on the readings

Exodus 24:3-8
Psalm 115
Hebrews 9:11-15
Mark 14:12-16, 22-26

In the reading from Exodus we hear about the original Covenant between God and his people. Moses tells them all God's commandments and laws, which they agree to keep, and the Covenant is sealed with the sacrifice of animals, their life-blood sprinkled both on the people and the altar. The practice of animal sacrifice may seem messy and barbaric to us, but its symbolism is very powerful. Everyone knows that flesh and blood show that something is alive, and an offering of life itself is a costly and precious sacrifice. For the ancient people of Israel, their national life was now bound up in the life of God through the Covenant of blood.

In the Gospel we find Jesus preparing to eat the Passover meal with his disciples. This was (and still is) a wonderful celebration meal, eaten by families and households to relive the great escape from slavery in Egypt. It was a last supper eaten before the walk to freedom. And this is the meal chosen for the new Covenant to be made – at the Last Supper before Jesus leads us to freedom through his death on the cross.

He uses all the traditions of the meal and fills them with new significance. The bread and the wine are blessed and offered as symbols of the life which he knows must be laid down in sacrifice – his own life. 'Take it,' he says. 'This is my body; this is my blood.'

What are we to make of this new Covenant, sealed with blood like the original one, and binding Jesus' life to the lives of the disciples, not only in that upper room but throughout Christian history?

The writer of Hebrews helps us to understand. Like a great high priest, Jesus the Messiah has come to be the reconciler and go-between to break the mould. The perfect high priest would have to be someone fully human but also divine, and no one, apart from Jesus himself, is that. Jesus' unique identity means that the sacrifice he offers is the real thing, rather than a hope for the future; as perfect priest and perfect victim the longed-for reconciliation between God and us is made possible.

Week by week, day by day, we as God's people can feed on the living bread and witness to the transforming of our lives by his.

Discussion starters

1. How can we ensure that familiarity with the Eucharist does not blunt our awareness of Christ's presence, but deepens it?

2. How would you explain to an enquirer the importance of the Eucharist for you?

All-stage talk

Show everyone a ten or twenty pound note, and ask a volunteer to read the promise on it: 'I promise to pay the bearer on demand the sum of twenty pounds.' This note may just look like a pretty piece of paper, but the reason it's a special piece of paper, worth treating carefully, is that it carries a real promise. At one time we could have gone to the Bank of England and demanded the real twenty pounds worth of gold. It's a bit more complicated than that now, of course, but in a way our whole financial system works on the promise, and we pay one another in promises of twenty pounds.

How do promises work? Collect ideas, and establish that when people make serious promises they mean what they say and it is understood that promises are not for breaking. We should never make promises we know we won't be able to keep, and if we do make a promise we should do our very best to keep it.

A Covenant is a legal promise between two people or two parties, often sealed by both people signing their names. Out in the desert, God had made a Covenant with the people of Israel. God promised to be their faithful God, and they promised to be his faithful people, living by God's law of love. As a kind of signing to seal the Covenant, animals were sacrificed, and their blood, the sign of their life, was sprinkled both on the people and on God's altar.

Today we are celebrating the new Covenant, or promise, which Jesus has made with God's people. In the bread and the wine Jesus says we can share his very life, and he seals that promise in blood – not by just signing his name, but by giving his life on the cross. That's quite a signature.

All-age ideas

- Give everyone a small piece of paper and a pen or pencil when they come in. Following the talk, or as part of the Penitential Rite, have a time of silence for people to look at the cross as Jesus' signature, sealing the promise of his life in us, and when they are ready suggest they recommit themselves to their part in that promise, signing their name on the paper as a sign of their life offered. Collect all these and stick them on to the shape of the cross.

- Have a longer than usual time of thanksgiving after Communion, either with quiet singing, with recorded music or with total stillness and silence, as people savour the gift of the sacrament.

Prayer of the Faithful

Celebrant
Gathered as the Body of Christ,
let us pray together to our heavenly Father.

Reader
We pray for all who celebrate
the Eucharistic mysteries,
all who administer the sacrament
of the body and blood of Christ,
and all who receive it, day by day,
week by week and year by year.
Through the loving nature of this feeding
may we all grow in holiness
and bring God's life to all we meet.

Silence

In our need, Lord:
we come to you.

We pray that all who know
their hunger and thirst for real feeding
may find the spiritual nourishment they crave,
and receive new and satisfying life
through Christ our Lord.
We pray that the world may know God's love for it.

Silence

In our need, Lord:
we come to you.

We pray for the spiritual feeding of our families,
and our parish family, through word and sacrament;
may we daily draw closer to the God who loves us,
and our lives become increasingly filled with his life as we feed on him.

Silence

In our need, Lord:
we come to you.

We pray for those who, through frailty or illness, receive the sacrament in their homes or in hospital; for all who are malnourished or starving, whether physically, emotionally or spiritually.

Silence

In our need, Lord:
we come to you.

We pray for those who have died,
that in mercy they may be brought
into the eternal joy of heaven.

Silence

In our need, Lord:
we come to you.

We make our prayers with Mary,
who brought the living bread into the world:
Hail, Mary . . .

Let us be still in the presence of God
and bring to him the needs and concerns
that weigh on our hearts.

Silence

Celebrant
Heavenly Father,
you nourish us by the body and blood of Jesus,
so that we can share in the life of heaven,
both now and at the end of time.
Hear our prayers and provide for us all.
Amen.

TREASURE SEEKERS, PEARL DIVERS AND GOLD PANNERS

It is likely that Corpus Christi services for schools will not need a separate programme for children and young people. However, in the books for TREASURE SEEKERS and PEARL DIVERS I have included worksheets for children in church today.

ORDINARY TIME

SECOND SUNDAY OF THE YEAR

Thought for the day

Christ calls us to follow him and walk his way through our lifetime.

Reflection on the readings

1 Samuel 3:3-10, 19
Psalm 39
1 Corinthians 6:13-15, 17-20
John 1:35-42

The child Samuel is clearly not expecting to hear so directly from God. Yet the experience is so real to him that he assumes it must be Eli calling, who has to instruct him hastily on how to respond. It is the start of a most wonderful lifetime of ministry; Samuel bravely speaks out this first prophecy he is given, and goes on to lead and coax the people of Israel for many years. What strikes us about Samuel's calling is his openness to hear even the unexpected, and his obedience to God. As many of us ruefully recognise, it is one thing to sense what God is wanting us to do, and quite another to agree to it.

The letter to the Corinthians helps us to understand the implications of hearing God's call and responding to it. Paul sees our calling as setting us apart for God's service, and it follows that our bodies, as temples where God's Spirit lives, are to be used with reverence throughout our lives. As he puts it, 'You are not your own property; you have been bought and paid for.' Remembering this can help encourage us in managing our bodies with respect and self-control.

Today's Gospel shows us the calling of three of the disciples, and their response. Once again, we find them ready to hear where they are being led, as John the Baptist points them in the right direction; and once again their response is eager obedience. Andrew turns into a fisher of men straightaway, passing on the news about the Christ to his own brother and pro-actively taking him to meet Jesus for himself. Those new to faith are often those most effective in spreading the Good News, perhaps because of the freshness of their enthusiasm and their still 'unchurchy' language.

The disciples spent time with Jesus informally, before they joined him as his students, and that, too, is a useful model for us to use. It may well be the informal contact with Christians in everyday life which sets the questions flowing and leads to realisation of calling and the challenge of commitment.

Discussion starters

1. Are there occasions when we sense God's call and direction but fail to run with it in case we are mistaken?

2. What makes people able to respond to God's call and what (and who) hinders them?

All-stage talk

Begin by giving out a few messages as if they are notices, rather like this. 'Is Ali Holden here? I've got a message from Molly, your neighbour's dog. She says when you next take her for a walk could you go past the swimming pool as there are some good smells around there. And then there's another message . . . this is for John Bendkowski. It's a message from the rope you used to climb the tree, asking for another high level outing as it enjoyed the view.' (Use inside information so that the messages match up with real life.)

What do we reckon – are those messages true or not? Does Ali take a dog called Molly out for walks? Did John use a rope to climb a tree? Yes! Then what makes us think the messages aren't quite right? It's because common sense tells us that dogs and ropes can't send messages like that, even if they wanted to. Today we are looking at the way God calls us, and how we can work out whether it's really God calling us, or not.

What first alerted Ali and John to the messages given out? It was their names. When God calls us, he gets our attention and speaks directly to us. Sometimes what happens is that we hear a reading at church, or read a passage of the Bible at home, and suddenly a particular bit hits home, and we know it's meant specially for us. It's as if it has our name on it. God spoke into Jonah's heart so that Jonah knew God had a message for him, whether he chose to obey it or not. The fishermen heard Jesus calling directly to them as they worked in the fishing boats. So one thing we can learn about God's call is that it feels personal to us.

The next thing to look at is this: is this the sort of message that God would give? With our messages from a dog and a rope, we knew they didn't ring true, so we could laugh at the messages and not take them seriously. But what other things might make us suspect that a call is not from God at all? If it's to do with anything unkind, violent, selfish, greedy, lazy, deceitful, or evil, then the call we think we are hearing is not coming from the God of truth and love. But if we feel God is calling us to something loving, selfless, thoughtful, kind, courageous, honest, or good, then it's likely that God is speaking into our hearts, and we should listen carefully.

Then what? Since Samuel realised that God was calling him, he bravely spoke out God's message to Eli, even though it wasn't very good news. As soon as Andrew heard about Jesus he went out of his way to follow him and introduce his brother Simon Peter to Jesus.

So we need to be ready to hear God calling in the quiet of our hearts, check with our experience of God that the call is true, and then be prepared to obey the call, going bravely wherever God is leading us.

All-age ideas

• The reading from 1 Samuel can be mimed as it's narrated.

• During the gospel, have a line of people (mixed ages) holding candles, which are lit one from another until all are alight.

Prayer of the Faithful

Celebrant
Let us pray to the God who has called us to be here, bringing to him the cares of our Church and our world.

Reader
We pray for deeper faith among Christians, and a readiness to respond to God's calling. For those being called to particular ministries and those called to change their way of living, we pray for courage, and the grace to obey.

Silence

Unfailing love is yours, Lord:
you are our rock of refuge.

We pray for all who feel pressurised
to conform to wrong values
in order to be accepted;
for a commitment to fight evil
and cultivate good in our world.

Silence

Unfailing love is yours, Lord:
you are our rock of refuge.

We pray for the households of this parish
and God's indwelling there;
for guidance in the everyday decisions
and the times of crisis.

Silence

Unfailing love is yours, Lord:
you are our rock of refuge.

We pray for the weak, the vulnerable,
the weary and the desolated;
for those entrenched in sin
and endangering others.

Silence

Unfailing love is yours, Lord:
you are our rock of refuge.

We pray for those who have died
in God's friendship,
and give thanks for their lives.
May they be called into the light of heaven.

Silence

Unfailing love is yours, Lord:
you are our rock of refuge.

We make our prayer with Mary,
who lovingly made herself available
to God's will:
Hail, Mary . . .

In silence filled with love,
we name our particular prayer burdens.

Silence

Celebrant
Loving Father,
we thank you for calling us,
and ask you to hear these prayers we offer,
through Christ, our Saviour.
Amen.

TREASURE SEEKERS

Aim: To know that God called Samuel when he was a child.

Starter

'Here I am!' Bring enough soft toy animals for every child to hold one. The leader is a very forgetful farmer/zoo keeper/pet owner who keeps losing things. While music plays all the children make their toys move about the room. When the music stops, they sit down and keep their toy out of sight. The leader says something like, 'Oh dear, oh dear, I've lost my little woolly bear. I don't know *where* she can be!' The child holding woolly bear makes her jump up and say, 'Here I am!' Then everyone moves around to the music again until the leader loses something else.

Teaching

Samuel was a little boy. He lived in the temple, which was a bit like a church. Eli, the old priest, looked after him, and Samuel had a bed in the holiest part of the temple. One night he got into bed as usual and lay down to go to sleep. As he lay there quietly in the darkness, he heard God calling him: 'Samuel! Samuel!' Samuel had no idea it was God and thought it must be Eli the old priest, so he got out of bed and trotted along to him. 'Here I am, Eli,' he said. 'What did you want me for?'

But Eli said, 'I didn't call you, Samuel. Go back to bed, there's a good boy.' So Samuel went back to bed and lay down in the darkness. Once again he heard God calling to him: 'Samuel! Samuel!' But he didn't know it was God. So he got up and went along to Eli. 'Here I am, Eli,' he said. 'I heard you call my name.' Eli was puzzled. 'I didn't call you, my child. Perhaps you're dreaming. Go back to bed and lie down.'

Samuel got back into bed and tried to go to sleep. He knew he hadn't been dreaming. Soon he heard the voice again! 'Samuel! Samuel!' But still Samuel didn't know it was God. So Samuel went to Eli again and told him that someone was calling him by name.

This time Eli realised that God must be calling to the child, so he said to Samuel, 'It must be God calling you by name, my child. Go back and lie down, and if you hear the voice again, say, "Speak, Lord, I am listening".'

Samuel went and lay down in bed and waited. Then God came close to him and called him by name again: 'Samuel! Samuel!'

'Here I am, Lord!' said Samuel. 'Speak, Lord, I am listening.' And as God spoke into his heart, Samuel listened. As he grew up, and all through his life, the Lord was with him. God could use Samuel for very important jobs because he was always ready to listen and do what God told him.

Praying

I am a child
(point to yourself)

and Jesus calls me.
(cup hand to ear)

I say, 'Here I am!'
(shout it, waving at the same time)

and run to his side.
(run on the spot)

Activities

Give each child a small lump of playdough to make a model of Samuel, and then they can retell the story using the 'stage-set' on the sheet.

Here is a recipe for playdough. Mix two teaspoons of cream of tartar, one cup of plain flour, half a cup of salt, one tablespoon of oil and one cup of water to form a smooth paste. Cook slowly in a saucepan until the dough comes away from the sides of the pan and forms a ball. When the dough is cool enough, take it out of the pan, add food colouring and knead for three or four minutes. (Store in an airtight container in the fridge.)

PEARL DIVERS

Aim: To look at being called and choosing to follow.

Starter

Pass the message on. Spread the group out over as big an area as possible and start off a message at one end. This person runs to the next and whispers the message, and so on until the last person brings it back to you. Time how long it takes for the message to spread all over the area, and try for the shortest time possible.

Teaching

What had to happen for the message to reach the end person? Everyone had to be

- looking out for their own runner
- listening carefully to the message
- ready to pass the message on

When God calls people to follow him, it's just the same. Remind the children of the boy called Samuel, who was ready to listen, listened carefully and then passed the message on. In today's Gospel (which is from John's Gospel) the calling of the first disciples follows the same pattern. In the other Gospels by Matthew, Mark and Luke we are told that the first disciples were fishermen, and Jesus called them from their fishing to be his students.

John tells it slightly differently. He doesn't mention that they were fishermen, for instance. (If we asked four people who had been for a day out to the zoo to tell us about it, one might talk about the polar bears, one the special offer on the extra-large ice creams, one how they got stung by a wasp and one about the elephant ride. It's rather like that when we read the four Gospels – they all talk about the same events differently because of being different people, and writing for different readers.)

What John notices about the calling of the first disciples is the way two of them are pointed towards Jesus by John the Baptist. 'Look, that's the one!' John the Baptist tells them. 'He's the one you need to follow because he's the one you've all been waiting for – the Messiah, or Christ.'

One of those first two disciples was Andrew, Simon Peter's brother. He and his friend listened to what John the Baptist said, and started walking along the road behind Jesus. Soon Jesus noticed, and turned round. 'What do you want?' he asked. Andrew and his friend didn't really know what to say to that, so they asked Jesus, 'Where do you live?' They just knew they wanted to spend some time with the one John the Baptist had pointed out to them. Jesus said to them, 'Come and see!' So they went back with Jesus to where he was staying and spent the rest of the day with him. We aren't told what they did or talked about, but we do know that, as a result of that afternoon together, Andrew and his friends became Jesus' followers. So they had followed the same pattern – looking out for where John the Baptist showed them to go, and listening carefully to Jesus' invitation.

The next day Andrew was very excited. Having been in Jesus' company for a while, he was pretty sure that John the Baptist was right, and this really was the promised Messiah. He couldn't wait to tell his brother about Jesus so that he could meet him as well.

So he went to Simon. 'Hey, you'll never guess who we've found!' said Andrew. 'It's the Messiah – the holy One we've been waiting for! Come on, I know where he lives and everything. I'll take you to him straightaway – you've just *got* to meet him!' Simon was used to his brother, and knew there was no point in arguing, and anyway he was very curious. Could this wandering prophet really be the Messiah? He certainly wasn't going to miss out on this.

So Andrew led Simon to Jesus, who recognised him straightaway. Perhaps Jesus had watched the fishermen working and listened to them talking. Jesus was glad to have Simon as his follower, and in calling him he gave him a new name to add to Simon. It was the name Peter, or Cephas, which means 'a rock'.

Andrew had immediately been ready to pass the message on. Who knows? It could well be that God is wanting to call another person to follow him, and the only way that person will hear about Jesus and be encouraged to start looking for his company, is by *you* telling them! We are all here today because someone listened to God, and then passed on the message.

Praying

Lord I don't want to miss out
on what you are saying to me.
I want to hear you speaking
in the quietness of my mind and heart.
I want to be ready to follow you
and lead others to know you too.
Amen.

Activities

There are instructions on the sheet for making a telephone for messages, and they are going to decode a semaphore message which points them towards Jesus. For the telephone each child will need two card beakers and a length of string.

GOLD PANNERS

Aim: To look at vocation and our response.

Starter

Give out a circled job advertisement in a newspaper, and prepare three or four simple profiles to give the applicants, including such facts as age, qualifications and experience. The rest of the group are the panel interviewing them for the job, and they decide which one to appoint.

Teaching

When God calls people for particular jobs he already knows all about them, and knows they will be perfectly suited to the work he is calling them to. (That's why it's such a sensible idea to consult God when we are thinking about jobs we might do.) But when God calls, it doesn't always look like what we were hoping to do.

Read the passage from 1 Samuel, pointing out that at first Samuel hadn't been trained by Eli to listen for God's call, and it took three goes for Eli's benefit for the penny to drop. Then the message Samuel was given wasn't a nice comforting one but saying very unpleasant things about Eli and his sons, so Samuel didn't at first want to tell Eli what God had said. Bravely he told him, and went on to become a really good shepherd of God's people.

Now look at the calling of the first disciples in today's Gospel. Andrew and his friend are ready and alert to take notice of what John the Baptist tells them about Jesus, and they make a point of seeking Jesus' company. Simon Peter is dragged along to meet Jesus by the enthusiasm of his brother Andrew, and so it goes on. Something in Jesus makes them sure that this wild and crazy idea of following a wandering preacher is a good one, if unusual and unexpected. They can feel how important it is, even though as yet they don't exactly know why.

When God calls us, he doesn't lay all the details out straightaway. He just lodges the conviction in us that we have to follow him in a particular direction, and, as we start to follow, the next bit of the job becomes clearer. He invites, but never pressurises. If, like Samuel, we don't recognise his call first time, he'll wait to get our attention again, and then quietly repeat the same call. If we agree to follow, he'll set off and expect us to keep up with him. Those first disciples were probably surprised it happened to be they who were called; we shouldn't be too surprised if we find God calling us!

Praying

Here I am, Lord!
I come to do your will.
You do not ask for sacrifice and offerings,
but an open ear.
You do not ask for holocaust and victim.
Instead, here am I.

(From Psalm 39)

Activities

On the sheet they are helped to see different ways God calls people, and to explore some of the reasons for listening or refusing to listen. They look at vocation in its broadest sense, both as long-term work and for particular tasks.

THIRD SUNDAY OF THE YEAR

Thought for the day

When we are called we need to respond with obedience so that many may be brought to repentance.

Reflection on the readings

Jonah 3:1-5, 10
Psalm 24
1 Corinthians 7:29-31
Mark 1:14-20

It's 'Take two' as far as Jonah is concerned, following the first calling which had resulted in his marching smartly away in the opposite direction, with fairly drastic consequences. Typically, God's call hasn't changed when he eventually gets Jonah's attention again; he just quietly repeats into Jonah's heart what Jonah knows is the right thing to do. And this time he obeys God's calling, with the result that the people of Nineveh come to a dramatic, collective repentance, and are saved from destruction.

The psalmist urges us to put our trust in God, whose way is faithful and protects us from evil. In comparison, all else is considered air-headed rubbish, bound to disappoint and let us down.

The passage from 1 Corinthians continues this train of thought, encouraging us to see the temporary nature of our life here in time, so that we will more readily trust in eternal, lasting things. Travelling light through life is the principle, rather than travelling possessively, cluttered with strivings, material comforts or heavy involvement in anything which is not going to last. Greater things are in store for us, and we need to leave ourselves space and energy to focus on what really, and eternally, matters.

The Gospel swings us back to Jesus first striding out into ministry, announcing the coming kingdom of God and urging repentance and belief in the good news. No sooner has he started to alert people, than he begins to gather workers for the harvest, calling fishermen from casting and mending their nets to reaching people and mending them through God's love. Their obedience to his call is vital for the saving of many.

Discussion starters

1. How can we live in the world without being drawn into its dealings at the expense of our spiritual development?

2. Why is it so important to repent? What does repenting involve?

All-stage talk

Point out that everyone is sitting with their bodies turned towards the person who's speaking. The same thing happens in a lecture theatre, at a play, and in the cinema. Why is this? Collect ideas, which may well include being able to see and hear better, helping concentration, and being polite. In the aisle provide a few chairs facing in the opposite direction and invite volunteers to sit in them.

Now start rustling a parcel and explaining that you are going to show everyone what's inside it – it's something you are sure they will all be able to enjoy. Slowly unwrap a new toy for the children's corner, and enthuse about it but don't mention what it is. Then address those sitting facing backwards, either pointing out the way they have turned their heads round to be as much facing the right way as possible, or giving them permission to turn round, as you are sure they are feeling they're missing out by facing the wrong way.

In our readings from the Bible today we heard the word *repent*. Jonah was giving God's message to the people of Nineveh to repent, and as Jesus starts his work among the people he goes around telling them to repent. So what does it mean to repent, and why are we told to do it?

To *repent* really means to turn round and start facing the right way. Ask the volunteers to pick up their chairs, turn them around and sit facing the front. It really isn't any fun facing the wrong direction – away from God's love. Sooner or later we shall feel we're missing out, somehow, and we'll be right. When we are facing away from God we *do* miss out. We cut ourselves off from seeing what God is doing and from hearing what he is saying. Sometimes we might swing our heads round to glance in God's direction, but that isn't repenting.

To *repent* we need to choose to turn ourselves round completely and face God. That may well be quite an upheaval for us. It will certainly mean that we'll be facing away from wrong (though perhaps pleasant and exciting) things we're involved with at the moment, and that takes courage. It may mean changing what we think of as most important. It may mean coming clean about some secret fault and apologising to certain people.

The good news is that facing the right way is wonderfully liberating, and takes all that weight and strain of our sin away. It lets us take advantage of all God's help and blessings again.

The disciples were called to help spread this message of Jesus which sets people free: *repent and believe.*

All-age ideas

- Have a flower arrangement focusing on the fishermen, using a flat mirror and some sand, stones and shells, driftwood and netting.

- Give everyone a stone as they come in and suggest they hold it during the Psalm and during the Prayer of the Faithful as a tactile reminder that God is our rock and refuge, whom we can always trust.

Prayer of the Faithful

Celebrant
Through the faithfulness of others
we have heard the good news.
In thankfulness, let us pray.

Reader
We thank God for all who have worked
to spread the good news in every generation,
so that we have been able to hear it.
May we, too, be faithful in passing on
the Gospel of God's love and forgiveness.

Silence

Make us lights:
to shine in the world.

We thank God for all
who have answered the call to repentance.
We pray for all peacemakers
and those striving to establish justice,
breaking the cycle of revenge with forgiveness.

Silence

Make us lights:
to shine in the world.

We thank God for every resolved conflict,
every heartfelt apology
and all open-hearted forgiveness.
We pray for all whom we have wronged
and those who have wronged us.

Silence

Make us lights:
to shine in the world.

We thank God
for the strength and wholeness he brings us,
and pray for all who are suffering.
May they be healed and comforted,
and may our hands be ready
to carry out God's loving care.

Silence

Make us lights:
to shine in the world.

We thank God for lives well lived;
for the example of those who have died
in his friendship.
May they come to know the joy of heaven.

Silence

Make us lights:
to shine in the world.

As we open our hearts to receive Jesus,
we remember Mary's receptive love,
and make our prayer with her:
Hail, Mary . . .

In silence we pray to God our Father
for our own intentions.

Silence

Celebrant
Rejoicing that we have been called
to serve you, Father,
we offer you these prayers,
along with our lives for you to use;
through Christ our Lord.
Amen.

TREASURE SEEKERS

Aim: To know that Jesus called the fishermen to follow him.

Starter

Play the fishing game, using either a commercial version or a homemade one – coloured paper fish with paperclips, and pea-stick fishing rods with string lines and opened paperclip hooks. Use a (dry) paddling pool, scatter the fish in it and stand each rod in a wellie. The children can hook the fish and throw them back in.

Teaching

Jesus lived beside a big lake which had lots of fish in it. That meant there were fishing boats, and fishermen who went and caught fish to sell. Invite the children to be fishermen, and do all the actions of mending the nets so there aren't any big holes, and scrubbing the boat out to keep it clean. Then they have to push the boat off from the shore, wade out and climb in the boat, hoist the sail and steer the boat. They let down the anchor, throw the fishing nets out into the water and wait. Then when the net is full of fish they haul the heavy net in, tip the fish into baskets at the bottom of the boat and sail back to the shore. They jump out of the boat and haul it up the beach. Then they have to carry the baskets full of fish to sell in the market. After all that they can lie down and have a bit of a rest while they listen to a story!

One morning a man called Jesus was walking along the beach. He was looking for some people to help him in his work, and he saw the fishermen. Some of them were throwing their nets into the water. (And we know how to do that, don't we?) Some of them were sitting on the beach mending their nets. (And we know how to do that, don't we?)

And Jesus thought fishermen, who are good at catching fish, would be just the people he needed to reach people for God. Fishermen who mended their nets would be just the people he needed to mend people through God's love. So he called them to follow him. 'Follow me!' he said.

And the fishermen were happy to follow Jesus and work with him.

Praying

If I was a fisherman
  (mime fishing)
and Jesus called me,
  (cup hand to ear)
I'd throw down my fishing nets
  (do that)

and run to his side.
  (run on the spot)
I am a child and Jesus calls me.
  (point to yourself, and cup hand to ear)
I say, 'Here I am!'
  (shout it, waving at the same time)
and run to his side.
  (run on the spot)

Activities

Each child will need a piece of old net fabric, about the size of a handkerchief. There are fish to colour and cut out on the sheet and these can be put in the net which is then tied up with a rubber band or length of string or wool.

PEARL DIVERS

Aim: To look at Jonah and the fishermen – being called and choosing to follow.

Starter

Have some water in washing-up bowls and three or four children to each bowl. Scatter some leaves and small sticks (such as spent matches) in the water and give each group a piece of the net which oranges come in from supermarkets. They have to work together to catch the 'fish' in the 'net'.

Teaching

As they might have guessed, some fishermen come into our teaching today! But we're not starting off with them; we're starting off with a very large fish. (Show a picture of Jonah being swallowed by it. Most children's Bibles include this picture.) Who is the man being swallowed by the enormous fish? It's Jonah, who heard God calling him and didn't want to do what God said, so he raced off in the opposite direction and got on a boat to Spain. After a terrible storm he ended up like this. Not a pretty sight. Did God give up on Jonah as a bad job? No! Three days later the fish spat Jonah out on to the beach. And once again he felt God calling him.

Was it a nicer message this time? No! It was exactly the same as before. God was calling Jonah to tell the people of the city of Nineveh to turn away from their evil ways and back to God.

Why didn't Jonah want to do it? Because Nineveh was an enemy city, and he didn't particularly want them to be saved. But this time when God called, Jonah listened and did what God wanted him to do. And as a result, the people realised they had done wrong, they told God how sorry they were and they really tried to do better. So God saved them from disaster.

So much for the big fish. Now back to the fishermen.

Andrew and Simon Peter were brothers. James and John were brothers. They all worked as fishermen on the sea of Galilee, which is a large, beautiful lake. And, just like Jonah, they were called by God. It happened like this.

Jesus was just starting out on his ministry of teaching and healing, and he needed some people to be his students. He was going to teach them over the next couple of years so that when he was no longer on the earth, they would be able to carry on his work in the world. Who would he choose? The religious teachers and leaders? No. Rich, powerful people who could get them into the posh places? No. Who then? Jesus watched the way the fishermen worked hard and stuck at it even when it was uncomfortable work. He saw their common sense and ordinariness, and the way they reached out for the fish and mended their nets. This was what Jesus needed – ordinary people who could talk to all the other ordinary people, and who knew what it was like to be exhausted after a day's work, and still go on. He wanted people who could reach out to others and knew about mending, because there are so many whose bodies, minds and spirits need mending.

So Jesus called them – 'Andrew and Simon, come and follow me. I will have you fishing for people instead of fish!' 'James and John, come and follow me!'

Did they do a Jonah and make excuses, or race off in their boats to the other side of the lake? No! They knew that God was calling them, and that it was important to follow Jesus. So they did. They left their boats and their nets, and set off to be Jesus' students, or disciples.

And Jesus still comes calling ordinary, practical people who can work hard, and talk to other ordinary people and help in their mending. Is he calling you? If you find he is, tell him in your prayer time that you are ready to do what he wants you to do, and then enjoy following wherever he leads you in your life. One thing's certain – you'll have an exciting life as one of Jesus' students!

Praying

Here I am, Lord,
ready to walk with you
and work with you.
I've got my L-plates
and I'm ready to go.
Lead on, my Lord!

Activities

There are pictures of different sounds to place in order of decibels, as they learn that Jesus' call can be very loud or very quiet. And they can read about some others who have heard God's call in their lives.

GOLD PANNERS

Aim: To look at the call to help people come to repentance.

Starter

Have a go at line dancing, where you are all changing direction as you do the set steps.

Teaching

Read the passage from Jonah, reminding them of what had happened the first time God wanted Jonah to call the citizens of Nineveh to repentance. In today's passage we find Jonah being obedient to his call, and the people also obedient to their calling. They decide to reject their evil ways and turn back to God. God knew that Jonah was the right person for the job, but he could only use him if Jonah willingly agreed. All kinds of good doesn't get done because the people God wants to call aren't listening.

Now read today's Gospel. We find Jesus starting out on his ministry, and his message is summed up by Mark as this: 'Repent and believe the good news.' The reason he needs to call the disciples is so that they can spread that same message far and wide. That way, the call to repent has reached millions of people in every generation since Jesus walked on the beach by the lake!

Talk over together what repentance means. It is a turning right round to face the right way – to face God rather than living with our backs to him. The reason God is so concerned that people hear the call to repent is because God knows that our only hope for lasting joy and fulfilment is to face this way. The last thing God wants is for people to miss out on the full and lasting life we are designed for.

Praying

Lord, make me know your ways.
Lord, teach me your paths.
Make me walk in your truth, and teach me:
for you are God my Saviour.
Amen.

(From Psalm 24)

Activities

The meaning of repentance is reinforced on the worksheet, and they are encouraged to look at how we can call one another to repentance in a loving, positive way. They also have a factfile for Jonah to fill in.

FOURTH SUNDAY OF THE YEAR

Thought for the day

Jesus displays all the signs that mark him out to be God's chosen One.

Reflection on the readings

Deuteronomy 18:15-20
Psalm 94
1 Corinthians 7:32-35
Mark 1:21-28

When Moses had approached God on the holy mountain, the people had watched all the signs of God's power and mystery and been so terrified of such a close encounter with the almighty One that they had trembled and begged Moses to act as intermediary for them. God's holiness threw their sinfulness into terrible focus and they knew they couldn't cope with such purity.

We find a similar reaction in today's Gospel, when a man in the congregation breaks the awed hush following Jesus' teaching, to scream out in the quiet synagogue. We can imagine the panic and horror expressed in that uncontrolled outburst. What could have set it off? Was the man merely a familiar local madman, used to disrupting the orderly services?

Mark suggests that this was something startlingly different from a mad heckler. Something has thrown the man into a frenzy of fear, and it seems to be linked with the way Jesus has been behaving. So what has Jesus been doing? We are told he has been teaching, and his teaching, unlike the usual preachers, has the distinct ring of authority.

Presumably so much of God's glory shone through Jesus' words and manner that it was highly challenging, and therefore offensive, to whatever in the man was evil, and in opposition to God's nature. He could not face the light of God's goodness shining into his soul and showing it up for what it really was. That carried with it a sense of horror at the destruction bound to come to that evil, if God were to get too close. So he screams out, seeing the loving God only in terms of cauterising purity.

And in one sense the man was right. Whatever we are – both the evil and the good – cannot be hidden from God, and as we allow him close, the evil cannot survive the power of his love. In Jesus, God's transcendent glory becomes immanent, in the only way this can happen without our destruction: in the complete self-giving of the cross.

Discussion starters

1. What signs of glory showed in Jesus?

2. How can we get the right balance between awesome reverence which verges on fear, and familiarity which borders on presumption?

All-stage talk

Strike a match and light a candle. Talk about how useful fire is to heat up food and cook it, to keep us warm, melt steel and make steam to generate power. But fire is very powerful, and so it can be very dangerous. Show a picture or a model of a fire engine, and enlist the children's help in talking about what happens when fires get out of control, and how the firemen fight the dangers. We need to have a healthy fear of fire to keep us safe.

God is very powerful. When you think of the power needed to create fire and oceans, ranges of mountains and galaxies of stars, you can't help but be a bit fearful at the thought of getting in touch with such a powerful person.

We are sensible to stand in awe of this great Being, on whom we depend for everything, including life itself. We are right to respect the Lord of life, and think carefully before we speak to him, and give him our full attention whenever we pray. We are right to humble ourselves in his presence and behave well during church services. God sees everything we do and knows everything we think, both the things we are pleased about and the things we are secretly rather ashamed of. Sometimes we behave as if God is more of an easygoing pet than the Lord of the entire universe. We need to take God seriously and recognise that he is very powerful indeed.

(Pick up the candle again.) But that great power of God is only part of the story. Just as a candle is a person-sized fire, which we can hold and which gives us light, but doesn't frighten us like a house on fire, so Jesus is the way we can approach the great creative God in person.

All-age ideas

- Have phrases describing God's power written up on the walls and pillars.

- Have the Gospel read by a group of people taking the different parts.

Prayer of the Faithful

Celebrant
As we gather in the presence
of the almighty, all-knowing God,
let us pray.

Reader
May the whole Church honour
and glorify God's holy name
in daily lives, private prayer and public worship.

Silence

Holy God:
may your will be done.

May the whole world resound with God's truth,
activate his compassion,
and be soaked in his peace.

Silence

Holy God:
may your will be done.

May all homes and households
make plenty of room for kindness and forgiveness;
clear the clutter of discontent,
and make us more thankful.

Silence

Holy God:
may your will be done.

May all who ache with sadness or physical pain
be comforted and cherished
by God's love for them.

Silence

Holy God:
may your will be done.

May the dying be surrounded with our prayers,
and those who have passed beyond death
remain safe for ever in God's keeping.

Silence

Holy God:
may your will be done.

With Mary, Mother of the Christian family,
we make our prayer:
Hail, Mary . . .

Now, in the space of silence,
we bring to God our Father
our private petitions.

Silence

Celebrant
Most merciful Father,
we ask you to accept these prayers,
through Jesus Christ.
Amen.

TREASURE SEEKERS

Aim: To explore the power and glory of God.

Starter

Take the children outside to look up at the sky and wonder at the clouds and the stars which are out there but which we can't see because the sun is shining. Draw their attention to the way they are breathing in the air that is all around them, and let them swish their arms around to feel it moving against them.

Teaching

Back inside, look at our hands and the skin on them which keeps our insides together, protects us so well and exactly fits us! All the things we have been looking at are the work of someone so amazing that our eyes can't even see him – we can only see the wonderful things he has made.

And his name is God. We are only alive here because God invented us. God invented the universe we live in. God sees everything that goes on. He is watching us now. He is listening to us now – not just to what we're saying, but to what we are all thinking as well! He hears us feeling sad when we're sad, grumpy when we're grumpy, and happy when we're happy. He knows when we try hard to be kind, even when we don't really want to. He knows when we feel sorry for someone and want to help them. He knows when we are being silly or unkind.

God knows each of us and every other person really well, even if we don't know that much about him yet. But as we get to know God more, we'll find out that he is completely good and completely loving as well as completely powerful.

Praying

Star maker, sky maker,
help me to see
that God who made everything
knows and loves ME!

Activities

Each child will need a large circle cut from half a black bin bag. There are instructions on the sheet for turning this into a prayer mat of the starry sky, using silver and gold tinsel, and silver foil. There is also a star-to-star picture to complete, and a picture to colour of some of the wonderful things God has thought of.

PEARL DIVERS

Aim: To recognise that the shining light of God's goodness shows up evil and challenges it.

Starter

Make the room as dark as possible, and have a powerful torch. The children start at one end of the room and try to creep up to you without you seeing them moving in the light of the torch, which you sweep like a searchlight slowly back and forth across the room. Anyone caught moving in the light has to come and help you check for other movers.

Teaching

Flash the torch around again and talk together about how light shows up things which are hidden in the darkness. When might we be pleased to have the light spotting us? (If we were shipwrecked and wanting to be rescued; if we were lost in a dark wood; if we're doing something we're proud of; if we're dressed in our coolest clothes.) When might we not want the light to spot us and show us up? (If we're doing something we know we shouldn't be doing; if we're wearing something awful; if we're up to no good.) The thing about light is that it can't help showing everything up clearly, both the good and the bad. Shine a torch into a dark cupboard and it might show up either a ten pound note or a dead mouse the cat has brought in!

When Jesus went about on earth, God's glory couldn't help shining out of him and lighting up people's souls to them, so they saw themselves clearly, as they really were. God's light showed up to them very clearly all their nastiness and sin, as well as all their loveliness and goodness. That wasn't always a very nice feeling. People who were behaving badly, but pretended they were behaving well, found Jesus' light showing up their lies and they hated it. People who longed to live well, but knew they weren't very good at it, found Jesus' light showing them hope and forgiveness, and so they loved the light.

God's light still shines. It still shows up to us our nastiness and sin, as well as our loveliness and goodness. How are we going to feel about that?

If we were to hate everything good, honest and right, then we would do our best to shut God's light out, so the evil in us could be safely hidden to fester and grow in darkness again. But if we see God's light as a way of helping the goodness and honesty in us to grow tall and strong, we'll be very happy to let it shine in us.

Praying

All-seeing God, all-knowing God,
shine in my heart,
so that the goodness grows strong
and no evil can take root.

Activities

On the sheet the children are helped to explore the story of today's Gospel, and in a colouring activity they can spot the signs which lead them to uncover a great truth.

GOLD PANNERS

Aim: To trace the prophecies through to the person of Jesus, displaying God's nature in his words and behaviour.

Starter

Play a card game in which you try to cheat, but if challenged you have to show whether you have been honest or not. One possibility is this. Deal out the cards equally. Players hide their hand of cards from everyone. Take it in turns to place cards face down in order of number, saying aloud what you are claiming it to be. If challenged, you must turn the card up, and if you are found to have cheated, you have to take all the cards laid on the table. First to be rid of all their cards wins.

Teaching

One of the top qualities of God is his complete integrity and honesty. God never pretends to us or cheats; his nature is full of truth. As people we often cheat, not just playfully in games but in our lives. We are quite good at doing wrong and pretending to ourselves that it is someone else's fault. If we don't like to think of ourselves as unkind, we'll sometimes pretend that we haven't been unkind, even though we secretly know we have.

That's why it has always been a bit unnerving when people have found God looking into their hearts, and realised that he sees what is really there, and not what we'd like him to find. His light shows up evil and wrong thinking as well as all the good stuff. Read the passage from Deuteronomy 18, noticing how the people even then were rather scared of close contact with the all-seeing God. Then go on to today's Gospel. In Jesus, God has come closer to his people than ever before, and there is a man in the congregation who finds this very distressing. Talk over why this might be, in view of what you read in the first reading.

Go back to the Deuteronomy passage and look at the verses about the prophet speaking God's word. Link this with Mark 1:22, so that they can pick up on the authority of Jesus as God's spokesman. Jesus is God's chosen One, and as he expresses God's thoughts and nature, people are bound to notice God's glory shining in him.

Praying

Lord Jesus, as we read about you in the Gospels
we can see that you are the Christ,
God's anointed, chosen Saviour.
We ask you to shine in us,
so that we are lit up by your truth and love.

Activities

On the sheet there is a role-play to try, and an identity markings activity which enables them to consider identity markings of the Messiah.

FIFTH SUNDAY OF THE YEAR

Thought for the day

The good news about God is far too good to keep to ourselves.

Reflection on the readings

Job 7:1-4, 6-7
Psalm 146
1 Corinthians 9:16-19, 22-23
Mark 1:29-39

Today's readings give us a dramatic contrast of mood. Poor Job wonders what it is all about. Life seems so hard and empty of joy – sentiments echoed by Thomas Hobbes who, in *The Leviathan*, said that 'the life of man is solitary, poor, nasty, brutish and short'. Job feels he is but a slave.

St Paul also feels like a slave, but with what a different outlook! He voluntarily made himself a slave of everyone. Why? Because he is so excited at spreading the good news about God that he is quite happy to devote his whole life and energy to it.

There is utter dedication to the cause in the way he does his research and fits his language and teaching programme to the diverse needs and backgrounds of his hearers.

Why is he so willing to adapt himself and put himself out? Because his encounter with the living God has revolutionised his own life; the God he has met personally through Jesus is simply so wonderful that he can't bear anyone to get through the rest of their life without knowing about him.

In today's Gospel we hear about Jesus' enthusiasm for spreading the good news. He has set Peter's mother-in-law free of her fever, and liberated all kinds of other visitors to the house from their mental, physical and spiritual suffering. We know that following this concentration of healing ministry, Jesus rises before it's light, in order to spend time in prayer, and when his friends find him, wanting to take him back to the community who are asking for him, he is instead concerned to move on. Having seen the look of liberation in the eyes of those set free in Capernaum, he cannot wait to spread the good news of God's freeing love far and wide.

It is whenever we get a fresh and breathtaking experience of who God is and what he is like, that we find ourselves longing for others to share what we have discovered, and cannot wait to pass the good news on.

Discussion starters

1. What would you most want people to know about God?

2. What do you think is the best way of telling them?

All-stage talk

Begin by having the following read out, or having it printed on the weekly sheet. It is an extract from *The Solitaire Mystery* by Jostein Gaarder.

'Tell me about Rainbow Fizz,' I said.
He raised his white eyebrows and whispered,
'It has to be tasted, my boy.'
'Can't you tell me what it tastes like?'
He shook his old head in despair.
'A normal fizzy drink tastes of orange or pear or raspberry – and that's that. That isn't the case with Rainbow Fizz, Albert. You taste all those flavours at the same time with this drink, and you even taste fruits and berries you've never been near with your tongue.'
'Then it must be good,' I said.
'Hah! It's more than just good. You can taste a normal fizzy drink only in your mouth . . . first on your tongue and the roof of your mouth, then a little

bit down your throat. You can taste Rainbow Fizz in your nose and head, down through your legs, and out through your arms.'

'I think you're pulling my leg,' I said.

'You think so?'

The old man looked almost dumbfounded, so I decided to ask something which was easier to answer.

'What colour is it?' I asked.

Baker Hans started to laugh. 'You're full of questions, aren't you, boy. And that's good, but it's not always easy to answer. I have to *show* you the drink, you see.'

(© H. Aschehoug & Co., Oslo. Reproduced by permission.)

Talk about how hard it is to describe something so wonderful that it is impossible to imagine; the only way Albert is really going to find out how wonderful Rainbow Fizz is, is to experience it for himself.

Today's Psalm is a bit like this. The psalmist is doing his best to describe to us how wonderful God is, but God is simply so incredibly amazing that we find it almost impossible to imagine. There's only one way to find out, and that is to experience God for ourselves. If you ask anyone who has become aware of the great, loving God working in their life, they'll agree that there really aren't any words to describe how wonderful and amazing he is. They just know because they've experienced him in action.

In the Gospel we heard how Jesus had been busy healing lots and lots of people at the house of Peter and Andrew, where he was staying. It started with Peter's mother-in-law, who had a bad fever and was very ill, and Jesus made her better. After she'd made them all supper, full of new energy, no doubt, crowds of visitors came, all wanting Jesus to heal them as well. So he did. Through Jesus, God was working right there in those people's lives, and making them more free and happy than they had ever felt before. It was so exciting to see! We can imagine how happy it made Jesus to see these people suddenly realising at last how wonderful God was! He couldn't wait for everyone else to find out.

Well, people are still finding out that our amazing God can set us free to live happy and joyful lives doing good and standing up for what is right and true. And how are they going to discover God? Only if those of us who have found out already how wonderful he is are prepared to tell them about him, and introduce them to him!

All-age ideas

- Try this wine tasting sketch:

Presenter Good morning, everyone, and welcome to today's pick of the bottles with our expert wine taster, Jelly Golden! Good morning, Jelly, it's nice to have you with us again for today's tasting.

Jelly Golden Gosh, yes, we've certainly got some super tastes here. Let's start with this delicious red – just look at that glowing, ruby colour. You can almost smell the sunshine through the glass, can't you?

Presenter If you say so, Jelly. Shall I pour some out for you?

JG (*Sniffs it*) Mmm! Wonderful aroma . . . warm summer days with a breath of a breeze . . . and just a faintest hint of honey. (*Tastes it*) Oh yes, it's so rich and mellow . . . I can taste loganberry, plum and, yes, strawberry as an exquisite aftertaste, all blended wonderfully in the grape. My word, it's really sun-packed . . . utterly delicious! It must be late summer 1992, and if I'm not mistaken, it's from that little valley a few kilometres north-west of Nuits St Georges. Here, you've simply got to try some for yourself! It's the only way to know how magnificent it really is!

Presenter OK, if you recommend it so highly, Jelly . . . Cheers!

- As a background to the reading from Job, play some music which speaks of pain and anguish, such as the theme music from *Schindler's List* or a slow movement from a Mahler or Shostakovich symphony.

Prayer of the Faithful

Celebrant
We have gathered in the presence
of the one, holy God,
from whom all things take their being.
Let us pray to him now.

Reader
Wherever the sparkle of our vision has dulled,
may the Lord set us glowing once again
at the very thought of him;
may he restore our longing to draw closer to him
until our lives reflect his shining.

Silence

Who is the King of glory?
It is the Lord our God.

Wherever important and far-reaching decisions
need to be made,
wherever wrongs need righting
and justice needs to be restored,
we pray for the holy breath
of wisdom and integrity.

Silence

Who is the King of glory?
It is the Lord our God.

Wherever ongoing family conflicts need resolving,
wherever communication has broken down,
we pray for the capacity for unconditional loving,
and appreciation of every 'other'
as another child of the Father's creating.

Silence

Who is the King of glory?
It is the Lord our God.

Wherever there is pain and suffering,
whether physical, emotional, mental or spiritual,
we pray for a fulsome and holy healing,
and ask for the courage and strength
to make ourselves available
and ready to help.

Silence

Who is the King of glory?
It is the Lord our God.

As we call to mind those who have recently died
and those who will die today,
we pray for each of them,
that in their dying
they may find the greatest healing of all,
as they come into the Father's holy presence for ever.

Silence

Who is the King of glory?
It is the Lord our God.

We join our prayers with those of Mary,
the Mother of our Saviour:
Hail, Mary . . .

Now, in silence,
we pray our individual petitions
to our heavenly Father,
who has promised to hear us.

Silence

Celebrant
Almighty Father, hear the prayers we offer,
and use our bodies, minds and spirits
in establishing your kingdom.
In the name of Jesus we pray.
Amen.

TREASURE SEEKERS

Aim: To look at how they can spread the good news of God's love.

Starter

Distribute the contents of a tube of Smarties around the group, or spread some slices of bread with butter and jam to make small sandwiches to give out at coffee time after church.

Teaching

Start with a news time, encouraging the children to share any good news they have, so that everyone can enjoy the good things with them.

The good news we all have to share is that our God is fantastic! Think together about some of the things about God which are wonderful and good.

Not everyone knows these things yet. Quite a lot of people don't know much about God at all, or they don't know how lovely and kind and loving he is. Point out that it seems a great pity that they don't yet know and we do – so how can we let them know our good news about God?

We can use our eyes (everyone points to their eyes) to notice when people need cheering up, or when they need some help, or when they need a hug, just as God notices our needs. We can use our ears (point to ears) to listen carefully, as God listens carefully to us. We can use our mouths (point to them) to speak words that are kind and friendly, and we can tell people about God. And we can use our hands (show them) to do things for people that are kind and loving and helpful.

Praying

I'm not going to keep it a secret – Shh!
I'M GOING TO SHOUT IT LOUD!
GOD IS REAL!
GOD'S THE ONE WHO MADE US ALL
AND GOD'S THE ONE WHO LOVES US ALL!

Activities

On the sheet there are pictures of different things to shout about, and they can work out what the good news is in each case. There is also a picture to colour of all kinds of people happy and dancing because they have just found out that God loves them all.

PEARL DIVERS

Aim: To see how keen Jesus is to spread the good news of God's kingdom.

Starter

In another room or behind a screen have an assembled picture based on the one below, composed of various sections of coloured paper arranged in layers. Beside the picture have all the component parts of a replica picture, already cut. (Have enough for several pictures if you have a large group, and sort the children into teams.)

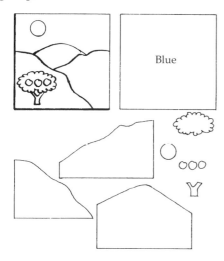

In the main room, explain that their task is to put together here the same picture as is hidden, and it must be made up in the right order. One child at a time can go and look at the finished picture and choose *one* piece to bring back, which they reckon is the next to be placed. Then another child can collect the next piece and so on. If they find the wrong piece has been collected, that must be returned before another piece is chosen. Eventually the two pictures can be shown together to check they are the same.

Teaching

Have two of the leaders pretending to be Peter and his mother-in-law. Mother-in-law is stirring a pot in which she's cooking supper, and Peter is sewing a sail. They talk about when supper will be ready, and start remembering the time when mother-in-law was so ill that she couldn't get up, and she had invited Jesus to supper. Together they chat their way through, remembering that amazing evening, with Jesus arriving, how he was so kind to her, and then how she felt when Jesus healed her. She can probably remember exactly what meal she cooked for them all! Then they remember all the other people coming, crowding round the door. (How did they know? Had mother-in-law met someone and told them what had happened to her?)

They go on to remember how Jesus was missing the next morning and Peter had gone looking for him and found him praying in the hills. What was it he said? Why was it he wanted to leave their town and go travelling around?

Make the conversation natural, asking each other questions and adding any character details that seem appropriate. Then freeze for a few seconds, leave the acting place and join the group as ordinary leaders again. Let the children relate to you what Jesus had been up to, and why he wanted to travel around. (So that lots of other people would be able to find out what it was like to know God's healing in their lives.)

In the picture we made earlier, we could only come back with the right information when we had seen the finished picture, and knew what we were doing. Jesus knew God so completely that he could show people exactly what God was like, even to the point of loving them to full health again. The closer we get to God, the more clearly we'll be able to show other people what God is like – by the way *we* are speaking and listening, looking, thinking and behaving. What will show is God's love.

Praying

Jesus, send us out to make God's love known,
so that more and more people
can meet you and enjoy living as your friend.

Activities

On the sheet there is a chart to help the children think through the methods of communication open to us, and which are most appropriate for giving information to small and large numbers of people. This leads them to think about how their lives can communicate God's love to others, rather than simply talking about God.

GOLD PANNERS

Aim: To focus on what the good news is and how we can spread it.

Starter

Have a selection of newspaper headlines and stories. These are to be sorted into different categories:
- Gossip
- The odd/unusual
- Important good news
- Important bad news

Teaching

Leading on from the starter, talk together about what we consider is news worth spreading around in our newspapers each day. Notice which kind of stories are considered most newsworthy, and whether good news is considered worth printing. If they were to become an editor, would they want to change what is thought worth spreading?

Now read today's Gospel, looking at why Jesus wants to move on from Capernaum. What is it that he has seen in the eyes of those he has healed which makes him anxious to spread the good news as widely as possible? (Such things as joy and freedom from pain or guilt; they look as if they have just been set free.) The news we have to tell about Jesus is worth telling because lives can be set free as a result of knowing it. People surely have a right to know something that has the power to change their lives for the better.

Read the passage from 1 Corinthians to see how, for Paul, too, telling people about God's real power and presence is an urgent matter – he can't bear for anyone to be left without the opportunity to know God and benefit from his saving love.

Praying

O God,
let no one miss out on knowing you
because I failed to let them know about you.
But rather let many be brought to love you
because of my words and actions.

Activities

On the sheet they are encouraged to think through the value of telling people certain information, both good and bad, and the responsibility of those who are in the know to inform other people of risks and benefits. They can then discuss what they want people to know about God, and how this might best be communicated to those who don't know God at all.

Sixth Sunday of the Year

Thought for the day

Jesus wants to heal us to wholeness, and to him no one is untouchable.

Reflection on the readings

Leviticus 13:1-2, 45-46
Psalm 31
1 Corinthians 10:31-11:1
Mark 1:40-45

To be considered untouchable is a terrible thing. To have people shrink away from you, either openly or more subtly, and to watch them draw their children out of your contaminating danger, inflicts deep wounds on the psyche, almost worse than the illness itself. It is not only leprosy; AIDS sufferers can meet the same kind of rejection, the Dalits of India are stamped with it from birth, and political regimes can concoct it legally and devastatingly, as, for example, in Apartheid. Any who live under tyranny and oppression, whether in police states or in dysfunctional family homes, are familiar with the erosive wearing-down of it. To some extent all minorities experience it, and only those who have been on the receiving end can have any idea of the effect it has on self-esteem and the capacity to relate positively with others.

Our readings today show us attitudes to untouchability in all its forms. In the reading from Leviticus we learn of the background to the exclusion of lepers, that hurt them more than the leprosy itself.

In the Gospel we meet a leper, in whom the years of untouchability have taken their toll. He can hardly believe that anyone would want to be bothered with him. He has come to see himself as others have treated him. Yet he senses that with Jesus there may be a spark of hope and, illegally, the man approaches him, doubting not his power but his desire to help. And how does Jesus react?

With anger. This comes as a shock, and some manuscripts have Jesus being moved with compassion, which is perhaps more what we might expect. But it is worth looking at the stern, strong words Jesus uses in reply. Emphatically he insists that of course he wants to heal the man. It may well be that he wants things done properly in keeping with the law, and that is why he directs the man to do what the law requires, going to show himself to the priest. But surely the overriding impression we are left with is of Jesus willingly touching what is considered untouchable, and making him whole, not only physically but holistically.

If this is God's nature, then it also needs to be ours. We cannot claim to be followers of Christ and live comfortably with any kind of marginalising, or any system which makes human beings out to be untouchable for any reason. If untouchability makes us angry, and urges us to do what we can to bring about change, then we shall be offering the touch of our healing God.

Discussion starters

1. Are there habits of social behaviour we have become so used to that we fail to see in them the marginalisation and degrading which is going on?

2. Do we ignore injustice when to act or speak out

might make us unpopular? As Christians, what can we do about this?

All-stage talk

Invite a volunteer to run up the aisle as if they really want to win a race. Then ask them (or another) to run as if they aren't much bothered whether they win or not. Everyone can pick out the differences in the two performances.

Paul tells us that in all we do, we must do it seriously, for the glory of God. What will that mean? We'll be taking our following of Jesus very seriously, and trying very hard at it, practising it every day and building up our stamina. We'll be like 'professionals' instead of wishy-washy drifters. And we'll be getting better and stronger as we practise. If we don't bother, and don't take it seriously, we won't make much progress.

Today in the Gospel we are given another example of what it means to be a follower of Jesus. Let's look at how Jesus behaves with the man who has leprosy. Then we can practise living like that, as we try to follow Jesus.

But first, what does it mean to be a leper? (Lepers and leopards both have spots, but there the similarity ends, so make this clear!) Leprosy is a skin disease. When people get leprosy, they first find they lose the feeling in a finger, or a bit of the foot, and gradually the skin turns very white in patches. It is a bad illness, and people die of it if they don't get the medicines which can cure it. In Jesus' time, lepers were sent off to live on their own because they were thought of as 'unclean'. No one else was allowed to touch them. If they did, the law said they would become unclean as well.

So what did Jesus do? There was the leper, knowing Jesus had the power to heal him, but not sure that Jesus would want to have anything to do with someone as unclean as he was. And there was Jesus, so much wanting the man to be healed that he did something very shocking. He reached out . . . and *touched* the leper! Jesus wasn't afraid of the law saying he would be unclean; he just knew that this man, who had been untouchable for years, more than anything needed to feel touchable again. We know what happened – the man's skin was made better straightaway, so he could go and show the priest and have it all made official; he was no longer unclean.

As Christians, we are followers of Jesus, so now we know a bit more about how we must try to live. We must try wanting the best for people, and we must try not to shut people off or have nothing to do with them just because they are poorer than us, or richer than us, ill, smelly or just different. Even if other people avoid them, as Christians we must never think of anyone as unclean or untouchable, because God made and loves every one of us.

All-age ideas

- Have some information displayed on leprosy aid, and have a collection for this important work. For more details contact: St Francis Leprosy Guild, 26 Inglis Road, London W5 3RL.

- Act out the Gospel, with the healed leper going down the aisle, telling individuals and groups in the congregation all about it at the end.

- Following the Gospel, try this mime. An 'untouchable' moves around in a group of people, who shrink away from him whenever he comes near, and turn their backs on him when he asks for their help. Then Jesus moves behind one of the group and gradually their actions fall in step with Jesus'. This time, when the untouchable comes near, Jesus stretches out his hands towards him, and so the person he is shadowing also reaches out. Through this touch, the untouchable realises he is accepted, and the others gradually come closer, losing their fear.

Prayer of the Faithful

Celebrant
Let us come to ask for the healing touch of our God in the Church and in the world.

Reader
The God of humility, in his desire to save us, was willing to share our human brokenness; as the Body of Christ, may the Church share that willingness to be vulnerable in order to serve in love.

Silence

Good physician:
heal us.

God's power and authority is gracious and merciful; may all those with authority in our world be inspired to act with mercy and compassion, so that the way may be opened for the kingdom to be established.

Silence

Good physician:
heal us.

May we all have the strength to drive far from our homes and communities all rejection and devaluing; all justification for barriers; and the courage to reach out in love.

Silence

Good physician:
heal us.

May God's compassion shock us
into seeing more clearly the ache of those
whom society rejects and overlooks;
the wounds of the discarded
and socially embarrassing.
May we reach out where others turn away.

Silence

Good physician:
heal us.

We remember those who, healed for ever,
live with God in the fullness of life.
We pray that we too may come
to share the life which has no ending.

Silence

Good physician:
heal us.

We pray with Mary,
solace and comforter:
Hail, Mary . . .

In silence filled with love,
we pray for those known to us
who need healing.

Silence

Celebrant
Father, your amazing compassion
fills us with wonder;
in joy and thankfulness we offer you
our praise and intercession
through the person of Jesus.
Amen.

TREASURE SEEKERS

Aim: To know that God enjoys helping us and making us better.

Starter

Cut out a number of spots of different colours (about 30 centimetres across) and spread them out on the floor. All round the room are placed small spots of the same colours, and the children go round spotting the spots and placing them on the matching large spot on the floor.

Teaching

Sometimes we get spots when we're ill. Does anyone remember having spots? (With chicken pox, for instance.) Today we are going to meet someone whose skin was covered in white spots because he had a skin illness. This man came to see Jesus.

Spread out carpet tiles or a couple of large towels

on the floor and tell the story of the Gospel (Mark 1:40-45) in your own words, using cut-out pictures of the characters based on the drawings below.

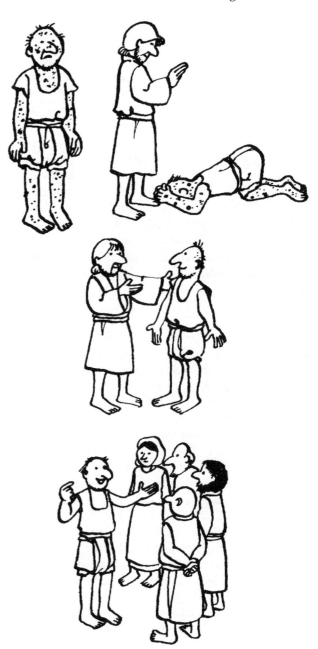

Praying

Dear Father God,
we pray for all the people
who are ill,
and for those who are looking after them.
Amen.

Activities

Using the sheet the children can put the pictures in the right order, and make the reversible model of the man to use as they tell the story at home.

PEARL DIVERS

Aim: To know the story of the healed leper.

Starter

Play 'Piggy in the middle' using soft balls or bean-bags.

Teaching

Begin by explaining to the children what leprosy is. (You can get posters and information from St Francis Leprosy Guild, 26 Inglis Road, London W5 3RL.) They also need to understand what the law said about those suffering from leprosy. They were considered 'unclean' and so was anyone who touched them, so all lepers had to live separately and warn people to keep away from them by calling out, 'Unclean! Unclean!' The law also said that if a leper got better, he had to show himself to the priest, who would officially pronounce him clean again.

Tell the story, or have it narrated, as you draw the events on a blackboard. You don't have to be brilliant at drawing – it just helps to focus their listening, and aids remembering. The advantage of a blackboard and chalk is that you can erase easily, not only mistakes, but also spots on cured lepers!

Praying

We pray for all the people
who are ill, or sad, or lonely,
and for those who no one
wants to be friends with.
Please help them, Jesus,
and help us to help them too.

Activities

On the sheet there are instructions for making a leper who gets healed, turning his life upside down (or rather down side up). Have some thin card for the children to mount the model for extra strength. They will also need access to a Bible for the references to today's story, and the activity to go with it.

GOLD PANNERS

Aim: To see how God feels about untouchables.

Starter

On separate pieces of card, write out the following: a tramp; a mother with a noisy baby; a white man; a black man; a person with flu; a person with leprosy; a tattooed skinhead; a pretty girl; a hand-some young man; an old lady who smells; a smoker; a disabled person; someone from a rival school.

Spread these cards out and let the group suggest a rating of 1-10 for their response to this question in each case: 'Would you be happy sitting on a crowded bus next to . . . ?'

Teaching

In the previous activity we could see that most of us have hang-ups about close contact with people in certain situations, for all kinds of reasons. It's easy to see why society clubs together to isolate certain groups, treating them as outsiders. Our readings today help us to see what God's attitude is to social outcasts and 'untouchables'.

Begin by reading the Gospel from Mark 1. Point out that in law this man was ritually unclean, and anyone touching him would be considered contaminated, and therefore unclean themselves. What was Jesus showing by touching the leper as part of the healing? Was it just the leprosy he was healing, or would the man have also been emotionally healed in some way by the touch?

Jesus' great desire to help the man to wholeness obviously overcame any thoughts of contamination; he reckoned it worth being 'contaminated', worth being thought 'unclean'. How does that link up with the idea of the Incarnation – 'Word of the Father, now in flesh appearing'? What does it all tell us about God and his attitude to us?

Now look at the passage from Corinthians, where Paul advises us all to check our own behaviour seriously. In view of today's Gospel, how do we measure up? Do we reach out to touch, or do we go along with what everyone else considers OK to ignore and avoid?

Praying

Lord God, make me willing
to reach out with your love
and touch the lives
and look into the eyes
of those whom the world despises and avoids.
Amen.

Activities

On the sheet there are examples of people working with the rejected and considering it a privilege as well as a responsibility. You could add to these with other examples, or invite someone in the parish who is working in such an area to join the group. There is also a thinking exercise to face the uncomfortable 'reasons' we have for rejecting and marginalising people. This week's teaching could well lead the group on to think of ways they can get more actively involved with local projects.

SEVENTH SUNDAY OF THE YEAR

Thought for the day

The Son of Man has authority on earth to forgive sins.

Reflection on the readings

Isaiah 43:18-19, 21-22, 24-25
Psalm 40
2 Corinthians 1:18-22
Mark 2:1-12

Most of us have at some point in life got stuck in a guilt zone. Whatever it was that we did or failed to do keeps washing around in our head and refuses to disappear. It alters our outlook and our attitude to the present, it distorts our capacity for walking freely into the future, and can, if we let it, actually drive us further into guilt-ridden places! The prophet speaking in today's passage from Isaiah obviously understands what it feels like to be trapped by guilt about the past. And so, of course, does the God who made us.

The passage is like a breath of fresh air: God is saying to us that we can stop thinking about all those past things, and put them behind us once and for all, because he is about to do something completely new. It is described in images of hope taken from the natural world – water in the wilderness and rivers in the desert. And why is God embarking on such a comprehensive forgiveness programme, erasing the guilt of the past in this way?

It is not because of anything his people have done to earn it, but simply because it is God's very nature to set people free like this. Since he is God he can't help doing it! And it is therefore not surprising that we find Jesus exercising authority over sin in the same way. The scribes, knowing their scripture, are quite right in observing that only God can forgive sins. They know that he alone has the authority over evil to erase it and render it powerless, thereby setting people free of its effects in the rest of their lives.

So when Jesus picks up on their thoughts and asks whether they think it is harder to forgive sins or make a paralysed body mobile again, he is leading them to the point where they will have proof of Jesus' identity. They are about to see, in the outward body, what only God is able to do in the realm of the human spirit. Just as the forgiveness has unlocked and liberated the man's spirit, so now his limbs are unlocked, setting him free also physically. Surely the authenticity of the one will convince them of the authenticity of the other? Only if they have eyes open to see.

In the passage from 2 Corinthians, Paul spells out the great truth which the scribes could not cope with: that all the promises of God have their 'Yes' in Christ. The liberating power of God's forgiveness is physically shown in the person of Jesus, and its vitalising effects continue to liberate prisoners two thousand years on.

Discussion starters

1. How can forgiveness be a healing?

2. In what way is Christ the eternal 'Yes'?

All-stage talk

Start by explaining that you have a list of hard things to do, and you are going to ask everyone which they think is easiest of two options. They can have a moment to think or confer, and then a show of hands should indicate their communal decision. Here are the options:

1. Learning to ride a bike, or learning to talk.

2. Earning money, or saving your money up without spending any.

3. Doing something brave, or doing something thoughtful.

4. Talking non-stop for an hour, or being completely quiet for an hour.

In today's Gospel we heard Jesus ask a similar question. Remind them of the circumstances – the crowds, the paralysed man let down through the roof, Jesus telling him his sins are forgiven, and the scribes, knowing that only God can forgive sins, horrified that Jesus has done what only God can do. This was his question – which is it easier to say to the paralysed man: 'Your sins are forgiven you' or 'Stand up, take your bed and walk'?

Let's try and work out an answer. First we need to make a few things clear. Who is the only one who can forgive sins? It's God. And what about a paralysed man suddenly being able to get up and walk home – who's the only one able to do that? Once again, it's God. So in a way, Jesus is saying to the scribes, 'Is it easier for me to act like God, or to act like God?' And what would be the answer to that? There'd be no difference; both are a natural way for God to behave.

The man's body was paralysed – that meant he couldn't make it move freely. When Jesus healed him he was free to move about again. It's like that when our lives are jammed by sin and guilt about bad things we've done in the past. When God forgives us completely, he unjams us, so we are free to live happily again.

All-age ideas

- Have the Isaiah passage read chorally, with a mixed group of voice tones – low, medium and high. Experiment with what helps unlock the mood of the words, using sometimes the whole group and sometimes one section, or one voice.

- Have the Gospel printed out, with movement directions, so everyone can join in. Jesus and the scribes know who they are beforehand. The scribes stand in a group a little apart from the congregation, and Jesus stands in the centre of the crowd. At verse 2 everyone moves out from their seats into the aisle. In verse 4 everyone looks up, and their eyes follow an imaginary bed as it comes down at Jesus' feet. Jesus says the words to the imaginary paralysed man, and the scribes pull their beards and look offended. Jesus looks over to them and says his words (verses 8-11). As the narrator reads about the man getting up, all the crowd gasp in amazement and say together their words in verse 12.

Prayer of the Faithful

Celebrant
In the sure knowledge that God cherishes us,
let us pray to him now.

Reader
Our heavenly Father is so full of forgiveness and mercy;
may the Church be filled to the brim with such holiness
that our understanding deepens daily,
and all our work and worship glorifies his name.

Silence

Holy God:
release in us your praise.

Our heavenly Father is so wise and perceptive;
may he give us the grace to share in the healing
between factions and nations,
guided by the Spirit.

Silence

Holy God:
release in us your praise.

Our heavenly Father is so comforting and kind;
may we notice the needs around us,
in our families, friends and colleagues,
and respond to them in love.

Silence

Holy God:
release in us your praise.

We bring to our heavenly Father
our sisters and brothers whose joints are stiff
and whose bodies cannot move freely;
we give thanks for their courage and example;
and pray that God will help their spirits to dance
and fill their hearts with joy.

Silence

Holy God:
release in us your praise.

We commend those who have recently died
to the everlasting care of the Father,
and may those who mourn their going
be comforted.

Silence

Holy God:
release in us your praise.

We make our prayer with Mary,
merciful Mother of Jesus:
Hail, Mary . . .

Confident in God's restoring love,
we pray silently now
for our personal concerns.

Silence

Celebrant
Heavenly Father, so full of power
and yet so personally involved with us,
accept these prayers
and let your will be done in our lives;
through Jesus Christ we pray.
Amen.

TREASURE SEEKERS

Aim: To know the story of the man let down through the roof.

Starter

Construct a pulley as shown in the diagram below, and let everyone help load the bricks that are on the top of our building down to the ground, taking it in turns to do the winding.

Teaching

In our story today, four friends were lowering something down from the roof on to the ground below – like we were, but it wasn't bricks!
    Use a prototype model from the worksheet, made from a shoe box as shown, and tell the children the

story of today's Gospel as you act it out with the working model.

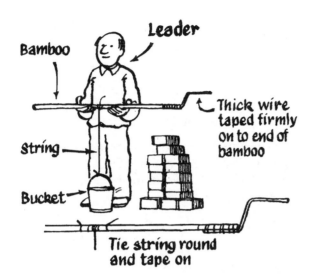

Praying

Thank you for the friends
who brought us to you, Jesus.
And thank you for legs to run with!
   (Run)
Amen.

Activities

Each child will need a cardboard box to make the model of the house. Have the hole in the roof already cut. They will also need some tape or wool to place under the man to lower him down through the roof, and plasticine or modelling clay to make the man.

PEARL DIVERS

Aim: To look at Jesus' authority to forgive sins.

Starter

Simon says. Point out that Simon is the only one with authority to tell us what to do.

Teaching

Act out the story of the paralysed man, with most children being the crowd, and a couple being scribes. The four friends climbing the outside stairs and making a hole in the roof is done with sound

effects, and everyone looks up and follows the (imaginary) man's journey down to the floor. Give the scribes their thought bubble card so they can read it out, and give Jesus his speech bubble card. Then gather in a circle.

Place the thought and speech bubbles in the centre of the group, and read the scribes' thoughts out again. Explain that forgiveness means drowning someone's sins in perfect goodness and love, so only someone who is perfect in goodness and love can do it.

Were the scribes right in thinking that only God can forgive sins? Yes, they were. (You could read the children verse 25 from Isaiah 43, where God is speaking, through his prophet.)

Now look at what Jesus said. Why was Jesus able to forgive the man's sins? Because he really was God's Son.

Praying

Jesus Christ,
we have come to see
that you must really be
the Son of God our Father.
You love as the Father loves
and you forgive as the Father forgives.

Activities

On the sheet there is a wordsearch which reinforces their thinking about Jesus' authority, and a wild and desolate desert for them to bring to life, following the Isaiah reading. They will need access to a Bible for this.

GOLD PANNERS

Aim: To explore the nature of God's forgiveness and Jesus' claims of identity.

Starter

Who am I? They have twenty questions in which to discover the identity of a chosen character. All questions can only be answered with a 'Yes' or 'No'.

Teaching

First read the Gospel together, with different people taking the parts and everyone reading the crowd's words. Look at what the scribes are thinking and wondering about. Why do they say, 'Only God can forgive sins'? Refer to the passage from Isaiah 43, seeing what God, through the prophet, has to say. Draw out that it is all part of God's loving goodness to forgive sins – his very nature is to do it. Look at what forgiveness actually means, using the sheet to focus your ideas, and then refer to 2 Corinthians 1:18-21. How does the Gospel show in action in verses 19 and 20? In Jesus forgiving the man's sins and healing him, he is acting out God's nature. So did he have the authority to forgive sins? Yes, because he was showing that he must indeed be the Son of God.

Praying

I'm accepted, I'm forgiven,
I am fathered by the true and living God.
I'm accepted, no condemnation,
I am loved by the true and living God.
There's no guilt or fear as I draw near
to the Saviour and Creator of the world.
There is joy and peace as I release
my worship to you, O Lord.

(Rob Hayward
© 1985 Kingsway's Thankyou Music)

Activities

On the sheet they are encouraged to look at what forgiveness is, when we need it and how it can change our lives. It is important that they realise Christians are not perfect just because they go to church, and the Church is full of redeemed sinners. They also need to know that the forgiveness is not a once-off event, after which we lose the chance of God forgiving us again. There is *always* the opportunity to confess our sin to God and know his healing forgiveness.

EIGHTH SUNDAY OF THE YEAR

Thought for the day

The long-expected bridegroom is Christ, and the Church is his bride. We cannot half-attend the wedding feast, but must wholeheartedly join in the celebrations.

Reflection on the readings

Hosea 2:16-17, 21-22
Psalm 102
2 Corinthians 3:1-6
Mark 2:18-22

The image of the bridegroom comes up on a number of occasions in the Bible, and it may be worth looking briefly at what his role was in the traditional Jewish marriage celebrations, so that we can better appreciate Jesus' teaching. One significant difference is that while we tend to think of the bridegroom already waiting in the church for the bride to arrive, this arrangement was reversed. The bride would wait with her bridesmaids at her own home for the bridegroom to come with his friends to ask for her. Then the happy couple would lead a lively procession through the streets to the bridegroom's house for the wedding feast.

So the image of the bridegroom is a lovely poetic way of thinking about the promised Messiah. Packed into the picture we have the alert expectancy about his coming, the careful preparations, the infectious love and joy which spreads through the whole community, and the sense of something new beginning – with the promise of new life and hope for the future.

No doubt Jesus had been to plenty of weddings, sometimes as one of the bridegroom's friends, and was happy to link himself with the bridegroom idea. In John's Gospel we are told that John the Baptist spoke of himself as being like Jesus the bridegroom's 'best man', happy to be there in all the preparations, but equally happy for Jesus to have the important role.

Now that we are in Hebrew marriage mode, the talk of patched cloaks and new wine makes more sense as well, since wedding garments and wine were a normal part of the festivities. With the Messiah walking the earth, we are celebrating something new, and can't expect to be part of it if we are still hanging on to what is old and in tatters; Jesus hasn't come to do a makeshift temporary fixit job, but a complete and deep transforming of us through God's love alive in us.

Discussion starters

1. Do we try to sew on the odd patch of God's new life to our familiar and comfortable cloaks of the old life, rather than accepting the completely new wedding garment which Jesus offers us?

2. Are we taking seriously the need to nurture new Christians, or do we concentrate on pouring in new wine without addressing the state of the wine skins?

All-stage talk

Bring along an old supermarket carrier bag, with the handles weak and split. Also some freshly bought glass bottles of wine or fruit juice – the posher the better. Beforehand, prepare a child or young person to interrupt you at the appropriate point. We'll call the person Phoebe. Give someone else in the congregation a strong new bag to have ready.

Show off your purchases and explain that you now need a bag to put them in to carry them home. Wave the old carrier bag around, mentioning how old it is and how the handles don't look too strong, but decide that it'll probably do, and start loading the bottles in, resting the bag on the ground as you load.

Now Phoebe comes and gets your attention, suggesting that it's stupid to put those new things in such a useless bag. Why? Well, it'll break, and then the bottles could break as well, and you'd have wasted all the wine and fruit juice!

Ask the rest of the congregation whether they think Phoebe is right. What would be more sensible? To put the new bottles in a strong new bag. Does anyone happen to have a strong new carrier bag? Well, that's a relief!

As you pack the bottles safely in this bag, explain that Jesus said it's no good – and can be dangerous – to think we can pack the new life of God into ourselves if we're still wanting to stay the same old bags we've always been! That won't work. We should never let Jesus into our hearts unless we are prepared for change.

Otherwise, after a quick froth of excitement as new Christians, we'll find it too much of a strain to be living a new life in an old lifestyle, and the danger is that we crack up, and end up feeling loads of guilt, loads of failure and think Jesus has let us down badly. In fact, all we need to do is go to Jesus and ask him to turn us into completely new containers to house the new life safely.

He's an expert at doing just that, and, however long or short time we've been Christians, we all regularly need God's transforming of our whole selves if we are to join fully in the celebration.

All-age ideas

• Have a flower arrangement on a wedding theme, focusing on the bridegroom aspect, with a button hole, top hat and gloves among the flowers, ribbon and wine.

• Invite everyone to share the celebration with a poster on the church notice board, made to look like a wedding invitation. The children will be providing some wedding garlands they have made.

Prayer of the Faithful

Celebrant
Let us pray to the God of glory,
revealed to us in his Son, Jesus.

Reader
As we listen to the Father's beloved Son,
we pray that we do not fail to hear his will for us
or share his longing for the world to be saved.

Silence

Let us worship the Lord:
in the beauty of holiness.

We pray for an increase in our desire
to enter into one another's suffering and hardship,
to share the world's resources fairly
with one another,
and recognise all humanity as brothers and sisters.

Silence

Let us worship the Lord:
in the beauty of holiness.

We pray for the grace
to not take one another for granted,
but wake each morning ready to notice the Christ
in each person we see and speak to;
and reverence the Father's hidden presence
in all creation.

Silence

Let us worship the Lord:
in the beauty of holiness.

In our prayer we stand alongside
all who are too weak to pray, or too confused;
may all who are suffering
sense the Father's love and comfort,
and be given strength to persevere,
and peace of mind and spirit.

Silence

Let us worship the Lord:
in the beauty of holiness.

We commend to God's eternal presence
those who have recently died,
that they may rest in peace and rise in glory.

Silence

Let us worship the Lord:
in the beauty of holiness.

We make our prayer with Mary,
the chosen one of God:
Hail, Mary . . .

Together in silence,
we name those known to us
who need our prayers.

Silence

Celebrant
Father, we have so often experienced
your loving kindness in our lives;
accept now these prayers and answer them
in the way that is best for your creation,
through Christ our Lord.
Amen.

TREASURE SEEKERS

Aim: To celebrate Jesus being with us.

Starter

Sitting in a circle, share news of when they have been very excited and happy to have someone they love (like family or friends) coming to stay. Talk together about how lovely it is when you first see them in the distance, getting off the train, getting out of the car, or wheeling their luggage trolley at the airport.

Teaching

People had been waiting for Jesus to come. Mary and Joseph had been looking forward to him being born, but before that Mary and Joseph's parents and grandparents and great grandparents had been waiting as well. People had waited for ages and ages and ages for God to send his Son into the world to live with us. They were looking forward to it, like we look forward to people we love coming to stay with us. 'One day he'll come,' they said to one another. 'One day God will send him.'

So when Jesus did come, and grew up and went about healing people, talking so lovingly to them and helping them, they were very, very pleased. It made them so happy that it felt like a wedding party!

And that party is still going on today. Every Sunday we all meet up at church to celebrate God sending his Son Jesus to be with us for ever.

Praying

Who's here? Jesus is!
Who's our best friend? Jesus is!
Who knows us? Jesus does!
Who loves us? Jesus does!

Activities

On the sheet there is a picture of a wedding party for them to colour. They can try spotting various things in the picture, some visible (like balloons) and others just as real, but invisible (like love).

PEARL DIVERS

Aim: To explore the image of Jesus as the bridegroom and our preparations for the wedding feast.

Starter

Tell everyone to sit still and imagine how long a minute is. When they think the minute is up they raise their hand. You have a stop watch and give no facial clues as to who is right or when the minute is really up, but make a note of the number of seconds each person suggests. Once everyone has made their claim, you can give a small prize to the person who was closest to estimating 60 seconds.

Teaching

While we are waiting for something, a minute can feel like a very long time indeed, but when we're given one minute more to play, it seems to be over in a flash! Time is like that – rather elastic and stretchy.

Explain (using some children to act it out as you go) that in Jesus' time and country, the bride and her bridesmaids had to stay at home, dressed ready, waiting for the bridegroom and his friends to come to the house. As they waited for the bridegroom to come the time probably dragged slowly past. Then, suddenly, they'd hear him coming and knocking at the door, and the time started to go faster as they all happily set off in a wedding procession down the street to the wedding feast at the bridegroom's house.

Now for a question – how is Jesus like a bridegroom? (Have the question clearly written out in lower case letters). He isn't getting married. He doesn't wear a flower in his buttonhole. Hint: think of the bride *waiting* for the bridegroom to come. Second hint: think about how everyone feels when the bridegroom arrives.

Jesus is sometimes thought of as being like a bridegroom because

a) the people knew he was definitely coming (the prophets had told them) . . . place a wedding invitation down.

b) they were playing the waiting game – waiting for him to arrive in person . . . place down a watch or clock.

c) his coming made everyone happy and meant that everyone could enjoy the wedding party . . . put down a smiley face.

Finally read from today's Gospel (up to verse 20), ensuring that the children know in advance what fasting means.

Praying

I will sing to the Lord
for his goodness to me,
I will sing the name
of the Lord, Most High!

Activities

On the sheet the children are introduced to the second part of the Gospel, about the need to match new life with new containers. They will also be filling in their acceptance card, which is printed on the sheet. These can then be offered at the offering of the gifts in church. They can also make string and tissue paper garlands to give out.

GOLD PANNERS

Aim: To explore the bridegroom imagery, and look at the importance of having new wineskins for the new wine of God's kingdom.

Starter

Have a few atlases and some wine bottles or labels. They are going to discover where each wine comes from.

Teaching

Look at some of the information on a wine label. We know where it comes from and how old it is, as well as what it tastes like and whether it will last. Explain how new wine is still very lively, and in Jesus' time it was important to put it in strong new skins, as otherwise it would burst the skins. One of the times when wine is often drunk is at weddings, and our readings today describe God's relationship with his people as rather like a bridegroom faithfully committing himself to his bride.

Read the passage from Hosea and pick up on the love and commitment of God to his people. Psalm 102 also celebrates the enormous forgiving love God has for us.

When Jesus came it was like the bridegroom coming in person, so that the wedding festivities could really begin. People did notice that Jesus wasn't leading his disciples in times of great fasting, like John the Baptist and the Pharisees, and they felt that as a holy man he ought to be fasting, rather than feasting. Read today's Gospel up to verse 20 to see how Jesus answers their criticism.

When did Jesus mean that his disciples would be fasting? After the crucifixion? What about once the Holy Spirit had filled them at Pentecost? What about now? In one way we have the bridegroom with us, and celebrate his real presence in the bread and wine at every Eucharist. At the same time we are looking forward to when Jesus returns in glory, so we are both with the bridegroom and waiting for him. This is reflected in our times of celebration and our times of fasting.

Now look at the second part of the Gospel. What is Jesus talking about? Patching old clothes with new unshrunk material certainly doesn't work, any more than putting new wine in old wineskins. But what is Jesus really talking about here? Remind them of God's total love and faithful commitment to his people. The new wine of the kingdom of God is the new risen life we are offered through Jesus saving us from sin and death. To have this in us we need to be remade as containers so that we can safely contain it.

Praying

Spirit of the living God, fall afresh on me!
Spirit of the living God, fall afresh on me!
Melt me, mould me, fill me, use me,
Spirit of the living God, fall afresh on me.

(Daniel Iverson
© 1963 Birdwing Music / Universal Songs / CopyCare)

Activities

On the sheet they look at the passage from 2 Corinthians, and how committed, renewed Christian people can be living letters of recommendation. They also look at how Christian lives shabbily lived can direct others away from God. They look at what real commitment is all about.

NINTH SUNDAY OF THE YEAR

Thought for the day

Jesus has the words of eternal life – he sheds light on a right attitude to the Law.

Reflection on the readings

Deuteronomy 5:12-15
Psalm 80
2 Corinthians 4:6-11
Mark 2:23-3:6

The satisfying thing about rules is that we can achieve a great sense of accomplishment when we have ticked them all off. The accompanying danger is that they can lull us into thinking we have done all that is necessary, simply because we have kept the letter of the law. The spirit of the law is far more open-ended, and cannot 'button up' our ethics in the same way at all.

Jesus teaching blows fresh air into the stale and hollow rule system which the sacred Law had become. In the reading from Deuteronomy we are given the background to the Sabbath Law, its origin in our relationship with God and with his creative and saving work. In today's Gospel we have instances of Jesus showing by example the Law lit, not from self-interested and narrow human perspective, but from God's perspective.

The keeping of the Sabbath was considered so important that intricate, detailed rules had been built up around it, till the sense of spending the day celebrating the good creation and joyfully worshipping the Creator was choked in small-print regulations. Jesus directs them to see it again as it really is. He asks them whether it is lawful to do good or evil on the Sabbath, which only allows the positive reply of actively doing good. To be tied down so tightly to the rules that your compassion has to be stamped on, can hardly be in keeping with the generous, caring Lord of Love.

This contrasted with the current thinking, which would probably have let the man's hand stay withered till the Sabbath rest was over. Jesus was not cancelling out the Law, or changing it; he was guiding his listeners back to its original freshness, and recognising that the whole Law is really about building a right and living relationship with God – loving God and loving one another.

In the reading from 2 Corinthians we are given a worked-out example of living by the Law lit up Jesus' way, with the full glory of God. What does such a life look like? We are shown a picture of extraordinary inner joy and vigour in spite of all the hardships and conflicts, dangers and threats. What is obvious is that these lives, rooted in God's grace, are not hemmed in but set free. Jesus has the words of eternal life, valid while we are still living here.

Discussion starters

1. 'Love God and do what you like.' Is this famous remark of St Augustine a helpful way of looking at the Commandments, or should we be taking the actual laws more seriously than we do?

2. What do you think might horrify Jesus today and need his teaching about a drastic re-think?

All-stage talk

Bring along a piggy bank and some money to put in it. Some people keep their treasure safe in one of these, adding to it each week. (Drop some more money in.) Sometimes people will get an ordinary jar and fill it up with coins, so that soon it's full of treasure. The pot or jar is often very ordinary – it's the treasure inside which makes it special. People in Roman times used to use clay pots to keep their silver jewellery safe – archaeologists have found them, still guarding their treasure!

In one of the letters Saint Paul wrote, he said he thought we were all a bit like clay pots holding special treasure. As people we're just ordinary, but we've got something as Christians which is extra-ordinary – real treasure. It's being friends with God through Jesus which changes our lives from being ordinary to extra-special, because we're actually holding in us the love of the living God.

What does that look like?

We saw a bit of what it looks like in today's Gospel. Jesus notices a man whose arm is withered and shrunk so he can't use it, and immediately his heart goes out to that man, and more than anything he wants to set the man's arm free to wave and lift things, touch and hold things. His love for the man makes Jesus sad for him having to struggle, and he sets about mending him.

What Jesus doesn't do is look at the man and think, 'Ah yes, a man with an arm which doesn't work. But it's the Sabbath, so that's too bad; he'll have to stay like that – I'm not going to break the rules and heal him today.'

Well, of course he wouldn't think like that, because you can't be full of God's love and yet shut off your compassion. What Jesus did was the Godly, loving thing – he used his power of healing and set that man free, there and then, rules or no rules. And that offended the teachers of the Law. They had become so keen to keep the Law that they'd actually blocked

God's light out, and couldn't see that Jesus was keeping the real spirit of the Law completely – love God and love one another.

So here we are as ordinary human pots, holding in us the light of God, and that's going to affect the way we live. We'll have to reach out in love and mercy to those around us, and that might mean we end up offending some people. But who cares? If we're living God's way, then we won't be offending God, and if living that way makes us unpopular sometimes, we'll be in very good company.

All-age ideas

• Collect the offering today in earthenware pots, such as unglazed flower pots.

• Have a flower arrangement expressing God's love and mercy, using warm colours and gentle, delicate foliage. Label it 'Jesus displays God's love and mercy'.

Prayer of the Faithful

Celebrant
Through Jesus
we are shown God's compassion and mercy;
let us pray to the Father for that love in our lives,
in the Church and in the world.

Reader
Let compassion and mercy
be the hallmarks of our church life
and all its activities;
may they shine in all our behaviour,
our conversations and activities.

Silence

Lord of love:
let only your will be done.

Let compassion and mercy
take root in every institution, policy and structure;
let them challenge accepted wrongs
and disturb complacency.

Silence

Lord of love:
let only your will be done.

Let compassion and mercy
guard every doorway and fill every room;
let them colour each encounter
and drive every decision.

Silence

Lord of love:
let only your will be done.

Let compassion and mercy
transform our attitudes
to all whose illness or frailty
makes them marginalised, ignored or despised.
Let there be healing of all damaged self-perception,
and restoration of jarred human dignity.

Silence

Lord of love:
let only your will be done.

Let compassion and mercy
accompany the dying
and welcome them into eternity.

Silence

Lord of love:
let only your will be done.

We join our prayers with those of Mary,
Mother of the Lord of the Sabbath:
Hail, Mary . . .

To the Lord who brings us life,
we pour out our private petitions
and thanksgivings.

Silence

Celebrant
In praise and gratitude
we offer you these prayers, Father,
through Jesus Christ.
Amen.

TREASURE SEEKERS

Aim: To know that we are like clay pots holding God's treasure.

Starter

Have a number of boxes, pots and tins with a different thing in each. Name one of the objects and let the children guess which container it's in. Open each one to look until you find the right one. With the next object they may have seen it already, so memory as well as guesswork comes into the choosing. Continue till all the objects have been found inside their containers.

Teaching

Talk about how all those ordinary containers held different treasures. We've got some more containers here in Treasure Seekers today. Count round the number of people present – we've got that number of treasure pots sitting here!

Each of us is like one of those ordinary pots, with secret treasure inside. The treasure is God's great love for us. (Gradually open up a huge red heart of paper.) Wherever we go and whatever we're doing, we know that God loves us, and that treasure makes us very special pots indeed! It means that we can be loving and kind, happy and strong because we haven't just got our loving in us – we've got God's as well.

Praying

I am filled with the love of Jesus –
love in my seeing,
  (*point to eyes*)

love in my speaking,
  (*point to mouth*)

love in all I do.
  (*open hands*)

Thank you, Jesus,
  (*raise arms*)

your love is ENORMOUS!
  (*stretch arms in huge circle*)

Activities

Give each child a really big piece of paper cut into a heart shape. With paints or crayons they can make it very beautiful, as it is God's love they are drawing. Then help them to fold it up really small, so it will fit into the envelope made from the sheet, on which they draw themselves.

PEARL DIVERS

Aim: To know the story of Jesus healing the man with the withered arm.

Starter

Give out soft balls, beanbags or rolled socks to each pair of children and ask them to practise throwing and catching to each other using only one hand at a time.

Teaching

Share how you all got on. It's hard to catch one-handed and it takes lots of practice. Today we're going to hear about a man who had to live one-handed because one of his arms didn't work.

We don't know his name. We do know that he had come to worship at the synagogue on the Sabbath with all the other Jewish people in his town. Remind them that Jewish people always worship on the Sabbath, which means seventh day, because of what God did on the seventh day of creation. (What did God do that day? Nothing! Having made the whole of the heavens and the earth, he rested on the seventh day, and so the people kept it holy, doing no work on it and worshipping God who had made everything so well.) So the Sabbath was *No Work* day, and we need to remember that because it's important in our story.

It so happened that Jesus was visiting their synagogue that Sabbath, and he noticed this man with his arm all shrunk and withered so he couldn't use it. Jesus saw how difficult it was for the man to manage like this, and, being Jesus, he felt very sorry for him. More than anything, he wanted to make the man's life easier; he wanted his arm to work as well as anyone else's.

Now, a few big questions . . .

- What day was it? (The Sabbath.)
- What was the rule about the Sabbath? (It's a *No Work* day.)
- Would it be work for Jesus to make the man better? (Take a vote on it.)
- So would it be right or wrong for Jesus to make the man better? (Take a vote on it.)

Now the teachers of the Law were hoping to catch Jesus doing something wrong, but they were finding that very difficult, because he never did! But this gave them something to pounce on. They pointed out that this was the Sabbath, and no work should be done on it. They were saying it would be breaking the Law for Jesus to heal the man.

So what would Jesus, the Lord of Love, think about that? (Collect their ideas.)

In fact, Jesus was angry at the teachers of the Law because they were so determined to keep the Law that they had stopped doing loving things like feeling sorry for a man with a useless arm, and wanting to make him better.

Jesus decided that the loving way of healing was keeping God's Law much more than sticking to picky detailed rules which shut love out. So he told the man to stretch out his poor withered arm, and, with all his healing love, he made that arm grow into a strong useful one again!

More questions . . .

- What do you think the man thought about Jesus healing him on the Sabbath? (Share ideas.)
- What do you think the teachers of the Law thought about it? (Share ideas.)

All the people were very happy that Jesus used the Sabbath to do great good, but the teachers were very offended.

Praying

Give me a loving heart, Jesus,
so that I want to help people
as you helped the man.
Make me brave enough
to go on loving and caring
even if people think I'm mad.
Amen.

Activities

On the sheet the Law of love has got cluttered with
lots of extra rules. They can clear these away to reveal
the real spirit of God's Law. Also there is a ruler to
make, with God's love to measure our thinking by.
Each child will need a strip of card for this.

GOLD PANNERS

Aim: To explore the nature of the Law and Jesus'
interpretation of it.

Starter

Using a softball play French cricket. The batsperson
stands in the centre with the others in a circle, passing
the ball and throwing it to aim at the batsperson's
legs. If they hit them, they take a turn in the centre.

Teaching

First read the passage from Deuteronomy 5, and
have a brief look at the ten commandments, which
are on the sheet. The spirit of the whole Law is love
for God and love for neighbour, and in an effort to
protect them and uphold them well, the teachers of
the Law had got hung up on all the details and had
lost sight of the real spirit of the Law.

Now go on to read today's Gospel, looking out
for the way Jesus is going to deal with this over-
zealous keeping of the letter of the Law, while
shutting out the loving spirit of it. At what level are
the teachers correct about Jesus breaking the Law,
and at what level are they mistaken? Notice how
Jesus doesn't draw away from doing what is right,
even when it makes him dangerously unpopular
with the authorities; never does he compromise
God's values in order to protect his position.

Finally look at 2 Corinthians 4:6-11. In a way it
interprets Jesus' actions in the Gospel, showing how
he shines God's light in our hearts so that we can
understand God better. That is bound to affect the
way we live. It should prevent us getting so set in
our ways and traditions that we stop bothering to
listen to God's directing; it should give us an ideal
by which to measure our attitudes to those in need.

Praying

Lord God, teach us your ways
of compassion and mercy,
so that the way we treat others
may be in line with the way you treat us.
Amen.

Activities

On the sheet there are the ten commandments and
Jesus' summary of the Law, to use as a daily guide
for right attitudes and behaviour. There is also
space to put down all the present involvement of
the parish with caring outreach. Any gaps can be
noted and prayed about regularly, with ideas for
action taken seriously.

TENTH SUNDAY OF THE YEAR

Thought for the day

Anyone who does God's will is considered a close
family member of Jesus.

Reflection on the readings

Genesis 3:9-15
Psalm 129
2 Corinthians 4:13-5:1
Mark 3:20-35

The terrible thing about sin is the rift and separation
it causes between people, and between God and
his people. As a result of Adam and Eve's wilful
disobedience, the natural relationship between the
Creator and his beloved creation goes horribly
wrong, and they are no longer comfortable in God's
presence, but hiding from him. So much self-deceit,
hidden agendas and complicated destructive living
is really to do with this hiding of ourselves from
God. So much of Jesus' teaching was showing
people how to feel comfortable in God's presence
once again.

Jesus is the great rift-healer. As Paul writes in 2
Corinthians, there is an ongoing healing for those
who live in Christ, which renews us spiritually even
as our physical bodies are wearing out. With the
eyes of a professional tentmaker he sees physical
death as merely a folding-up of one's tent, which
has provided temporary accommodation during
our journey through earthly life. The permanent

house is a spiritual one, prepared for us in God's heaven. Paul adjusts our view to revel in the marvellous reality of what is unseen, rather than wasting time concentrating our attention only on the seen, temporary world.

At first sight today's Gospel does not look like Jesus in healing mode at all. He is being spoken of as using demonic powers to set people free from demons, and his family is concerned for his sanity, hearing the reports about him. These are very serious accusations and Jesus treats them seriously. To be God's chosen One, living out God's love, yet accused of being Love's destroyer, must have given Jesus intense, sharp pain. Surely this was all part of the sword Simeon had predicted, and here is Mary sharing it, just as he said she would.

As Jesus looks into the eyes of those around him, in that typical, straight encounter with people and affection for them, he is cherishing the wideness of close family. In God's love, our family extends and is no longer tied simply to blood and genes. Spiritually we are bound together in God's great family, as close to Jesus as his own flesh and blood.

Discussion starters

1. It is quite an honour to be considered Jesus' close relatives! Do we behave as if this is true? Do we show any family likenesses?

2. What does it mean in practical terms to pray to God our Father: 'Let your will be done on earth as it is done in heaven'?

All-stage talk

Whether we live on our own or with others, most of us have family; we may not see them that often, or we may see them every day. Some of them may no longer be alive, but they are still our family. Mothers and fathers, stepmothers and stepfathers, parents-in-law and children-in-law, sons and daughters, grandchildren and grandparents, aunts and uncles, brothers, sisters and cousins, are all family. We share the same genes (and sometimes the same jeans).

In every family there is something called a family resemblance – a family likeness. (Some family members may be willing to demonstrate this likeness.) The DNA within our families shows up right across the generations; in my family there's the Morris nose, the Rackett musicality, and the Orme stubborn determination, for instance!

In our Gospel reading today, Jesus says something rather amazing. He's sitting teaching, surrounded by a closely packed circle of faces, people from all kinds of different families and backgrounds, with all kinds of different looks and personalities. They are there because they sense that in Jesus they can get closer to the true, living God than they've ever been before. They are so keen that they are hanging on every word Jesus speaks, listening to him intently.

And as he looks around at them sitting there, and sees in their eyes their love of God, Jesus happily counts all of them – and everyone else who does the will of God – as members of his close family. He is saying that any of us, however ordinary or damaged, whatever natural family we belong to, or are separated from, are close members of Jesus' family! So you can think of yourself as closely related to Jesus. And that makes all of us in the Church part of the same family, distinguished by the family likeness of doing God's will – living the loving way.

All-age ideas

- As a Penitential Rite:
  Father, there have been times
  when we have seen your will but failed to do it.

  Lord, have mercy.
  Lord, have mercy.

  Jesus, there have been times
  when we have behaved more as your enemies
  than members of your close family.

  Christ, have mercy.
  Christ, have mercy.

  Spirit, there have been times
  when we have ignored your prompting
  and preferred to live selfishly.

  Lord, have mercy.
  Lord, have mercy.

- Have the reading from Genesis read by a group of people, so that the different voices are clearly brought out.

Prayer of the Faithful

Celebrant
As members of God's family,
let us pray together to our heavenly Father.

Reader
That as family members of the Church of God
we may show his likeness by doing his will;
that those visiting our churches
may find there God's beauty and truth,
open-hearted loving and a unity of purpose.

Silence

Father:
let your will be done.

That as members of the human race
we may work together, share resources,
respect and learn from one another.

That leaders may inspire collective good,
and those with vision be valued and heard.

Silence

Father:
let your will be done.

That we may give both support and space
to those we love and nurture;
that those of our own families
who do not yet know God
may come to understand the depth
of his love for them.

Silence

Father:
let your will be done.

That all who come to Jesus in need
may find in him forgiveness, healing
and wholeness of body, mind and spirit,
strength to cope with their difficulties
and a constant inner renewing.

Silence

Father:
let your will be done.

That as those coming to death
roll up the tents of their earthly existence,
they may be welcomed into the eternal home
prepared for them by their loving God.

Silence

Father:
let your will be done.

We pray now with Mary,
whose willing obedience
made our salvation possible:
Hail, Mary . . .

In silence, now,
we approach our loving Father
with our private petitions.

Silence

Celebrant
Most merciful Father,
who knows us so well,
accept our prayers
through Christ Jesus.
Amen.

TREASURE SEEKERS

Aim: To know that Jesus thinks of us as family when we do God's will.

Starter

Part of the family. Stand in a circle. Tell each group in turn the way to move in the circle, like this: 'If you are a brother, run in the circle; if you are a sister, skip round the circle; if you have an uncle, stand still in the circle; if you have a grandma, walk about in the circle.'

Teaching

Talk about the way we look a bit like other people in our family, and look for family likenesses in children from the same family, or with families everyone in the group knows well. Sometimes we are alike in the way we look and sometimes in how we walk, fiddle with our fingers, or laugh. Sometimes we are like other people in our family in being quiet or noisy, losing our temper or liking music.

One day Jesus was sitting talking to a circle of his friends, rather like we are sitting now. Someone told him that his mother, brothers and sisters were outside. Jesus looked around at all the people and told them he thought of everyone living God's way as part of his close family!

So that means us as well. We are part of Jesus' family, and when we are living God's way we're showing the family likeness.

Praying

(To the tune of *Twinkle, twinkle, little star*)

Jesus, Jesus, can I be
in your loving family?
When I live the loving way,
loving others every day,
Jesus, Jesus, I can be
in your loving family!

Activities

On the sheet there is a picture of Jesus sitting in a house surrounded by people who are listening to him. They add themselves to the group, and other people who are living as Jesus' friends. Also there is a praying space in which they can draw someone who doesn't know Jesus yet. As they draw this person meeting Jesus, they will be thinking of them and that is very real prayer.

PEARL DIVERS

Aim: To look at why Jesus' family were worried about him, and what Jesus means by his remark about who is 'family'.

Starter

Play happy families. Give out the cards equally. The children go round swapping cards until they end up with complete family sets. (You can either give a time limit or continue till all sets are complete.)

Teaching

The people in our own families are special to us. Sometimes we have good times together, sometimes the people in our families make us cross and we make them cross. But people in a family are bound together closely because we are physically related to each other. We often look alike and family members will usually stick up for one another, even if we don't always get along easily. In our story today we are going to meet some people in Jesus' family, at a tricky family meeting.

First, let's meet the family. Give out speech bubbles to various children to read in turn, explaining that, in the Gospel, 'brothers and sisters' means 'kinsfolk'. Close families in those days, living in one place, included cousins and uncles and aunts who were referred to as 'brothers and sisters'. Jesus was Mary's only child.

Mary	Hello, I'm Mary. My son is called Jesus. I'm very worried about him.

(Hold up a sign for all the children to read)

All	Why are you worried about Jesus, Mary?
Mary	Well, there are such big crowds of people with him all the time. Some of them have evil spirits. He makes them better, but some people say he's mad.
Jesus' brothers	We are Jesus' brothers. We want to come and take Jesus home with us. It isn't safe to live like he is.
Jesus' sisters	We are Jesus' sisters. It isn't normal to go round healing and teaching great crowds of people. He doesn't even have time to eat! We want to tell Jesus to come home and just be our brother again.
All	But Jesus has very important work to do while he is on earth, you know.
Brothers	But we are his FAMILY!

Thank the readers and explain that when Jesus' mother, brothers and sisters arrived at the house where Jesus was, they found it packed with people, all listening to Jesus. They couldn't get near him, so they told one of Jesus' disciples that they were there, and asked them to tell Jesus.

When Jesus was told that his mother, brothers and sisters had come to take him away home, he looked around at all the faces of the crowd. He could see that they all needed him. He knew he had important work to do with lots of people, and couldn't just live with his family. 'Do you know,' he said, 'who my family is? My family isn't just my mother, brothers and sisters, but every single person who is trying to live God's way.'

Jesus' family had to learn that although Jesus belonged to them in one way, he also belonged to everyone, because his work was to gather lots of people into the family of God.

Praying

Jesus, thank you for letting us
be part of your family.
We hope the family grows and grows
until everyone is living God's way.

Activities

On the sheet there is a pop-up model to make of Jesus in the house with all his huge 'family', and they can draw themselves in it as well. They are also helped to see how Jesus' family extends right over the world and the generations.

GOLD PANNERS

Aim: To look at the scribes' accusations and Jesus' response.

Starter

Play 'netball' using a blow-up beach ball and a bucket or bin for the net. Play first with even sides, and then with everyone on the same side, and no opponents. Compare the scores!

Teaching

It is so much easier to score goals when we don't have any opposition! Today we are going to look at some opposition Jesus was faced with, and how he dealt with it.

It wasn't just when Jesus was around that people hit against God's way of love. Read the passage from Genesis to see that, right from the beginning, people have been self-willed, and their sin creates a rift between themselves and God; they no longer feel comfortable in his company. That is just as true now; we only feel comfortable in God's company when we are choosing to face his way and are being honest with him. Otherwise we try to hide from him, and avoid his company.

Now read today's Gospel, looking out for any friction and opposition to his work. There are two main areas in this reading – the accusation of the scribes, and the concerned family, coming to 'take charge' of Jesus.

What do the scribes accuse Jesus of doing? (Casting out demons by the power of demons.) Would this make logical sense? How does Jesus respond to what they are saying about him? (If Satan was fighting against himself in that way, his power would crash.) Logic proves that Jesus cannot be in league with Satan if he is overcoming evil spirits in people.

What about his family – why have they come, and why doesn't Jesus rush off home with them as they would like? Having heard the reports of the crowds surrounding Jesus all the time, giving him no time even to eat, and all the casting-out of evil spirits, they are anxious for him and don't understand that his work on earth is very important, and needs to be done, even if it's sometimes dangerous. He can't spend his life living quietly at home with his immediate family, or the saving work would not get done.

Sometimes families have to share their loved ones with a wider circle of people, and Jesus wants to include as close family all those who are doing their best to live God's way. That is the 'family likeness' which marks many people out to be members of Jesus' family.

Praying

Make me a channel of your peace.
Where there is hatred, let me bring your love.
Where there is injury, your pardon, Lord,
and where there's doubt, true faith in you.

(Taken from the song by Sebastian Temple,
based on the Prayer of St Francis
© 1967 OCP Publications, USA)

Activities

On the sheet there is space to put in an imagined subscript of Jesus' family, in order to put Jesus' reply in context. They can also draw a cartoon to get at the meaning of the scribes' accusations and Jesus' response. Some comments by those struggling with family expectations and God's calling can be used as discussion starters.

ELEVENTH SUNDAY OF THE YEAR

Thought for the day

From small beginnings, and by God's power, the kingdom of heaven grows.

Reflection on the readings

Ezekiel 17:22-24
Psalm 91
2 Corinthians 5:6-10
Mark 4:26-34

One of the things we all find difficult to do is relinquish power. We may consider that we don't possess much of that commodity, but just listen to yourself and others protesting as soon as our own way of doing something is challenged, or things are suddenly changed without us being told or even our opinion being asked. We bridle! Today's readings remind us that God is in charge, and can work in all kinds of ways and through all kinds of people whom we may not choose. He goes on working even when we are on holiday, ill, or asleep; though we are important in the growth of the kingdom, the whole thing will not fall apart whenever we are not personally involved. Today we are challenged to recognise that the growth of the kingdom of heaven is not entirely down to our conscientious activity, and we can and should let go and let God.

The reading from Ezekiel shows us God acting with typical care and forward planning in a dynamic new way. God acts with deep wisdom, startling diversity and breadth of vision, and the power rather like that of a superb orchestra playing softly. God has his power under control and uses it with perfect love and integrity.

Extraordinary as it may seem, we can share in that. As Paul points out in 2 Corinthians, everyone was included in Christ's death so that everyone can also be included in his resurrection life, where our whole focus and aim runs in line with what God wants and longs for.

The seed in today's parable does not rely on the farmer's constant attention – it is quite capable of growing wonderfully on its own, simply because it is living seed. Whenever we sow the seed of God's love or his Word in someone's heart, God will continue his work of growth there, using all the circumstances of that person's experience to develop the growing. And what begins so small can grow beyond our imagining. We must never forget that all growth is God's doing. As Christians we are not in the business of empire-building for Christ, but praying for God's kingdom to come.

Discussion starters

1. Do we sometimes block God's growing kingdom by wanting it to happen in a particular way for us, our family, or our church?

2. Is it possible to work too hard for the coming of the kingdom?

All-stage talk

Ask everyone to look at the mustard seeds they were given when they came into church (see All-age Ideas), and have a couple of tall people (or children on chairs) to stand back to back, spreading their arms out. In Israel, where Jesus was living, mustard seeds often grow as big as this, and local people will even use the mustard branches for firewood, so that tiny seed really does grow into a spreading tree, and all the birds love to sit in the shelter of its branches. The mustard plant provides spicy flavour, fuel and shelter.

Why did Jesus talk to the people about mustard? He often used things that were all around to help describe spiritual things which can't be seen. Perhaps there was a shady mustard plant right there where they were sitting, and some of its seeds scattered on the ground.

Anyway, Jesus said that the way God's kingdom grows is a bit like the way a mustard seed grows. It starts off very little, and gradually grows very big. The little seed may be an act of kindness you do which makes someone think to themselves, 'I wonder! She's become a Christian, and it seems to be changing her for the better. Perhaps there's something in this Jesus person after all!' Or perhaps you're the one in the office who insists on honesty, even if you'd gain from being less than honest, and someone notices and starts thinking. Or perhaps someone notices that you aren't that impressed by the labels people are wearing, even though you're cool.

The little seed of God's kingdom is someone opening themselves up a tiny bit to the possibility of God being real and active in their lives. Gradually it grows in them. Perhaps they begin to ask more questions about God, perhaps they read some Bible stories or start coming with you to church sometimes. Then they start to pray! Now that little seed can really begin to grow, because God can lead the person step by step as they get in touch with him more and more. Sometimes the kingdom of God grows gradually as they pick up teaching week by week, or look at God's world with new eyes. At other times there's a sudden growth spurt. Perhaps a verse of scripture hits home and they realise how their life needs to change, or they suddenly sense God real and close to them in a time of sadness or joy.

Perhaps over a few years, or a lifetime, that little seed has grown in the person until they are so full of God in their life that they are standing tall and strong in faith, and many come to them, now, for spiritual help and comfort, like the birds coming to the mustard plant's spreading branches.

How is the kingdom of God's growing coming on in us? Is it still a tiny seed, full of hope but not yet developed very much? Has it just started to sprout, putting out roots and shoots? Is it not growing very much at all at the moment, or has it recently had a big surge of growth and is excitedly stretching upwards and outwards in the knowledge of God's love and forgiveness? Or is it already tall and strong, providing spiritual shelter for others, scattering other seeds all around, and happy to be full of God's life?

What a world it would be, with churchfuls of people in it, in whom the kingdom of God was growing strong as mustard trees! It could happen. The people could be us.

All-age ideas

- Have bowls of mustard seeds and invite people to take one as they come in. They can plant their mustard seed when they get home.

- If practical, include some mustard plant in one of the flower arrangements.

Prayer of the Faithful

Celebrant
Let us pray to the God of heaven and earth
for the growth of the kingdom.

Reader
May the kingdom grow
in clusters of Christians all over the world;
may it grow as hearts are warmed
by encounter with the living God;
nourished by word and sacrament,
private prayer and public worship.

Silence

Lord of heaven:
let the kingdom grow!

May the kingdom grow
in states, empires and monarchies,

in the crowded streets of cities
and in the scattered rural communities;
in all decision-making and all spending.

Silence

Lord of heaven:
let the kingdom grow!

May the kingdom grow
in every human shelter and home,
every place of work and education,
in each conversation and
in our mutual care of one another.

Silence

Lord of heaven:
let the kingdom grow!

May the kingdom grow
to bring peace and healing
wherever there is pain or sadness;
to bring reassurance, comfort, courage and hope.

Silence

Lord of heaven:
let the kingdom grow!

In the knowledge that we must all face judgement,
we pray for those who have died,
thanking God for his loving mercy,
and entrusting our loved ones
to God's safe keeping.

Silence

Lord of heaven:
let the kingdom grow!

We pray with Mary,
who nurtured our Lord in his earthly life:
Hail, Mary . . .

Knowing that God our Father is listening,
we pray in silence
for our own needs and cares.

Silence

Celebrant
Father, we lay our needs and cares before you,
and ask you to hear us,
through Christ.
Amen.

TREASURE SEEKERS

Aim: To know that God's love grows and grows in his people.

Starter

Play with very soapy water, making bubbles by blowing through your hands. (Ordinary bubble mix is the rather boring substitute!) As you play, talk about the bubbles growing bigger and bigger, and see who can make the biggest.

Teaching

How did we make our bubbles grow? We had to blow very carefully and gently. Show the children some little seeds and pictures of what they grow into. Show them some real 'grown' examples as well if this is practical. In the story of *Jack and the beanstalk*, the beans grew up overnight into a huge plant, but usually the growing goes on bit by bit, day by day, until instead of a tiny seed you find a big tall plant, or even a tree.

Bubbles and plants aren't the only things which grow. We grow too! Let them stand up as tall as they can and remember when they were only very short. In the world God has made, there is lots and lots of growing that goes on.

Jesus told his friends one day that, just like the other things that grow, the kingdom of heaven grows and grows. Bit by bit God's love and goodness is growing and spreading. Once there were just a few of Jesus' followers, but now there are friends of Jesus all over the place. We know a few of them, because they are with us in our church. (Name some of them.) Then there are Jesus' friends in all the other churches, not just in this country, but all over the world.

Praying

Pray for each other by name:

Lord Jesus, bless . . . .
Let your love in her/him grow and grow
a bit more every day of her/his life.

Activities

When they have coloured and cut out the plant on the sheet, they can fold it as shown so that they can make it 'grow' like Jesus' love in us. They can also match the seed to the tree pictures.

PEARL DIVERS

Aim: To know the parables of the growing seed and the mustard seed.

Starter

Bring a variety of leaves and have some reference books available so that they can be identified, together with their 'seeds'.

Teaching

Talk about what has been discovered in the opening activity, and how small seeds grow into huge plants. Jesus loved using the world around us to help us understand spiritual things, and today we're going to hear how Jesus used growing seeds to explain spiritual truths for us.

First, he looked at the way seeds grow. (As you speak get a flower pot, fill it with earth and plant a seed in it.) Gardeners will talk about growing vegetables and flowers, but what do they actually do? They get the seeds and they put them in the earth. Then what happens? They water them and put them in a suitable place. Then what? Do they have to sit and watch all the time? Is it no more TV until the vegetables are ready? No, the seeds just grow, more or less on their own! They don't need the gardener to be there fussing over them every minute of the day. Wild plants don't have gardeners and they still manage to grow.

Jesus says that the kingdom of heaven grows rather like that. Just as we can look back and remember that we've grown taller over the last few years, and our knowledge of maths has grown, we've also been growing spiritually. We understand a bit more about who Jesus is now; we are getting more used to talking things over with God in our prayers; we are able to ask some of the big questions about what God is like and how the miracles happened. We are starting to think about what happens when people die, about right and wrong, about what it costs to be a follower of Jesus.

All this proves that the kingdom of God is growing in you, just as seeds grow in the earth. All that growing is God's doing.

There's another thing about seeds. They start off so small and can end up a huge plant. Jesus noticed that the mustard seed is specially good at that – it's one of the tiniest seeds (show some) and yet it can grow to the size of a tree, with lots of big, spreading branches where the birds love to come and shelter.

He said that the kingdom of heaven grows rather like a mustard seed. Explain that you're not going to tell them what that meant. What do they think he meant by that? (Talk over their ideas. The value of Jesus' parables was to get people thinking for themselves, rather than giving out the answers straightaway.)

Praying

Our Father in heaven,
let your kingdom come.
Let it come in me and my family.
Let it come in my school and my church.
All over the world, Father,
let your kingdom come.

(*Jesus, reign in me* can also be sung as a prayer today.)

Activities

Today's teaching can be read in a picture story on the sheet, and there is a map to plot and colour in the gradual spreading of the kingdom from Jerusalem outwards across the Roman world.

GOLD PANNERS

Aim: To look at Jesus' teaching on the growth of the kingdom of heaven.

Starter

If you have one of those Christmas ornaments where lit candles make angels move round and round, this is ideal for them to set up and watch, working out what keeps the movement going. Other appropriate 'machines' would be lamps where globules of oil float gracefully up and down, driven by the heat, or kites.

Teaching

First have a look at the Old Testament passage from Ezekiel. Explain first that King Nebuchadnezzar had taken the important people of Israel off into Babylon, and the prophet had described this as a great eagle tearing off the top branches of a cedar tree and planting it in a land of traders. Now, in contrast to the worldly way of doing things, we look at God's way of renewing and redeeming a hopeless situation.

Bring out the point that God decides what he will do and does it, for greatest good. We are called to work with him, rather than just following our own whims and fancies; the important thing is to check constantly with God what his will actually is. That way we will be less likely to find ourselves working in opposition to God.

Now read Mark 4:26-34. Look out for where the growing power lies. (Farmers and gardeners don't create the growth themselves, but work with the creative God to allow God's natural growing power to happen.) God can't *only* work where we are busying about his business. If we do our best to provide the best conditions for people's faith to grow, the actual growth of the kingdom is going to happen through the loving God's power and will.

Finally look at this week's section of 2 Corinthians. Whether we are in this life or the next, our only goal is to please God. It is the love of Christ in us that controls us, enabling us to live fruitfully – his freely given gift rather than our hard work.

Praying

It is a good thing to give thanks to the Lord,
and to sing praises to your name, O Most High;
to tell of your loving kindness early in the morning
and of your faithfulness in the night season.

(From Psalm 91)

Activities

There is a short sketch on the sheet about a sun-bathing farmer who is busy growing his crop, and they are encouraged to explore the quiet, hidden growing of the kingdom of God. There is also a checklist for looking at signs of spiritual growing, both as individuals and in their church community.

TWELFTH SUNDAY OF THE YEAR

Thought for the day

What kind of person is this? Even the wind and waves obey him.

Reflection on the readings

Job 38:1, 8-11
Psalm 106
2 Corinthians 5:14-17
Mark 4:35-41

Although we perhaps know that God is all-mighty, the way we live often shows that we don't take this terribly seriously. Many claiming belief in God speak of him as a slightly ridiculous, inept but well-meaning gentleman, part security blanket and part Father Christmas. Any God with real power, many believe, would act to prevent pain and suffering, and design creation differently so that things didn't go wrong. For the most part God is ignored, much of the time even by his supposed friends and worshippers, and we live our daily lives with an occasional glance in God's direction. Praying is generally the last resort – 'All we can do now is pray'.

Today's readings bring us the shock of ordinary people brought suddenly into close contact with God's power in their ordinary lives. In the Gospel the disciples are floating in their solid, wooden-hulled fishing boat, with its smell of salt, damp and stale fish. The stained and wet sails are straining under the increasing wind, and the ropes creaking. All so normal and familiar.

But as the power of wind and waves increases out of control, and Jesus is woken up in their anxious panic, they suddenly witness a much greater power and authority than anything in the created world. The dramatically hushed and tamed sailing conditions shock the disciples into new questions about Jesus' full identity; they have just witnessed God's power in action, and it shakes them.

Other examples have been shown to us today in the Old Testament reading, of God demonstrating his power and authority. Whenever people glimpse it, they are brought to a new reverence and respect for God, as they suddenly see him in all his awesome greatness, and our condescending, human-sized impressions of him are shown up to be shamefully inappropriate.

The continued readings from 2 Corinthians show us Paul, still dazed from his encounter with the living Jesus, recognising the miracle of God's vitality and power working in the ordinariness of human beings, and the extraordinary effect of this in people's lives. It is, after all, a universe-builder we're talking about, an all-knowing, all-seeing God, whose reality should bring us frequently to our knees in utter wonder and adoration.

Discussion starters

1. When were you last stunned by the awesome power of the living God? Share your experiences and how they affected your understanding of God.

2. If people know something of what God is really like, how is it likely to affect the way they pray?

All-stage talk

If practical, arrange for a couple of people to bring their (well-controlled) pet into church this morning. If this isn't possible, interview a couple of pet owners.

Look at the animals and talk to the owners about what they like to eat, and how they like to play. Then ask them about how their pets behave when they are frightened or feel threatened, and how they calm them down.

It isn't just pets who get worried, angry and upset – it's humans as well. Today we heard about a time when Jesus' friends were so frightened they were panicking, and we saw how Jesus calmed them down. Remind them that Jesus was actually asleep, and the disciples woke him up to tell him to start worrying! With the stormy waves pitching the boat up and down, and the water coming in over the side it was beginning to look like a *Titanic* situation, and there was Jesus fast asleep in the bottom of the boat!

Sometimes we do that, too, if life seems very scary, and everything seems to be going wildly out of control. We scream out to Jesus, demanding that he notices and *does* something, instead of being so calm about it all. It's almost as if we want him to panic as well.

Jesus, once he's been thoroughly shaken awake, doesn't seem to be caught up in the excitement. But he can see that it isn't only the disciples who are churned up – it's the weather as well. And perhaps he sees here a good way to help the disciples understand more about who is. The disciples are so scared at the moment that they can't take anything in. So instead of calming them down, Jesus calms the wind and the waves. As the howling wind eases and settles quietly again, and the pounding waves flatten back to a gentle lapping around the battered boat, the disciples calm down as well. In this lull they recover themselves and stop panicking.

What does Jesus do next – wait for their applause? Go back to sleep? In fact we find he now starts teaching them, because they are now calm enough to listen. He talks to them about trusting God, even in the middle of raging storms.

Often in life we will find that when we have invited Jesus into our boat – into our life – we don't get so thrown by all the stormy problems (things like quarrels in friendships, loved ones moving away, financial problems, pressure and stress at work). And if we're panicking about them so much that we can't hear Jesus helping us to weather the storm, then often we'll find we're given a breather – a bit of space – where things are calmed down long enough for us to realise that, with God in charge, we don't actually need to be terrified.

All-age ideas

- As an introduction to the talk, try this eye-opener to the wonder of God:

  Voice 1   The highest waterfall on earth is Angel in Venezuela, where the water plunges down 979 metres. The River Nile in Africa is 6,695 kilometres long. At its greatest depth the Pacific Ocean is 11,034 metres deep.
  What a universe.
  What a God!

  Voice 2   Adult salmon in the open sea find their way by rivers and streams and up waterfalls, to the actual pool they hatched in, years before.
  What a universe.
  What a God!

  Voice 3   Our Milky Way galaxy is one of thousands of millions of galaxies, all apparently rushing away from one another at tremendous speeds. The nearest neighbour star to our solar system is 24 million million miles away.
  What a universe.
  What a God!

- During the reading of the Gospel, some of the children can interpret the mood of the sea by moving a length of blue fabric, first gently, then increasingly stormily until Jesus' calming of the waves, to which they quickly react, restoring the gentle calm once more.

Prayer of the Faithful

Celebrant
As residents of God's universe,
let us pray now to our loving Creator.

Reader
We pray for those in positions of authority
in the Church all over the world
and in each gathered community;
that in all the storms
we may be enabled to hear God's calming voice
and deepen our trust in him.

Silence

Lord of all truth and goodness,
calm our fears:
and teach us your peace.

We pray for those with political and military power,
and all whose decisions affect many lives.
May they speak the Spirit's truth into motives,
the Son's honour into actions,
and the Father's vision of peace into every conflict.

Silence

Lord of great power and majesty,
calm our fears:
and teach us your peace.

We pray for all single people,
couples, communal groups and families,
as they weather their storms
and learn from them;
may all who have the care of others
be given the capacity to bring peace and calm fears.

Silence

Lord of all compassion and mercy,
calm our fears:
and teach us your peace.

We pray for those
whose minds and hearts are in turmoil,
whose lives lurch from crisis to crisis;
for those who find their lives shattered
by illness or injury;
for peace in those threatening storms
and a settling of all anxiety.

Silence

Lord of all healing,
calm our fears:
and teach us your peace.

We pray for those who are dying alone,
unnoticed or unprepared;
we commend those who have died
to God's merciful forgiveness
and eternal tranquillity.

Silence

Lord of eternity,
calm our fears:
and teach us your peace.

We pray with Mary,
who served God fearlessly:
Hail, Mary . . .

Trusting in God our Father,
we name our particular prayer burdens.

Silence

Celebrant
Father, rejoicing that you are in overall charge
of all creation,
we offer these prayers,
through Christ Jesus.
Amen.

TREASURE SEEKERS

Aim: To know that Jesus calms our fears.

Starter

Bring either a small parachute or a large sheet and stand everyone around the outside, holding the edge. They can now make a flat calm, then build up through very gentle ripples to a full-blown storm, before making it die down again, ending with a gentle peace.

Teaching

Talk about what happens when we're frightened and about the people who calm us down and make us feel better. Also talk about any people and pets we calm down and comfort, when they're feeling frightened or worried.

Jesus is like that. When we are frightened or scared or upset, whether we're children or grown-ups, we can all come to Jesus and he will help to calm us down and comfort us. He may do that through your family, and he may use *your* words and arms to comfort other people or other creatures!

Sometimes you will find that as you ask Jesus to help you calm down, you will suddenly feel inside like our sheet was at the end of our pretend storm – all gentle and peaceful. Jesus is very good at bringing us peace, and all we have to do is ask for his help.

Praying

Give me your peace,
O Jesus Christ, my brother,
give me your peace,
O Jesus Christ, my Lord!

Activities

On the sheet there are pictures of a storm and a calm sea, children fighting and the same children playing together. Use these for spotting the differences, not just in the detail, but in what's going on. There is also space for them to draw in the calmed version of the pictured panic zone. Actively drawing the peace will help them work through the next conflict, Jesus' way.

PEARL DIVERS

Aim: To know the story of the calming of the wind and waves.

Starter

Sit everyone in a circle on chairs. You are going to create a storm with actions and sounds. Each 'round', the leader starts off a new action, the person on the right joins in and so on around the circle. When it gets to the leader again, a new action is started. It's important that people carry on with the previous action until the person next to them changes – that makes for a gradual build-up instead of a sudden change.

Here are the 'rounds':

1. Flick fingers, so they brush against one another (both hands at once).
2. Tap lightly with two fingers on the palm of other hand.
3. Clap lightly with fingers on palm.
4. Clap fast and louder.
5. Slap thighs with hands – left hand, right hand alternately and quickly.
6. Stamp with feet on the floor.
7. Still stamping, clap while you make wind noises.

(Then work your way back through the numbers to a calm.)

Teaching

Our story today is about a sudden storm, rather like the one we've just made, so we're well practised for providing all the sound effects for it.

Last week we heard a couple of the stories Jesus told – about mustard growing from a tiny seed into a wide spreading tree. Well, Jesus had spent all day out in the open air telling those stories, and teaching and healing people. He used to sit in one of the boats to talk, with the water lapping * the odd fly buzzing around * and all the crowds sitting quietly on the beach. That way they could all see Jesus and hear him, and he could see them. But now it was evening, and there was Jesus sitting in the boat with the water lapping * and he was really tired *. All the crowds had crunched their way home along the beach *.

So he said to his followers, 'Come with me across the lake'. They used the boat Jesus was already sitting in, and some other boats as well. They waded into the water *, pushed the boat further out * and clambered aboard *. They felt which way the wind was blowing by licking a finger and holding it up * and then hoisted the sail *.

Soon they were moving through the water, with the waves making a wash behind them *. Jesus lay down with his head on a pillow in the bottom of the boat and fell asleep *.

But then the wind started to whip up strongly * and that made the waves bigger and higher, crashing around the boat *. The water started to trickle in over the side of the boat * and they had to pull down the sail *. The disciples were getting frightened. 'Oh my goodness, this is terrible! Our boat is going to be completely swamped!' they shouted. They were scooping the water out as best they could, but the wind was still howling * and the sea was still churning and rolling all around and all over the boat *.

Then they noticed that Jesus was still fast asleep in the bottom of the boat! 'Wake up, Jesus', they said, shaking him, 'Do you care about us or not? We're going to drown soon if this weather goes on.'

Jesus woke up, looked at his friends, and saw the fear in their eyes. He heard the sounds of the angry wind * and the boiling, churning waves (*** above the next part of the story). He stood up in the boat and commanded the wind and waves to stop – he called out to them: 'Quiet! Be still!' * Then the wind stopped and the lake became calm, lapping gently around them again *.

Jesus looked round at his disciples. Their faces, hair and beards were soaked with sea spray, they were still panting from the effort of shouting and bailing out water, and they were standing ankle deep in water that had poured into the boat. They were completely stunned by what they had just seen. Who could this Jesus be if he could even take charge of the wind and waves? It was frightening to see such power in action.

Jesus said to them, 'Why are you afraid? Do you still have no faith?'

And they didn't really know what to say to him. One thing they had realised – that Jesus must be something more than an ordinary teacher – it was as if he had God's power.

They hoisted the sail again *, bailed out the rest of the water *, and sailed over the calm lake, with the water lapping the bow.

Praying

Jesus, we see in you the power and love of God.
When we are like stormy water, calm us down;
When we are frightened and panicking,
give us your peace, we pray.

Activities

Using the sheet they can make a model of the boat. Each child will need the right sized square of fabric (cut from an old sheet or shirt) so they can paint it and wrinkle it into waves. The boat is made from the cut-out drawings, with a used matchstick fixed in for the mast.

GOLD PANNERS

Aim: To explore the implications of the calming of the storm.

Starter

What are we? Explain that they are some kind of group with some kind of leader, and they can work out what they are by asking the leader questions (yes/no answers only). They may be objects, animals or people, or a combination. To start them off they are given one clue.

Here are some possible scenarios:

- A group of planes at different flying levels, waiting to be given permission to land from ground control. (Clue: boiled sweets and travel wrist bands/travel pills)

- Swallows perched on a telegraph wire gathering in the autumn for their leader to set them off on migration to Africa. (Clue: a feather)

- Members of a morris dance team with the leader playing an accordion. (Clue: bells and a white hanky)

- A mountain rescue team in thick fog on Snowdon guided by the compass. (Clue: A map and a first aid kit)

Teaching

What does it mean for God to be in charge? First read the chosen Old Testament passage, looking at it from this point of view. Notice what it does and doesn't mean – responsible loving, picking up pieces, drawing together and planning, yet following natural laws and allowing us the freedom of choice.

Now read from Mark's Gospel the account of Jesus calming the wind and waves.

Why do they think the disciples woke Jesus up?

Do they think they would all have drowned if Jesus hadn't commanded the weather to calm down?

Why might Jesus have chosen to do this instead of comforting the disciples and cheering them through the difficult situation? (Feeling compassion for them/showing a sign?/fighting with evil?)

What did it help the disciples to understand about Jesus in a very dramatic lesson?

What does it help us to see about Jesus as we read the account nearly two thousand years later?

Share ideas and other questions they may have.

Praying

Lead us, heavenly Father, lead us
o'er the world's tempestuous sea.
Guard us, guide us, keep us, feed us,
for we have no help but thee.
Yet possessing every blessing
if our God our Father be.

Activities

On the sheet there are some of the questions people ask about God intervening, and hints and references are given to help them work out possible answers. They are also invited to look at possible storms into which Jesus speaks calm – in their own lives, in the Church and in the news. This can all lead on to prayer and action.

THIRTEENTH SUNDAY OF THE YEAR

Thought for the day

God's power can reach even into death and draw out life.

Reflection on the readings

Wisdom of Solomon 1:13-15; 2:23-24
Psalm 29
2 Corinthians 8:7, 9, 13-15
Mark 5:21-43

Everything about death looks final. The body we knew laughing, anxious, angry or intrigued is stilled; all the memories and stories locked inside and out of our reach. It seems to be the end of responding, thinking, feeling and moving. Clustered around it are other endings – the cupboards to be cleared, possessions and clothing now redundant; terrible gaps in family, friendships, committees and rotas, the particular pew. The tragedy of death is its terrible finality – it is like a violent rejection of what was previously so very much alive; a slap in the face to life itself. With King David, our gut reaction to death is the grieving of endings – 'Look how the mighty are fallen'.

Yet with God walking this planet in person as Jesus, we discover in his ministry several cases of death's finality being challenged and reversed. Jairus' twelve-year-old daughter had left the living world and yet Jesus speaks into death and calls her out of it, back into the world of life again. She hears his call to her ('Talitha, koum!') and follows it through a journey we can only imagine, emerging to stand up in the world she had left, no longer full of fever as before, but in full health and very hungry.

As with last week's miracle, we might ask why, if Jesus' compassion drove him to do such acts contrary to nature then, does he not continue to reverse natural laws daily and universally on grounds of compassion today? In fact, of course, there must have been many hundreds of other people dying during Jesus' ministry on earth, none of whom were raised from the dead. There are other reasons for Jesus acting like this in these particular situations; reasons to do with signs and pointers to Jesus' true identity.

But we are also challenged by the great faith shown in today's Gospel. In Jesus' encounter with the woman in the crowd, finally healed after twelve years of miserable ill health and uncleanness, according to the law, she is told that it is her faith which has healed her, even though Jesus knows that power has gone out of him. Did her faith draw that healing power out?

Certainly we do need to be expectant, considering God-incidences perfectly possible, allowing God permission for his kingdom to be unleashed in each situation. We choose whether or not to unbolt the door from the inside.

Discussion starters

1. The situation in the Gospel of urgent business being interrupted by another crisis is all too familiar! What can we learn from Jesus' way of dealing with it?

2. Paul talks of us giving generously within our means (2 Corinthians). What does this mean in terms not just of money but time, commitment and even faith and trust?

All-stage talk

Make a circle of chairs near where you are talking, or a circle of rope – something which is clearly visible.

Explain that this circle is like our life here on earth. How do we get into it? By being born. (Invite a couple of people to make their way in.) While we're here what do we do? We eat, play, work, talk, make friends (and perhaps some enemies), watch TV, learn things and so on. (Everyone can add to the list.) Invite the people in the circle of life to mime some of those things as they are suggested.

How do we get out of the circle of life? By being born backwards? We get out of this life by dying. (The volunteers make their way out of the circle.) Point out that they're not in the circle any more, but

they're in a huge space, much bigger than they might have imagined, if they'd only ever known life in the circle. And outside this space is the whole outdoors, stretching outwards and upwards, and full of light and colour, better than anything we could imagine if we'd only ever known the circle as 'life'. Just as the circle isn't the only place, so this earthly life isn't all there is to complete life – Jesus told us that life after our death can be full, rich and wonderful; and it's Jesus who has made that possible for us.

Remind everyone of the story in today's Gospel, about a twelve-year-old girl dying. Everyone is specially sad when a young person dies, because they haven't had a chance to live very long here and enjoy our world. But Jesus brings that young girl back to life again. It's as if from inside the circle of life he calls to her on the outside and she comes back in again, completely better, and hungry. He could do that because Jesus *is* life. When she next died, perhaps after a long and happy time on earth, she closed her eyes on earthly life and heard Jesus calling her name again into life – but this time from heaven, into the life with Jesus that lasts for ever.

When we get to the point of our death, Jesus will be there, calling us out into that life, and welcoming us. And because we know his voice, from a lifetime of prayer, we'll be very happy to move towards it and find him, waiting for us there.

All-age ideas

• Act out the Gospel for today, either miming it as it is narrated, or preparing it with spoken parts.

• As a reflective preparation for a penitential rite try this dialogue:

Left side	If we were praying for rain, would we bring our umbrellas?
All	Forgive us, Lord; we place limitations on what is possible with you.
Right side	If we pray for others, are we ready to be part of the answer?
All	Forgive us, Lord; we mark off boundaries where your kingdom is not welcome, because it makes demands on our time.

Play some reflective music during which the following is said:

Voice 1	Come, Holy Spirit and draw us into full life.
Voice 2	Come, Holy Spirit and melt our hearts of stone.

Prayer of the Faithful

Celebrant
As God has called us by name
out into full, abundant life,
let us lay before him now our concerns
for the Church and for the world.

Reader
May all the built-up layers
of complacency or despondency,
of over-comfortable familiarity
or under-active expectation
be removed from the Church
and from our lives,
until we see again
with the freshness and wonder of deepened faith.

Silence

Lord, we believe:
help our unbelief.

We call to mind societies and systems of our world.
May our assumptions be questioned
and our destructive choices challenged;
may the unnoticed scales of prejudice which blind us
be broken away,
so that our world may increasingly come
under the reign of justice, righteousness and love.

Silence

Lord, we believe:
help our unbelief.

May our pride be replaced with humility
until we learn from young children
the lessons of wonder and trust.
May the childlike be kept as a living flame
in all of us, whatever our age,
and enable us to rediscover God's glory
all around us.

Silence

Lord, we believe:
help our unbelief.

As the sick were brought to Jesus
by their loved ones,
so now in prayer we bring all those
whom we long to be healed.
May they hear the Lord's voice
and sense his touch.

Silence

Lord, we believe:
help our unbelief.

Earth-bound, we grieve
at the loss of loved ones through death;
yet we also rejoice
that they have been called by the Lord
into the fullness of everlasting life.

Silence

Lord, we believe:
help our unbelief.

With Mary who gave us her Son,
we make our prayer:
Hail, Mary . . .

In the silence of God's generous love,
we name those known to us
who need our prayers.

Silence

Celebrant
Father, we thank you
for drawing us here to pray,
and ask you to hear us,
through Jesus Christ.
Amen.

TREASURE SEEKERS

Aim: To know that Jesus is never too busy to bother with them.

Starter

Play the singing game *Here we go round the mulberry bush*, with lots of busy verses, such as 'This is the way we clean the car/carry the shopping/hoover the hall/make the packed lunches'.

Teaching

Talk together about being busy, and all the things that need to be done each day and each week. Sometimes we have to wait to tell our news or talk over a worry we have because people are too busy to listen straightaway. They might say, 'Just wait till I've got the dinner on', or 'till I've driven round this roundabout', or 'till we've paid at the check-out'.

But Jesus is always ready to listen to us, because he isn't stuck in time like us. He can give us his full attention straightaway, wherever we are. He never rushes us or tells us to wait. He's always ready to listen to our worries and fears, and enjoy our news and jokes with us.

Praying

Thank you, Jesus,
for listening when we pray.
You're never too busy to hear what we say.

Activities

There are pictures of some very busy animal life – ants, birds, bees and spiders – to talk about, with an observation activity. There is also someone telling some news, and they draw in a friend who is really listening to what she's saying. This discussion of what good listening involves will help the children become better at the skill themselves, as well as helping them understand that Jesus is the very best listener ever.

PEARL DIVERS

Aim: To know the story of Jairus' daughter and the healing which 'interrupts' Jesus on his way to the house.

Starter

Provide all kinds of dressing-up clothes, including some thick gloves. Everyone sits in a circle, and a dice is passed round. When someone throws a six they run and start dressing up in all the clothes. As soon as someone else throws a six, they interrupt the first person and take the clothes for themselves.

Teaching

There's an interruption in our story today. Remind the children that Mark has written his Gospel to show us who Jesus is, and we've seen Jesus healing people, teaching people with his stories, and making the wind and waves do what he tells them. The disciples are beginning to realise that this is no ordinary teacher and healer – he seems to have the power of God in all he says and does.

Today we are going to travel with Jesus and his friends and see what happens. (Gather them all up and walk around, outside if possible, with you telling the story as you go.)

Explain that Jesus would often set off with his followers like this, walking from town to village to town. They would have passed by hills with sheep on them, fields growing barley and wheat, vineyards full of grapes, and farms with hens and their chicks. At the towns it became very crowded as the streets were narrow, and everyone came out to join them and see Jesus. Rumours about him being able to make people better meant that people would bring their sick friends and family out (stop walking), and Jesus would lay his hands on them and make them well again. Then everyone would be so happy, and join in the crowd! (Start walking again.)

Sometimes, instead of walking, Jesus and his friends would travel by boat across the lake. (Everyone climbs into a big 'fishing boat' and make the noises of the water. They look across at the shore – at the (pretend) crowd of people waiting for them. Everyone climbs out of the boat and stops.)

One man came up to Jesus and bowed. His name was Jairus, and he told Jesus that his twelve-year-old daughter was very ill, and asked Jesus to come and lay his hands on her so that she would be healed and live. So Jesus and his followers started to walk with Jairus to his house, down the narrow street. (Start walking.) But suddenly Jesus stopped walking and looked around. (Stop.) 'Who touched me?' he was asking. His friends said, 'Well, it's so crowded here that everyone is squashed against everyone else!' But Jesus had felt healing power go out of him and knew that someone had touched him wanting to be made better.

Then one of the women in the crowd came up to Jesus. 'It was me, teacher,' she said. 'I touched your clothes because I wanted to be made well – I've been ill for twelve years, you see. And thank you, Jesus, because you *have* made me better!'

So everyone went on walking to Jairus' house. (Start walking.) But then they were stopped again. (Stop.) Some men from the house came up to Jairus and whispered to him. Jairus burst into tears. (Can the children guess what the men had told him?) But Jesus paid no attention to what the men had said. He put his arm round Jairus. 'Don't be afraid,' he said. 'All you have to do is believe.'

Jesus told all the crowd to wait here, and only Peter, James and John, and Jairus and his wife were allowed to go on with him. (A leader takes three children and leaves the group to walk just out of sight.) So we'll stay here and wait for them to come back. (Sit down together, looking down towards the house. The healing party let out loud, excited shouts and come running back to the full group. Everyone gets up and crowds around them. The other leader continues the story. S/He excitedly explains how Jesus went into the house where the little girl was lying.) He held her hand, saying to her, 'Little girl, I tell you to stand up!' And sure enough she opened her eyes again and stood up, perfectly well, and Jesus had told her parents to give her something to eat!

Praying

Jesus, Jesus, we have come to see
that you must really be
the Son of God our Father.
We've been with you and we all agree
that you're the only person
who can really set us free!

Activities

On the sheet there is a wordsearch to reinforce the teaching, and they can make a game to play which helps them imagine a typical day in Jesus' ministry. They will need some thin card on which to mount the game and pieces, once they have coloured them and cut them out.

GOLD PANNERS

Aim: To explore the implications of this healing from death.

Starter

Use a stopwatch and set someone off talking for one minute on a particular subject. They can be interrupted and challenged for repetitions or hesitations, after which the challenger continues the talk. Whoever is talking at time-up is the winner.

Teaching

Talk a little together about how sad it is when someone we know and love dies, and how we miss seeing them.

Now make a point of moving to the New Testament, and find Mark's Gospel. Read this with different voices taking the various parts. Are they surprised at Jesus actually raising the dead? What does this show his followers? Why do they think only a few were allowed to be present?

Also look at the healing which takes place on the way to Jairus' house. How do they think Jairus might have been feeling while Jesus took time to talk to the woman? How do they cope with urgent interruptions? What if the interruption was the reason the little girl was already dead – might this be why Jesus was prepared to bring her back from the dead?

Finally look at what Mark shows us about faith. Where does faith and believing come up in the two healings of today's Gospel? What does Jesus say about it?

Praying

Be still, for the power of the Lord
is moving in this place;

he comes to cleanse and heal, to minister his grace.
No work too hard for him,
in faith receive from him.
Be still, for the power of the Lord
is moving in this place.

(Taken from the song *Be still, for the presence* by David J. Evans © 1986 Kingsway's Thankyou Music)

Activities

There is a role-play on the sheet to help them see today's Gospel from various different standpoints, and there is space for them to record what this account reveals of the nature of Jesus and his mission.

FOURTEENTH SUNDAY OF THE YEAR

Thought for the day

If we are not ready to listen to the truth, we will not hear it.

Reflection on the readings

Ezekiel 2:2-5
Psalm 122
2 Corinthians 12:7-10
Mark 6:1-6

Discreet rebellion does not go unnoticed by God. Whatever we proclaim with our lips, whatever we claim to believe, and however cleverly we disguise our rebellion from others, God sees and knows where our hearts really are, and which way we are really facing. This isn't something to make us scared of approaching God. It's actually quite a relief to find there's no point in pretending or trying to impress him. Those who, like me, tend to live in a certain amount of clutter, know there are some people whose visits spur us to a spate of frantic tidying, and others who know us so well that this isn't really necessary – they know and love us well exactly as we are!

When God has something to say to us which may involve opening us up more to his grace, challenging a fixed or self-centred attitude or behaviour, or a little spiritual growing-up, then he will tell us. But if we aren't ready or prepared to hear what he has to say, then there's no way we'll hear it. Later we might look back and wonder why we couldn't see the obvious! But at the time we're far more likely to react with hostility and defensiveness, rather like those in Jesus' home town. We can hear their indignant, self-righteous wounded egos as they mutter their complaints about Jesus. When they look at the facts, he's not even on a level with them for background; so what right has he to be displaying more wisdom and miracle-working than any of them? It is quite usual to resent holiness, or any other gift, in those close to us – holiness in strangers is far easier to cope with as we don't take that as personal criticism.

Discussion starters

1. How genuinely receptive are we to God's word? Do we mark out 'no-go' areas where God is concerned?

2. How might our gut reactions alert us to God trying to tell us something important, which we don't really want to hear?

All-stage talk

You will need a sieve – either a culinary or a gardening one. Also some appropriate thing to sieve – such as flour or earth.

First talk about the way we tend to hear if someone offers us a second chocolate biscuit, a raise in our pay, or a special discount, but not if we're being told to clean out the rabbit, work late, empty the washing machine or make a dental appointment. As the saying goes, 'There's none so deaf as those who won't hear'.

Explain that what our minds do is to sieve information which comes in through the ears and the eyes. Produce the sieve and start sieving so that everyone can see this process in action. The holes are a particular size so that everything is sorted automatically. Big lumps are not wanted, so they won't fit through the holes. Fine flour or earth can get through quite easily. The rest only gets through if we process it a bit first (breaking it down to a suitable size) and if it can't be broken down (like stones in the earth or a free sticker in the flour) then it doesn't get through the sieve at all.

In just the same way we are selective about what we hear, and mostly that is very useful to us. It stops us turning into nervous wrecks by the daily news items, for instance.

But sometimes we try to keep out what God is trying to make us hear. Just because it may mean us changing something in our lives, we treat it as a threat, and shut it out, when really it is helping us to get rid of a way of thinking or behaving which is not healthy to us or others, physically, mentally or spiritually. What we need is to have 'God's Word'-shaped holes in our sieves, so that God's Word can always get through.

All-age ideas

- As a response to the all-stage talk, suggest that we trace the cross on our ears and eyes (or do this to one another) as a sign that we really want to see and hear what God is telling us, whether it is comforting or challenging.

- Cover the base of a flat sieve with paper which has a cross cut out of it. Place this where people will see it as they come to receive Communion, or as they leave the church, and label it: 'Lord, may we hear and receive your Word'.

- In the Ezekiel reading, mime the prophet walking about trying to tell people good news. Each in turn starts to listen, but some shrug and shake their heads, getting on with what they were doing before, and others look affronted or angry, and deliberately turn their backs on the prophet, folding their arms and sticking their chins in the air.

Prayer of the Faithful

Celebrant
God has drawn us down many different routes
to this shared worship today.
Let us still our bodies
and alert our minds and hearts in his presence.

Reader
We are the Body of Christ
because the Spirit binds us together.
We pray for a real concern
and love for one another,
supportive and encouraging,
without malice or bickering,
so that we can be sent out
strong in our weakness and littleness.

Silence

Heavenly Father, give us your grace:
to hear your word with joy.

All the kingdoms and states
are answerable to divine authority,
and much evil is allowed to flourish
through the silence of good people;
we pray for the courage to speak out the truth,
whether it is popular or not.

Silence

Heavenly Father, give us your grace:
to hear your word with joy.

May all our listening
at home, on the phone, at school and at work
be done with our full attention to God's voice
and to one another,
happy to grow wiser through each conversation.

Silence

Heavenly Father, give us your grace:
to hear your word with joy.

We pray for those
whose pain screams silently and incessantly;
for those who have no one to confide in,
no one to listen.
May the love of the Lord enfold them,
his peace calm them
and his healing transform them.

Silence

Heavenly Father, give us your grace:
to hear your word with joy.

In all our life and in all our living
may we be prepared for the life to come;
we commend to the Lord's keeping all those
who have recently made their journey through death.

Silence

Heavenly Father, give us your grace:
to hear your word with joy.

Mary showed us how to listen;
we join our prayers with hers:
Hail, Mary . . .

We bring our personal petitions now
to God our Father, who hears us.

Silence

Celebrant
Father, we ask you to fulfil our prayers
to your glory;
in Jesus' name we pray.
Amen.

TREASURE SEEKERS

Aim: To know that God talks to us and teaches us,
and to learn about listening.

Starter

Explain that you are going to do a spot of listening today. Give out to the children pictures or models of different animals. Ask them all to shout to you the name of their animal or the noise it makes, and you will listen to what they are telling you. Finding that very hard, ask them instead to tell you one by one, so that you can hear them better.

Teaching

Point out how much easier it is to listen when we are quiet and still, without lots of other noises going on. One of the ways we pray to God is by making ourselves very quiet and still, so that we can listen to God's love, and feel him close to us.

Try being very quiet and still and listening for a pin to drop. Then try being still and quiet, with eyes closed (they can lie face down for this if they like), while you read this to them:

Imagine you are walking along beside a high wall and you see a little door in it. Over the door there is a picture of you and your name is written there. You turn the handle and the door opens. You walk inside and find a sunny day with soft green grass under your feet, and flowers growing there. You feel happy and safe in this place, and take off your shoes and run across the grass, enjoying the coloured flowers and the butterflies. You come to a sandy beach, and the sea is lapping against it, so you sit down and listen to the waves. Although you can't see him, you know that Jesus is here with you, and you sit quietly in the sunshine together by the sea, with the seagulls calling.

After a while you get up and walk back across the beach and the grass, put on your shoes and make your way to the door. As you go out of the door you know that you can come back to this garden of prayer whenever you like.

(Put on some very quiet music as you tell the children to sit up slowly and open their eyes. Pray today's prayer together while the music plays.)

Praying

O Jesus, we love to be with you!
Thank you so much for being our special friend,
always here with us and always loving us.
Amen.

Activities

On the sheet there are lots of sounds 'pictured'. They look at the pictures and make the sounds. There is a checklist for top listeners – what do our eyes, ears, hands, brains, feet and heart do when we are really listening? They can also draw their own garden of prayer with Jesus there.

PEARL DIVERS

Aim: To learn about Jesus being listened to by some and not by others.

Starter

Sit in a circle so everyone is visible to everyone else. Choose someone present but don't let on who this is. Say, 'I'm thinking of someone who . . .', giving one clue at a time until the identity of the person has been guessed. The guesser carries on the game, until all the children who want to have had a go. With older children you could include some people who are in the church community.

Teaching

The people we have been describing are well known to us. Some of them we have known since they or we were babies. We perhaps go to the same school. That's how the people of Nazareth felt about Jesus – how could he be so special? To them he was just the ordinary Jesus they had always known, whose mother's name was Mary and whose father was the town's carpenter. They knew his brothers and sisters. They were happy for Jesus to make their furniture or repair their houses, but they didn't want to think of him as someone special who could teach them God's thoughts.

And because they didn't want to hear, they found they couldn't understand what Jesus was talking about. (We sometimes block our ears if there's something we don't want to hear.) Read the children Mark 6:1-6.

That was in Jesus' home town. What happened in all the other villages and towns? All the people crowded round to listen to him because when they heard him they felt close to God, and that felt really good. Jesus knew he'd never be able to get round everywhere for everyone to hear him so he had a plan. How many disciples were there? Twelve. (Lay down twelve simple paper cut-outs of people as you say this.) Jesus split them into pairs (a child can do this), so how many pairs were there? Six.

He sent each pair of disciples out to the different villages and towns to preach to the people, encouraging them to change their hearts and their lives, to heal those who were ill and comfort those who were sad. (Spread the pairs out all over the floor.) And Jesus told them to go out just as they were, without money or luggage or insurance policies. They were to live simply and joyfully, and God would do the rest.

What do you think happened? There were still some who refused to listen, just as there are today. But lots and lots of people did listen to what they said, and turned back to God, and lots were healed.

Praying

Lord Jesus, help me to listen
with my heart as well as my ears.
Lord Jesus, speak into my thoughts and hopes,
my questions and my fears.
Amen.

Activities

On the sheet there are some pictures to help the children explore the way we tend to choose what we want to hear and stop listening if we don't want to hear what is being said. There is also a word-search reinforcing today's teaching.

GOLD PANNERS

Aim: To look at how the message is to be preached, whether people want to listen or not.

Starter

Play 'pick-up-sticks', either with a commercial set, or by tipping a pile of cutlery on to the table and taking it in turns to lift off one item at a time very carefully, so as not to wobble the rest.

Teaching

That was a bit how it feels to be talking about our faith to someone who is determined not to believe a word of what we're saying! We have to go very carefully and sensitively, looking out for where those people are coming from, so we can talk into their questions and help them understand. Today we are reading about the way the people in Jesus' home town reacted to him. Read Mark 6:1-6 and look out for why they rejected him.

Now read the passage from Ezekiel, where the prophet is told to tell out God's words, even though he knows there will be many who refuse to listen. Talk together about our own lives and the people we know. How are they to be told about the God who made them and longs for them to live freely in his forgiving love, instead of living just for material things and personal comfort?

Pray for one another in the group about particular situations that come up in the conversation, and particular people they want to help hear God's message.

Praying

Lord, help me to listen properly
so that I hear your voice, your will for me,
your comfort and your challenges.

And help me to speak out your good news
so others may hear your voice, your will for them,
your comfort and your challenges.
Amen.

Activities

On the sheet there is a short script to draw their attention to different ways of not listening, and some help with training ourselves into a habit of daily prayer. They are also encouraged to look at how the call to pass on God's message affects them.

FIFTEENTH SUNDAY OF THE YEAR

Thought for the day

Those who speak out God's will are bound to be vulnerable to rejection and abuse.

Reflection on the readings

Amos 7:12-15
Psalm 84
Ephesians 1:3-14
Mark 6:7-13

Today's readings pulverise any suspicions we might have had that walking God's way is the comfortable option for wimps. We hear story after story of the reality – that those who speak out God's will are quite likely to find themselves rejected and abused, insulted and scorned. Perhaps Bibles should have a safety warning pasted on the front cover: 'Following the God you meet through these pages is usually dangerous.'

We hear of Amos, told to push off and go back to his farming because he spoke out a message from God which his listeners did not want to hear. Never mind how right and wise God's advice is, those brave enough to speak it, when a community or a relationship needs changing, are bound to be treated as attackers, and are frequently fended off aggressively, at least initially. As a species we do not take criticism positively, but beat it off at all costs, even though it can help us grow. It is a mark of great maturity to be able to welcome criticism in order to learn from it.

When Jesus sends out his disciples it is in the support of pairs, and they are to preach repentance, whether the people are ready to listen or not. Jesus prepares his disciples for the likelihood of stubborn rebellious natures not taking kindly to the challenge.

Brushing the dust from their feet is not a vindictive move, but a visual sign – a testimony – that the Gospel of repentance has been offered and refused. It is also important from the disciples' point of view, and ours. There are times when it is right to move on and leave the Holy Spirit to continue working in people's hearts through the subsequent events and conversations, without feeling weighed down by the rejection.

We need to pray for the courage to speak out as God's people, and get on with the work we have been chosen to do, however we are received. All too often the first hint of opposition or waning popularity shuts us up, and we persuade ourselves that we shouldn't mention such things again. But if the early Church had followed a similar line, how many of us would ever have heard the good news of God's love?

Discussion starters

1. How ready are we to speak out God's truth and God's values when we know they will make us unpopular?
2. How can we best support and encourage the young people as they live and work in environments often openly hostile to God?

All-stage talk

As everyone comes into church give them a length of thin wool or string and a paper clip.

Begin by inviting everyone to fix one end of the wool or string into the paper-clip so that they have made a plumb-line. Explain that this can be used to check whether things which are supposed to be upright are as straight as they should be. (They can try out their plumb-lines on the pews and chairs around them, and some volunteers can check other uprights in the building.)

Suppose we were to find that one of our upright walls was actually leaning over – would it be useful to know that? Yes, because then we could get in the workmen and pay them to put it right.

Suppose we just got angry and offended at being told our wall wasn't as upright as it should be? We could tell the person with the plumb-line to go away and not talk about it to us any more. That way we could go on pretending our wall was upright, and we wouldn't have to pay to put it right. But if we did that, the upright wall might go on leaning more and more until in the end the whole building crashed down in rubble.

Plumb-lines for checking how straight and upright things are can be very useful indeed. Being told where things aren't as upright as they should be can also be very useful indeed.

One of the things prophets do is draw our attention to places in our lives or our society or our church community which are leaning dangerously and are nowhere near as upright as they should be. How do people react to being told? We heard today how the people shouted at the prophet Amos to go and leave them alone. They didn't want to hear, because they didn't want the bother of putting things right. We also hear how Jesus prepares the disciples for rejection and not to be surprised when people don't want to listen to them. People don't want to hear because they don't want to put things right.

How good are we at hearing God whispering lovingly into our hearts about the places in our lives that should be standing tall and upright but are instead leaning a little, or leaning dangerously? Do we thank him for showing it to us so we can quickly put things right again, or do we get sulky or angry and pretend we haven't heard?

All-age ideas

- On upright pillars or walls stick strips of coloured paper with Bible verses on them which emphasise the importance and joy of living upright lives in God's love and strength. Here are some possible verses: Psalm 84:11 – Love and faithfulness meet together; Psalm 23:1 – The earth is the Lord's and everything in it; Psalm 31:11 – Sing, all you who are upright in heart; Psalm 111:2 – The generation of the upright will be blessed; Proverbs 3:32 – The Lord takes the upright into his confidence; Ephesians 1:4 – He chose us in him before the creation of the world to be holy and blameless in his sight; Matthew 22:37-39 – Love God and love one another.

- Have a display with a pair of sandals, a staff and, separately, a tunic, or jacket, a bag, bread and some copper coins, with the note, 'Leave behind'.

Prayer of the Faithful

Celebrant
In humility and love
let us draw near to our God
and pray to him now.

Reader
We pray that our lives
may be upright and holy;
that our church communities may shine
with goodness and love, humility and truth;
we pray for all leaning lives to be straightened up
through your merciful forgiveness.

Silence

Holy God, scatter all darkness:
and bathe our world in your light.

We pray that many may be empowered
to recognise evil and fight against it;
to discern warning signs and speak them out;
to notice the sparks of love and goodness
and celebrate them.

Silence

Holy God, scatter all darkness:
and bathe our world in your light.

We pray that our households
and neighbourhoods,
our places of work and leisure,
may be arenas of praise and thankfulness,
not only in the comfort zones
but particularly through the disturbed
and difficult times.

Silence

Holy God, scatter all darkness:
and bathe our world in your light.

We pray for those in prison;
for those leading cruel and violent lives;
for all victims of oppression or abuse;
for all who suffer mental anguish or physical pain.

Silence

Holy God, scatter all darkness:
and bathe our world in your light.

We pray for those who have died,
that they, and we in our turn, may be given
merciful judgement through Jesus our Saviour,
and brought into the unquenchable light of heaven.

Silence

Holy God, scatter all darkness:
and bathe our world in your light.

We pray with Mary,
who mothered the Son of God:
Hail, Mary . . .

In silence now,
we bring to God's love
the special needs and concerns
known to us individually.

Silence

Celebrant
With great joy, Father,
in the knowledge
that we can trust you unconditionally,
we offer you our prayers,
through Jesus Christ.
Amen.

TREASURE SEEKERS

Aim: To know that in Jesus they can stand up tall and upright for what is right in God's eyes.

Starter

Choose three different sounds (such as a bell, a shaker and a drum), and a grand, regal piece of music on tape such as *Land of hope and glory*. They move in a different way for each sound – such as crawling, jumping and bunny-hopping – but when the grand music plays they stand up tall and strong, like a good king or queen.

Teaching

Talk together about behaving well and being good (both adults and children), so that the children are telling you all they know about this. In voicing these good and noble things they will be reinforcing their own expectations of behaviour and beginning to own those values. Don't make any comments which contrast any of this with unacceptable behaviour, or the times we don't do it – we are simply celebrating the good we know about. Talk about how we behave well in different situations, such as in the car, at meal times, when playing with friends, when doing jobs at home. Help them to see that what they are describing is loving behaviour, thinking of other people and being kind and generous, honest and brave. It's Jesus behaviour, and it makes God very happy to see us doing it.

Praying

In your love, Lord Jesus,
I can stand up tall –
do what's right,
do what's good,
live the way I know I should.
In your love, Lord Jesus,
I can stand up tall!
Amen.

Activities

On the sheet there is a person to colour, cut out and fold so they stand happy and upright, living Jesus' way in the world. The whole sheet ends up being a landscape. Some of the children will need help with the cutting, and it's a good idea to have completed one sheet beforehand to show them what theirs will look like.

PEARL DIVERS

Aim: To know how Jesus sent the disciples out, and the instructions they were given.

Starter

Have quite a number of large, bulky cartons in two piles at one end of the room. Split the group into two teams. Team members have to take it in turns to carry as many boxes as possible in one go across to the other end of the room and back without dropping any. A checker counts the number of boxes transported by each team member. A dropped box means that the number of boxes is counted only as one. The winning team is the one with most boxes transported.

Teaching

In our starter game we were struggling to carry huge, bulky loads, and sometimes life can feel complicated like that, so that we don't have enough time for people any more. Jesus knew that there was only one of him, and loads of towns and villages full of people needing to hear the good news of God's love. If he were to try and do all of this work on his own he'd be racing around the countryside non-stop, with no time to do the work of listening, healing, praying and preaching.

So he sends out his disciples in pairs with these instructions.

(Lay down a rucksack, a wallet with money in it, a loaf of bread, a staff, a spare set of clothes and some sandals.)

Jesus told his disciples they weren't to take anything for the journey except a staff and sandals. (Gather these from the assortment and push the others away as you mention each item.) No bread, no rucksack, no money, and no extra clothes.

Why do they think he wanted them to travel light like this, instead of having lots of luggage with them? Collect their ideas on a blackboard, whiteboard or sheet of paper. Draw them to see that travelling so light was sensible because . . .

- they wouldn't be worrying about their possessions, or getting robbed

- it forced them to depend on God and those they worked with for food and shelter
- it gave the people lots of opportunities to be caring and generous towards them
- it was clear that they weren't out to make money
- by being as poor as the poorest people, they were sharing their hardships and showing that God loves and looks after everyone
- this was the 'uniform' of prophets and holy men

They were to teach everyone, encouraging them to change their hearts and their lives, and they were to heal those who were ill and comfort the sad. The disciples were told to go out simply and joyfully to the people, and God would do the rest. Some people didn't listen, but lots did.

Praying

Send us out
in the power of your Spirit
to live and work
to your praise and glory.

Activities

On the sheet there are village doors to cut open. Like the pairs of disciples, they can knock at all the doors to tell the people of God's love for them, and some will open while others remain shut. They are also helped to remember the instructions Jesus gave to the disciples as they set out.

GOLD PANNERS

Aim: To look at why speaking out God's truth is often dangerous.

Starter

Tie a length of string across the room at just above head height and provide two different coloured balloons. Split the group either side of the string, each with a balloon. Both sides aim to get their balloon to touch the floor on the other side, while preventing the other balloon from coming to land on their own side.

Teaching

Draw attention to the way we all did our best to hit that approaching balloon back where it came from. We do just the same in arguments. If someone says something about us that we don't want to hear, we hit it back as fast as we can. Today we are reading about the way prophets are treated when they go on speaking out God's words which people don't want to hear.

Read the Amos passage, noticing in both how faithfulness to God is despised and rejected. Then read today's Gospel, where Jesus tells his disciples that people may not want to listen to them. Suppose instead of shutting their ears to what the disciples had to say, they did listen. What might happen?

When we shut our ears to hearing what God wants us to know, we shut out all kinds of possible good in our lives, and open up all kinds of possibilities of evil.

If you have time, look at Ephesians 1:3-14. It is Christ's life in us, and the forgiveness of our sins that makes it possible for us to live God's way – we can't do it on our own without his grace. Also it's important that they understand God's love for us doesn't depend on how well we behave. Getting our lives upright in God's sight is our response to the love God lavishes on us, not the way to earn his love.

Praying

Refiner's fire,
my heart's one desire is to be holy,
set apart for you, Lord.
I choose to be holy,
set apart for you, my Master,
ready to do your will.

(Taken from the song *Purify my heart* by Brian Doerksen © 1990 Mercy/Vineyard Publishing/Music Services/CopyCare)

Activities

On the sheet there are some quotations from people imprisoned for continuing to live God's way even when it is dangerous, and they are looking at what they can do to support those in prison at the moment for their faith, or other Christians locally who could do with some encouragement.

SIXTEENTH SUNDAY OF THE YEAR

Thought for the day

Like a good shepherd, Jesus sees the needs of his people and always responds with love.

Reflection on the readings

Jeremiah 23:1-6
Psalm 22
Ephesians 2:13-18
Mark 6:30-34

The reading from Jeremiah shows God lamenting the destructive effect of bad leadership of his chosen people. As he sees them scattering in all directions, confused and undisciplined, the promise is made of the plan to draw them back under wholesome leadership, into the peace and settled spirit of God's charge.

In today's section of the letter to the Christians in Ephesus, Paul sets out the important aspect of Jesus' leadership: the breaking down of barriers between people, and the drawing together of those from different traditions and backgrounds into unity through the Christ.

Then in the Gospel we find Jesus doing just that, his heart of God aching to see the vulnerability of the crowds. In Jesus the image of the good shepherd king becomes a practical reality, and the people sense it, watching his every move, racing ahead of the boat to be at the other side of the lake when he arrives, ceaselessly demanding as they recognise their need of healing at all levels. They gravitate to the one whose words and works make contact with their deep, unconscious drive to be at one with the living God.

How does the humanness of Jesus cope with such overwhelming demands? Loving with God's love makes him responsive without reserve, and he is never recorded in the Gospels as turning anyone away. However, he is obviously aware of his human need for rest and refreshment, and we do pick up on the weariness and exhaustion of ministry on such a scale. His early morning walks into the hills for solitary prayer are vital to him, and there is evidence that part of his leadership responsibility was aiming to provide periods of rest and retreat for his close disciples and himself. Presumably there were at least some occasions when they managed these oases of quiet, without the crowds catching up with them!

All this enables us to look at the question of demands in ministry, and the provision we make for our own leaders' spiritual refreshment and quiet reflection. We need to look both at the extent of our willingness to put ourselves out for others, and also at the dangers of overworking with insufficient support or rest. We are challenged to see the way crowds naturally flock to where they sense God being proclaimed in the person of Jesus, and check that visitors to our churches are enabled to meet with the living Christ there.

Discussion starters

1. Jesus tried to ensure that his disciples had times of rest and spiritual refreshment. Do we follow that example in our church community?

2. Why were the crowds going out of their way to flock to Jesus?

All-stage talk

Bring along a crowded diary or calendar, and other gadgets for coping with busy lifestyles, such as a computerised notebook, a laptop, mobile phone, alarm clock or fax message.

Ask a few children to walk up and down pretending to be talking on their mobiles or driving their cars, while you talk about the way we can now continue our office work walking along the High Street or on the train. We can send messages by e-mail or fax so that they get there almost immediately. All this enables us to spend more and more of our time being fully at work if we happen to have a job, with increasing pressure and decreasing space in our lives. People have either far too much work than is healthy or none at all, and leisure activities often have to slot in some frantic physical activity to compensate for all the physically inactive work of brain and adrenaline. Advertisements shout at us to buy this, choose that, look like them; the newspapers and magazines advise us what to think and how to behave, and often we believe their lies. We are like a scattered flock of sheep racing in different directions, without knowing where we are or where we are going.

(Stop the children and have them sit down very still wherever they are.)

Today we heard in the Gospel about Jesus' busy ministry of teaching and healing, listening and encouraging. When he and his disciples had been hard at work for days, and were really tired and drained, they'd get into a boat to sail across the lake for a bit of peace and quiet – only to find all the crowds had run round the edge of the lake and were already there waiting for them! Jesus didn't send them away and tell them what the office hours were, or put them on hold. He didn't ask Peter to change course and sail off somewhere else instead.

Instead, Jesus saw the lost and struggling lives, the need for reassurance and practical, wise teaching, the longing for healing and wholeness, and the hearts attracted to God but needing help to find him. And seeing all that, he loved them, with the deep affection of God's love; he climbed wearily out of the boat and fed them with the teaching and comforting they so badly needed. From stories like this of Jesus' ministry we know with certainty that God never ever turns any of us away. None of our needs or wounds or sorrows are hidden from him. Whenever we run around the lake to be there waiting for him, he will step on to our beach and minister to us, because he loves us. Like a good shepherd he is concerned for our well-being and leads us carefully and safely through time into the eternity of heaven.

All-age ideas

- Have a time of peace and reflection after the talk, where people can simply be still and settle themselves in God's loving company. Music is helpful at such times – possibly the music group singing *Be still, for the presence of the Lord*, or a recording of Beethoven's *Pastoral Symphony* (No. 6) – the song of thanksgiving after the storm, for instance.

- Consider a parish away-day for some relaxation and spiritual refreshment together.

Prayer of the Faithful

Celebrant
Knowing God's love and concern for us all,
let us settle ourselves in his presence
and pray to him now.

Reader
Recognising the brokenness and disunity
of Christ's Church,
we pray that he may draw us closer to one another
as we draw closer to him;
we pray for all our Christian brothers and sisters
in this neighbourhood,
and for all who are searching
for meaning in their lives.

Silence

The Lord is my shepherd:
there is nothing I shall want.

With the noise of global conflicts
and human deprivation
thundering in our ears,
with the questions and doubts clamouring,
we pray that the Lord may shepherd our humanness
and lead us in the secret places of the heart.

Silence

The Lord is my shepherd:
there is nothing I shall want.

With the statistics of family life
challenging our values,
and with the pressures to conform to norms
in conflict with God's will,
we pray for a sound and centred wisdom
in all our daily living and life choices.

Silence

The Lord is my shepherd:
there is nothing I shall want.

With the stressed and overburdened,
the overworked and the unemployed,
we pray for balanced lives;
for physical, mental and spiritual health;
for patience in times of trouble,
and direction in times of confusion.

Silence

The Lord is my shepherd:
there is nothing I shall want.

As we remember with love and gratitude
the lives of those who have died in faith,
we commend them to eternal rest in the Lord
and his unchanging affection.

Silence

The Lord is my shepherd:
there is nothing I shall want.

We pray with Mary,
whose Son became our Good Shepherd:
Hail, Mary . . .

God our Father loves us;
in this silence
we name our particular petitions.

Silence

Celebrant
Father, in the sure knowledge
of your promise to answer the prayers
of all who are faithful,
we offer you our cares and concerns,
through Jesus Christ.
Amen.

TREASURE SEEKERS

Aim: To know that Jesus likes them, enjoys their company and knows their needs.

Starter

Have a selection of toys and construction bricks (or boxes) to play with, and enjoy a time of playing together or alongside each other, while quiet music is playing.

Teaching

Talk about how lovely it is to enjoy time playing together, knowing we are safe and in God's good care. We didn't have to talk to each other – it was nice just to be there in the Treasure Seekers group.

God enjoys spending time with us. It makes him really happy when we want to be in his company, when we chat to him about our ideas and when we sing our songs of praise to him. (You could sing one now.)

Talk about how our mums and dads often seem to know when we're feeling a bit sad, when we're thirsty, or when we are frightened. That's because they love us. God loves all of us, and so he knows all about the times we feel happy and sad, excited or frightened. He is like a good, kind, strong shepherd and we are like his lambs and sheep.

Praying

Sing this to the tune in the song of thanksgiving after the storm from Beethoven's *Pastoral Symphony*. (The melody line for this may be found on page 236.)

Jesus, you love me,
you love me very much;
I love you, Jesus,
I love you very much!
Amen.

Activities

On the sheet there is a picture of Jesus with space for the children to draw in themselves, playing in Jesus' company. There are also pictures of different times of day with speech bubbles of prayers the children are chatting to God. These can be cut out and hung on lengths of wool ready to be put up all over the place at home.

PEARL DIVERS

Aim: To know what a typical day in Jesus' ministry would have been like.

Starter

Have a clock face and arrange with the children that when it says 7 o'clock it's time to get up, 9 o'clock it's working time at school, 12 o'clock it's lunchtime, 4 o'clock is watching television, and at midnight everyone is fast asleep. When the clock time is displayed and called out, they do the appropriate actions.

Teaching

Beforehand prepare a blue sheet to look like a motorway sign for services, based on the picture below.

You will also need a 30 mph sign and a sign for a carpenter's shop, together with a few wood-working tools and bits of wood, and a pair of sandals.

Begin by sharing a couple of different typical days from the group, one child and one adult, starting at waking-up time and going through to bedtime. Today we are going to take a look at a typical day in the life of Jesus during the years of his ministry.

Jesus grew up helping Joseph in the carpentry business the family owned. (Place down the carpenter's sign, the wood and the tools.) When he was grown-up he carried on working as a carpenter, sawing wood, hammering in nails, measuring, sanding down and polishing. During this time he lived at home, probably eating with the rest of his family in the evening after work.

When he reached the age of thirty (place down the 30 mph sign) things changed. Jesus stopped being a carpenter (pack the tools and wood away) and started the work God needed him to do among the people. Instead of living at home and being sure of a bed to sleep on and food to eat, Jesus set out walking around the country (place down the sandals), staying with friends, or sleeping rough.

(Now refer to the service station sign.) Jesus ate and drank wherever he and his disciples were invited, and whatever they were given. Sometimes this would be grand parties at the houses of rich, important people, sometimes they might be crowded into poor people's homes, laughing and talking late into the night, and sometimes they might go hungry. Sometimes they would stay for a few days or a few weeks with people, and sometimes there wouldn't be any shelter provided. Jesus once said, 'Foxes have holes and the birds have their nests but the Son of Man has nowhere to lay his head.' They never knew for certain in the morning where they might be that evening as Jesus just went where he sensed God wanted him to go. For transport they used feet, walking along the roads and tracks between the towns and villages.

So what was the work Jesus was doing for these two or three years? There were people who needed healing and comforting, forgiving and setting free from evil spirits. There were people living in the darkness of evil who needed to have God's light brought into their lives. There was lots to tell people about God so they understood how lovely he was, and there was the work of helping people learn to love one another and help one another. All of this was like the job of a shepherd – caring for the people and guiding them wisely.

And if we had lived in one of the towns or villages around the lake of Galilee at that time – nearly two thousand years ago, we'd have met Jesus; perhaps he would have eaten with us, or stayed at our house, or healed one of our friends, or played with us.

Praying

Be with us in the morning –
from the first yawn to the coco pops.
Be with us in school –
from 2+2 till the last full stop.
Be with us in the evening –
from the children's programmes till bedtime.
Be with us while we sleep –
from starlight to the new day's dawn.
Amen.

Activities

The children can make a day-round prayer with their usual day on one side, and a day in Jesus' ministry on the other. They will each need a paper fastener, and some thin card for strengthening the circles.

GOLD PANNERS

Aim: To see how Jesus' ministry as leader and shepherd fulfilled the prophecies.

Starter

What's my line? Take it in turns to mime a job while the others try to work out what job it is.

Teaching

Begin by reading what God thought of the job being done by the leaders of his people during the time of Jeremiah, not long before they were taken off into Babylon as exiles. On the sheet there is space to jot down the reasons why God is going to punish these irresponsible leaders. Also draw attention to the love God has for his people as he talks of a future leader who will take proper care of them. That would be quite a job, and only one person could do it.

Look next at the Gospel to see Jesus in action, and the passage from Ephesians. Jot down what everyone notices about his ministry, as if you are compiling a job description. (For example: on call 24 hours a day; no guaranteed regular holiday.

Accommodation and food variable according to availability and others' hospitality; salary £00.00. Highly demanding but highly rewarding work.)

Praying

The Lord is my shepherd,
I have everything I need.
He gives me rest in green pastures.
He leads me to calm water.
He gives me new strength.
True to his name
he leads me on paths that are right.

(From Psalm 22)

Activities

There is space on the sheet to record the needs of God's people, suffering under bad leaders, and the practical loving shepherding that Jesus provides, reflecting the Father's love. They are encouraged to imagine what such a ministry would feel like as a disciple, as Jesus himself, and as someone among the crowds.

SEVENTEENTH SUNDAY OF THE YEAR

Thought for the day

Out of God's riches, a great crowd is fed and satisfied from a small offering of food.

Reflection on the readings

2 Kings 4:42-44
Psalm 144
Ephesians 4:1-6
John 6:1-15

Great evil and great good do not simply happen out of the blue; both begin in small, barely noticed incidents, whose significance only becomes apparent once the evil or goodness has snowballed. Huge international conflicts can be traced back to a number of small-scale wrongs or misguided attitudes, or an early absence of real communication. Thankfully the same is true of goodness, and today we are celebrating the way that small acts of generosity and love can be blessed and transformed for great, widespread good. It is like watching a parable of the growth of the kingdom of heaven in action.

First we read about the distribution of twenty barley loaves among a hundred people – a combination of one man's generosity and Elisha's close and faithful relationship with God – so close that he can discern God's will and acts obediently. As a result, many more people are blessed by the original gift than could have been imagined.

The reading from Ephesians reinforces this lavish nature of God's provision. Paul knows from experience that with his power working in us God can do so much more than anything we can ask or imagine, and Paul longs for his readers to take this on board so that they too can live in the fulfilment of God's faithful promises.

In today's Gospel one boy's offer of lunch is accepted with thanks, blessed and used so that thousands are fed. It is always a temptation to look at huge needs and dismiss what we are able to do as being pathetically inadequate so that we end up being too discouraged even to use what we do have. The work of Mother Theresa was sometimes dismissed as being too little to make any difference, but, as far as she was concerned, every little act of loving kindness was something beautiful for God, and infinitely worth doing. That 'little' has been so greatly blessed and brought hope and joy to so many all over the world.

Each of us has a lifetime's worth of moments to offer, each very small but each there to give. Anything that we offer for God to use, however small or insignificant it may seem to be, is gathered up, blessed and redistributed for blessing beyond our imagining.

Discussion starters

1. When faced with our next problem which looks insurmountable, how can today's Gospel help us do things God's way?

2. Why do you think John mentions that the feeding of the five thousand takes place at the time of the Jewish Passover? What other meal would Jesus preside over at Passover?

All-stage talk

If you have an ancient building you can direct people to look at how steps or pews are worn away by generations of people simply walking on the step or holding the end of the pew. Or you could show a well-used copy of a Bible, worn out and falling apart just by being handled and read every day. (It is said that Bibles which are falling apart are read by people who are not.) You could show an old and well-loved teddy, threadbare through daily loving.

Each step, each picking up of a book, each cuddling of a bear is in itself only a slight action which we can't imagine would do much. But day by day, over the years, the effect of all those little actions starts to show quite dramatically. Little actions turn out to be very important. Even a smile can spread wider than we might think. There's an old children's poem about that:

> Smile awhile, and when you smile
> another smiles, and soon
> there's miles and miles of smiles
> and life's worthwhile
> because you smile!

Today we heard about one boy and his packed lunch. What was the point of him offering that when there were so many thousands of people to feed? Perhaps we think he might as well have just eaten it himself! But look at what happened when, instead of that, the boy wanted to offer what he had to share. Jesus used it. He blessed the gift that was offered and then all the people were fed, with some left over.

Those who have been God's friends for a long time will have noticed that God is very good at giving us more than we asked for, and giving in ways we hadn't thought of! But he does need us to offer what we have, whether that's time, money or talents and skills. Basically what we have to offer is ourselves. And when we do that, God can use the rest of our life here in ways we haven't even thought of, blessing people who perhaps we haven't even met yet, and may not meet till heaven. If we offer ourselves at the start of every day, then every day can be used for some wonderful good that wouldn't otherwise happen.

All-age ideas

- Have written on the day's handout, or displayed on a board or OHP, the words from John 6:14 – 'This must be the Prophet who's to come into the world!' Ask everyone to turn to those round them when you get to that section of the Gospel and whisper these words to one another a few times, getting louder each time.

- Have a flower arrangement incorporating a child's lunch box.

Prayer of the Faithful

Celebrant
Knowing that our loving God
supplies all our needs,
let us pray to him now
on behalf of the Church and the world.

Reader
We pray for the Church
with all its varied ministries;
for the youngest to the oldest baptised members;
for those of mellow faith
and those who struggle with doubts.

Silence

Loving Father:
give us today our daily bread.

We pray for the strength
of a new commitment within ourselves
to pray the news each day
and share the pain we read about,
longing for peace and justice
in a world tense with aggression
and distorted with selfishness.

Silence

Loving Father:
give us today our daily bread.

We pray that the Lord may work in,
and transform, our homes and our relationships.
In all our meetings and conflicts
and all differences of opinion
may we work to the glory of God.

Silence

Loving Father:
give us today our daily bread.

We pray for all who suffer
or are heavily burdened;
we pray for their comfort and refreshment,
wholeness and restoration,
but above all for the consciousness
of Christ's presence in their pain,
and his love for them.

Silence

Loving Father:
give us today our daily bread.

We pray for the faithful souls
entering by the gate of physical death
that they may have eternal life.

Silence

Loving Father:
give us today our daily bread.

We make our prayer with Mary,
who fed and clothed her precious Son:
Hail, Mary . . .

As God our Father listens with love,
we name those we know
who are in any particular need.

Silence

Celebrant
Father, your generosity draws us
to love more deeply;
hear us as we pray,
and use us in fulfilling our prayers.
We pray through Jesus Christ.
Amen.

TREASURE SEEKERS

Aim: To know the story of the feeding of the crowd of people.

Starter

Prepare enough different coloured paper shapes for each child in the group to have one of each. There need to be as many different categories as there are children. Give each child a pile of a particular coloured shape so that everyone has a pile. (They can set up their own 'base', or have their shapes in a yoghurt pot.) All the children go round sharing the shapes out until they end up with a pile of different ones. These are arranged into a pattern on the floor in front of them.

Teaching

Admire everyone's patterns and talk about how we have all been sharing what we were given so that we could all make our lovely pictures. Today we are going to hear about a child who offered to share his lunch with Jesus.

Spread out a sheet or bath towel on the floor and sit around it. Place on it some blue material or paper to be a lake, and stand a few plants in pots around as bushes and trees. Place a model boat on the lake. Talk about the landscape you are making as you add the items, and let the children help.

One day Jesus and his friends went over the lake in a boat. All the crowds of people walked round the side of the lake (everyone finger walks), so they could be there when the boat arrived. Jesus climbed out of the boat and taught the people, telling them stories to help them understand how much God loved them.

Soon they were all very hungry, but they were a long way from their homes. One boy had some packed lunch with him. (Produce a packed lunch box.) He could have just sat and eaten it, but he knew the others were hungry too, and he heard Jesus talking to his friends about how to feed all these people.

So he went up to Andrew, one of Jesus' friends.

'Excuse me,' he said, 'but is this any use? There's five barley loaves and two small fish.'

Andrew took the boy and his lunch to Jesus, and Jesus looked very happy and thanked the boy very much for offering to share his food. 'Because you've been so kind, you've given enough here for everyone!' Jesus whispered to the boy. 'Watch carefully!'

Everyone sat down on the grass and Jesus gave thanks for the little lunch; he thanked God for providing enough for everyone, but the boy couldn't think how there would be enough. Jesus started breaking up the bread and the fish, and his friends kept taking it to the groups of people. Somehow the food went on and on, until everyone had eaten as much as they needed. And there was even some left over!

Praying

(This can be prayed before we eat.)

Thank you, God, for food we eat,
that keeps us strong and healthy.
Amen.

Activities

The Treasure Seekers are going to make sandwiches, which can be cut up and shared with the rest of the congregation. If you want to be authentic you can have tuna or sardine sandwiches, but other fillings would be fine! On the sheet there is also a dot-to-dot picture of the boy's lunch, and a map for them to walk round with their fingers.

PEARL DIVERS

Aim: To look at the meaning of the feeding of the five thousand.

Starter

Teach the children the song *5000+ hungry folk* with actions as shown below.

5 0 0 0+ hungry folk,
(five fingers on one hand, make ring with other hand which is shown three times, then rub tummies)
came 4 2 listen 2 Jesus. *(cup hand to ear)*

The 6 x 2 said O O O,
(use fingers for each number and for the O)
where can we get some food from?
(shrug shoulders and open hands, moving head from side to side)
Just 1 had 1 2 3 4 5, *(use fingers)*
loaves and 1 2 fishes. *(count with fingers)*
When Jesus blessed the 5 + 2
(hands face down as if blessing; count with fingers)
they were increased many x over.
(roly-poly with hands going upwards)
5 0 0 0+ 8 it up, *(use fingers, then pretend to eat)*
with 1 2 3 4 5 6 7 8 9 10 11 12 basketfuls left over.
(count on fingers and stamp each foot for 11 and 12)

(Ian Smale
© Copyright 1985 Kingsway's Thankyou Music)

Teaching

Beforehand prepare some pieces of card or paper with questions on one side and the Bible references on the other. Arrange them question side up over a picture of the feeding of the crowd, based on the drawing below.

Here are the questions and references for finding the answers:

1. What lake did Jesus sail over? John 6:1

2. What time of year was it? John 6:4

3. What did Jesus say to Philip? John 6:5

4. What did Philip reply? John 6:7

5. What food did the boy offer? John 6:9

6. What did Jesus tell the people to do? John 6:10

7. How many people were there? John 6:10

8. What two things did Jesus do with the food? John 6:11

9. What happened to the food left over? John 6:12-13

10. What did this miracle make the people want to do? John 6:15

Give out Bibles and help everyone to find John chapter 6. Then as each question is asked, the children can tell the story, checking with the Bible as they go. As each question is answered, take it off the picture and lay it at the side, until you are left with the whole picture and the whole story revealed.

Praying

Loving Father,
thank you for feeding us
with food for our bodies and our souls,
making us strong
so we can live good, loving lives.
Amen.

Activities

On the sheet there is a coded message to crack, and the link is made with another time Jesus broke bread at the Passover, so they can see how that bread goes on being broken to feed Christians in every generation all over the world.

GOLD PANNERS

Aim: To see how this feeding prefigures the feeding of the Last Supper and the Eucharist.

Starter

Bring a selection of breads from different parts of the world, together with an atlas or world map. Find where each bread comes from and sample it. All over the world bread of some kind is basic food.

Teaching

Begin by reading the passage from 2 Kings, where Elisha feeds a hundred people with a gift of bread. Notice the generosity (in offering the bread) and Elisha's careful listening to God's will, and his wholehearted obedience to it.

Now look at the feeding of the five thousand in John's Gospel. Draw attention to the timing – it's about Passover time. (Another meal, just before the escape from slavery.) Look at what Jesus does with the food – he accepts the gift, gives thanks to God for it, breaks it in pieces and gives it out to the people to feed them when they are hungry.

Link this with what Jesus started at the Passover meal he shared with his disciples before his death, and which goes on happening in all our churches right through the centuries and the generations, all over the world. That is quite a crowd being fed! And we are part of that same blessing, breaking and giving out which has been going on for about two thousand years. It's a record-breaking meal.

Praying

(From Ephesians 3, a prayer to pray for each other)

I pray that Christ will live in your hearts
because of your faith.
I pray that your life will be strong in love
and built on love.
And I pray that you and all God's holy people
will have the power to understand
the greatness of Christ's love –
how wide and high, long and deep that love is.

Activities

On the sheet there are pictures of Christians from different times in history and different countries, all taking part in God's feeding programme. The actions of Jesus are linked with what happens in church at the Eucharist.

EIGHTEENTH SUNDAY OF THE YEAR

Thought for the day

Jesus is the Bread of Life who satisfies our hunger and sustains us on our journey to heaven.

Reflection on the readings

Exodus 16:2-4, 12-15
Psalm 77
Ephesians 4:17, 20-24
John 6:24-35

In our Exodus reading the people were finding their hunger dampening their pioneering spirit considerably, and the provision of quails and manna saved the day, as well as proclaiming God's care for his people.

Most of us start getting irritable and short-tempered when our bodies need food. Complicated or demanding decisions are always best left till after a meal, rather than trying to rush into them when we return home weary and hungry, and in mountain-climbing the hot drinks and food are first on the agenda when setting up camp at the end of the day. We are all deeply affected by the appalling sight of real hunger and starvation. Since we all have bodies which run on the fuel of food, we all instinctively know the importance of feeding, right from screaming our hunger at birth. Food is simply a matter of life and death.

This makes it an ideal image for describing how important Jesus is to us. When he says, 'I am the Bread of Life', we understand the life and death nature of the relationship; it implies that Jesus brings us life, and without him we die. That is why it is linked with the Resurrection – the risen nature of Christ. All we are to do is believe in Jesus and we will be taken with him through death into the fullness of life with God for ever. Believing is attaching ourselves to him so that wherever Jesus goes we end up being taken as well.

What saddened Jesus in today's Gospel was that the people were there clinging to his every move, but for the wrong reasons. They were there for what they got out of it – in their case, being fed with bread and fish. We can sometimes get into the same 'craving rather than believing' mode if we are locked into receiving the spiritual or sacramental gifts for ourselves because they make us feel good. Jesus is not a restaurant where we indulge ourselves and eventually roll out home to bed; he is the Bread of Life, and supplies us with the food we need in order to live out his risen life among the people we are led to.

In Ephesians we are given an inspiring picture of such a life worked out in practical terms, enabled through our spiritual feeding to be built up in a co-ordinated body, displaying the characteristics of God's loving and humility.

Discussion starters

1. Do we realise our need of Jesus' feeding, or think of it more as an optional extra?

2. How can our God-given work in life just be to believe in Jesus? (What difference does that belief make to everything else we do?)

All-stage talk

Ask who had a meal yesterday, and express surprise that they are thinking of having another meal today – some have already eaten today and are still planning to eat lunch! They can explain to you that our bodies need food every day for them to stay strong and healthy, and for the children to grow. We run on food like a car runs on petrol.

Remind everyone of how Jesus had fed all those people with enough bread and fish, and they had all enjoyed their meal. Now they are all running after Jesus the next day as well. Some of them want to hear what Jesus says, some want to come and be healed, some want to come because it's exciting going where everyone else is going and they don't want to miss out on anything. And lots are going because they remember those nice tuna sandwiches – the meal they ate with Jesus.

Why does Jesus want them to have come? Collect various ideas, and draw out that Jesus wants them to be there because they know they will meet with God if they're here with Jesus.

But Jesus knows all too well why some of them have really come, and he tells them so – 'You're looking for me because you ate the bread and were satisfied.'

And then he helps them to understand how God feeds us not just with bread for our bodies, while we live on this earth for seventy years or so, but in another way as well. He gives us spiritual food which keeps us alive through this life and right on into life beyond physical death. With that feeding we won't be finishing as soon as we die, but going on living for ever.

The people thought that sounded pretty good bread to have, and asked Jesus if he would give them some, so they could be fed spiritually as well as physically. And Jesus told them, 'I am the Bread of Life!' So it's Jesus himself who we feed on.

What does that mean? Obviously we're not like cannibals, eating Jesus up – he didn't mean that. But if we think how satisfied we feel when we have been very hungry and then eat a good meal, that's how our spirits feel when we spend time with Jesus and receive him in the Eucharist – contented and satisfied, happy and full of energy and health. And just as we need to keep eating ordinary food every day, so we need to keep spending time with Jesus every day, so that, spiritually as well as physically, we will be growing strong and healthy, and we'll stay that way even when our physical bodies get old and weak, and when they stop working so that we die. Even then we'll be spiritually bounding with life and energy, ready to spend eternity alive in God's company.

All-age ideas

- Have wheat and bread as the focus of one of the flower arrangements today.

- Have the words of the Gospel written out in full, with the people's words in bold, and the priest or deacon reading the words of Jesus, so that the Gospel becomes a lively teaching conversation.

Prayer of the Faithful

Celebrant
Let us pray to the God who loves us,
knows our needs, and provides for us.

Reader
As the travelling people of God,
we pray for a deepening hunger
for the things of God
and a loosening of our grip
on all the wants and expectations
which prevent us from moving forward God's way.

Silence

Feed us, Father:
with the Bread of Life.

As brothers and sisters with the whole of creation,
we pray for respect and reverence among people
regardless of wealth or status;
for responsible sharing of resources
and consideration for the natural world
of our fragile and beautiful planet.

Silence

Feed us, Father:
with the Bread of Life.

As we prepare and eat our food each day,
we pray for those who grow and manufacture it,
distribute and sell it, shop for it and cook it,
and for those with whom we share food.
May we all be built up with the spiritual feeding
which sustains us for ever.

Silence

Feed us, Father:
with the Bread of Life.

As we ask for daily bread,
we pray for those who are physically starving,
for all who hunger emotionally
or try to survive on spiritual junk food;
for those who mistrust God's feeding.

Silence

Feed us, Father:
with the Bread of Life.

As we remember with love
those who have journeyed through physical death,
we pray that, nourished by the Bread of Life,
they may travel on eagles' wings
into the brightness of eternal life.

Silence

Feed us, Father:
with the Bread of Life.

We pray now with Mary,
who so tenderly nurtured her holy child:
Hail, Mary . . .

Meeting our heavenly Father
in the stillness of silence,
let us bring to him
our own particular cares and concerns.

Silence

Celebrant
Father, we can never thank you enough
for what you have done for us,
and for the way you are transforming our lives;
with grateful hearts we offer you these prayers,
through Jesus Christ.
Amen.

TREASURE SEEKERS

Aim: To know that God gave the people of Israel food in the desert.

Starter

Manna? – What is it? Teach the children some Hebrew – that 'manna?' means 'what is it?' and then show them some items, mostly hidden in a bag or by a cloth. As you draw out a bit of a teddy, a jumper or an orange, you say to them, 'Manna?' so they can give the answer – 'It's a teddy!' Then a child can be the person who asks, 'Manna?'

Teaching

Remind the children, using a Moses basket, a crown, a whip of plaited string and a piece of blue cloth, that Moses was the baby who had been put in a basket and floated down the river to keep him safe when all God's people were slaves in Egypt. He was brought up by Pharaoh's daughter in the palace. When he grew up he had seen how his own people were badly treated as slaves. God used Moses to lead his people out of slavery. They had crossed through the middle of the Red Sea on dry land and now they were travelling in the desert, with Moses leading them.

And they got very hungry, so they all started grumbling. (Perhaps they start grumbling when they're hungry as well.) They said, 'It's not fair, Moses! If we were back in Egypt we could be eating nice stews and casseroles.' And they all got very grouchy with Moses.

Moses went off to talk with God about it. 'Lord, they're all moaning and grumbling about not having any food to eat,' he said. 'What should I do?'

God told Moses to let the people know that God knew they needed food and would be getting them some, so the people waited to see what would happen. That evening a flock of quails flew over. Some of the birds couldn't manage to fly any further, and they fell down dead on the ground. So the people picked them up and made a kind of chicken stew with them, and everybody enjoyed it very much.

Next morning there were white flakes all over the ground (scatter some pieces of white paper all over the floor). The people didn't know what it was, so they said to Moses, 'Manna? Manna?' And Moses said, 'This is the food God promised you!' So all the people took bowls (give out little pots) and gathered the white flakes. (The children go and gather it up in their bowls. When they've finished, they sit down again in the story circle.) Explain that our white flakes are just pieces of paper, but the flakes the people gathered up were food which tasted sweet – a bit like honey. And because no one knew what it was really called, they all called it 'manna'.

Praying

Thank you, God,
for giving us food each day.
Thank you for the farmers who grew it,
the shops that sell it,
and the people who cook it for us!
Amen.

Activities

Using a paper plate the children can make a plate of their favourite food out of playdough. Prepare some brown, green, yellow, red and white – most food can be made from roughly those colours! On the sheet there is a place mat to make for them to use at home. (There is a recipe for playdough on page 109.)

PEARL DIVERS

Aim: To look at what it means for Jesus to be the Bread of Life.

Starter

Beforehand draw pictures of several different meals (or cut pictures from magazines). Cut these into wedge-shaped servings and scatter them all around the room. The children find the separate pieces and put them together so they end up with complete meals.

Teaching

Look at the different kinds of meals we have made, and at the variety we like to eat during the week and during each day. If we put all the things we ate in a week together, it would be quite a lot, and even though we feel nice and satisfied just after we've eaten breakfast, we're still looking forward to lunch by the end of the morning and tea by the evening.

God has provided us with a rich planet to live on which has plenty of food for us to eat – there's enough for everyone if only we were better at sharing. We use the fruits, roots and vegetables that grow in it, and the animals, birds and fish that live there. God has provided wonderfully for our bodies.

Remind the children of last week when Jesus fed that huge crowd of five thousand people with bread and fish. That was a different kind of feeding in a way, because Jesus was looking after them spiritually as well as physically. The next day after that the people went out searching for Jesus again. They had been very impressed by all that bread and fish and they were hoping for some more.

But Jesus said, 'Don't just run after the kind of food that satisfies the body. The body won't last for ever – some time it will die. A much better idea is to run after the kind of bread which will feed you spiritually, so that you'll stay spiritually alive and healthy, even after you're dead.'

So the people thought that sounded the best kind of bread, but they didn't know how to get hold of it. They'd never seen any in the baker's. They said to Jesus, 'Give us this kind of bread, sir. We'd like to live on that bread which gives life which lasts for ever.'

Then Jesus looked round at them and said, 'My Father has given you the true bread from heaven to give life to the world, and it's standing right here in front of you. It's me! I am the bread that gives you life!'

Jesus meant that just as ordinary bread is very good at satisfying us and keeping us physically alive and healthy, so Jesus himself is the one we need to believe in and be with for spiritual life which goes on whether we're still alive here or whether our bodies have worn out and died. In Jesus we can go on being very much alive for ever, just as Jesus is.

Praying

Jesus, I know that you were born as a baby,
lived and worked among us,
showing us God's love,
that you died on the cross and rose again to life.
I know you are alive for ever
and I want to stay close to you
right through this life
and on into heaven. Amen.

Activities

On the sheet there are different ways of 'feeding on Jesus, the Bread of Life' which the children can do. Help them to get around their Bibles so they know exactly where to find the Gospels – there are references of familiar events for them to practise looking them up. Some of the children may already have made their First Communion; for others this is something for the future.

GOLD PANNERS

Aim: To explore the significance of Jesus describing himself as the Bread of Life.

Starter

This person . . . Sit in a circle, and take it in turns to describe someone (who may be famous, or someone everyone knows), not by looks but by different things they do or have done. Whoever guesses the identity can have the next go.

Teaching

We managed to work out who those people were without knowing anything about their appearance. We know hardly anything about Jesus' appearance, but we can tell a great deal about him by what he said and did. Today we're going to look at one of the ways Jesus described himself.

Read today's Gospel, writing 'I am the Bread of Life' on a large sheet as it comes up. Talk about what Jesus might have meant by this. (Look at what bread does for our physical bodies and then look at how Jesus does this in a spiritual way, especially in the gift of Holy Communion – feeding, satisfying hunger, providing essentials for growth and health and energy, and so on.)

Now look back to the Exodus passage and Psalm 77, referred to in the Gospel, so that they can see the connection and the background to the way Jesus was thinking. Who did the people think had provided them with manna in the desert? (Look at Jesus' reply in John 6:32.) Remembering how the crowd had just recently been miraculously fed by Jesus, talk about what they might have meant in verse 30 of John 6. What does it mean to 'believe in the one God sent'? (Verse 29)

Point out that we all walk straight past things we're not prepared or expecting to see, and some of the people couldn't believe that Jesus could be anywhere near as holy as Moses, the holy figure from the past. They didn't realise that Moses had been pointing towards this moment, and that they happened to be alive at the very time God's Son came to the earth.

Finally look at Ephesians, where we are shown how this risen life, nourished by the Bread of Life, works out in practice. Notice anything they recognise from their own experience of Christians, and anything which they feel our own community is falling short on.

Praying

Lord Jesus Christ,
I would come to you,
live my life for you,
Son of God.
All your commands I know are true,
your many gifts will make me new,
into my life your power breaks through,
living Lord.

(Taken from the song *Lord Jesus Christ* by Patrick Appleford © 1960 Josef Weinberger)

Activities

On the sheet today's teaching is reinforced with space to record the qualities of bread which help us understand about the nature of Jesus. They are also helped to see the links between God's feeding of his people in the desert and our feeding as a travelling people.

NINETEENTH SUNDAY OF THE YEAR

Thought for the day

Just as bread is the visible form of life-giving nourishment, so Jesus is the visible form of God's life-giving love.

Reflection on the readings

1 Kings 19:4-8
Psalm 33
Ephesians 4:30-5:2
John 6:41-51

There are times when we have something important which needs saying, but we know that it will be difficult to say without being misunderstood. Jesus knew that what he was saying would be hard for many to accept or understand, yet he also knew it had to be said. The problem is that, unlike young children, we all carry so much luggage and hurt from our past that our listening is impaired.

However good our hearing, we block out and distort whatever we are not wanting to receive, focus on the negatives and recycle explanations as ammunition.

Much of praying and spiritual growth is to do with learning to listen, deliberately putting down our preconceptions, pride and status, so that we are able to take in what God is whispering into the humility of our unladen hearts. And, sooner or later, that will always lead us to Jesus. Our Gospel today homes in on a listening crisis, where the preparatory work could all have been done, if those religious leaders had been practising their Godly listening. Had that been the case, they would have found themselves drawn, like the wise and elderly Simeon, to see what God had been preparing them for throughout their history: to recognise Jesus as the Bread from heaven – the visible expression of God's life and feeding.

In 1 Kings 19, Elijah is strengthened and refreshed on his journey to the mountain of God, and recognises that the baked loaf of bread and the jar of water are part of God's caring provision for him; even though he is emotionally drained and spiritually burnt out, he knows that it is God who is leading and feeding him. How wonderful it would have been if, on hearing those extraordinary words of Jesus – 'I am the bread that came down from heaven' – the religious leaders could have seen all the sense and truth of God's plan being worked out in front of their very eyes and in their hearing! But as it was, their habit of loaded listening prevented them from understanding.

The passage from Ephesians continues its practical advice to keep us open to God and able to listen with Godly understanding. There are marvellous hints like not letting the sun go down on our anger, and not letting the devil get even a toehold. There is much talk of shedding whatever prevents us from being built up in the life of Christ. The great news of hope which Jesus proclaims is that full life is possible as we recognise Jesus for who he is, and gladly receive his feeding.

Discussion starters

1. Are we aware of when we are listening to learn and understand, and when we are not? Do we really want to hear whatever God says to us?

2. Are we taking Jesus up on his offer of feeding, and relying on it for dear life, or do we tend to glance at the Bread of Life but commit ourselves to spiritual junk food – or spiritual starvation?

All-stage talk

Tell everyone that you are about to show them some vitamin B and some energy, some life-giving essence and some potential penicillin. Have a drum roll or dramatic chords on the organ as you whip out of a supermarket bag a loaf of bread.

But this is just an ordinary loaf of bread – how can something so natural and ordinary be all that clever, invisible, scientific stuff? Well, it is! If we were really hungry we could try it and find out how much better it made our bodies feel. (A hungry person can do this.) We eat our way through loaves and loaves of bread every day because we have found that it does us so much good and comes in a form we can easily take naturally – by eating!

So bread is the visible form of all kinds of goodness and life-giving nourishment. And when Jesus talked of himself being the Bread of Life, he was describing how he is the invisible God in visible form – in the familiar shape of a human being, who we can talk to, watch, touch and listen to.

So why couldn't the religious leaders understand? Why did they find it offensive that Jesus said this?

- Jesus seemed too normal and familiar – they knew him as their carpenter.

- They thought the Son of God should look greater than Moses.

- Their expectations blinded them to seeing the very person they had been waiting generations to meet, when he was standing there right in front of their eyes.

We too need to make sure we don't miss God in the ordinary. In fact, God made everything, so nothing is just ordinary, and God can speak to us through his creation, as long as we are ready to notice and listen. Here are some examples.

We often see heavy rain, but usually just moan about it spoiling our hair or stopping a match. Suppose we start actually looking at it and seeing there a picture of how generous and fulsome God is; so many individual droplets of rain – or petals in a tree full of blossom!

Or think of the wide night sky describing God's overarching love; the regular days, nights and seasons showing his faithfulness.

In a dog's dogginess and a young child's openness we can see God showing us the importance of being honestly ourselves; when we see weeds and wild flowers growing over a rubbish dump we see God telling us about redemption, and how everything can be made new and beautiful.

All we need to do is train our spiritual eyes to look, so that we don't miss out on anything God is wanting to say to us, even through the ordinary things.

All-age ideas

- Try this dance/mime of having our eyes and ears opened to notice God. Have a group (of mixed ages and genders) being very bustly and busy – perhaps miming the jobs they themselves do during the week. Walking around between them is someone who keeps tapping people on the arm to show them something, but they are just brushed aside, in a rather irritated way. Finally one person is alerted and shown a flower, so that they really look at it and then in wonder upwards, giving God thanks and praise. They too now wander around trying to alert others, until one by one they are all able to enjoy the world and recognise God's love in it. The mime ends with all raising their hands in worship and moving off back to their places, looking expectantly around them as they go.

- The Penitential Rite could be based on the reading from Ephesians:

Therefore each of you must put off falsehood and speak truthfully to his neighbour.

Lord, have mercy.
Lord, have mercy.

Do not let the sun go down
while you are still angry,
and do not give the devil a foothold.

Christ, have mercy.
Christ, have mercy.

Do not let any unwholesome talk
come out of your mouths,
but only what is helpful for building others up.

Lord, have mercy.
Lord, have mercy.

Prayer of the Faithful

Celebrant
Let us pray to our God
as we worship him in Spirit and in truth.

Reader
We pray for all who are commissioned and called
to work as leaders and prophets in the Church.
We pray for greater discernment
of the Lord's presence
and his will in our Christian communities,
and a clearing away of all that obscures our vision.

Silence

Heavenly Father, open our eyes:
to see your glory.

We pray against the cynicism
and complacency that deaden wonder.
In the ordinary things of life
may we detect love and wisdom;
through the everyday events
may we encounter Christ, walking alongside us.

Silence

Heavenly Father, open our eyes:
to see your glory.

We pray for breadwinners
and sandwich makers, and all food growers;
for the Spirit's presence in kitchens, dining rooms,
canteens, restaurants and bars;
wherever people gather to eat together.

Silence

Heavenly Father, open our eyes:
to see your glory.

We pray for those whose emotional damage
makes trusting and receiving
seem threatening and dangerous.
We pray for peace of mind for the anxious,
and hope for all who are close to despair.

Silence

Heavenly Father, open our eyes:
to see your glory.

We pray for those
who have reached the boundary of death,
that in faith they may journey through it
and out into the unconfined space
and joy of heaven.

Silence

Heavenly Father, open our eyes:
to see your glory.

We pray with Mary,
our spiritual Mother:
Hail, Mary . . .

Upheld by God's grace,
we pray now in silence
for any who specially need our prayer.

Silence

Celebrant
Father, we acknowledge
our total dependence on you,
and ask you to hear us as we pray,
through Jesus Christ.
Amen.

TREASURE SEEKERS

Aim: To see God in the ordinary.

Starter

Share some ordinary things and look at them carefully. For example, bring a rosehip, break it open and look at all the seeds inside, a peapod with its neatly arranged peas, a selection of bright colours in feathers, flowers, stones and shells. Look up at the huge sky and the clouds, or the rain or shadows. Feel some wool, our hair. Work out how many sunrises there have been since they were born.

Teaching

Everything that we know and make, here in our exciting and beautiful universe, comes from something God has made. If we look carefully we can see God's love all around us in the things he has made. Look at all the objects again, helping the children to see how the great big sky over all of us is like the great big love God has for all of us. In the rosehip and the peapod we can see the loving way that God is careful with all the little things as well as the huge things. Each tiny seed and pea, each tiny baby, young child and little old woman is important to God.

God's love shines in our lives and warms our hearts, just as the sun shines on our bodies and warms us. The rain shows us how God showers us with blessings and happiness, without checking up first on how good we have been. And just as the sun rises day after day after day, so God is faithful and reliable, and we know we can trust him.

Praying

Your love is deeper than the sea
and wider than the sky.
You shower us with love
like you shower us with your rain –
lots and lots and lots of it!
The warm sun is just like
the warmth of your love.
And day after day after day
you forgive us
again and again and again!
Amen.

Activities

Provide some tubes for the children to look down, so they can focus on signs of God's love. They can also look through a magnifying glass at various things. On the sheet there is a magnified butterfly wing to colour in (or use collage), and they are encouraged to be observant, both physically and spiritually, in the 'What can you see?' activity.

PEARL DIVERS

Aim: To look at how God leads and feeds us.

Starter

Have a variety of ordinary objects laid out. As you tell them a particular use, they choose which item is most suitable for the job. Ideas for objects: a toothbrush, an umbrella, an egg cup, a loaf of bread, a crayon and a washing-up bowl. The uses will be the obvious ones, but also include some for which no object is available, but for which one of the objects might possibly be pressed into use. For example, 'having a drink in' might be linked with the egg cup or the washing up-bowl, and 'writing a book' might use a crayon, though this wouldn't be terribly efficient.

Teaching

We don't always want the jobs we're given in life, because they're not always easy. Mostly, jobs we are given turn out to be a mixture of bits we enjoy very much and bits we'd rather not be doing, because they are difficult. A clown may enjoy doing silly things to make everyone laugh, but not enjoy getting all his make-up off before he goes to bed. A drummer in a group may love practising and performing, but hate having to get up really early to travel on to the next concert.

One of the questions humans often ask is this: 'Who am I and what am I here for?' (Have this written out clearly.) If toothbrushes and egg cups could ask that question it would be quite easy to answer – 'You're a toothbrush and you exist to brush teeth.'

As human beings we need to work together with God our Maker to answer that question, as God has plans for each of us, and work he hopes we will want to share with him during the time we are given to live on this earth.

Today we are going to look at one of God's friends from the Old Testament who wasn't finding life very easy, and was wondering what it was all about. (Spread out a large sheet or towel on the floor and tell the story with the help of cut-out pictures, based on those below.)

next time the Lord told him to eat and drink again, so that he'd have the energy for the journey God wanted him to make. Elijah sat up and ate and drank, and started to feel better. He knew God was calling him to walk to the holy mountain, and he knew that he could trust God to look after him, even through the very worst and most tiring times.

Many centuries later, Jesus talked of himself as being 'the Bread of Life'. Like Elijah, we may find that the life God calls us to is not always easy, and we will sometimes find it tiring and hard work. But God will always look after us through those times, leading us and also feeding us with whatever strength, energy and rest we need. If we keep our spiritual eyes and ears open, we will notice the way God looks after us, leads us and feeds us.

Praying

Lord God, what would you like me
to see and hear this week?
What would you like me to notice?
Keep my eyes open and my ears pinned back
so that I don't miss you speaking
through all the ordinary things of my life.
Amen.

Activities

On the sheet there are two 'noticing' activities, one looking out for particular things in the picture and the other noticing with the eye of faith how God's nature is shown in the natural world.

GOLD PANNERS

Aim: To explore ways in which we can read God's signs.

Starter

Use the road signs below and write up the 'spiritual' meanings separately. Fix them all around the walls. Send everyone round to match them up.

Elijah had been working hard telling people about God, and showing them how wonderful and powerful and real he is. That had got him on the wrong side of the wicked queen Jezebel, so Elijah had to run for his life and escape into the desert. He felt lonely, exhausted and depressed. He was also starving hungry and very thirsty. Elijah sat down under a bush and wanted to die, he felt so bad. 'I've had enough, Lord,' he prayed. 'Let me die. I'm no better than my ancestors!'

God felt very sorry for his friend Elijah. He knew the job he had given him to do was a hard one, and he understood why Elijah was feeling so fed-up with it all. But God knew that Elijah was still the one he wanted to speak his word to the people of Israel – what Elijah needed at the moment was a good night's sleep, some rest, something to eat and drink and a bit of peace and quiet. (There are times we all need that.)

So first of all God gave a lovely gift of sleep to Elijah. He slept and slept for hours, under the shade of a tree. Then God sent a messenger to give Elijah some food. When Elijah opened his eyes, there was a warm, freshly baked loaf of bread and a jar of clear water. That cheered Elijah up. He ate and drank and then lay down and went back to sleep again. He was *so* tired! When he woke up

Cast your cares
on the Lord.
(Psalm 55:22)

Come unto me all who
labour and are heavy
laden, and I will give
you rest.
(Matthew 11:28)

He will not suffer your
foot to be moved.
(Psalm 121:3)

He owns the cattle on a
thousand hills.
(Psalm 50:10)

He will direct your paths.
(Proverbs 3:6)

Small is the gate and
narrow the road that
leads to life.
(Matthew 7:13)

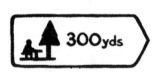

I am the bread of life.
(John 6:35)

Be self-controlled
and alert.
(1 Peter 5:8)

Life's an uphill struggle
without Jesus.

Teaching

Read the passage from 1 Kings 19, where Elijah is provided with the rest, food and drink he needs to continue in God's calling. Elijah is exhausted and depressed as he walks into the desert, and he recognises that God is providing for him in the shady tree, the much-needed sleep, the bread and the water. He understands these things as signs of God's love, because he is already used to being attentive to God and expecting God to communicate with him. Too often we don't notice God's care of us through the ordinary things of life, but actually every meal, every shower when we're hot and sticky, every clean bed we collapse into, every patch of shade . . . all of these ordinary, everyday things are signs to us of God's love for us, and we just take it all for granted, unless we've recently had to do without such luxuries! God's practical provision enables us to do the work he calls us into.

Jesus' commission is to be our Saviour, acting out God's total love in words and actions throughout his life. Sometimes this must have been uplifting and thrilling, as great crowds began to understand how God was reaching out to them. But at other times the message had to continue to be proclaimed in the face of hostility, as in today's Gospel. (Read that now.)

Jesus is claiming a very special relationship with God, which has been backed up by signs and miracles of many different kinds. The stage is set for the religious leaders to hail him as the true Messiah, for whom they have been waiting for generations, and towards whom Moses and the prophets had carefully directed their hearers and readers.

But the religious leaders cannot and do not read the signs.

Now read the passage from Ephesians, which gives some excellent advice for keeping ourselves ready to notice God's signs. It is all to do with regularly cleaning up after ourselves, recognising that we need to check our position and direction with God, several times in each day. Knowing God's love for us has the effect of making us actually want to keep coming back like this – we do it not out of fear or a burdensome duty, but out of love and gratitude, knowing that so much more of the positives can happen, and life feels right when we are right with God.

Praying

A man that looks on glass,
on it may stay his eye;
or, if he chooses, through it pass,
and thus the heavens espy.
Lord, in all the outward things,
let me see you and learn from you.
Amen.

Activities

On the sheet there are various signs to read, and they are encouraged to read the signs of the natural world which tell us of God's nature. They also look at some of the everyday signs of God's practical caring, linking Elijah's feeding with Jesus coming to us as 'Bread from heaven'.

TWENTIETH SUNDAY OF THE YEAR

Thought for the day

God's wisdom may appear foolishness without the God-given grace to understand.

Reflection on the readings

Proverbs 9:1-6
Psalm 33
Ephesians 5:15-20
John 6:51-58

In the passage from Proverbs the lady Wisdom calls out to those who recognise that they are simple, and want to increase their wisdom, which is in contrast to the lady Folly, who is encouraging people to drown out any higher calling and indulge their instincts and pleasure drives instead. Too late they will realise that her misleading call was to death, whereas Wisdom will lead her followers into a life of order and inner harmony.

In today's reading from Ephesians, too, we are advised to live wisely, making good use of every opportunity since the times are evil. The inference is that unless we are consciously walking positively in God's direction, we can so easily find ourselves sucked into the foolishness of living contrary to God's will for us. Wisdom is seen as living in inner peace and harmony with the God of our making.

If we are to get anywhere near such a state, we will need to walk expectantly and as disciples, rather than experts defending our position, and feeling offended every time we are tutored or instructed. In our Gospel for today, the religious leaders' status and learning was an enormous block to wisdom. They had too much to protect to risk walking in the nakedness of honesty.

We need to check any areas where we consider ourselves, or others consider us, experts or professionals, since these are precisely the areas where we shall find it hardest to place ourselves in the humility of discipleship.

It is hard for these learned religious teachers to understand his message, hung up as they are on precise detail instead of seeing the whole vision. They would hear Jesus' words not as a wonderful metaphor for God becoming one with his people through his Son, with all the wholesome nourishment and life-giving that the idea of bread contains; rather, they would hear it as a shocking blasphemy, with this wandering teacher aligning himself with the sacrificial Passover lamb and claiming to bring eternal freeing from sin. So they end up rejecting the fulfilment of the very idea they have studied and taught for years – that one day God will be 'with us' in person, and save us from our sin.

Discussion starters

1. What is the difference between being clever, learned and knowledgeable, and being wise?

2. Why do learned and clever people often find it harder to understand God's wisdom? Should this affect the way our children are 'taught'?

All-stage talk

Begin with the short quiz given in the All-age Ideas.

Are the people who knew the answers to our quiz necessarily the wisest people here? No. (Though of course they may be!) Real wisdom is different from knowing lots of facts. Remind everyone of the Brownie story about the wise owl. The children are sent to her because they want to find out who will be the little people who do secret good turns all around their house, and wise owl tells them to go to a pond in the woods and recite a poem. (Any Brownies, present and past, can join in the poem!)

Twist me and turn me and show me the elf;
I looked in the water and there saw . . . MYSELF!

The owl had been very wise because she had been able to help the children understand a deep kind of magic – whenever they did their good turns, they would be not just Imogen and Rebecca, but real Brownies! And they'd go on being Brownies whenever they did their good turns, long after they'd become Guides and grown up and had their own children who were learning the wisdom of the wise owl!

Wise people are good to go to when you want to talk things over, but you don't want to be told exactly what to do. Wise people are those who really listen to you – to how you are feeling inside as well as what you are saying. Wise people think carefully before they speak, and like learning from their mistakes.

We could say that WISDOM is all about
Walking In Simplicity Dreaming Of More
or we could say that to become WISE we need to
Wonder and ask questions
Imagine
Seek God
Expect to learn from him

All-age ideas

- Have lady Wisdom and lady Folly both calling out to invite people their way, as a group walks up and down deciding, one by one. Each lady has a big sign on a stick. On the front these say 'Wisdom' and 'Folly', and on the back there are pictures of a rising sun with rays of light, and a skull. As each person decides to go down one way or the other, the lady in the chosen place turns her notice around so that the person can't see it but the rest of the congregation can.

- The quiz:
  1. What is H_2O?
  2. How many legs does a spider have?
  3. What animal pretended to be Red Riding Hood's grandma?
  4. What is the current exchange rate for dollars?
  5. What do you call a cake made with eggs, flour and sugar but no fat?
  6. Who scored for Manchester United in their last match?
  7. What are nine sevens?
  8. What comes straight after a red light?
  9. What is another name for Rose of Sharon?
  10. How many balls in one over?

(Answers: 1. water; 2. 8; 3. wolf; 4. check in newspaper; 5. sponge; 6. check in newspaper; 7. 63; 8. red and amber; 9. St John's Wort/hypericum; 10. 6)

Prayer of the Faithful

Celebrant
As we gather, conscious of our need of wisdom,
let us pray to our wise and loving God.

Reader
In all the decision-making,
problems and challenges of our church,
we ask for wise counsel and encouragement;
in all our worship and outreach.

Silence

Wise and loving God:
quieten us to hear your voice.

In all the clashes of needs and wants,
the half-forgotten hurts that drive aggression,
the half-remembered grievances,
barbed with revenge,
in all the world's raging and protesting,
we pray for the spirit of peace and reconciliation.

Silence

Wise and loving God:
quieten us to hear your voice.

In the daily batch of misunderstandings,
conflicting loyalties, negotiations and compromise,
may the Spirit walk among us
in our homes and places of work,
whispering sanity and mutual respect.

Silence

Wise and loving God:
quieten us to hear your voice.

For those engulfed by pain
or enslaved by addiction,
we pray for hope and healing;
may the Lord bless all those
whose minds think simply
and rely on others for basic care.

Silence

Wise and loving God:
quieten us to hear your voice.

May all who have left this life
in the Father's friendship
be gathered into his keeping for ever;
we pray too for those approaching death,
that they may know his love
surrounding them across time and eternity.

Silence

Wise and loving God:
quieten us to hear your voice.

We join our prayers with those of Mary,
whose spirit was always peaceful:
Hail, Mary . . .

Together in silence now,
we make our private petitions.

Silence

Celebrant
Most loving and merciful Father,
we ask you to take over our lives
and live through them,
and accept these our prayers
in the name of Jesus.
Amen.

TREASURE SEEKERS

Aim: To know that God helps us understand, and that he understands everything.

Starter

Have a time of sharing news, or let different children share with the others something they have learnt how to do.

Teaching

Spread all the pieces from a jigsaw puzzle over the floor in the circle, but don't show a picture of the completed puzzle. Talk about how we can put it together. First we can look for pieces with straight edges as they will make the edge of the picture. (Do this in turns.) Point out how much easier it would be if we had a picture to help us.

There are lots of things in life which are a big puzzle to us, and we find them very hard to understand. Perhaps we don't understand how dogs bark, why grown-ups talk so long on the phone, what makes heavy planes stay up in the sky, why Mum was cross with us that time, why Dad wasn't cross with us last week, how some people can be cruel to animals, why some people have asthma, why some people are very rich and others very poor.

Our life is full of puzzles. And we are always trying to work the puzzles out.

God understands all the puzzles, and knows why everything is as it is, and how. It's as if God holds the finished picture. So when we're puzzled about anything at all in life, we can ask God to help us understand. (Produce the jigsaw picture.) Bit by bit, if we keep working with God and with each other (talk as you work together on the puzzle), we'll start to understand some of those puzzles, even before we get to heaven!

Praying

Over the earth is a mat of green
over the green is dew,
over the dew are the arching trees,
over the trees, the blue.
Across the blue are scudding clouds,
over the clouds, the sun,
over it all is the love of God,
blessing us every one.

(Ruth Brown
© Oxford University Press)

Activities

The sheet can be made into a hanging model of today's prayer. Each child will need a circle of green paper stuck on thin card. The prayer is stuck on to this and the other layers made into circles as shown and fastened together with wool.

PEARL DIVERS

Aim: To know that God is wise.

Starter

Tell or read a story which illustrates wisdom, such as the Emperor's new clothes, or the crowded house story, where a man complaining of his pokey home is advised by a wise man to get all kinds of animals to live in it with him. Then he is told to let them all go, and he ends up discovering how much space he has.

Teaching

The child who spoke out and said the Emperor was really wearing no clothes at all was wise because he stuck with what he knew was real and true. The man who advised the farmer to fill his home up with animals and then have it to himself again was wise because he knew about people. He knew that we grumble when we want something we can't have, and that we're happy if what we have is better than what we used to have.

So we can be wise even if we don't get top marks for our spellings every week. We can be wise whether we are grown-up or still children. And sometimes children are a lot better at being wise than grown-ups! In fact, some of the wisest grown ups are the ones who still go on thinking like children, still asking questions and marvelling at the world, still saying what they know is true.

As you can imagine, our great God is full of wisdom. That doesn't mean that he knows everything (although he does), but it means that God really understands why people act the way they do, and what makes each of us like we are. And because God is wise, he also knows the best way for things to happen. If we pray every day for God's will to be done on earth just as it is in heaven, then we can be sure that God will work with all the events of the day for good. He is so wise that he can even work with the bad things that happen, the arguments and fights, the disappointments and wrong choices people make.

(Place a large question mark on the floor.) If we are not at all sure how to put things right when we've made mistakes (place a cross over the question mark), our wise God can help us. (Place the question mark down again.) If we are bothered by things that are happening at school or at our club or at home (place the cross over the question mark), our wise God knows how to work in that place so that things are sorted out for good.

As God's children we are to live wisely as well. How do we do that? We need to go through life looking and listening. We need to seek God out every day. And we need to make good use of every opportunity we have for playing on God's team, fighting evil and working for good.

Praying

Jesus, did I hear you needed players on your team?
Well, here I am!
Did I hear you needed volunteers?
That's me!
I want to be on your side, Jesus,
fighting for good against evil,
fighting for justice and truth
with weapons of love and hope.
Who's for Jesus?
ME!

Activities

On the sheet there is a picture in which to spot the opportunities for doing good. These are not all immediately obvious, just as real opportunities are often hard to spot. Help the children to see the situations where conditions might be improved, people in difficulty helped, and others comforted or befriended. There is also a kind of crossword puzzle containing practical advice for anyone wanting to be wise.

GOLD PANNERS

Aim: To see how God's wisdom is sometimes seen as foolishness.

Starter

Sing one of those silly songs with actions, such as 'Did you ever see a zombie come to tea? Take a look at me – a zombie you will see.' With each verse an extra action is added: marching with feet, right arm up and down, left arm up and down, nod head, blink.

Teaching

Now we have all made ourselves look ridiculous! Today we are going to look at how God's wisdom is often seen as complete foolishness. Perhaps they

have already been made to feel foolish for believing in God and talking to him. It is never a nice experience, and can set us wondering why we bother with God if it's going to make some people laugh at us and think we're stupid. (Of course, God is there whether we bother with him or not, so it won't make God disappear if we deny him. Nor will it help those who are doing the scoffing. But we do need to support one another with our prayers, and to know that Jesus received the same scorn from his contemporaries.)

Read the passage from Proverbs, telling them also about the lady Folly, in contrast to Wisdom. At first sight Folly can look like a good idea, appealing to our instincts and cravings, rather like much of the media does today. Only after people have made their choice is it clear that this leads to death, whereas the path of Wisdom leads to life-giving nourishment and fulfilment.

Go on to read the passage from Ephesians, discussing what 'living wisely' means for us. Draw out the need to be actively involved in goodness, rather than just not doing anyone any harm.

Now look at today's Gospel, where the religious leaders are finding it impossible to see Jesus' words as wisdom, but only as foolishness and blasphemy. What stops them seeing the truth of Jesus' words? (Look at their expectations of the Messiah, their attention to precise detail at the expense of the wider vision, and their status as learned, respected leaders in the community.)

Praying

Be thou my wisdom, be thou my true word,
I ever with thee and thou with me, Lord;
thou my great Father, and I thy true heir;
thou in me dwelling, and I in thy care.

(From a song translated from the Irish
by Mary Byrne and Eleanor Hull
© Copyright Control)

Activities

On the sheet they are helped to look at some of the things which those who cannot accept God find foolishness, and to see how they are in fact wisdom, though contrasting to the world's values. They are also encouraged to see how they can live wisely, making the most of every opportunity to do good and fight against evil.

TWENTY-FIRST SUNDAY OF THE YEAR

Thought for the day

'To whom else could we go? You alone have the words of eternal life.'

Reflection on the readings

Joshua 24:1-2a, 15-18
Psalm 33
Ephesians 5:21-32
John 6:60-69

Most choices we make in life are fairly unimportant. It will probably make little difference whether we choose vanilla or raspberry ripple, ten o'clock or ten fifteen, chrysanthemums or asters. But the big important decision, which drives everything else we decide, is the direction we choose to face as we walk through life.

In our reading from Joshua, the significance of this commitment is made thoroughly clear to the people, since Joshua wants to be sure that everyone really knows what they are voting for, together with the potential cost as well as the benefits. Having laid out the facts, Joshua then gives the lead. He is not opting out of leadership and suggesting that either choice is as good as the other but offers one direction as choosing life, the other death, and takes his stand on the good choice as he declares, 'As for me and my household, we will serve the Lord.' The people wholeheartedly agree, basing their commitment on their actual experience of God's consistent loving care of them.

In a genuine but over-enthusiastic desire to allow freedom and engender mutual respect, our own age tends now to distrust any absolutes, preferring to think of all truth as relative and a matter of individual choice. In such a climate it takes courage to profess our faith in Jesus Christ, and we may often find ourselves in the minority, or actively disputing widely accepted moral principles which run contrary to God's law of love.

So we hear with empathy today's Gospel reading, with many disciples walking away from Jesus now that he claims such a close relationship with the transcendent God. It is too much for them to come to terms with, and they conclude that Jesus has overstepped the mark. We too are faced with the same challenge. Either Jesus, as a good and gifted human being, has overreached his sanity, or he is speaking the truth. If the latter is so, he must indeed be the Holy One of God, with all that this implies for us in terms of commitment.

Discussion starters

1. What do we actually believe Jesus to be, and how does this affect our life?
2. Why do you think Jesus made no attempt to persuade those who turned away to return?

All-stage talk

Have a show of hands for a few choices – Who's for football, who's for rugby? Who's a lark and loves the early mornings, who's an owl and loves to stay up late? Who's a 'dog' person, who's a 'cat' person?

All these are a matter of choice, and happily we are all different so we all like to choose different toppings on our pizzas, different music to listen to and different colours to wear. It's wonderful and important that we are all different.

But there are some things we can't choose, because it's been decided that there is a collective good way of going on. So we all drive on the same side of the road whatever part of the country we're in; we all go to school and learn how to read and write and do maths and science; we all pay taxes on what we earn so everyone, both poor and rich, can use schools and hospitals and so on.

In our first reading, from the Old Testament, Joshua wants the people to decide, before they go in to the promised land, whether they really do want to serve the Lord their God or not. He makes it quite clear that they will only be choosing wisely if they do choose to worship God, as he is real and powerful, and the other gods are not. It's a little bit like asking a football team if they are going to choose to play with a football or a matchbox in an international match. There really isn't much point in playing with anything other than the real thing!

In the Gospel we heard of some of the crowds choosing not to walk with Jesus any more because he seemed to be making out that he was the Holy One of God. Jesus asked his disciples if they were going to turn away as well, and Peter spoke for them all, and for us as well. 'Lord, who else could we go to,' he asked, 'seeing that you are the one with the words of eternal life?' When we know that God is real, and that Jesus really is the Holy One of God, what else can we do but make the sensible, wise choice and commit ourselves to following him? That's the wisest, most important choice we make in the whole of our life.

All-age ideas

- As a follow-up to the All-stage Talk, it may be helpful to provide the opportunity for making a renewed commitment to serve God and become a follower of Jesus Christ. Depending on the style and tradition of your church this could involve a time of worship before the Blessed Sacrament; or you could have a time of silent reflection followed by the baptismal declaration of faith.

- With the focus in the reading from Ephesians being on marriage, have a display of photographs of the couples in the parish preparing for marriage, or of those celebrating particular anniversaries.

Prayer of the Faithful

Celebrant
We have chosen to serve the Lord.
Let us pray to him now.

Reader
We pray for those whose faith
is being challenged or undermined
by inner doubts or outside influences.
We pray for those who build up our faith
and all who strive to proclaim the Gospel
in language that people understand.

Silence

Holy God, we believe:
help our unbelief.

We pray for our torn and fragmented world,
wrestling to equate the deep yearning for peace
with the instinctive urge
for gratification and power;
that many may have the courage
to walk God's way.

Silence

Holy God, we believe:
help our unbelief.

We pray for our loved ones;
for those who lift our hearts
and those who turn our hair grey.
We pray for those we instinctively warm to
and those with whom
there are frequent misunderstandings.

Silence

Holy God, we believe:
help our unbelief.

We pray for all who are marginalised,
scorned or rejected;
for those isolated through illness or imprisonment;
for those who feel that no one understands.
May the Lord surround them all with such love
that they may know they are precious.

Silence

Holy God, we believe:
help our unbelief.

We pray for those approaching death,
that through our prayers
they may know themselves
accompanied with love on that journey.
We pray for those who have died,
that they may come to know the full joy of heaven.

Silence

Holy God, we believe:
help our unbelief.

Now we join our prayers with those of Mary,
the Mother of Jesus:
Hail, Mary . . .

In silence, we name any we know
who especially need our prayer.

Silence

Celebrant
In great thankfulness
for all your blessings to us,
heavenly Father,
we offer you these prayers,
through Jesus Christ.
Amen.

TREASURE SEEKERS

Aim: To know that God gives us spiritual armour to protect us from evil.

Starter

Give the children lots of rolled-up balls of newspaper as snowballs and have either a leader or a child who volunteers to be the one everyone is trying to hit with the paper. However, this person is given a tray as a shield, to protect themselves.

Teaching

Talk about how much better it was to have the tray as a shield. It really helped to protect the person being pelted with snowballs! Have a look at some other things we use to protect ourselves – overalls and aprons protect our clothes from paint and glue, umbrellas and wet weather clothes protect us from getting too soaked, sunglasses protect our eyes from the glaring sun. If possible, have a look at some toy Roman armour, or a picture of a Roman soldier.

God knows that it isn't always easy to be loving and good, honest and kind. And he knows that sometimes people are hurt by bad things that happen, like wars, or someone being nasty to them, or frightening them, or making them feel silly. God hates to see any of his children getting hurt by any kind of evil, or hurting others. So he gives us armour to protect us from evil.

The armour is God's love, and if we imagine ourselves getting dressed in God's love every day, we'll be wearing his special armour to help us live God's way and fight against evil.

Praying

I am wearing the armour of God
to help me fight against evil.
I am carrying the shield of faith
'cos God wants me to be safe.
Yes, God wants me to be safe and strong,
and I belong to him!

Activities

On the sheet there is a picture of a Roman soldier and the children can dress him up in his armour by sticking on the cut-out sections. Talk with them about God's armour of love, goodness and faith as they work.

PEARL DIVERS

Aim: To know that some of Jesus' followers turned away and only those who recognised him as the Holy One of God stayed with him.

Starter

Play 'follow my leader' with different children taking the lead in dancing to some music. They all do what the leader does.

Teaching

Lay out the following items to serve as memory joggers: a packet of mustard seed (or any small seeds), a coin and a toy sheep. Remind everyone that while Jesus was travelling around the countryside during the two or three years of his ministry, he did lots of teaching by telling stories. Use the objects for them to recall the kingdom growing like a tiny seed grows into a big tree, God searching for sinners like a woman searches for one lost coin and a shepherd for one lost sheep. The people were used to hearing Jesus explaining things like this.

Perhaps they can remember Mum or Dad telling them it must be about bedtime. They know that probably means that they needn't jump up and go just yet. But if the tone of voice changes and gets serious, they know that means they have to go straightaway, as this time it's for real! They have been told not in a gentle, roundabout way, but very clearly and directly.

Now place down a loaf of bread. When Jesus started telling the people that he was living bread from heaven, he was talking to them very clearly and directly. He was showing them that he really was the Holy One of God.

That left them with quite a challenge. (Place down two separate cards, one labelled 'Jesus must be a liar!' and the other 'Jesus must really be the Holy One of God'. Place a question mark between the two cards. They could see that they either had to believe him, and recognise him as the Christ, or not believe him, in which case he must be a liar who had let them down.

How would they choose? (Place down a picture of an eye.) They could think over all the things they had seen Jesus do. Did they point to him being a liar or the Christ? (Place down a picture of an ear.) They could think over all the teaching they had heard, and the way he had talked to people. Did his words point to him being a liar or the Christ? (Place down a scroll.) They could think over what their prophets had said about the Christ. Did Jesus fit in with those ideas or not?

We are told that for many of those people the thought of this Jesus they knew being the Christ was just too difficult to accept, and they turned away and walked off. For other people, although it seemed incredible that the Christ was actually standing on the grass beside them, they realised that everything pointed to Jesus telling the truth, so he must really be the Holy One of God. And that made them very happy and excited indeed!

When Jesus saw some of the crowd moving away, he turned and looked at his disciples and asked them if they would be going as well. Let's find out what they said. (Look up John 6:67-69 and read it out.)

Praying

Jesus, Jesus, we have come to see
that you must really be
the Son of God our Father.
We've been with you and we all agree
that only in your service
can the world be truly free!

Activities

On the sheet there is a puzzle to work out so that they come to discover Peter's words – 'You are the Holy One of God'. They are also encouraged to think through the reasons for claiming that Jesus was declaring the truth about himself.

GOLD PANNERS

Aim: To explore why the split happened at this point.

Starter

Why? (This is a variation on *Call my bluff*.) Split the group into two teams and give each some kind of bell or other noise item. Whoever is first with the right choice wins the round. Here are some ideas to start you off.

1. Why did the campanologist climb the stairs? (a) Because he was camping at the top of a mountain; (b) because he was campaigning in highrise flats; (c) because the bells he was ringing were in a tower.

2. Why was the kleptomaniac arrested? (a) Because she was a compulsive clog dancer; (b) because she was a compulsive thief; (c) because she was a compulsive stalker.

3. Why did Jeremiah not have sore armpits? (a) Because his friends padded them with rags; (b) because he never shaved them; (c) because he used Oil of Ulay every day.

4. Why did the student need his portfolio? (a) Because he was going to sea; (b) because he wanted to choose some wine to celebrate passing his exams; (c) because his artwork was carried in it.

Teaching

Why do we do the things we do? Often there isn't just one reason but lots of little reasons and events that come together. (Why, for instance, is each person here today?) Today we are looking at people making important decisions, and why they made them.

Read the passage from Joshua, with the people's choice based on their personal experience of Yahweh's care and their trust in what Joshua, their leader, advises. Then read the Gospel for today. Why did they find what Jesus was saying so hard that it made them decide to walk no more with him? Share ideas about this, and help them to see that in making those statements, Jesus was saying that he was the Holy One of God, and this was a very hard thing to accept, especially for Jewish people who thought of God as so awesome that they never even allowed themselves to say his name. The thought of the transcendent God walking among them in sandals was mind blowing, so they came to the conclusion that Jesus must either have gone OTT or was a liar.

But if he really was telling the truth – and all the evidence pointed to that – then God's Son was actually standing with them, breathing the same air.

Praying

Yes, Lord, I believe that you are the Christ,
the Son of God who has come into the world.
I have decided to follow you,
for you alone have the words of eternal life.

Activities

On the sheet there are different reasons for believing that the world is flat/round. They can use these to see how we come to conclusions which others would challenge unless they have plenty of evidence. They then compare Peter and the disciples' reasons for concluding that Jesus is the Holy One of God, compared with those who turn away.

TWENTY-SECOND SUNDAY OF THE YEAR

Thought for the day

We need to be careful never to replace the timeless commands of God with man-made traditions.

Reflection on the readings

Deuteronomy 4:1-2, 6-8
Psalm 14
James 1:17-18, 21-22, 27
Mark 7:1-8, 14-15, 21-23

In the reading from Deuteronomy the people are given reasons for valuing and upholding the Law of God as encapsulated in the ten commandments. One reason is that a community living according to such a Law will look very impressive to all the surrounding peoples, and point to the nation being full of wisdom and understanding. Another reason is that such a relationship with the living God will make all observers respect the obvious greatness of a nation so greatly blessed. However, this does depend on the people actually keeping the Law, and passing it down through the generations. That is crucial.

When we come to the passage from Mark, we find that a very human corruption of truth has been eating away at that wonderful ideal. We always find it so much easier to reduce vibrant truth to rigid, narrow rules. Insidiously the rules surrounding the truth take over in importance and are given permission to reign through the name of tradition, which is then reverenced, tragically at the expense of the original glorious, liberating vision. It is not just in Jewish religious teaching that this happens, but everywhere.

Jesus, with the clear insight of the Son of God, sees the terrible reality gap and its consequences. So corrupted has the perception of the Law become, that the very teachers are preventing the truth from catching hold of people's imagination, and in many cases the real meaning has been turned completely on its head. Jesus is not so much turning the world upside down by his teaching as turning it right side up again, the way God intended it to be.

Far from not keeping the Law, Jesus is reverencing it with his whole being, while the teachers have let go of the essence of God's truth and are left hanging on to scraggy handfuls of dry rules.

The reading from James is particularly helpful today since it comes from the Jewish tradition, with the fresh life of the Spirit breathed into it. Like the ancient prophets, the writer grounds God's truth in compassion and practical caring, coupled with a rigorous checking of personal purity so as to live in the wide freedom of God's law of love, which is altogether more demanding but also infinitely more fulfilling.

Discussion starters

1. Is there anything in the Church today – which is the Body of Christ – that Jesus might be unhappy with?

2. Do we still accept Jesus' teaching that the 'uncleanness' which so often leads to sin comes from the inside of people, or is responsibility for sin being replaced by genetics and other circumstances beyond our control?

All-stage talk

Probably quite a lot of us washed before we came out today. Why do we keep ourselves clean by regular washing? (Collect ideas and reasons.) Conclude that there are good reasons for washing. It's all to do with keeping healthy as well as being pleasant to sit next to! Our Gospel reading today was talking about what makes us unclean. If we are talking about our bodies, what sort of things make us unclean, or dirty? (Collect a few ideas.)

Now it was traditional for Jewish religious people to do lots and lots of washing. Some of this was to keep everything clean and healthy, and, having lived as wandering nomads in hot desert country, all that was very important. But there was another kind of 'being unclean' which wasn't to do

with bodies but souls. Sin is your soul, or spiritual nature, being unclean and in need of a good clean-up. They believed that eating certain foods or not following special rituals would make you unclean.

But whereas it's *outside* things that make our bodies unclean and in need of washing, Jesus explained that with our souls it's thoughts and wants from deep *inside* us that often lead us into sin, making us unclean. Like what, for instance?

- Like when we have mean, unkind thoughts;
- when we feel like hating or despising people because they've got what we want;
- whenever we want what we know is wrong and against God's way of living;
- when it seems like a clever idea to lie our way out of trouble;
- when doing something unselfish seems too much hard work and we can't be bothered with it.

When we are baptised, we're dunked in water, partly as a sign that we're being washed clean from sin. (The priest washes his hands just after the bread and wine are brought to the altar, as an outward sign that he wants God to wash him clean of sin, ready for this special part of the service.)

So if those wrong and bad thoughts and drives make us sin, so that our souls are unclean, how on earth can we get clean again? Can we scrub our souls with soap and water, or soak all our nastiness away in a hot bath? No, we can't. But there is a way of getting our souls clean without leaving any stain of sin at all. It's a two-stage washing process, rather like putting stuff out for the laundry because we know it's dirty, and then having it washed clean. And it's called *repentance* and *forgiveness*.

Once we realise that our souls are messy and dirty with sin, and that makes us sad, we bring all of it to Jesus, tell him how sorry we are and how we would love our souls to be completely clean again. That's *repentance*.

What Jesus does is to take our souls and soak away all the sin in a wonderful bath of *forgiveness*, that leaves us feeling free and happy and spiritually clean.

All-age ideas

- Have an arrangement of washing products, such as a laundry bag with some clothes in it, washing powder/liquid, a laundry basket and some pegs.
- Give everyone a peg to hold. While a song or hymn is sung, focusing on repentance and forgiveness, suggest we all look over our souls to see what needs a good wash, and bring it to Jesus for his cleansing forgiveness.

Prayer of the Faithful

Celebrant
Our God is the source of all holiness;
with the needs of the Church and the world
close to our hearts,
let us pray to the only one
who can renew and redeem.

Reader
Aware of our temptation
to place our trust in rules and traditions,
we pray for a release in the Church
of such a desire to serve the living God
that nothing is allowed to get in the way of that.

Silence

Into your hands, O Lord:
we commit the future.

We recognise in ourselves
the universal dangerous wants and cravings
which are cultivated because they make money.
May we have such a loathing of evil
that there will be international co-operation
and individual responsibility in fighting it
and building one another up in love.

Silence

Into your hands, O Lord:
we commit the future.

May our homes, schools and churches
reflect and engender the Godly values
of mutual care, respect and responsibility,
of integrity and forgiveness.

Silence

Into your hands, O Lord:
we commit the future.

We stand alongside all who are hurting
in body, mind or spirit;
all who need courage, support or practical help.
May we be willing to become
part of God's answer
to our prayers for them.

Silence

Into your hands, O Lord:
we commit the future.

We commit to the Father's keeping
those who have died to this life;
that, freed from all pain, and forgiven,
they may live in the peace and joy of heaven.

Silence

Into your hands, O Lord:
we commit the future.

Encouraged by Mary's example of obedience,
we make our prayer with her:
Hail, Mary . . .

As God's stillness fills our hearts,
we pray for our own particular needs and concerns.

Silence

Celebrant
Heavenly Father,
in your love and mercy hear our prayers,
through the mediation of Jesus Christ.
Amen.

TREASURE SEEKERS

Aim: To look at how we can say 'thank you' to God with our lives as well as our voices.

Starter

Sit in a circle and pass round a paper plate or a broom stick. Each person mimes with the object to show what it is. (Examples might be a steering wheel or a fishing rod.)

Teaching

Point out how we managed to say what the plate or stick was, using not words but actions. In the circle try out some more telling actions, such as showing by our faces that we're pleased or grumpy, interested or scared.

Today we are going to look at some of the ways we can say 'thank you' to God for making us and such a lovely world, for forgiving us and looking after us.

We can say our thanks to God. Go round the circle with the children who want to, thanking God for different things.

We can silently say our thanks to God. Suggest everyone shuts their eyes and puts their hands together, as we all thank God silently for something or someone special to us.

We can sing and shout and dance our thanks to God! Play and sing a favourite praise song, with the children singing along, dancing and playing instruments.

So we can tell God our thanks by saying aloud, saying silently, singing, shouting, dancing and playing . . . *and* by living our thanks.

How do we live our thanks?

Well, if we want to tell God how happy we are that he has made a lovely world, we can show him our thanks by being careful to look after it. (Chat together about ways this might be done.)

If we want to tell God how happy we are that he has given us loving people to look after us, we can show him our thanks by being helpful to those people. (Again, talk over examples.)

If we want to tell God how happy we are that he forgives us when we do things wrong, we can show him our thanks by forgiving other people.

Praying

Father God, we want to thank you
for your loving kindness,
and to show you that we thank you
we will live our thanks each day.
Watch our living and you will see
how loving and kind we'll try to be!
Amen.

Activities

On the sheet there are pictures to discuss and colour in of two friends of Jesus whose lives said a big 'thank you' to God. They are Saint Francis and Saint Clare, looking after the lepers, enjoying the lovely world and living simply.

PEARL DIVERS

Aim: To understand that, as far as God is concerned, the 'inside' is more important than the outward appearance.

Starter

Fix down a few sheets of paper to the floor and tell everyone they are in a land belonging to the great king. They can move around to the music but on no account are they to step on one of the sheets, as these belong to the king's enemy. Gradually add more sheets so that it becomes harder to walk freely. Anyone touching the king's enemy's land has to stay banished on that sheet, as they are now too 'unclean' to tread on the great king's land.

Teaching

Talk together about some of the ritual rules we make, sometimes as games and sometimes for real, like not letting ourselves step on the cracks in the pavement, or stopping all the children playing with their toys by saying some special word, like 'Poop Nincom' (but they can when you reverse it and say 'Nincom Poop'!). Share any ritual rules the children have used. You could also read them A. A. Milne's poem about cracks in the pavement. Today we are looking at some rules which are worth keeping and some that aren't.

Remind them of the ten commandments given by God to Moses when the people of Israel had escaped from being slaves in Egypt. Basically, these ten commandments were all saying two main things: Love God and love one another. They were very good rules to keep and live by.

But over the years people had added all sorts of other ritual rules. To show you loved God, you kept yourself 'clean' by all sorts of rules like not touching dead bodies, not eating certain food, and never eating without a special washing ceremony that had to be done in exactly the right order. (What do they think God thought about those kind of rules? Would they really show that the people loved him? Or would they just show that the people had a lot of rules?)

Read from Mark 7, verses 1, 2 and 5. So Jesus, the Son of God, wasn't keeping all the little tiny rules as the religious leaders thought he ought to. When they picked him up on it, Jesus told them this: 'You think it's more important to follow your own rules than God's commandments! But it's God's commandments which are really important.'

(And what are God's commandments? To love God and to love one another.)

That's just as true for us as it was for them. We may have got ourselves clean and smart to come to church, because we want to show God he's important. But God's more interested in whether we've got ready to meet him by being kind and helpful this morning, whether we've been in touch with God at all by praying during the week, whether we're wanting to show off or not. Those things may not show on the outside, but they show up very clearly to God. The best-looking and the best-dressed people here as far as God is concerned, are those who are really trying to live the way of love.

Praying

Lord, I want to show my love and thanks
in the way I live my life.
I want everything I think, say and do
to be in line with your Law of love.
Lord, help me to be more concerned
with the state of my soul before you
than with my efforts to impress other people.
Amen.

Activities

On the sheet there are different people needing advice, and the group can think of how they could help. There are also pictures of various people together with a brief description of their attitudes and lifestyle. The children can look out for some marks of 'true religion' in them.

GOLD PANNERS

Aim: To look at the benefits and dangers of tradition in the Church.

Starter

On separate pieces of card write down various traditions, which they sort into 'Very important', 'Non-essential' and 'Chuck'. Here are some ideas: Christmas pudding; a white wedding; wearing black at funerals; school uniform; dinner before dessert; milk poured in before the tea; standing for the national anthem; salt and vinegar with chips; homework; wearing best clothes to church; ladies first.

Teaching

Lots of our traditions are so much part of life that we only notice them when we travel abroad and find they're not there. Sometimes we take it for granted that anything we're used to doing must be right. Today we're going to look at that and question it, as Jesus did.

First read the passage from Deuteronomy, reminding them of the basic principles of the Law – Love God and love one another. Make a list of the advantages of having traditions in place to help keep the Law. Use the sheet to see how the extra 'fence' of rules and regulations became part of the tradition, from the best of motives, but having the effect of shifting priorities in people's minds.

Now read the Gospel passage from Mark 7, picking out the dangers and disadvantages of having intricately worked-out traditional customs. What had happened to the way the people thought of religious duty?

Finally, talk over the traditions of our own church, looking at what is obviously very precious and important, and what seems to them to be rather in line with some of the religious teachers' rules and regulations.

Praying

Lord, I want to show my love and thanks
in the way I live my life.
I want everything I think, say and do
to be in line with your Law of love.
Lord, help me to be more concerned
with the state of my soul before you,
than with my efforts to impress other people.
Amen.

Activities

There is space on the sheet to work out quantities of time, energy and money spent on various things in life, in order to assess what our life is actually displaying. And they are helped to see how the build-up of regulations grew out of a genuine desire to keep the Law faithfully.

TWENTY-THIRD SUNDAY OF THE YEAR

Thought for the day

Jesus comes fulfilling the hope of healing to wholeness; he shows that mercy has triumphed over judgement.

Reflection on the readings

Isaiah 35:4-7a
Psalm 145
James 2:1-5
Mark 7:31-37

In the Old Testament prophecies describing a healing Messiah, we sense the huge waves of longing for the whole nation to be restored and beautiful in God's sight, in full and vigorous health morally, elementally, physically and spiritually. Everything is pictured as bursting into new life and vitality through the direct touch of God's presence.

The reading from James picks up on the kind of healthy attitudes which are free from prejudice and discrimination, recognising that in the fullness of God our thinking is to be reworked until it reflects God's character, and we celebrate the triumph of mercy over judgement.

Today's Gospel shows Jesus acting all this out in person. He doesn't advertise for custom, so as to force the events to fit the promises of scripture; on the contrary, people drag their loved ones to him and beg him to work God's healing in them. Even as he sighed, 'Ephphatha!', longing in love for the man's ears to be opened, it is as if he is longing for the ears of the whole people of God to be opened so that they may hear and understand.

Jesus' action in healing the deaf and dumb man inspired 'unbounded admiration', despite his insistence that they keep quiet about this miraculous event. There is much debate as to why, in St Mark's Gospel, Jesus so often tells people to keep quiet and not say anything. It would surely be hard for anyone to imagine how someone who had been deaf would not want to communicate their joy at being able to hear, or how someone who was dumb would not be bursting to use their new-found capacity for speech.

If Jesus touched and healed the big problem in our lives, could we keep quiet about it?

Discussion starters

1. Can we appreciate mercy unless we first appreciate the judgement we deserve?
2. How do we stand, as Church and as a nation, in relation to issues of discrimination and prejudice?

All-stage talk

Introduce the talk with the short sketch given in the All-age Ideas. Bring along a couple of different masks and ask volunteers to come and put them on. Point out how Farouk has now turned into a fierce tiger, and we might be scared of him; Mazin is now a clown and looks even funnier than usual! Thank the volunteers and restore them to their normal identities.

One of the things that all grown-ups do is to put on different masks for different people. We need to learn from the children, especially the very young children, how not to. What sort of masks do grown-ups wear? Not usually animal or clown masks, but masks all the same!

Like the woman answering the phone in the sketch, we put on a special voice for people we want to impress, we wear special clothes and try to give the other person the impression that we are efficient, cool, witty, deep or dependable. Why do we do that? Because we know that most people are influenced by outward appearances, and most people are fairly judgemental. If we can persuade them that we are worth respecting, then we reckon they will be more likely to listen to us and take notice of us.

Is that how we want it to be? Think instead of young children, who simply act as themselves, and haven't yet learnt the game of pretending who they are. You can see in the direct look in a young child's eyes that there is something there which grown-ups call innocence, because they are real; and we all regret losing that in all the clever pretending and wearing of masks.

As Christians, we are called to break that destructive cycle. We are *not* to judge from outward appearances, or just be friendly and respectful to wealthy, important-looking people. For us it's different because we know that every person we set eyes on is made and loved by God. And if we treat every person with the respect and love which they deserve as God-made human beings, they won't feel that they need to put on masks when they are with us. We will be joining Jesus in allowing people to be who they are, so that they are helped to wholeness and integrity.

All-age ideas

- Here is the sketch to introduce the All-stage Talk.

Pauline Carter is sitting at her office desk working and answering the telephone. She can have the script in front of her, so she won't have to learn it.

(Phone rings. Pauline answers it in bored, automatic voice.)

Good morning, Pauline Carter speaking, how can I help you? . . . *(Suddenly sits up straight and adjusts hair, changes voice to be very efficient and respectful.)* Oh Mr Townsend, good morning. How can I be of assistance? . . . Yes, certainly, I'm sure that would be convenient . . . I'll just check the date . . . Yes, Monday at eleven forty would be fine . . . Certainly, I'll arrange that . . . And you, too, Mr Townsend . . . Thank you so much . . . Goodbye.

(Carries on working. Phone rings again. Pauline answers it in efficient, friendly mode.)

Good morning! It's Pauline Carter here. How can I help you? . . . *(Suddenly raises eyebrows and slumps back in seat, getting on with work while the other person talks. She's obviously not really listening.)* Ah . . . oh, hi . . . mmm . . . ah . . . ah . . . no . . . look, I'm really busy here . . . yeah. OK . . . Bye.

(Carries on working. Phone rings again. Pauline answers it in bored auto voice.)

Good morning. Pauline Carter here. How can I help you?

- Beneath the words of the Alleluia verse have a display. To one side have a radio, some newspapers and a TV listings guide. On the other side have an open Bible. In the middle of the display have a question mark.

Prayer of the Faithful

Celebrant
Let us pray to our loving and merciful God.

Reader
In gratitude for the richness and diversity
of each unique identity,
we pray for the separate members
of this Body of Christ, and our corporate nature,
that we may be filled at every level
with the living breath of God.

Silence

Father of mercy:
let your kingdom come.

In gratitude for the beauty and variety
of our landscapes and cultures, all over the world;
for starscapes and the wideness of space,
we pray that we may cherish and respect
this universe we inhabit,
and respect all those who look or sound
different from ourselves.

Silence

Father of mercy:
let your kingdom come.

In gratitude for the hope
each newborn child brings;
for the gentle gifts of laughter and friendship,
thoughtfulness and sympathy,
we pray that our eyes may see all others
with God's affection.

Silence

Father of mercy:
let your kingdom come.

In gratitude for the patient endurance
of so many who suffer so much,
we pray that they may come to know
Christ's wholeness and refreshing,
his upholding and healing.

Silence

Father of mercy:
let your kingdom come.

In gratitude for the promise of mercy
triumphing over judgement,
we commend to God's love for ever
our own loved ones who have died.

Silence

Father of mercy:
let your kingdom come.

We join our prayers with those of Mary,
who was full of compassion for others:
Hail, Mary . . .

In this silence,
we bring our particular petitions
to God our Father.

Silence

Celebrant
Father, your character is so rich in mercy;
please hear our prayers
which we offer in the name of Jesus.
Amen.

TREASURE SEEKERS

Aim: To look at how we can use our tongues to speak for good.

Starter

Tongue twisters. Try saying some of these: 'She sells sea shells on the sea shore'; 'red lorry, yellow lorry'; 'thirty thousand feathers on a thrush's throat'.

Teaching

Our tongues are very useful for talking. There are lots of sounds we can only make if we use our tongues – like ddd, ttt, nnn, ng, kkk, lll, sss. They can try making these sounds, noticing where their tongues go. Talking is a wonderful skill to have, and we start learning how to do it as soon as we are born. (Perhaps some of them have baby brothers and sisters who are just beginning to say the odd word.)

So now that we have learnt how to use our tongues for talking, what can we do with our talking? We can ask for exactly what we want or need, instead of crying and hoping someone will understand. We can tell other people what we are thinking. We can tell jokes. We can chat to our friends and we can pray to Jesus. We can cheer people up. We can help other people by telling them how to do something. (They can think of examples for all of these.) Put down a happy face and point out that we can use our tongues for saying all kinds of good and useful things.

Is that the only way we can use our tongues in talking? No, we could choose to use our tongues to say nasty, unkind things, or to be rude and disobedient, or to tell lies, or make someone cry. (Show an unhappy face.) But what a waste of a good tongue that would be. God has given us a wonderful gift of speaking. Let's use that gift to make the world a happier place.

Praying

Chatter, chatter, chatter,
thank you, God, for tongues to talk with,
tongues to tell the truth with,
tongues to speak kind words with,
tongues to pray and tongues to say,
chatter, chatter, chatter!

Activities

There are pictures on the sheet for the children to 'read' the sound effects, and also some situations with empty speech bubbles, where the children can work out what words could be said there.

PEARL DIVERS

Aim: To know the healing events of today's Gospel.

Starter

Give out some instruments for some of the children to play and ask the others to close and open their ears so they can feel what it is like to be shut off from the sounds. Swap the instruments around so the others can have a go.

Teaching

Today we are going to hear about someone who couldn't hear anything at all, and he couldn't speak either. When he was trying to listen to someone, this is what it sounded like: (mime the words, but let no sound come out). Sometimes he could tell that people wanted him to do something but it was hard to work out what. (Mime the words 'please can you get me a chair' several times, getting more irritated as no one gets it, gradually adding gestures to help them understand.) People helped him as much as they could but it still felt very lonely being unable to hear. Sometimes he would see people saying something to each other and laughing, but he didn't get the joke as he couldn't hear the words. He hoped they weren't laughing about him.

One day his family said to him: (only mime the words) 'We're taking you to Jesus. He can make your ears better.' (Say it several times with increasing actions till they work it out.) The man was very pleased. He had seen Jesus before and thought he looked kind. Of course he hadn't been able to hear what Jesus had been saying but he had seen how interested the crowds were and how carefully they listened. He had even seen Jesus put his hands on people with eyes and legs that didn't work, and watched them shouting and laughing as they were made better. He could hardly wait to go to Jesus himself.

His family took him to where Jesus was, pushed through the crowd and said to Jesus (mime it only), 'Please, Jesus . . . put your hands . . . on him and make his ears better.' The man saw them speaking and worked out what they were saying, just as you have done. He watched Jesus nod and look straight at him, smiling. The man smiled back and tried to say, 'Hello, Jesus', but he couldn't speak so just some sounds came out. Jesus led the man away from all the people to be with him on his own. The man watched as Jesus put his fingers into the man's ears. He could feel them there but couldn't hear anything, like we usually do. Then Jesus spat and touched the man's tongue. Doctors at that time quite often used saliva in healing so to them this was quite an ordinary thing to do.

Now the really exciting bit happened. The man watched Jesus looking up to heaven and praying (mime only), 'Be opened! Be opened! Be opened!' Suddenly the man realised he had just *heard* what Jesus was saying, as well as *seen* what he said! He could hear everything, and a very noisy world it was, too. He could hear the birds all screeching and singing, the crowd in the distance, the leaves rattling in the wind and everything. The man started to say, 'Oh good heavens, I can hear!' And suddenly he heard his own voice speaking. Jesus had healed his speaking as well!

Praying

Father God, we want to pray
for all the people who can't hear properly.
We pray for those who are working
to mend their hearing
and making hearing aids to help them hear better.
Amen.

Activities

The sheet is arranged like a computer page, so that they can help create a web site about the man who was given his hearing and speech by Jesus.

GOLD PANNERS

Aim: To look at the Christian attitude to prejudice and discrimination.

Starter

Size, shape, colour. All work together (or in smaller groups) on the puzzle shown below. No adjoining shapes can have more than one thing in common.

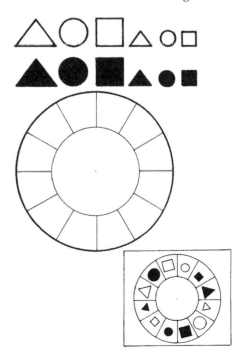

Teaching

Being able to discriminate between things is an important skill which we need to have. But often our society is full of discrimination of the wrong sort, selecting those who are acceptable and those who are not; those we respect and those we can despise. There's also lots of prejudice (the word means judging before you've even met) and today's readings help us discover what Jesus' views are.

First read the prophecy from Isaiah, noticing the wide-ranging healing it describes, with nothing and no one excluded or shut off by physical disabilities.

Then read the passage from James, looking out for some advice for us about discrimination and prejudice. As one of the proverbs says, the thing that rich and poor have in common is that God made them both! This passage challenges our attitudes as individuals, as the Church and as members of a nation. Draw attention to mercy triumphing over judgement.

Now read the Gospel for today. This is the story of a man who was shut off, or excluded, before being welcomed in, through the silence of hearing loss. Notice how the prophecy is being fulfilled without Jesus forcing things to happen, but simply responding to needs as they present themselves. Mercy has triumphed over judgement.

Praying

Father we pray for all who are cut off
from the world of sight and hearing,
and for those who just feel
cut off and left out.
Jesus didn't leave anyone out.
Teach us to live that way too.
Amen.

Activities

On the sheet there are various hot potatoes to look at in the Church and in society concerning discrimination and prejudice, and they are helped to look at these in the light of the Gospel. They are drawing up a few guidelines for challenging the rest of us as well, and these could perhaps be printed in the magazine or the local newspaper.

TWENTY-FOURTH SUNDAY OF THE YEAR

Thought for the day

Loving obedience to God is shown by Jesus to be a quality rich in courage and wisdom, a quality to be highly respected.

Reflection on the readings

Isaiah 50:5-9
Psalm 114
James 2:14-18
Mark 8:27-35

Obedience is currently rather a despised quality, and certainly not one which most people would strive to develop. Rather the opposite, since it has connotations for us of being somewhat immature and not yet our own, independent person if we claim to place any store by it. Not surprisingly, children pick this up in adults and copy it. Children learn discipline and self-control from disciplined, self-controlled adults, who value obedience themselves.

As the prophet in the book of Isaiah speaks of the figure of the Servant in complete loving obedience to God, his hearers would understand that here is someone of perfect wisdom and harmony with God, humble and courageous enough to do what is required as Saviour, whatever the personal cost. Though the people might well rebel in full-blooded human style, they recognised the importance and good sense of obedience.

In the letter of James the early Church is encouraged to put the example of Jesus' obedience in faith into practical application. The intellectual aspect of faith means nothing unless the hands get dirty by attending the basic needs of others.

As always, our example is Jesus, and today we meet him at the point when his disciples are beginning to grasp who he is, so he starts to explain what this will involve. It's too much for his friends. If Jesus isn't going to protest, then they will. Satan is quite happy to use well-meant persuasion to tempt us away from obedience. Thankfully Jesus stands firm, and lays out the obedience needed for all potential followers. Are we prepared to take him up on it?

Discussion starters

1. Has the time come to take another look at obedience and see if we've grown up enough to consider it a Godly quality worth developing?

2. Why does Jesus say that following him is bound to involve taking up our cross as he did?

All-stage talk

Ask for some volunteers and spread them around. Explain that all you want is for them to do as they're told. Then give a series of instructions, such as right hand in the air, stand still, run on the spot, stretch arms out to the sides, touch your toes, touch your nose, and so on. Hardly give them time to think. Finish by telling them to go back to their seats and everyone can give them a round of applause for giving us such a stunning example of perfect obedience.

Point out that it's quite easy to be obedient when someone's shouting out instructions, and the things aren't too hard. But if you had told them to push everyone off their chairs, or give all their money to the priest, would they have rushed to be obedient and carry out the instructions? Hopefully not! God forbid that we should be so keen to obey anyone that we fall in with any dangerous or wrong instruction. Teachers often come across children who have done something really stupid, and give the excuse that their friend told them to. Is that a good excuse? No, of course it isn't, because we have to think when we are asked to do anything, and refuse to do it if it seems selfish, dangerous or wrong. (It isn't just children, either – grown-ups will give as an excuse that everybody else does it, which is just as foolish an excuse, since everybody else could well be doing something dangerous or wrong.)

So where have we got to with obedience? That we are not meant to leave our brains and consciences behind. That means we are measuring every instruction up against the one we really trust to know what is right and good – underneath all the other obedient things we do there is a deep solid rock of obedience to God. That is what keeps us obedient wherever the instructions we are given are sensible and good, because measured up against the solid rock of our God we can see clearly that it's right to do what we're told here. In being obedient we are also being obedient to God.

And it's also what stops us obeying foolish, dangerous or wrong instructions which we might get from other people. Because when measured up against the solid rock of our God we can see clearly that to obey in those cases would make us disobedient to God.

Obedience to God is what matters more than anything, and Jesus showed us that.

All-age ideas

- Have different voices reading today's Gospel.
- Use part of the letter of James as the basis for a Penitential Rite.

For the times when we have failed to respond to the needs of our neighbour,

Lord, have mercy.
Lord, have mercy.

For the times when we have failed to clothe the naked,

Christ, have mercy.
Christ, have mercy.

For the times when we have failed to feed the hungry.

Lord, have mercy.
Lord, have mercy.

Prayer of the Faithful

Celebrant
As sons and daughters of our heavenly Father, responding to his call,
let us bring to him our needs and concerns.

Reader
That we may all learn to think God's way
and desire to do his will above everything else;
that we may be ready to suffer if necessary,
and put ourselves out, and do that cheerfully,
considering it a privilege.

Silence

Lord, in the spirit of obedience:
we ask your guidance.

That the craving to be most powerful
may be transformed into a yearning
for mutual respect and harmony;
that wealth may not shout louder than right,
and the whisper of truth may be heard
above the clamour of expediency.

Silence

Lord, in the spirit of obedience:
we ask your guidance.

That within our homes and places of work
we may practise self-discipline in all that we say,
and in the way it is said,
using our mouths to speak wisely and positively
with love in both hearts and voices.

Silence

Lord, in the spirit of obedience:
we ask your guidance.

That those whose bodies or spirits
are heavy with suffering

may be given courage and hope,
ease from the pain, and healing to wholeness.
That we may know how best to help them.

Silence

Lord, in the spirit of obedience:
we ask your guidance.

That those who have died in faith
may rise to eternal life,
and that we may so live on earth
that we are all prepared
for meeting the Father face to face in heaven.

Silence

Lord, in the spirit of obedience:
we ask your guidance.

We make our prayer with Mary,
Mother of Jesus, the Christ:
Hail, Mary . . .

In the knowledge
that God our Father hears us,
let us name our own particular petitions.

Silence

Celebrant
Father of mercy, hear our prayers
which we offer through Jesus, the Christ.
Amen.

TREASURE SEEKERS

Aim: To know that God loves everyone whatever
they look like and however rich or poor they are.

Starter

Have enough small gifts as prizes for each child to
have one. Keep these hidden. Put some folded
pieces of paper in a hat and tell the children that
whoever picks the piece of paper with a smiley face
on it will be able to have a prize! Hype this up a bit
so they are all really hoping to be the lucky one.
Pass round the hat, and tell each child to pick a
piece of paper but not to open it until you say.
When everyone has their paper, let them all open
them up and discover that they have all won a
prize. Give out the prizes with love from the
church.

Teaching

Talk about what it feels like to be left out, and how
it feels when we are the chosen ones. With our God
no one is ever left out and we are all special to him,
even though we are all different. God doesn't just

love those with long hair in bunches, because God
loves everyone! He doesn't just love those who are
wearing stripes, because God loves everyone! Or
those who eat without making a mess, because
God loves everyone! He doesn't just love those
who go to our church, or those on television. Why
not? Because God loves everyone! He doesn't just
love those who are good at football, or those who
live with both Mum and Dad. Why not? Because
God loves everyone! He doesn't just love nice
people. He doesn't just love good people. Do you
know why? *Because God loves everyone!*

Praying

Every person I can see
is loved by Jesus, just like me!
Whoever I am, whatever I do,
you love me, Jesus! And that's true.

Activities

On the sheet there is a picture of the earth with
people all over it. The children can work out which
ones Jesus loves by following a wiggly line with their
finger. They can also make fingerprint pictures with
their own special fingerprints that no one else has.

PEARL DIVERS

Aim: To see the importance and value of Jesus' (and
our) loving obedience.

Starter

Dogs and owners. Everyone gets into pairs, and takes
it in turns to be the dog and its owner at obedience
classes. They are all directed to get their pet to walk
to heel, sit, lie down, beg and stay. They are told to
give lots of praise and encouragement to their pet
as soon at it obeys the instruction.

Teaching

Some of the children may have had experience of
training a pet or watching working dogs, such as
sheepdogs or police dogs. There always has to be a
good friendship between the dog and its owner, so
that the dog is obeying and working hard because
it wants to please the owner it loves. How is that
different from a dog who is badly treated and
beaten? That just makes the dog crouch down
frightened, or it might turn round and attack the
owner. Real obedience is working together out of
love. There are lots of stories of dogs who have
done all kinds of brave and dangerous things, just
because they love their owners.

Read Isaiah 50:5 from the Bible, preferably in a clear children's version, explaining that the prophet is talking about God's obedient Servant, who turned out to be Jesus. Jesus was obedient to everything the Father told him, not because he was scared of punishment, but because he loved his heavenly Father so much.

Praying

Father God, we want to obey you
because we love you,
and know that you love us.
Your loving kindness
is all around us in this world
and we choose to come to you and say,
'Let your will be done in us.'

Activities

The children will need access to a Bible for looking up references which give examples of Jesus' loving obedience, and they can also make a communal collage entitled, 'Let your kingdom come, let your will be done on earth as it is in heaven.' Help them to see that every time we pray this we are placing ourselves in obedience to God.

GOLD PANNERS

Aim: To explore the value and importance of Jesus' loving obedience, and its implications for us as his followers.

Starter

Collect some snails and stage a snail race down a premarked sheet of A4 paper.

Teaching

However much we shouted encouragement at our snails, they weren't able to be particularly obedient either to us, or the ruled lines marking their lanes. They still have no idea of what they were supposed to be doing. Today we are going to look at what obedience really is.

Begin by reading the passage from Isaiah 50, describing God's obedient Servant, willing to go along with God's guidance even in the face of violent opposition. Who does it sound like? For us, living after Jesus' coming, the passage points very significantly to Jesus, describing the kind of loving obedience he showed during all his life and particularly in his trial and crucifixion. This kind of obedience came from the way Jesus was always so close to his Father – at one with him, so that God's will was also Jesus' will.

Now look at today's Gospel from Mark 8. Jesus is making it plain that part of being the Christ is the necessity to go through the suffering foretold by the prophets. That loving obedience is all part of Jesus' identity as the Messiah, or holy, anointed One of God. And Jesus goes further; it's also part of being someone who claims to be one of Christ's followers, like us. If we mean what we say, it will involve a daily willingness to walk the way of the cross (verse 34).

Have the words of the Lord's Prayer available, and draw their attention to the way the first section of the prayer is placing ourselves in that loving obedience, whenever we say, 'Let your kingdom come; let your will be done on earth as it is in heaven.' Do we realise what we are saying here? We need to do that conscious placing of ourselves in obedience to God every single time we say those words – and say them at least morning, afternoon and evening every day.

Praying

Our Father, who art in heaven,
hallowed be thy name;
thy kingdom come;
thy will be done on earth as it is in heaven.

Activities

On the sheet there is an example of how the tongue can be a powerful instrument for spreading both trouble and good. Examples of Jesus' loving obedience are used to help us in our obedience, and they are encouraged to work out what obedience involves.

TWENTY-FIFTH SUNDAY OF THE YEAR

Thought for the day

The truly great in God's eyes are those who are prepared to be last of all and servant of all.

Reflection on the readings

Wisdom of Solomon 2:12, 17-20
Psalm 53
James 3:16-4:3
Mark 9:30-37

Plato reckoned that the only people suitable for leadership and positions of power were those who would never want to do it. The corrupting influence of power is clear for all to see, and we can all think of people in positions of greatness who are there through their ambition rather than their suitability for the office! In today's candid Gospel the disciples are not spared the gaze of the world at their petty arguing about which of them is most important, carrying most status. As we recall our own (probably private) conversations about what people think of us, we can humble ourselves with them as we listen to Jesus' teaching.

The kind of values we usually set store by are upended by Jesus' criteria for greatness. Being the last of all and the servant of all is, for a start, likely to go unnoticed and unappreciated most of the time. But we usually would expect praise and acknowledgement for humble service, and grumble if it wasn't forthcoming. Jesus is talking about enjoying working for others without recognition; keeping such service secret as far as possible.

The little child is a dramatic visual aid of the vulnerable and those of lowest status, without rights or wealth or power. And Jesus is suggesting that we consider ourselves servants with fewer rights than these little ones. We are to gather up all our ambitions about wealth, power and status, which are bound to affect our attitudes to others, and scatter them on the wind, leaving us free and unburdened, so that we can simply serve others in humility and love. We have the shining example of such a life in Jesus himself.

All the battles and strife which James talks about stem from this drive to be considered best, or to be better than other people. Often we ground this drive in our desire to possess money, things, qualifications, people, or any kind of trophy. Sadly, none of it impresses God, and none of it helps us fulfil our true selves, even though Satan persuades us that it will give us what we crave. As James suggests, we need to stand up to Satan and then we will find he slinks away, and we are already totally valued, so there was no need to strive after any of those things. Loving and obedient service, in simple humility, is what gladdens the heart of God, who already loves us completely.

Discussion starters

1. Why does Jesus use a child as a focus for talking about greatness?

2. Look at examples of arguments and strife – personally, locally and internationally – and see if they do come from what Jesus and James suggest.

All-stage talk

You will need to bring along a Christening gift of some kind (Peter Rabbit bowl, silver spoon or locket), a 5 or 10 metre swimming badge, an item of school uniform, several cups or trophies, a graduation certificate or gown, and a driving licence, a few brown envelopes and a clock.

Ask for a volunteer to help take everyone on a whistlestop tour of a lifetime. Work through a person's life (you can call them the name of the volunteer), presenting them with the trophies which mark each stage of the climb to power and greatness. As a baby they are presented with special presents. As they grow up they start doing clever things like swimming and riding bikes. They wear special clothes to show they're old enough and clever enough to be going to school and learning loads more things every morning. Perhaps they have a hobby – in sport or music – and they do so well that they keep winning cups and trophies for it. As they get older still, they're off to university, and a few years later, here they are at their graduation. It's congratulations time again. And then there are the driving lessons and the practice and the extra insurance, and suddenly it's the test, and a smart new driving licence. All they need now is the car to drive. But the work's going well and the money's coming in, so they can buy all the things they've always wanted, and here are the bills to prove it. And then, after a good many years of work, this highly respected person is old enough to retire. They have become a powerful and important pillar of society.

The volunteer is now loaded. Help unload them and thank them for their assistance.

We all have ambitions; we all hope our lives will turn out like our dreams. We want to be successful, liked, appreciated, fit and good-looking. And often we secretly want to be best. Jesus sees all of our dreams, even the secret ones. He knew what the disciples had been muttering about on their way as they walked along. They probably hoped he couldn't hear, because, like all of us, they had a strong suspicion that discussing who had most status was not really Jesus talk. Jesus really didn't care if the important people disapproved of him. He wasn't out to impress anybody, or work his way up, or gain status – he was just there to get on with the work of loving people to wholeness.

And that's what he wants for his followers as well. He wants us to have that freedom, so we can get on with what's really important, instead of wasting our time and energy empire-building in our particular area, impressing people, or collecting status symbols to wear or drive in. What do they matter when we compare them with God's values? Let's learn to be happy and content with nothing but being last, being unnoticed and the servant of all.

All-age ideas

- Act out the Gospel while it is narrated, using a young child. Have the child's parent taking Jesus' part.
- *Secrets.* Give everyone a small piece of paper and invite them to think of some act of loving service they could do without anyone knowing. When they have thought, they fold the pieces of paper up and bring them out to a collection point near the cross. They can enjoy carrying this out during the coming week – a secret between them and God.

Prayer of the Faithful

Celebrant
Let us pray to the God of glory
in whom we live and move and have our being.

Reader
We pray that the Church may hold true
to the teaching of Jesus,
free from the worldly values of status and ambition.
We pray for a spirit of humility
to deflate all pomposity and arrogance.

Silence

Yours, Lord, is the kingdom:
yours the power and yours the glory.

We pray that all in positions of power,
authority and influence in our world
may recognise their calling to servanthood
and never lose their identity
with the needs and longings of those they serve.

Silence

Yours, Lord, is the kingdom:
yours the power and yours the glory.

We pray that all communities
may look after one another,
supporting the vulnerable, encouraging the timid,
providing practical help for all who need it,
and nurturing the young in a climate of trust.

Silence

Yours, Lord, is the kingdom:
yours the power and yours the glory.

We pray that none may be considered expendable,
or beyond our cherishing;
we pray for all who have lost heart,
through pain, suffering or sin,
that God's redeeming power may work its wonders
in the very darkest situations.

Silence

Yours, Lord, is the kingdom:
yours the power and yours the glory.

We pray that all who have wearily
struggled to death
may know the joy of burdens laid down,
and new, lasting life transforming them
through the eternal love of God.

Silence

Yours, Lord, is the kingdom:
yours the power and yours the glory.

We make our prayer with Mary,
who shared her Son's sorrows:
Hail, Mary . . .

Trustingly, we pray in silence
to our loving Lord,
who considers each one of us special.

Silence

Celebrant
Father, you always give us far more
than we can ever deserve;
please fulfil our prayers
in the way that is best for us.
We ask in the name of Jesus Christ.
Amen.

TREASURE SEEKERS

Aim: To know that God loves to see us looking after one another's needs.

Starter

Think of someone in the church community who would appreciate receiving a special 'get well soon' card from the Treasure Seekers group (or whatever the need is). Explain this to the children and bring a suitable card along. Give each child a small piece of paper on which to draw a message, write the children's names on their drawings and stick them all into the card. The children can help put the card into its envelope and see it addressed and stamped.

Teaching

The Treasure Seekers have done a very kind thing this morning, and that card will certainly cheer someone up. God loves to see us looking after one another's needs like that. It makes him very happy indeed!

Jesus always noticed what people were wanting, and went out of his way to help them. If he saw that someone was sad and lonely he would go and talk to them. When people came to him with their legs or backs not working, Jesus loved to mend their bodies and put them right. Jesus calls all his followers (and that's *us!*) to do the same thing – to look after one another's needs.

So how can we do that? What kind things could we do? Talk over their ideas and write them down. (It doesn't matter that they can't read them; they can see that you think they are important.) Read the list of suggestions back to them and give each of them a secret sign on their hand and your own (draw a smiley face) to remind you all of the kind things you and God are planning to do together. Suggest they do them as a secret between them and God.

Praying

Father God, we want to pray
for those who are sad or lonely,
for those who are ill,
for those who are very busy
and get tired from all their jobs.
Please help us to help them.
Amen.

Activities

The children can do another kind thing by making a scrap book of pictures and prayers to be passed around among those who would enjoy such a book. Provide a scrap book and some pictures for the children to cut out and stick in, and scribe for each child so that their prayers are also included. The pictures on the sheet can be coloured and added to the book.

PEARL DIVERS

Aim: To know about Jesus teaching the disciples that being servants is the way of true greatness.

Starter

VIP spaghetti quiz. Have a pot with some different length pieces of string in it. Split the children into teams, and ask the questions. If a question is answered correctly, that team takes a piece of spaghetti. At the end of the quiz, each team ties its pieces of spaghetti together. The longest wins. Here are some ideas for questions:

1. Who is the Prime Minister of England?
2. Who is the headteacher of (school)?
3. Who is the parish priest?
4. Who is the captain of Liverpool?
5. Who is number one in the charts this week?
6. Who runs the Brownies here?
7. Who invented the telephone?
8. Which king had six wives?
9. Who plays (part) in (soap)?
10. Who introduces (animal programme)?

Teaching

What makes some people important and famous? Talk this over, looking at such things as being rich, clever, good-looking, speaking for the rest of us, being specially bad or good. What about God – if he were to draw up a list of important people, would it look the same? What kind of things might God be more concerned with? You could remind them of what happened when Samuel was choosing a king from Jesse's sons – God didn't go for the tall, handsome ones but for David, the youngest, in charge of the sheep. People look at the outward appearance, but God looks at the heart of a person.

One day some of Jesus' disciples were walking along the road having a bit of an argument. Was it about who had to do the washing-up? No. Was it about something Jesus had been teaching them? No. Was it about the road they needed to take? No. They were arguing about which of them ought to be the most important – the greatest of the disciples. Perhaps it went something like this. (Give out different 'scripts' to various children who can read.) Perhaps Peter was saying . . . (Peter reads out: 'I am best. I am very good at fishing. Jesus likes my fish.') Perhaps Andrew was saying . . . (Andrew reads out: 'I am best. I was one of the first to be called by Jesus.') Perhaps James was saying . . . (James reads out: 'I am best. My name starts with a J and so does Jesus.')

They all had their reasons for thinking they ought to be the greatest, most important disciple of all. That evening, Jesus asked them what they had been arguing about, and they all felt rather silly. It didn't seem to matter who was best when Jesus was there. But Jesus wanted to teach them something very important. And it's important for us to learn as well, because we are all Jesus' followers. Jesus explained that the way to be greatest in the kingdom of God was to be the last of all and the servant of all! Not richest, not best-looking, not sporting champion, but the last of all and the servant of all.

Praying

Lord, teach me the joy
of serving others for no reward
apart from knowing that I am making you happy.

Activities

On the sheet there is a maze to construct and follow. All the usual worldly status symbols turn out to be dead ends, but the right route is going by the way of loving service. They will need thin card to reinforce the bottom of the maze and the uprights.

GOLD PANNERS

Aim: To understand Jesus' teaching about greatness and servanthood.

Starter

Have a number of pictures of famous people from newspapers and magazines cut out and stuck around the room, numbered. Give out sheets of paper. Everyone goes round writing down the names of those pictured. The one with most right gets to wear a posh hat to show how clever they are.

Teaching

All the people in those pictures were famous, for all sorts of reasons. They were all 'the greatest' in their particular area. Now read today's Gospel, where the disciples have been arguing about which of them should be the greatest. Why were they ashamed to admit to Jesus what they had been talking about? Why might their argument have disturbed Jesus? (He knew that they were going to be the leaders of the Church, and here they were behaving like pagan leaders, full of boasting and jealousy.) Notice how Jesus both explains and shows them, with the little child, what he means. Children were vulnerable, and with no status at all, so to accept Jesus by accepting them suggests that he is prepared to think of himself on a level with what most people would consider the very lowest of the low. (How do we choose our friends? Would we feel embarrassed to be seen with some people because our other friends despise them?)

Now read the passage from James. There are more arguments here, and James is helping his hearers understand where all this strife comes from. That makes it easier to sort out, provided we genuinely want it sorted. Sometimes people enjoy having their battles and moans. Look at the sound advice James gives. He helps us see that Satan fools us into thinking he's big and powerful, but if we really stand our ground and fix our feet in what we know is right and good, Satan's power trickles out of him, and he slinks away. This is a very useful image for when we find ourselves being tempted, and it always works.

Praying

The world wants the wealth to live in state,
but you show us a new way to be great:
like a servant you came
and if we do the same
we'll be turning the world upside down.

(Taken from the song *O Lord, all the world* by Patrick Appleford © 1965 Josef Weinberger)

Activities

There is a short sketch to look at the reasons for arguments, linked with the James reading, and some information about status so that they can better grasp what Jesus is saying in today's Gospel. There are some different life ambitions to consider.

TWENTY-SIXTH SUNDAY OF THE YEAR

Thought for the day

Don't let your body lead you into sin and risk exchanging eternal life for eternal punishment.

Reflection on the readings

Numbers 11:25-29
Psalm 18
James 5:1-6
Mark 9:38-43, 45, 47-48

Nobody talks much about hell. We have moved away from the graphic fire and brimstone images of the medieval artists, and tend to pass over Jesus' teaching about it. But sometimes we have to address it, and today is one of those days.

Jesus had a lot of hard sayings for his disciples to swallow. They needed to understand and accept, for instance, that God doesn't rigidly limit his spirit to work within the Church. Joshua had been just as offended by the seventy elders all prophesying, and Moses had to remind him that as far as he was concerned he'd be happy for the whole community to be filled with the Spirit of God. God doesn't limit his power to those of specific groups. We, too, need have no problem with Christian work being done by those outside the Church.

And then there is the hard but clear teaching on the importance of self-control. Jesus is not pretending temptation is easy to cope with. He knew from personal experience that it was agonisingly difficult. It is always a struggle to resist temptation, and fighting it can feel as drastic as chopping off hands or feet, or plucking out eyes. Even hearts, if they are causing us to sin and distracting us from God. It is because we don't take temptation seriously enough that we so often fall into sin. Jesus, in his agony in the garden, as he watches and prays desperately to resist the temptation to opt out of the work of salvation, urges Peter and the others to do the same, so that they will not fall when the onslaught of temptation engulfs them, but they sleep instead.

The reason for Jesus' urgent concern for us is that sin has eternal terrible consequences that we can barely imagine. It is forfeiting eternal life we are talking about, and some kind of eternal punishment which certainly fills Jesus with horror to think of. If he was taking it that seriously, then surely we would be wise to do the same.

Discussion starters

1. Do we believe that prayer is truly effective or not? If not, what may be blocking the power?

2. Jesus is very serious about not leading the vulnerable into sin. What can we actively do in our society as those concerned for the eternal well-being of souls?

All-stage talk

Bring along some scissors and some thick garden wire, and something which has been ruined by being used in the wrong way – such as a spoon, buckled after being used as a trowel, or a tray which has gone rusty from being used under the Christmas tree.

Ask people what they think would happen if you were to use this good pair of scissors to cut the wire. Although you'd probably be able to cut through it eventually, you'd probably spoil the scissors for ever – they aren't made to cut wire, so the wire would ruin them. Show your example of something you have already ruined through using it in a way it wasn't designed for.

It's just the same with human beings. We were all made in the image and likeness of our loving God. We were designed to love God and love one another, and we work at our best like this.

But our readings today are full of the sad truth that we often live in a selfish and wrong way. If we insist on living this wrong way again and again, we're setting out on a self-destruction course. Jesus wants all his followers (including us) to know that it isn't worth choosing wrong ways of living all the time because that way we'll end up being destroyed instead of having the wonderful everlasting life we were made for, and Jesus wants the very best for us all.

And there's another thing. God is very concerned about all the other people who don't realise how dangerous and destructive it is to live wrongly, and he needs those who know God's love to help them all. God badly needs some volunteers living in this world, and this parish, going to the local school, shopping in the local supermarket, working wherever you work, and belonging to the clubs you belong to.

To be of any use, we'll need God to sort out our own sin, and we mustn't let our minds or bodies lead us into wrong thinking and doing. We need to get that done, however much it hurts and however difficult it seems – even if it feels as painful as chopping off a hand or a foot. Turning from sin hurts, but it won't kill your eternal life, like the sin will. Let's live instead as we were designed to live – growing in love day by day, looking out for one another's needs, and working together for the coming of God's kingdom.

All-age ideas

- Have a display with, on one side, a moth-eaten or very grubby garment, with the sign 'Original price £xxx – value now £???'. On the other side have a glass of water with the caption 'Your gift to a thirsty person' and the sign 'Value £???'.

- As a poster or banner, have a selection of many and various pictures of people, with the words: 'Humans – designed for loving'.

- For the Penitential Rite give everyone a piece of paper with a '1' written on it. Invite them to reflect on what they have made number 1 in their time, loving and spending, instead of putting God first.

Prayer of the Faithful

Celebrant
Conscious of our need for God's power
in our lives, our Church and our world,
let us pray to him now.

Reader
We pray for the courage
to reject sin and evil in our own lives.
May our churches be powerhouses of the Spirit,
training and upholding us
as we live the Father's life and love in the world.

Silence

Your Law, O Lord, is perfect:
it revives the soul.

We pray for a greater awareness
of what damages souls and encourages evil,
and for widespread commitment
to addressing the dangers.
We pray for all who earn their living
through selling what destroys lives.

Silence

Your Law, O Lord, is perfect:
it revives the soul.

We pray for the young,
and the vulnerable in every community,
for all in positions of trust,
for child-minders, playgroups and schools,
for loving nurture and protection from all evil.

Silence

Your Law, O Lord, is perfect:
it revives the soul.

We pray for all long-term carers
and those they look after,
for all who are having
to learn dependence gracefully,
and those who are imprisoned by their guilt.
May the Lord work his healing love in them all,
reassuring them of his presence.

Silence

Your Law, O Lord, is perfect:
it revives the soul.

We pray that no one may be lost eternally,
that all may turn from their sin
and trust in God's mercy;
that physical death may be but the gate to heaven.
We commend to God's loving mercy
those who have recently died.

Silence

Your Law, O Lord, is perfect:
it revives the soul.

Encouraged by Mary's steadfast example,
we make our prayer with her:
Hail, Mary . . .

In silence filled with love,
we name our particular prayer burdens.

Silence

Celebrant
With thankfulness and praise
for all your blessings to us, Father,
we offer you these prayers,
through Jesus Christ.
Amen.

TREASURE SEEKERS

Aim: To know that it's good to pray for one another.

Starter

Prepare a prayer area which looks beautiful and special, with lights and flowers, pictures and a cross. It might include a mirror lying flat so that everything is reflected. Have quiet music playing and gather the children to sit round, to sing a quiet worship song such as *Jesus, reign in me* or *Jesus, I adore you*. Then all pray for each of the children in turn by name, like this:

> Jesus, we ask you to bless Sean
> with your love in his life.
> We thank you for his funny jokes
> and the way he cheers us up.
> We ask you to help him and his family
> as they get ready to move house soon.
> Be with Sean every day of his life.
> Amen.

The other children can stretch one hand up to God and the other towards the child being prayed for to remind them 'in body' that they are being channels of God's love as they pray.

Teaching

It's good to pray for one another. It's good to know that other Christians are praying for us. Praying is the way that God helps us look after one another and deepen our love for one another. Today we're going to learn a bit more about how to pray.

Show the children a walking stick, zimmer frame or crutches, and talk with them about who uses these and why. Imagine together what it must be like just to need help walking, and to be in pain, let alone losing the use of your legs. When we pray for people, we need to imagine what it's like for them, and feel sorry for them. Then we ask our lovely Jesus to help those people. (Do this.) Jesus has lots of ways of helping someone. Sometimes he helps by making their legs strong again so they work. Sometimes he makes the person happy and peaceful even though their legs still don't work. Whatever is best and right, Jesus will do when we pray, trusting him.

Show the children a watering can, with water inside. When we pray, Jesus can pour out his love through us so that it reaches other people who don't pray. (Pour out the water so it sprinkles over a plant.) When we pray we are like channels of God's love. We reach up to God (reach up one hand), letting him fill us with his love, and send it out over the places and people in the world who need it (stretch out other hand). As they are in this position ask them to close their eyes and think of God's love coming into them and them pouring that love over the people who are sad at the moment, all over the world. 'Jesus, fill us now with your love. Let that love pour out over all the people who are sad, so that they feel your love and peace instead of their sadness. Amen.'

You can tell them that children are specially good at praying because they are so good at trusting God. God enjoys working with children of their age – they don't have to wait until they're older.

Now they can practise, talking about people they feel need praying for, and all the children praying together in their own words, for this person or situation. Thank God for answering all our prayers and letting us work with him to spread his love and peace.

Praying

Jesus, show me
who to pray for
and what to pray for.
Thank you for having me
on your prayer team. Amen.

Activities

The sheet can be made into a prayer corner for their bedroom. They will need thin card to strengthen it and a hole punch and some cord or wool to fasten it.

PEARL DIVERS

Aim: To explore the meaning of Jesus' teaching about cutting off hands and feet.

Starter

Make up some salt dough, with different children adding the ingredients and everyone having a go at the kneading. Here is the recipe: two cups of flour, one cup of salt, water to mix. Make impressions of hands and bare feet in the dough.

Teaching

In our Gospel today we find Jesus warning us about hands and feet – and eyes. Let's first listen to what he was saying and then we'll try to work out what he meant. (Read Mark 9:42-47.) Did they hear how much Jesus wanted the children to be kept safe? That's because Jesus loves you and really cares about you.

But what was all that about chopping off hands and feet and taking out eyes? What on earth is Jesus talking about.

(Lay the impressions of feet and hands down so everyone can see them.) Jesus knew something we have all probably found out. Sometimes it's our hands that can lead us into wrong, cruel or unkind behaviour. What kind of ways are we able to use our hands for wrong, cruel or unkind things? (Collect suggestions. They may mention such things as hurting someone, stealing what doesn't belong to us, or spoiling something.) Talk about feet and eyes in the same way.

Jesus was warning us to get tough with our eyes, hands and feet whenever we find them leading us into what we know is bad, wrong and unloving. Of course he doesn't mean that we're to actually chop them off – that's a jokey way of putting it to make the point! But we *are* to get tough with ourselves and not *let* our eyes or hands or feet lead us away from the right and loving way to live.

Sometimes temptations to do the wrong thing are really strong and hard to fight off. We need to fight temptation with God's armour on, and with God's weapons of love and truth, prayer and praise. It's a battle, fighting temptation, but God's power is always stronger than evil, so if we stick with God, we'll win. And if we do fall into sin and evil, it's important that we sort things out with God as soon as we possibly can, so that God can forgive us and help us put things right.

Praying

Forgive us our trespasses,
as we forgive those who trespass against us;
and lead us not into temptation,
but deliver us from evil.
Amen.

Activities

The children will need Bibles to do the activities based on Mark 9 and James 5, and some salt dough to make the models suggested.

GOLD PANNERS

Aim: To look at the importance of being prepared for temptation.

Starter

Press flour into a pudding basin with a coin somewhere inside and carefully upend it so you have a pudding-shape of flour. People take turns at slicing the 'pudding' without making it collapse, and without dislodging the coin. Continue until one of those things happens, and the one who was cutting a slice at the time has to clear it all away. But they can keep the coin!

Teaching

Today we're looking at resisting temptation. If we're not well prepared for it, we're more likely to find our good intentions collapsing in a cloud of dust, like our flour pudding. We're taking temptation seriously because Jesus did. He was tempted very severely just after his Baptism, during his ministry and in the garden of Gethsemane, just before he was arrested, and he urgently warned his disciples to watch and pray so that they wouldn't give way to temptation. They didn't realise how important it was, and ended up scattering, and leaving Jesus when he most needed them.

Begin by reading today's Gospel, from Mark 9, picking up on how seriously Jesus is wanting us to take this teaching. He uses strong, violent examples to make us think, and to help us recognise what a real battle it can be to resist evil; it isn't something to treat casually because the effects are so lasting and so damaging, both to ourselves and others, not just in this life but after death as well. Jesus is suggesting that we take strong action to turn our backs on temptation before it drags us into sin. As soon as a sin looks attractive to us – tempting – our danger lights should start flashing and that's when we need to take action. If we don't, the temptation will just get stronger, and harder to resist. Temptation is well worth resisting, because sin is long-term destructive.

Now look at the passage from Numbers, seeing how temptation works on the people, and the trouble it causes. Also notice the link between Joshua's protest and the disciples' protest in Mark 9:38, and the similarity between Moses' and Jesus' replies.

Praying

The dearest idol I have known,
whatever that idol be,
help me to tear it from thy throne
and worship only thee.

Activities

On the sheet the passage from James draws attention to faithful prayer and its effectiveness. There is also a diagram showing how temptation works and how we can short circuit it in God's strength.

TWENTY-SEVENTH SUNDAY OF THE YEAR

Thought for the day

Human beings are made responsible for the care of creation but are subject to God in all aspects of their lives.

Reflection on the readings

Genesis 2:18-24
Psalm 127
Hebrews 2:9-11
Mark 10:2-16

In the Genesis reading we look at the ancient and primitive of the creation stories, with Adam being taken around the freshly made world, naming the animals and thus being established as responsible for the care of creation. No animal being suitable as a helpmate, woman is created from Adam, though for this 'birthing' Adam is anaesthetised and spared the pain! (Floating ribs would have become separated in skeletons seen around at the time of writing, possibly giving rise to the idea of woman being created from a spare rib.)

The deep truth of the story lies in God creating people who are given responsibility while remaining subject to God, their creator. The 'God with man and woman' teamwork is established right at the start of history. It is just as fresh and definite now, and we must not shirk that responsibility, under God, to care for the universe we inhabit. We are not called to dominate it and squeeze it dry for our own short-sighted indulgence, but to be careful stewards in every generation.

That careful stewardship extends to our own lives as well, and all our relationships, particularly marriage. Choosing life partners is a serious matter for God and us to consider carefully together, and the upholding of marriage is the responsibility of the whole community. Jesus takes his disciples back to this basic established pattern when he reinforces the importance of lifelong faithfulness in marriage. We cannot tear these verses out of the Gospel simply because they are at variance with society's norms. Jesus is describing God's good intention for those called to marriage to live in the security and comfort of lifelong partnership under his banner of love.

Of course there will be cases where, due to our hardness of heart, our wrong choices or through other pressures, the ideal falters and relationships break down. Those are occasions of deep sadness for the whole community, for a recognition of our brokenness, for repentance and forgiveness. They do not alter the wonderful provision God has made for us.

Discussion starters

1. Should our aim in life for ourselves and our children be happiness or goodness? How will this affect our attitude to life's troubles and hardships?

2. What are the difficulties involved in taking Jesus' teaching on marriage seriously?

All-stage talk

Invite people to share what jobs they are responsible for, including household chores, professional responsibilities and so on. Have people of all ages contributing so that it is clear that we all have responsibilities of some sort, whatever our age. You could also draw attention to those responsible for particular jobs in church, making it an opportunity for everyone to thank the flower arrangers, servers and choir, cleaners and pastoral team.

Point out that right from the beginning, when Adam was naming the animals, God has made us human beings responsible for looking after this world and each other. That is the important job that God has given us to do. If we all did our bit and everyone acted responsibly to the planet and to one another, under God's guiding hand, we would find that our life together here would be greatly blessed. People would have enough to eat, and many disasters and much suffering would be avoided.

So why doesn't that happen, when it seems such good sense for us to live according to the Maker's instructions?

The trouble is that we all let our own wants and selfishness get in the way. If we, as rich nations, started acting more responsibly, then things we've become used to getting cheaply would be more expensive, and we might have to make do with less. Our greed stops us acting responsibly. So does our short-sightedness, when we want 'lots, now!' instead of considering those who haven't yet been born.

It's even the same in our friendships and marriages. If we are responsible in these, we will be caring for the other person and looking after their needs, sensitive to their feelings and wanting to help them. If one or other or both stop doing that, the relationship becomes hurtful and wearing instead of rewarding. The answer may not be to get out of the friendship or marriage, but change our way of behaving with each other, talking things over with each other and with God, learning to be responsible again. It is grown-up and sensible to know that life can't always be happy, and the person we love can't always agree with us. Giving one

another space, understanding that we all have bad days, forgiving one another and working at our friendships – all this is part of being the responsible people God created us to be.

He doesn't expect us to do it without help. God is there with us in all the bad patches as well as the easy rides, and as a community we are to look after one another properly, making sure we're all OK and coming to the rescue whenever someone isn't.

All-age ideas

- If the church hasn't already got a system for community caring, today is a good time to start one. This might involve grouping people to keep an eye on one another's needs, looking out for them and being there for them in any rough patches. Spreading the responsibility like this makes for a realistic expectation of care without overload.

- Married couples may like to affirm their marriage vows today, with the whole community affirming their commitment to the support and nurture of families.

Prayer of the Faithful

Celebrant
Let us come before God our Maker,
making our prayers to him,
through Jesus and in the power of the Holy Spirit.

Reader
We pray that the Church may be alive
to God's beckoning,
quick to obey his will
and always ready to act in his loving service
for the good of the world.

Silence

Lord of heaven:
let your will be done.

We pray that all leaders and heads of state
may take wise advice and act responsibly
for the well-being of all.
We pray for God's guidance
in the way we manage and care for this planet,
its resources, riches and inhabitants.

Silence

Lord of heaven:
let your will be done.

We pray for all marriages,
for those seeking marriage partners
and those whose marriages are under strain.

We pray for all in close relationships,
that there may be mutual love and respect.

Silence

Lord of heaven:
let your will be done.

We pray for all who are suffering
through illness, accident or deliberate cruelty;
for refugees and all who are abused;
that through the caring of human hands
they may experience the caring hands of God.

Silence

Lord of heaven:
let your will be done.

We pray for all who have died violently
or suddenly, or with no one to miss them.
May all who have died in faith
be judged with mercy
and welcomed into eternal life.

Silence

Lord of heaven:
let your will be done.

We pray with Mary,
the Mother of the Lord:
Hail, Mary . . .

Knowing that God our Father
hears the cries of his children,
we pray in silence
for our needs and cares.

Silence

Celebrant
Father of compassion and mercy,
accept our prayers,
through the person of Jesus Christ.
Amen.

TREASURE SEEKERS

Aim: To know that God wants us to look after the world.

Starter

Scatter around some fallen leaves. The children gather them up one at a time and bring them to place them on brown, red, orange, yellow or green paper, matching the leaf to the approximate colour of the paper.

Teaching

Talk about the lovely colours of our world in all the different seasons, and show them different coloured pieces of paper. What do the colours remind them of? (The blue of sky and sea and forget-me-nots, the pink of sunsets and roses, and so on.) Celebrate the colourful world God has made.

When God made people, he gave us an important job to do. We are to look after this world, and all the universe, as carefully as we possibly can. We are to look after the ground (place down a chunk of rock) and all the minerals of our planet like gold and silver, iron and copper, calcium and sulphur. We are to look after all the growing plants (place down a potted plant) like rain forests and cactus, fruits, flowers and herbs. We are to look after all the animals (place down a book of animals and turn through some of the pages) like horses, fish, birds, spiders and worms.

And we are to look after one another (place down a book with pictures of people from all different parts of the world and flick through it), sharing so that everyone has enough to eat, and taking care of one another.

Are there any Treasure Seekers who are ready to help God look after the world? That's good! Could we start today? How? Talk over their ideas and do your best to put into practice any that are practical. (What about giving each child a bag to collect litter in and cleaning up this patch of the world together? Or recycling their newspapers, bottles, stamps and cans?) The ideas could be written down and perhaps put in the parish newsletter.

Praying

Father God, we love this world
that you have made.
We are old enough to help look after it
and we're going to start by . . .

Activities

Use the leaves from the starter activity to stick on the sheet and make leaf pictures. There is also a picture of a rain forest so they can go on safari, hunting for hidden plants, fruit and creatures.

PEARL DIVERS

Aim: To know that we are responsible for looking after the world and under God's authority.

Starter

Name the animal. Have a number of pictures of animals spread out on the floor or wall so everyone can see them. One person decides on an animal but doesn't say which it is. This person starts to describe the animal, one fact at a time, and the others try to guess which one it is. Whoever names it first has next go.

Teaching

Explain that the Bible has included two versions of the story of how the world was made, one an even older story than the other. Show them the story we know best, the one at the very beginning of the Bible, with the world being made stage by stage, in six days, or ages. Adam and Eve – the first people – were made on day six, and they were told to look after the world.

Today's reading is from Genesis chapter 2. (Show them this.) And this version of the same story is even older than the other one. Both stories give us the same truth – that God made the world, and people, and gave them the responsibility of looking after it all. Read today's reading from the Bible. Remind them of Adam being taken around to name all the animals. What did he call the animal with long ears and a fluffy tail which hops about? What did he call the animal that is furry and striped, has sharp teeth and runs fast?

What the writer of the story is telling us is that, as human beings, we have the important, responsible job of taking good care of creation. How do they think we are doing? When do humans make a good job of looking after the world? Where do we mess up the job God has given us to do? On a sheet of paper or a blackboard, jot down their ideas in tick and cross columns. Talk through any ideas they have for ways we could do better, locally and internationally. (Look, for instance, at recycling our litter, asking for simpler packaging, using feet and bikes and public transport more instead of cars.)

We have to look after one another as well – our friends and the people in our families. How? Again, share ideas.

Praying

All good gifts around us
are sent from heaven above;
so thank the Lord, O thank the Lord,
for all his love!

Activities

On the sheet there are pictures of animals nearing extinction, forests being cut down and industry polluting the environment. They can talk over what we can do to protect the world from such damage. They are also encouraged to see how they might help others in the world who have no fresh water. Addresses are given for letters and gifts to be sent.

GOLD PANNERS

Aim: To explore responsibility and faithfulness in caring for our world and in our relationships.

Starter

Play consequences. Each section is written and passed on around the circle, before the disjointed stories are read out. (Girl) met (boy) at (place). He said to her (. . .), she said to him (. . .), and the consequence was (. . .).

Teaching

Practically every book, film and soap is about people and their relationships, falling in and out of love, marrying, divorcing, quarrelling, making up and messing up. Today we are going to look at what the Bible teaches us about faithfulness and responsibility, both with one another and with the natural world.

Begin by reading the passage from Genesis, looking at the way humankind, in the person of Adam, is placed in a position of responsibility, to care for the world and look after it. Notice how life-long partnership is seen as God's way of providing us with companionship and help, as we work under God's rule for the good of the world.

Now read today's Gospel, where Jesus is teaching his disciples about divorce. He reminds them of the Genesis passage we have just read, reinforcing that God's way of faithfulness and responsibility in a lifelong relationship is good and rewarding. What does that mean for us as Christians, living in a time of easy divorce? It means we're going to need really serious thought and lots of prayer as we go about choosing a partner with whom we're expecting to have to spend the rest of our life, through the difficult times and broken nights, and financial worries and growing children, as well as the high spots and romantic bliss!

Praying

Lord, for ourselves;
in living power remake us –
self on the cross
and Christ upon the throne,
past put behind us,
for the future take us,
Lord of our lives,
to live for Christ alone.

(Taken from the song *Lord, for the years* by Timothy Dudley-Smith © Timothy Dudley-Smith)

Activities

On the sheet there is a questionnaire to help them look at choosing a marriage partner for life, as a basis for discussion about this issue. Other callings in life are also explored. There is also space given to the responsible care of our universe, with examples of good and bad stewardship.

TWENTY-EIGHTH SUNDAY OF THE YEAR

Thought for the day

The most valuable possession is not the wealth that owns us, but is Christ, the Wisdom of God, who gives us untold riches.

Reflection on the readings

Wisdom 7:7-11
Psalm 89
Hebrews 4:12-13
Mark 10:17-30

The author of the Book of Wisdom is on a quest, a quest for God. Such a search for God alters our whole outlook on life. It isn't a casual hobby, or a weekend interest. While we actively seek God, we will be listening and looking attentively, and this will move us to question our own motives for doing things, and the way we behave. We cannot be seeking God, for instance, if we are trampling on all that is right and good, despising those who tell the truth and crushing the poor. If we are honest and serious in our search, the very seeking will begin to change us, by changing our hearts.

The writer of Hebrews has obviously seen and experienced this process, and likens the power of the word of God to a sharp sword – or perhaps for us the image of a surgeon's scalpel – with its precise, clean cut, enabling the healing work to be done. Once the thoughts and attitudes of our hearts are being transformed, through God's power, then the impossible business of conquering sin becomes a distinct possibility; hope is in sight for us at last!

The young man in today's Gospel is keen. He comes running up to Jesus, wanting to know how he can inherit eternal life. Typically, Jesus doesn't answer directly, but picks up on the young man's thinking, as shown in calling Jesus 'good'. His seeking has already led him to recognise goodness in this preacher, and Jesus helps him further along, to look at what God's ideas of goodness are, and where that challenges the young man's life. When

he moves away frowning, it isn't that he disagrees with Jesus, but that he has just realised he is right.

Like the young man, we who seek will find Jesus challenging us, and then we have to choose whether to go on with the search, or press cancel.

Discussion starters

1. How can we help one another through the dark times when God does not seem to be answering us or making himself known?

2. What makes it so incredibly worthwhile to follow Jesus, in spite of the difficulties?

All-stage talk

Beforehand set up a kind of treasure hunt, like this. Prepare the following envelopes, numbered clearly, and place them all around the church.

1. Contains the reference Wisdom 7:7 and a Bible with a bookmark in the right place.

2. Contains a charity envelope with a description of the need for fresh water in many villages, or an immediate crisis concern.

3. Contains a flag of our nation.

Ask for a couple of volunteers, old enough to read, and send them off to search for envelope number 1. When they bring it back, ask them to open it and look up the reference in the Bible. This was part of our first reading today, and in order to understand what seeking God involves, we're doing it. The author knew that seeking God actually changes us, helping us to find God. Already our search has led us to pick up a Bible and read it. All of us need to do that – it's no good having a Bible at home if we never open it up and read it! As we heard in our second reading today, the word of God is living and active. If we are really seeking God, we'll have to find out what the word of God says, every day.

Ask for another couple of volunteers to search for envelope number 2. They open it and show the contents. Either describe the needs in the present crisis, or explain how (CAFOD) is trying to provide the basic need of fresh water for villages in Africa and India, where the children die because the water is so bad. We have fresh water there in our taps all the time! What can we do to help these people? God is leading us to see with his eyes of compassion and love. Explain how the parish may already be responding through its concern for the developing world.

Another couple of volunteers search for envelope number 3. Inside is the national flag. Invite people to think about their country – the things that make them happy about it and the things which sadden them. As we seek God's goodness, truth and justice, we'll find that we notice things that need to be changed. Our country needs us to stand up for what is right and fight what is evil. Are we doing that, or leaving it to other people?

The young man in the Gospel was seeking God, and Jesus helped him. The next stage of that young man's journey into God would be to change things in his life. If we set out to seek God, we must expect the same.

All-age ideas

- Outside the church have a large sign with an arrow, saying, 'God-seekers this way!'
- Have the Gospel acted out, with people taking parts.

Prayer of the Faithful

Celebrant
Let us lay down our own agendas
and seek the face of God,
and his will for the Church and for the world.

Reader
We pray for all who are seeking God,
and for the nurturing process in this parish.
We pray for opportunities to share God's love
and draw others to meet him.

Silence

Father, your will be done:
on earth as in heaven.

We pray for all who are fighting against evil
for goodness, truth and justice,
both those who make the world news
and those whose battles are known only to God.
We pray for our country and its leaders,
that this nation may seek God.

Silence

Father, your will be done:
on earth as in heaven.

We pray that wealth and comfort may not divert us
from searching out the heart of God;
that we may hear God's challenging
and gladly respond to him;
that our homes and communities
may sparkle with God's glory.

Silence

Father, your will be done:
on earth as in heaven.

We pray for the disillusioned and depressed
and all who have lost their way in life;
we pray for those corrupted by evil,
trained in hatred and twisted by bitterness.
We pray for the transforming of these lives.

Silence

Father, your will be done:
on earth as in heaven.

We pray for those whose earthly life
has come to an end,
and for those who mourn their going.
May the dead rest in the peace and joy of heaven.

Silence

Father, your will be done:
on earth as in heaven.

We join our prayer with Mary,
who laid up treasure in heaven:
Hail, Mary . . .

As our loving Father listens in love,
we share with him our personal burdens,
joys and sorrows.

Silence

Celebrant
Father, in your great mercy,
hear these prayers we offer,
through Jesus Christ.
Amen.

TREASURE SEEKERS

Aim: To know that we are to seek God and find him, and help others to do the same.

Starter

Set up an edible treasure hunt, leading the children from one numbered box to the next. Spread the boxes around the edges of the room. Give them each a length of string, with a twiglet tied to one end. (This stops them losing the other things off the end.) In numerical order they thread on an object from each box. They should each end up with their strings looking identically threaded. Box one contains hula hoops (the edible sort) box two has polos, box three has jelly rings and box four has biscuits with a hole in the middle. Those with the right order on the string can eat their necklace.

Teaching

Talk about our funny treasure hunt. We had to seek for the right number on the box, and get that right. Then we had to do something with what we found. That led us on to the next thing to seek   we found the treasure as we went along, didn't we? And it was treasure that tasted good.

The Bible tells us that we are to seek God as we live our lives. It's a bit like our treasure hunt. We seek, or search, for God by looking out for his love, just as we looked out for the numbers on the boxes. We might find God's love in helping someone, being friendly, enjoying God's beautiful world or talking over our fears and worries with God. There are lots of different ways we can find God's love around, just as there were lots of different tasty things to thread on our string. Our strings were filled up with all sorts of tasty things, and our lives will be filled up with the love of God as we seek him.

Seeking God will help us to know what is right and good, and that will make us happy as Jesus' friends.

Ask if any of them helped someone to find any of the boxes. Thank them for doing that. God wants us to help others to seek him as well. We could invite them to Living Water, or lend them one of our favourite Bible stories, and we can pray for them. That way we will be helping them to get to know our lovely God.

Praying

As I get to know you, Jesus,
I love you more and more.
You're kind and good,
you're strong and brave,
and I'm glad you are my friend.

Activities

On the sheet there are pictures of children who are seeking God in different ways, and they can circle the ones they do as well, or want to start doing. There is space for them to draw a person they want to help to seek God.

PEARL DIVERS

Aim: To know the story of the rich young man, and Jesus' teaching about entering the kingdom.

Starter

Creeping with the keys. Sit in a circle, with one person in the centre, blindfolded. Someone is given a bunch of keys, and they creep all round the outside of the circle, trying to get back in and to the person in the middle without being heard. If the blindfolded person hears the keys, she points in the direction of the sound. If that is the right place, she joins the circle and someone else becomes blindfolded in the centre.

Teaching

God is never blindfolded – he sees everything. Sometimes people creep around the world doing what they know is evil and wrong, thinking that God can't see and doesn't know, but God knows all about their evil, and he knows why they are doing it. So God can see everything about us – both our outsides and our innermost secret thoughts. But we can't see God, can we? That's because God is Spirit, and so bright with goodness and love that we wouldn't be able to cope with seeing him just yet. But he does want us to seek for him, searching him out so that we get to know him really well. Today we're going to hear about someone who was seeking God for all he was worth.

You will need two of the leaders, two of the young people, or a leader and a rehearsed child to prepare the script. The actors can be dressed up.

(Jesus walks into the room and the young-man runs up to him, kneeling before him.)

Young man Good Teacher, what must I do to get eternal life?

(Jesus looks thoughtful, looks at the man, and helps him up.)

Jesus Why are you calling me good?

(Young man looks puzzled.)

Jesus No one is good, only God. You know the commandments? *(Young man nods, pleased, and counts them on his fingers as Jesus says them.)* Don't murder, don't commit adultery, don't steal, don't lie, don't cheat . . . *(The man looks puzzled again as this isn't one of the commandments.)* honour your father and mother . . .

Young man Yes, teacher, I know all that. I've been keeping the commandments since I was a little boy! But I still feel I'm missing out somewhere. It's more than just obeying the rules, isn't it?

(Jesus looks at him and smiles, placing his hands on the young man's shoulders.)

Jesus Yes, you're right, my son, there is more. There's something else you need to do

– but it won't be easy for you. *(The young man looks pleased and ready to do anything. Jesus stands back and looks at him very seriously.)* Go and sell whatever you own and give it to the poor. All the treasure you have then will be treasure in heaven. Oh and then . . . *(Jesus smiles)* come and follow me!

Young man *(Half to himself)* Sell everything . . . EVERYTHING! Oh my goodness. *(His face clouds over and he looks at Jesus, shaking his head in disbelief before walking away, muttering to himself.)*

(Jesus walks towards the Pearl Divers group, shaking his head sadly.)

Jesus Oh dear, he's so attached to all the things he owns, you see. Do you realise how difficult it is to enter God's kingdom? Especially if you're used to having lots of nice things around you. I reckon it's easier for a camel to get through the eye of a needle than for the rich to get into God's kingdom.

(Now you walk up to Jesus.)

You Goodness, Jesus, in that case who has any chance at all of entering the kingdom of God?

Jesus *(Shrugs)* Well, if you're talking about getting into God's kingdom all by yourself, I'd say no one has any chance at all! *(He smiles)* But if you let God do it in you – that's a very different matter. The impossible becomes possible!

You But some people give up everything to follow you, Jesus.

Jesus *(Nods)* That's right. And I can assure you that no one who sacrifices house, family or friends or land because of me will ever lose out. They'll get it all back many times over, in a different way, with eternal life thrown in!

Praying

It's so hard to enter the kingdom of God
but I want so much to do it;
harder than threading a camel through a needle,
but I want so much to be there.
Your kingdom of love and joy and peace
is the place I want to be,
and I know that only through God my Saviour
can I enter it and be free!
Amen.

Activities

The sheet can be made into a card which enables us to get into the kingdom through the grace of God. They will need a Bible to work out the puzzle about the word of God.

GOLD PANNERS

Aim: To ask the young man's question.

Starter

Have two people turning a long skipping rope. The others have to try getting through the turning rope without getting entangled.

Teaching

Have the words of the young man written down and explain that this was a question put to Jesus by a young man. Talk over what they would say to the young man if they were asked the question.

Now read today's Gospel, with different people taking the various parts. How does Jesus' response compare with ours? Notice how he doesn't answer directly, but addresses what is going on in the man's mind as well as what he actually asks.

Next read the passage from Wisdom, looking at the importance of seeking God. God is found through the seeking. Go back to the Gospel where the disciples ask how anyone at all can be saved, and see how Jesus tells them that this is impossible for us to do for ourselves; we need God for it, and then it becomes possible.

Finally read the passage from Hebrews, and think about what effect Jesus' words had on the young man, both immediately and possibly after he had calmed down a bit. The word of God is just as challenging to us, and just as effective, if we listen to it.

Praying

All that I dream, all that I pray,
all that I'll ever make I give to you today.
Take and sanctify these gifts
for your honour, Lord,
Knowing that I love and serve you
is enough reward.
All that I am, all that I do,
all that I'll ever have I offer now to you.

(Taken from the song *All that I am* by Sebastian Temple © 1967 OCP Publications, USA)

Activities

The sheet reinforces the teaching in the Gospel, with them taking a look at the things in their own lives that would be hard to give up, and a look at Christians who can witness to how they have gained through sacrificing things for Jesus.

TWENTY-NINE SUNDAY OF THE YEAR

Thought for the day

Even the Son of Man himself came not to be served but to serve, and to give his life as a ransom for many.

Reflection on the readings

Isaiah 53:10-11
Psalm 32
Hebrews 4:14-16
Mark 10:35-45

In the Isaiah reading we have one of the extraordinary prophecies about God's suffering servant, which we, in the light of the Gospels, see as so perceptive in grasping the inevitable suffering of God's Saviour, Jesus. The writer of Hebrews helps us to understand it. Although the Messiah figure for many was seen as a national leader who would establish his reign and drive out oppressors, the more spiritual Messianic dream was that he would be a priestly king, mystically anointed with the power of Yahweh himself, taking on the suffering of the people with God's blessing, so that they may be saved.

Humans find it so hard to break away from the power and hierarchy models of thinking. Even though James and John have spent two or three years living and working with Jesus, have gone out on mission preaching the kingdom and experiencing many miracles, being dragged off to meals with rich and poor, socially elite and social outcasts alike, they are still thinking in worldly terms of greatness and status.

I suspect they might, at the time, have protested at that, and believed they were asking to sit at Jesus' right and left for noble reasons, like feeling themselves so close to their master, and wanting that to continue for ever. Who knows. Jesus is wonderfully forgiving of their inane suggestion, so alien to all he is. We can imagine him shaking his head helplessly as he says, 'You don't know what you're asking!' James and John are like so many of us, arrogant in our ignorant enthusiasm.

Today's message is really to do with that humble obedience which comes through suffering and persevering when the going is tough, and eventually makes us wise enough to listen with our hearts to what is really important.

Discussion starters

1. Even if we grasp the idea of being servants, how can we stop ourselves striving to be the most important and highly honoured servants of Christ?

2. Is Jesus' model for leadership practical? Do we practise it in the Church and in our lives?

All-stage talk

Have three chairs placed in front of the altar, in the obvious place of honour. Prepare three 'Reserved' signs.

In the Gospel today we watched two of Jesus' disciples – James and John – coming up to him with a question they wanted to ask. They wanted to make sure Jesus would give them what they wanted, so instead of starting with the real question, they first said, 'We want you to do for us whatever we ask.' Perhaps we try that one with parents or spouses, or the boss sometimes. Like this.

Invite a child and adult to come and read the following script:

Child Dad, you love me, don't you?

Dad Yes, son.

Child You'd give me anything I wanted, wouldn't you?

Dad Mmm . . . maybe I would.

Child Well, can I have this really good educational computer game?

Dad No.

Child Oh, but Dad, you said . . .

Dad I only said maybe!

Child Oh well, it was worth a try.

Jesus didn't say yes either. He asked James and John what they wanted, and was pretty gobsmacked by what it was. Invite two children to read out James and John's question – have it printed out in large, clear letters for them: 'Let one of us sit at your right and the other at your left in your glory.'

What on earth was Jesus to say to that? Point out the three chairs, and have someone place a reserved sign on the main, middle one. Who was this place in glory reserved for? Jesus. Had he pushed for it or even asked for it? No! He was given it by Almighty God, his Father. It was being a servant and being willing to give up his life for us all that brought Jesus to reign in glory. If James and John were to be granted their wish (invite them to go and sit either side of the main seat), what would it show about them, and about Jesus? (Collect ideas. It might show that they were the most important of the disciples, that Jesus liked them better than the others, that pushy people get their way in God's kingdom, for instance.)

Jesus pointed out to them that those places are not his to give anyway as they have reserved signs on them. (Invite someone to move James and John off the thrones and place reserved signs on them.) No one, not even Jesus, knew who they are reserved for. It could be for someone here! What we can be sure of is that the people they're reserved for would be the very last people to ask to sit there, or count themselves more worthy than anyone else!

Jesus tells us that we are all here to bother about serving others, not to bother about being served. Even Jesus himself, the Son of the living God, came as a servant, and gave up his life for the good of others. That's the example we're to follow, not resigning ourselves to it, grudgingly, but happy to have the honour of giving up our lives to serve others in love.

All-age ideas

- The Gospel works well read with different voices, especially if the readers have prepared by studying the text and thinking through the sub-script, rather as actors would, so that they can act it in the expressions and body language, pauses and so on, as well as the words themselves.

- While the first reading is read, have a cross brought from the back to the front of the church, or project an image of the cross from a painting on an OHP screen.

Prayer of the Faithful

Celebrant
In humility and love, let us pray together
to the God of our making and redeeming.

Reader
That all Christians may fulfil their vocation
to be servants, caring for the needs of others,
obedient to their Lord in all things

and supportive of one another
in worship, prayer and deepening faith.

Silence

Into your hands, O Lord:
we commit our prayers.

That those who govern and advise
may seek out God's will
and the good of all
in each crisis, dilemma and debate.

Silence

Into your hands, O Lord:
we commit our prayers.

That we may develop the habit
of rejoicing in the opportunities to serve,
and to put ourselves out for others,
laying down our craving for praise
and importance.

Silence

Into your hands, O Lord:
we commit our prayers.

That those who suffer in mind, body and spirit
may sense the Christ close beside them,
knowing his healing and resting in his love.

Silence

Into your hands, O Lord:
we commit our prayers.

That those who have died in faith
may be welcomed into the light of heaven,
and that all who are walking in sin today
may turn away from evil, and live.

Silence

Into your hands, O Lord:
we commit our prayers.

We pray with Mary,
who knew the reality of suffering:
Hail, Mary . . .

God our Father loves us;
in silence now,
we bring our personal petitions to him.

Silence

Celebrant
Father, in your unfailing mercy,
we ask you to accept these prayers,
through Jesus Christ.
Amen.

TREASURE SEEKERS

Aim: To know that Jesus is a Servant King.

Starter

Yes, your majesty. You will need a small handbell. One child is the king (or queen) and wears a crown. The others are all the king's servants, and they do all the work at the palace. Whenever the king rings his bell, the servants have to run up to where he is and bow or curtsey. Then the king gives his command (with the leader's help) and the servants rush about doing what he says. A leader takes the king to different parts of the palace for ringing the bell. Commands are household jobs, such as 'Sweep the floor!', 'Make the bed!', 'Clean the windows!' and 'Peel the potatoes!'

Teaching

Put down the crown, and a dustpan and brush. Hold the appropriate symbol as you refer to kings and servants. What is a king? A king is the person who rules over a land and is in charge of it. (We're thinking about traditional, storybook kings here, as this is in keeping with the imagery Jesus uses.) He's the one who gives the orders and tells everyone else what to do. He knows he is powerful and expects everyone to bow or curtsey to him, and say, 'Yes, your majesty!' to him. (The children can try that out, with another child wearing the crown and strutting about importantly.)

What is a servant? They are the ones who do the work, looking after the king and his family, and making sure he has all the things he needs. The servants cook and clean, and do the washing, and tidy up, and buy the food, and weed the garden, and clean out the gerbils, and put out the rubbish, and polish the tables, and scrape mud off the shoes . . . ! (The children can try all these out in quick succession, till everyone is out of breath.)

Who would they rather be – the king or a servant?

Now Jesus is our King, but he isn't anything like the sort of king we've been talking about, is he? It's true he is very important. It's true he is powerful and reigns over us all. But Jesus came into our world as a tiny baby, living in an ordinary family, like ours, without any palace or power. He worked as an ordinary carpenter, making things out of wood. In fact, Jesus is a king, but he behaves like a servant! He went around looking after people, making them better and cheering them up. He looks after us now, helping us wherever we need help.

(Put the crown over the dustpan and brush.) So Jesus is both a king *and* a servant, not bossing us around but caring for us all because he loves us.

Praying

Leader: We pray for kings and queens
and presidents and everyone in charge.
All: Lord, make them wise and good.
Leader: We pray for those who clean and cook
and everyone not in charge.
All: Lord, make them wise and good.
Leader: Our Servant King, we pray for each other.
All: Lord, make us wise and good. Amen.

Activities

On the sheet is a game to play with the king giving orders to the players who are the servants. They mime the jobs pictured when they land on those squares. The children can mount the sheet on thin card and make the pieces to play with from coloured playdough. Provide a plastic envelope for each complete game.

PEARL DIVERS

Aim: To know the story of John and James' question, and Jesus' teaching about servanthood in leadership.

Starter

Write out a set of questions and a set of answers, all on different pieces of card. Spread them around and turn them blank side up, so the children can play pairs with them, turning over any two at a time and keeping them if they match. Only one go each in a round.

Ideas for questions:

- What are the colours of the rainbow?
- How far is the sun from the earth?
- What two colours make purple?
- Why is it dangerous to look straight at the sun?
- What is steel made of?
- How fast can leopards run?
- What are the seasons called?
- Which month comes straight after July?
- What is the capital city of France?
- When was the battle of Hastings?

Teaching

Who learnt something from that game which they didn't know before? We all learn by asking questions, and anyone with younger brothers and sisters will know that they are always asking, 'Why?' Sometimes we ask questions which are so difficult that we can't understand the answers. (Perhaps like our question of how far away the sun is from the earth.) It's good to ask questions all through our lives.

One day, two of Jesus' disciples, John and James, asked Jesus a question which he couldn't answer. It wasn't because the question was too hard, but because it was the sort of question that shouldn't have been asked in the first place. And this was it (have it written out large and clear for everyone to read): 'Can one of us sit at your right hand and the other at your left in your glory?'

What had Jesus been trying to show his disciples about the way to live? (Collect their ideas, writing them down on a sheet titled: 'If you want to be my followers you must . . .' They might include things like loving one another, loving God, looking after one another, being the servant of all and trying to do God's will.)

That question of James and John shows that they hadn't really understood this teaching yet, had they? They were still interested in how important they would be and how much respect they could expect.

What do they think Jesus might have said to that question? Share ideas and then read it in the passage from Mark 10.

Praying

Take my love; my Lord, I pour
at thy feet its treasure-store;
take myself, and I will be
ever, only, all for thee.
Amen.

Activities

There are instructions on the sheet for making another 'pairs' game, based on Jesus' teaching. They will need to colour the sheet, mount it on card, and cut the cards out.

GOLD PANNERS

Aim: To explore the concept of Jesus being a Servant King.

Starter

Human sculpture. One person is the sculptor, and the others are his medium to work with. He explains where he wants each person to be and how to arrange their body, until the whole group has turned into a sculpture. Then someone else can be the sculptor.

Teaching

Begin by reading the Isaiah passage. Here we see God's chosen One as a servant, suffering, humbled and broken, laying aside his majesty for the good of the world.

Go on to the reading from Hebrews, explaining that the Jewish priests were appointed to represent the people and offer sacrifices to God on their behalf. The writer points out that, owing to their own sinfulness, they needed to include themselves in this. Jesus, like a high priest, is also appointed by God, and becomes the perfect sacrifice to take away the sins of the whole world. (Link this with the Agnus Dei – 'Lamb of God, you take away the sins of the world'.)

Now read Mark 10:35-45, seeing how Jesus' calling to be the suffering servant ties in with the prophecies, and jars against what James and John are wanting. Like Jesus, we are called to the servant role.

Praying

My song is love unknown,
my Saviour's love for me,
love to the loveless shown,
that they may lovely be.
O who am I, that for my sake,
my Lord should take frail flesh and die?

Activities

On the sheet they are helped to explore the concept of the suffering servant, which Jesus recognised as his route to save the world. There are also some examples of leadership to consider in the light of Jesus' teaching.

THIRTIETH SUNDAY OF THE YEAR

Thought for the day

In Jesus, God gathers his scattered people and opens their eyes to see.

Reflection on the readings

Jeremiah 31:7-9
Psalm 125
Hebrews 5:1-6
Mark 10:46-52

In the passage from Jeremiah, the prophet longs for the people to find again a close, personal relationship with the living God. No more empty, formalised religious practice, but a real reverence and tender returning to the Lord who loves them. He describes it as if it is happening, with streams of scattered people, all with their needs and frailty, being drawn from the ends of the earth, weeping and praying as they realise who they are, and whose they are.

The writer of Hebrews reinforces this joy of finding in Jesus the Saviour who meets our needs, providing for us what we by ourselves cannot achieve. Only Jesus, as the go-between, priestly figure of all time, is holy, blameless, pure, and set apart from sinners, yet willingly taking their part.

The Gospel reading catapults us into the kingdom longed for by the prophets. Here, in the dusty main street on the way out of Jericho town, we find the promised Christ going about his healing business of giving sight to the blind. Bartimaeus is anxious not to miss out on this opportunity, and it is his faith, Jesus tells him, which heals his sight. In the reality of this beggar, happy and freed from blindness, choosing to follow Jesus, we glimpse the wider vision of the whole of the world returning, with tears of joy running down their faces, to the God who never gives up on them and longs to gather them to himself.

Discussion starters

1. In what way do Jesus' disciples help (or hinder) Bartimaeus from coming to Jesus for healing?

2. How do we help (or hinder) people from coming to Jesus?

All-stage talk

Begin by asking people to imagine a child who has gone outside to play. She has been learning to ride her bike, and is quite good at it now, with a few wobbles. She's happy out there, riding up and down, until she takes a corner a bit steeply, brakes sharply, and she and the bike crash down. The child has a nasty graze on her leg, and is upset and a bit frightened by the fall. All she can think of is getting back home, to the person she knows will make it all better, and there she is, limping up the road, with her leg bleeding, crying out for her mum as she goes.

Most of us have been there. Whenever we're badly hurt, even when we've grown up, there's a young child inside us limping back home, crying, to the place we feel safe, and to the person we know will look after us and make it all better.

It's a good picture of our loving parent God, who is always there, waiting for his hurt and limping children to walk back home to the one who can and does make it all better, however old or young we are, and however we got our wounds. What

that walk back home shows is that the child trusts. What our walk back to God shows is that we know and love and trust God to help us.

In today's Gospel we met a blind man called Bartimaeus. He knew he was blind. He knew he missed out in life because he couldn't see. When he heard that Jesus was passing by, he shouted and kept on shouting, so he wouldn't miss his chance. Never mind if the disciples told him to be quiet, he knew this was too important an opportunity to miss, and he shouted hard until Jesus himself heard him. That gave him the chance to do his 'limping home' – he made his way to the person he knew could help him. And, sure enough, Jesus did just that.

All-age ideas

- The reading from Jeremiah can be read chorally, with a group of voices such as men, women and children, or a mixed group of high, medium and low voice tones. Work through the passage experimenting with who reads what, bearing in mind that the object is to help bring out the meaning in the best way.

- The Gospel can be acted out, with a narrator and mime, or with the different voices. In a small group, everyone could be involved by creating the Jericho street scene, with the people all standing there, crowding round the action as it happens.

Prayer of the Faithful

Celebrant
As children of our heavenly Father,
trusting in his will and capacity to care for us all,
let us pray.

Reader
We pray for all pastoral care in the Church,
for the ministries of listening and counselling;
the sharing of grief; the freeing from guilt.
We pray for the grace to accompany
others to Christ's healing love.

Silence

What do you want God to do for you?
Lord, we want to see.

We pray for the healing of the nations;
for a recognition of our need of God
and a turning away from all that is evil.
We pray for all in authority and worldly power,
that they may be guided along right paths.

Silence

What do you want God to do for you?
Lord, we want to see.

We pray for an increase in love for one another,
that we may be better at recognising needs
and responding to them;
that we may give more time to those we love.

Silence

What do you want God to do for you?
Lord, we want to see.

We pray for those who are blind
or partially sighted,
and those who are spiritually or emotionally blind.
We pray for the opening of eyes to see God's way
and faith to trust him through good and ill.

Silence

What do you want God to do for you?
Lord, we want to see.

We pray for those whose eyes
have shut to this world,
that they may open to the brightness
and joy of heaven.

Silence

What do you want God to do for you?
Lord, we want to see.

We pray with Mary,
whose spiritual vision was clear:
Hail, Mary . . .

To God, our heavenly Father,
we pray for our own intentions.

Silence

Celebrant
Father,
you pour out your blessings so richly on us;
with thankful hearts we praise you,
and ask you to hear our prayers,
through Jesus Christ.
Amen.

TREASURE SEEKERS

Aim: To know that Jesus helped a blind man to see.

Starter

I spy with my little eye . . . using either colours, or
letter sounds.

Teaching

Tell the story of Bartimaeus while you (or an assis-
tant!) draw it on a black or white board, rubbing
out and changing things as you go. Very simple
drawings are fine, and most effective. The visuals
are there to aid imagination, not replace it. Basically you'll be drawing Bartimaeus begging by the
road, a crowd of people coming in a cloud of dust
down the road, the disciples' cross faces, the disciples turning friendly, Bartimaeus meeting Jesus,
and Bartimaeus happy and able to see.

Praying

With my eyes, Lord, I can see
all the love you have for me.
Help me spread your love to others,
friends and parents, sisters, brothers,
till the world is full of love.

Activities

On the sheet the children can make a face with
closed eyes which open. There are also hidden things
for them to use their eyes to find in the picture.

PEARL DIVERS

Aim: To look at what we can learn from the way
Bartimaeus is healed.

Starter

Blindfold everybody and stand them all over the
room. Ask everyone to move about, and, when
they find someone else, to hold hands and go on
together, till they find someone else to join up with.
When you can see that everyone is joined up
together, tell everyone to freeze and open their
eyes. They will be surprised to find that they are all
linked up.

Teaching

We are all going to act today's Gospel. Get to know
the Gospel account really well, so that you can narrate it, directing various children to do the actions
as they happen.

Put up a sign which says 'To Jericho' and choose
someone to be Bartimaeus. Direct them to sit by the
roadside and give them a begging bowl to hold.
Bartimaeus is blindfolded. Choose someone to be
Jesus and two others to be disciples. Gather the
crowd at Jericho and explain that we are all following Jesus, who has been teaching and healing in the
town.

All the crowd are walking on the spot. We're just
leaving the city, and Bartimaeus can hear us coming, so he's shouting out at the top of his voice,
'Jesus, son of David, have mercy on me!' Now a
few people are going ahead, trying to make the
blind man be quiet. But the man is shouting even

louder, the same thing again. This time Jesus stops, and we all stop as well. Jesus tells the disciples to call the blind man. They go over to him and cheer him up, telling him that Jesus is calling him. The blind man jumps up, not bothering to pick up his cloak, and comes across to Jesus. (The disciples might well be guiding him.)

Jesus says to Bartimaeus, 'What do you want me to do for you?' Bartimaeus says to Jesus, 'Teacher, I want to see.' Jesus says to him, 'Go, your faith has healed you,' and suddenly the man finds he can see. (Jesus helps him to take off the blindfold.) The crowd moves off down the road, very happy for the man, and Bartimaeus is walking with Jesus, looking around at things for the first time ever.

Praying

Jesus, you made the blind to see,
open my eyes to see your love.
Jesus, you made the deaf to hear,
open my ears to hear your truth.
All we need we find in you;
your love is total, your words are true.

Activities

On the sheet they are taken through the story of the Gospel stage by stage, with questions which help them deepen their understanding of how God works in our lives and in our needs. They will need a Bible to help them with this.

GOLD PANNERS

Aim: To see how, in Jesus, God gathers his scattered people back and opens their eyes to see.

Starter

Make a tape of assorted sounds. They have to work out what the sounds are.

Teaching

With the aid of biblical maps, show how the split north kingdom of Israel was overcome by the Assyrians and the people taken into exile. Soon after that Assyria was attacked and conquered by the Babylonians.

Jeremiah lived in the south kingdom of Judah just after this, when Judah was caught in the middle between the Egyptians and the Babylonians. Before long Jerusalem itself would be captured and all except the poorest people of Judah deported to Babylon. Not happy times. Jeremiah was trying hard to warn the people that they really needed to unite under God's law, committing themselves to him completely.

Now read the passage from Jeremiah, with its picture of people returning to God with all their hearts. As we know, the people didn't listen, and they were taken into exile, eventually returning to a ruined city. But the hope developed that one day, a 'son of king David' would be a special king, filled with God's power, who would lead his people back to God's ways.

Next look at the Gospel, with different people reading the various parts. Here we have the blind man calling out to Jesus as 'son of David'. In Jesus that great hope has become a real person, walking around Jericho and the other cities, towns and villages, bringing people back to God and healing them. Today we have yet another example of such healing.

Praying

Praise, my soul, the King of heaven!
To his feet thy tribute bring;
ransomed, healed, restored, forgiven,
who like me his praise should sing?
Praise him! Praise him!
Praise him! Praise him!
Praise the everlasting King!

Activities

On the sheet there are examples of people returning after deportation, and they are encouraged to imagine the feelings at such a time. There are also examples of those who have returned to God after a long time of self-imposed exile, and how they feel. They can make a collage of returning with joy, using pictures, words and colours to express the sense of Psalm 125.

THIRTY-FIRST SUNDAY OF THE YEAR

Thought for the day

To love the living God with heart, soul and strength, and to love our neighbour as ourselves means far more than any sacrificial offerings.

Reflection on the readings

Deuteronomy 6:2-6
Psalm 17
Hebrews 7:23-28
Mark 12:28-34

We might wonder why a scribe, highly educated in the law, should ask Jesus the seemingly obvious question: 'Which is the first among all the commandments?' Surely he knows that? But, as in any discipline, the simplest sounding questions are often the most complex to experts, and the Jewish academics spent much time puzzling over the huge number of accumulated laws, so it had become hard to see the wood for the trees. Genuinely this scribe is wanting to search out right priorities – or indeed to establish whether any prioritising would be insulting to God.

Jesus' answer, coming after the discussions with those out to trick and test him, responds to this scribe's honest searching with perhaps the most powerful statement of faith ever uttered. Here is the Son of the living God, standing among his own people, in direct line from the patriarchs, prophets and King David, proclaiming the Shema: 'Hear, O Israel! The Lord our God is the one Lord!' To all Jewish people, this expression of faith is profoundly precious, a kind of 'passport into paradise' for every child of Abraham, spoken three times every day by every believer. What must it have sounded like in this context, spoken by this voice? I would love to have been there!

All the love, all the obedience, all the authority, inspired the scribe to recognise, with fresh understanding, the wonder of those words, and the following summary of the law. We can hear in his excited response that he has seen the fresh colours of God's law again, as if the accumulated varnish from generations has been cleaned away, and the original beauty and brightness is startlingly visible.

Right back in the Deuteronomy reading, the significance and importance of this statement and law was urged upon the people. They were to wear it, tie it on gates and attach it to door-posts, passing it on to their children and grandchildren so as to ensure its continued obedience, and the psalmists meditated on the joy and blessing resulting from keeping God at the heart of our lives.

The writer of Hebrews, speaking to a Jewish audience, explores the work of Jesus in terms of Jewish sacrifices, right at the heart of their worship of the one true God. Time and again the priests needed to offer sacrifices on behalf of the people; in Jesus, both high priest and sacrificial victim, the total sacrifice is accomplished once and for all.

Discussion starters

1. Jesus answers the seeking scribe's question not with argument but with a statement of faith. What can we learn from this?

2. What is our priority in life?

All-stage talk

Beforehand ask three people to practise saying the same sentence, each emphasising a different word so that the meaning is slightly changed.

- WE go to church on Sunday – (as opposed to other people)
- We go to CHURCH on Sunday – (that's our destination)
- We go to church on SUNDAY – (rather than another day)

Also they need to practise saying the same sentence meaning something different.

- Yes, I believe so – (but you're not at all sure about it)
- Yes, I believe so – (automatically because it's written for you to say, but absent-mindedly)
- Yes, I believe so – (after much thought and with deep conviction)

Begin by pointing out how jokes can be really funny if you tell them right, but fall completely flat if you don't. How we say things is as important as what we say. Somebody can be saying nice things but you know they really don't like you and are trying to be nasty. Your friend could say the same things and you'd be happy and pleased instead of upset.

Invite the sentence-speakers to the front and invite everyone to spot the difference in what they are saying. (We go to church on Sunday.) Through stressing different words, they changed the meaning, even though the words stayed the same.

In the Gospel today we met a well-educated person, who had been quoting the scriptures every day of his life for a good number of years. He was thought of as fairly expert in his field of understanding God's law. He's been sitting listening to Jesus discussing the matters of law and faith with other experts, and he's impressed. He thinks it sounds as if Jesus really knows what he's talking about. He's so impressed that he asks Jesus a question, addressing him very respectfully as Rabbi, or Teacher. And the question he asks is this (have a volunteer, or everyone, read it out clearly and loudly): 'Which is the most important of the Commandments?'

The trouble was there were so many commandments now (as you speak, gradually unroll a very long roll of paper labelled 'Commandments') that it was all rather complicated and confusing. The scribe needed some help to sort it all out.

And what Jesus does is this. He recites the

special statement of faith which every Jewish person knew by heart from childhood. It was this (everyone reads it out clearly): 'Hear, O Israel! The Lord our God is the one Lord.'

Just imagine how God's Son, a Jewish young man, would say that! The scribe could hear, in the way he said it, all Jesus' complete trust in God. He could tell it meant everything to Jesus, and he wasn't just rattling it off by heart. He meant it, completely and joyfully. And that got the scribe excited about his own faith – Jesus' love of God was catching!

When we talk about Jesus, does our love for him show?

All-age ideas

- A credal statement today could be this:

  The Lord our God is the one Lord,
  and Jesus is Lord!
  Glory be to the Father and to the Son
  and to the Holy Spirit,
  as God was in the beginning,
  is now and shall be for ever. Amen.

- The summary of the law can be sung to the tune of *London's burning*, in a round:

  You shall love the Lord your God with
  all your heart and all your mind and
  all your strength! All your strength!
  And love your neighbour,
  and love your neighbour.

Prayer of the Faithful

Celebrant
As God's people, gathered in his presence,
let us pray.

Reader
For all who preach and teach the Gospel
in word and sacrament
throughout the worldwide Church.
For those who lead prayer groups
and Bible studies,
and all who gossip their faith to others.

Silence

O Lord our God:
in you we trust.

For all who are tortured or persecuted
for what they believe;
for the voiceless and powerless,
for the powerful and coercive.

Silence

O Lord our God:
in you we trust.

For greater respect for one another
as children of God's making;
for God's presence in each conversation,
discussion and debate,
each concern and celebration.

Silence

O Lord our God:
in you we trust.

For healing and wholeness,
mending and comforting,
calming and refreshing,
wherever lives and bodies ache.

Silence

O Lord our God:
in you we trust.

For everlasting peace in the arms of God
for those who have come to the end
of their life on earth
and comfort for all who grieve.

Silence

O Lord our God:
in you we trust.

Mary faithfully loved God and her neighbour;
let us join our prayers with hers:
Hail, Mary . . .

In the silence of our hearts,
we pray for any needs known to us personally.

Silence

Celebrant
Father, with grateful hearts for the gift of life,
we offer you these prayers,
together with ourselves
for your service;
in Jesus' name we pray.
Amen.

TREASURE SEEKERS

Aim: To learn the summary of the law.

Starter

Have lots of building bricks or cartons for the children to play with, balancing one on another to construct towers and buildings.

Teaching

We were building on the good strong floor, and that helped us build good strong towers. The Bible tells us two good strong rules to build our lives on, and we're going to learn them off by heart, so that we'll always have them inside our minds, and won't lose them or drop them.

The first and most important is to love God (point up), with all our hearts (hands on heart), with all our mind (hands hold head), and with all our strength (flex arm muscles). And the second is to love other people as we love ourselves.

Teach the children to sing this summary of the law to the tune of *London's burning*. The accompanying actions will help them to learn the words and understand them.

You shall love the
(hands on heart)

Lord your God with
(point upwards)

all your heart and
(hands on heart)

all your mind and
(hold head with hands)

all your strength! All your strength!
(show biceps)

And love each other, and love each other.
(arms round one another's shoulders)

Read verses 4-6 in Deuteronomy 6 to them, explaining that grown-ups have been passing on this rule to their children and grandchildren and great-grandchildren for thousands of years, and now you are passing it on to them. When they grow up and have children they are to pass it on to their children and their grandchildren to make sure that everybody knows it really well, and can live by God's love every day. If you read on to verses 7-9 of Deuteronomy 6, you can show them how this rule was made a practical part of everyday life.

Praying

I love you, Lord God,
with all my heart and mind and strength!
Amen.

Activities

The children can decorate the summary of the law with stickers, printing or stencils. It can then be tied on to a chair or door at home to remind them of God's rule of love.

PEARL DIVERS

Aim: To know about the scribe's question and Jesus' answer.

Starter

Have some playdough and a number of different shapes to press the dough into so that they mould it. Ideas for shapes: shells, lids, buttons, shortbread moulds, coins.

(There is a recipe for playdough on page 109.)

Teaching

Look at all the created shapes, and point out how the playdough was soft enough to take on the shape of the firm moulds. If we think of ourselves as a lump of playdough (!), then having God's law of love to live by helps us take on the shape of God's love in our lives. For that to happen we can't be so set in our ways that we're like playdough that's hardened in the air. We need to stay flexible in God's hands to be moulded to his likeness.

What turns us into the shape of loving people is keeping to the rule of love that Jesus gave us: Love God and love one another. Read it out in full from Mark 12:30-31. Go over it again slowly with actions to help them remember it. If we wriggle ourselves into the shape of those commandments every day, we shall find our lives full of God's blessing as we get closer to him and our love grows.

One day when Jesus was teaching and answering people's questions, a scribe came and asked him what was the first among all the commandments. As a scribe, he would have studied the scriptures and God's law very thoroughly. He wasn't trying to trick Jesus, but really wanted to understand God better. Jesus answered the scribe by quoting the scriptures to him, which he knew well, and showing him what they really meant. They weren't really about rules at all but about loving God!

The scribe could see how right that was, and this is what he said: (read Mark 12:32-33). And Jesus was happy for the scribe and told him he was close to the kingdom of God.

Praying

Lord, we pray for those
who don't yet know you.
We pray that they will find you
and discover how lovely you are.
Amen.

Activities

On the sheet the children learn about the sacrifices offered by the priests, so that they can better understand the scribe's concern to get back to real, heartfelt worship, rather than going through the motions. They are encouraged to say the Lord's prayer every day, thinking carefully about the words as they say them.

GOLD PANNERS

Aim: To see the priority of loving God.

Starter

Everyone makes their own favourite design paper plane, adjusting it for optimum flying. See whose can fly best and furthest.

Teaching

With the paper planes, the basic design was important, and also aligning and balancing, adjusting the shape to stop it crashing. Today we are looking at getting our lives aligned and adjusted in keeping with the best design of all.

Read the passage from Deuteronomy, explaining that the people were just about to cross over into the Promised Land. What was their 'design for living' going to be? How were they going to make sure it never got forgotten?

Tell them about the way the priests, on behalf of the people, regularly sacrificed animals, sprinkling the people with the animals' blood and offering the burnt sacrifice to God as a way of cleansing the people from sin. Show them some pictures of this. Now look at Hebrews 7:23-28, seeing how Jesus, being both the priest figure and the sacrificial victim (the Lamb of God), was able to do the cleansing of the people's sin once and for all. The people would understand about being 'made clean' by the blood of animal sacrifices, so it made sense to them that the blood of Jesus, poured out for us on the cross, was able to cleanse us of sin completely.

Now explain how some of that offering of sacrifices had become empty ritual over the years, with the people doing all the actions, and having lots of rules about correct procedures, but living lives which were not in a loving relationship with God. The scribe in today's Gospel was one of those who recognised this and worried about what really was important.

Read the Gospel, so they can see how Jesus cut through all the accumulated complications, right to the very heart of the matter – loving the one true God with our whole heart and soul and mind and strength.

Praying

Be thou my vision, O Lord of my heart,
naught be all else to me save that thou art;
thou my best thought in the day and the night,
waking or sleeping, thy presence my light.

(From a song translated from the Irish
by Mary Byrne and Eleanor Hull
© Copyright Control)

Activities

On the sheet there is a picture of the sacrifices being offered, together with the scribe's words in verse 33 of Mark 12. They are encouraged to explore the difference between correct practices and a loving relationship. They also learn about the Shema, and the effect of Jesus reciting it in the context of his teaching.

THIRTY-SECOND SUNDAY OF THE YEAR

Thought for the day

Loving generosity is the hallmark of Godly giving.

Reflection on the readings

1 Kings 17:10-16
Psalm 145
Hebrews 9:24-28
Mark 12:38-44

The widow gathering sticks was the first person Elijah met when he reached the city gates of Sidon, and, in spite of her probably obvious lack of wealth, it is this woman Elijah approaches for hospitality. If we were on a journey to a city we may be rather more likely to walk around seeking out the best place to find food and accommodation, picking out the best and most comfortable option. Elijah's method is echoed in Jesus' sending out of the disciples, as he tells them to stay in the first place they are offered at each town and village.

When we live our lives constantly in God's company it is not so much a question of asking God's guidance to choose well, but rather of waiting on him to reveal his provision for us. The widow was God's choice, recognised by Elijah, and there was great blessing from her generosity, both for Elijah and the woman herself and her son.

It makes us wonder what opportunities we have missed out on in life through failing to notice calls for generous giving of our money, our hospitality, or our time. All too easily we can fill our lives so full of business that we simply do not notice needs.

Part of a generous spirit is the noticing; only then can we go on to decide to help or give.

In the Gospel we are shown another example of costly giving. Jesus is struck by the shining generosity of the widow as she contributes her two small coins. Her willingness to give out of love for God all that she has poignantly contrasts with the pomposity and self-assurance of the flamboyant scribes. Without a fuss, and with no expectation of praise or acclaim, the woman quietly gives the equivalent of millions.

The fact that Jesus notices reinforces for us God's delight in every act of goodness and kindness and generosity. His criteria are quite different from the worldly ones. He does not account worth with wealth. We can all learn so much from this unnamed widow, and what we learn should challenge us to look again at our own criteria for giving.

Discussion starters

1. Is it practical to live in the world without being taken over by worldly values?

2. Are there any ways we can take more seriously the call to practise hospitality?

All-stage talk

Ask for two or three volunteers and give each of them a thick wad of monopoly money, a posh hat to wear, and a car key for a posh car (an ordinary key with a flashy cardboard key ring marked Rolls or BMW, for instance). Explain to everyone that they have their hats and flashy car keys because they all have lots and lots of money. Now invite another person and give them a supermarket bag and two pennies. This is all she has left for the week.

Have another volunteer holding the collection plate, and go over the Gospel with the rich people miming their giving (several notes from their wad). Encourage everyone to be impressed by how much each one has given. When the poor person comes to the collection plate, she gives two pennies (everyone listens to hear them clatter in). That isn't nearly as much as the others gave, is it? But Jesus reckoned the woman who gave two coins had given most. Why?

Collect their ideas and draw out Jesus' reasoning. God is not interested in the actual amount we give but in how lovingly generous we are, and that turns our way of thinking upside down. Sacrificial, or costly giving, out of love, will vary enormously in the actual amount. And there's another thing, too. Sometimes we are tempted to spend much more than we can afford, not really because we're so generous, but through a kind of pride. We feel pressurised to give the same quantity and quality of presents at Christmas, for instance, or all the trimmings at weddings, which richer people can easily afford. Many end up working themselves ill to keep up such giving, or running up huge credit card bills with massive interest to pay.

That is not what Jesus means by generosity.

If our giving is sliding in that direction we need to check our motives in giving. Are we giving so that our children will like us better, or stop nagging us? Are we hoping for other people's respect and admiration? If so, we need to ask God in to change things. Loving generosity is a way of thinking, of giving time and attention to others, as well as looking after needs. It is even learning the humility to receive as well as give, and to love without being possessive.

The readings today teach us how to give in a Godly way – freely and willingly, not through pressure but through love.

All-age ideas

- Have the children singing *Love is something if you give it away* at the offering of the gifts.

- Have the first reading read by three people – Elijah, the widow and the narrator.

Prayer of the Faithful

Celebrant
Let us pray to our loving and generous God.

Reader
We pray that God will transform our giving
and provide us with the courage
to renounce all meanness of spirit,
until we are glad to give freely and lovingly.

Silence

Give us today our daily bread:
give us – and forgive us.

We pray that we may be good stewards
of this planet we are given to inhabit;
that all may learn to share what we have here
and look after it well for those who come after us.

Silence

Give us today our daily bread:
give us – and forgive us.

We pray that we may be more generous
in the attention we give to one another;
in allowing others to be themselves,
different from us but just as valid.

Silence

Give us today our daily bread:
give us – and forgive us.

We pray for the poor and for the rich,
for all whose lives are somehow impoverished.
We pray for those in debt
and all who are finding finances a great worry.

Silence

Give us today our daily bread:
give us – and forgive us.

We pray for those who have died,
that in God's mercy they may be welcomed
into the peace and joy of heaven.

Silence

Give us today our daily bread:
give us – and forgive us.

We join our prayers with those of Mary,
who gave of herself without stinting:
Hail, Mary . . .

In quietness now,
we pray for our own particular needs
and concerns.

Silence

Celebrant
Father, we thank you for bringing us here today,
and ask you to accept our prayers
through Jesus Christ.
Amen.

TREASURE SEEKERS

Aim: To look at being generous.

Starter

Pass round a pound coin in the circle. If we were going to spend this on someone as a present, what would we buy for them? Each child can give their choice, choosing a gift for someone from their family or friends.

Teaching

Celebrate all the good ideas the children have had, and enjoy thinking about what fun it is to give presents we know someone will really like. Share together some of the things they have chosen to make or buy for other people.

Now show them some pictures of fruit trees, and try counting the fruit. There is so much it's hard to count! In our world we can see that God is very generous, and loves giving us things. He gives us lots of sunshine, lots of rain to make our food grow, lots of apples on the trees, lots of potatoes growing in the earth.

When we are being generous, and enjoy giving, we're being just like our loving, generous Father God.

Praying

All God's gifts around us
are sent from heaven above
so thank the Lord,
O thank the Lord
for all his love!

Activities

There is space for the children to make rubbings of different coins, and they will be making sweets to put on the paper basket on the sheet to give away. Any no-baking sweets would be nice, such as peppermint creams or dates stuffed with marzipan.

PEARL DIVERS

Aim: To know the story of the widow's two coins.

Starter

Have a number of different play coins fixed around the room on walls, tables and window sills. The children walk around counting the money (or for some children the number of coins). When they think they've worked it out, they bring you their answer and the one nearest to the correct amount is given a real coin as a prize.

Teaching

Give out wads of play money notes to some children and varying amounts of coins to others. In real life it's like this – some people are very rich and have lots of money all the time, some have enough to live on and others are very poor, and can't even afford to buy food or clothing. There are lots of reasons why some are rich and some are poor, and God doesn't think it's very important at all. He's much more bothered about the kind of people we are. Rich people, as far as God is concerned, are those who are rich in love and goodness; poor people, as far as God is concerned, are those who are hardly loving at all.

One day Jesus was watching the people putting their gifts of money in the collection plate as they went into the synagogue. Some of the rich people had loads of money. What do you think they put in the plate? (Children with big wads of notes can hold up what they reckon.) Pass round a plate for them to put their money in. It certainly looks a lot of money here, doesn't it? But did it mean they would have to go without something themselves now because they had given this much away? No – they had so much money that although they'd given a lot, they hadn't been particularly generous, really.

Then Jesus watched a widow going in. Widows are women whose husbands have died, and in Jesus' time they were often very poor. She only had two coins. That was everything she possessed. (Identify the person in the group with only two coins.) So what do you think she did? Do you think she went past the plate, knowing God would understand that she had nothing to spare? Or did she stop and give something? (Collect their ideas.) Well, those who said she still gave something were right. In fact the woman put in both the coins she had! And Jesus happened to see her doing it.

He was very impressed by how generous the widow was, and told his disciples about it. 'Look at that!' he said to them. 'This woman has really given far more than all the rich people put together, because they could easily afford what they gave, but she's given everything she had!'

Praying

When I'm feeling mean, Jesus,
help me to be generous instead.
When I feel like pleasing myself,
help me to be unselfish instead.
When I'm feeling grumpy and fed up,
help me to do something kind for someone else.

Activities

There are some examples of ways different amounts of time and money can be spent, and they can talk about these, choosing some project to give to as a group. The story of the generous widow who fed Elijah is also included.

GOLD PANNERS

Aim: To look at God's view of generosity.

Starter

Bring along something everyone enjoys eating, and say that as you were feeling generous today you thought you'd like to treat everyone. Share out the food to be eaten later, and enjoy the sudden burst of generosity!

Teaching

In our readings today we are going to be looking at God's view of generosity, and we're starting with a story of a generous-hearted widow in the Old Testament. Read the passage from 1 Kings 17, with different voices reading the parts of Elijah and the woman. It was the woman's remarkable generosity to Elijah that ended up by blessing her and her son.

Now look at today's Gospel, with another widow story. (Widows were very often poor and destitute.) Why was this woman commended for her generosity when she'd given such a little? Discuss what connection generosity has to amount and attitude, drawing out the way God is most concerned about the loving, wholeheartedness of our giving.

Finally look at the amazing example in Hebrews of loving generosity shown in Christ offering nothing less than himself. How can we respond to this amount of generous love?

Praying

Were the whole realm of nature mine,
that were an offering far too small;
love so amazing, so divine,
demands my soul, my life, my all.

Activities

On the sheet the story of Elijah and the widow encourages them to go behind the spoken words to the possible thought processes. They also look at how seeming generosity can actually be pride, ambition or boasting, and explore what qualities mark genuine generosity.

THIRTY-THIRD SUNDAY OF THE YEAR

Thought for the day

We are to be on our guard; great anguish will accompany the last days, but all that is good and loving, wise and true will be saved and celebrated for ever.

Reflection on the readings

Daniel 12:1-3
Psalm 15
Hebrews 10:11-14, 18
Mark 13:24-32

As the darkness crowds further into each day for those of us in the northern hemisphere, we have a powerful reminder of the gathering evil which it is foretold will accompany the heralding in of the last days. Jesus smelt it with the nose of a prophet, and although no exact dates can be given, he is very concerned for his disciples to understand the importance for them and us to be on our guard. We do indeed need to take great care as we walk and drive through our time on earth. All around us are subtle and powerful temptations to steer us off course, and distract us from our calling.

As we begin to experience the effects of our shrinking world, and recognise our interdependence, we are aware of the opportunities provided for mutual damage and instability as well as positive partnership. Large-scale damage of evil is increasingly possible and harder to prevent.

All is not gloom and doom, however. For those already living the risen life, the fear of annihilation is actually irrelevant, and the last day should fill us with excitement and hope, rather than terror, since at that time of accomplishment, all goodness, love, wisdom and truth will be revealed for what it is, shining and beautiful, and lasting for ever.

The psalmist describes his spiritual inheritance as if he is walking around the pleasant farmland which he knows will become his own as soon as he comes of age. He is pleased with the patch God has chosen for him and enjoys it in the present as well as for the future. Perhaps that gives us a model to work with.

We know and are thrilled that Jesus Christ has secured salvation for us, and our hope for that last day is not in our own ragged and scarred lives, but in the victory of the cross. The reason for being on our guard in these last days is not that the promise of salvation may suddenly be snatched away from us, but that in all the evil we may choose to throw away our hope of salvation. If we stay faithful through all the troubles which there are bound to be, we have nothing to fear at all, but rather a celebration to look forward to.

how well loved he is! He bears the signs of being well loved. Probably most of us older ones feel a bit like this – loving has worn us to the shape we are, a bit threadbare and squashed maybe, but perhaps a little wiser and softer and less selfish as a result. Although we know from experience that loving hasn't always been easy, we can say with certainty that it's well worth living lovingly.

Our readings today are helping us to look forward to the end of time, when the sky is wrapped up and the moon folded away. It can sound very frightening, to think of everything we know coming to an end. Whenever there are terrible disasters and famines and wars it can feel as if things are spinning out of control – even out of God's control. Is the end going to be some huge ghastly mistake, brought about by our greed and selfishness?

The Bible reassures us that, however it may look as evil grows and temporarily gains the upper hand, God is always ultimately in charge. As we know, God's way is not to crash into our blundering and force us to change so that disasters are prevented. He has given us that great gift of free will, so that we can choose good or evil in the small and large decisions of life. He longs for us to choose the good that will bring us blessing and peace, but is always there weeping with us in the chaos and suffering that evil leads to, ready to redeem it for good.

And it is that buffeted and battered loving which will last and last for ever. The prophet Daniel gives us a lovely picture of that. All those who have guided others in the right path, he says, will shine like the stars of heaven for ever. All the wise leaders will show up brightly for all to see. If we have set ourselves to live lives of faith and love, there is no way we need be frightened by the last days. After the feeding of the five thousand Jesus told his disciples to gather up the fragments so that nothing is lost. That's how it will be at the end; every scrap of goodness and love will be gathered safely in, so that nothing of it is lost.

Discussion starters

1. Are we worried about the right things, or about things which needn't concern us?

2. Do today's readings affect our attitude to evangelisation?

All-stage talk

Bring along a well-loved and very well-worn companion – teddy or pyjama case. Introduce him to everyone and point out how we can all see just

All-age ideas

- Have a display with the well-loved friend, together with a sign which reads 'Love remains for ever'.

- Have the passage from Daniel read by a group of adults and children, reading alternately, like this:

Children: Verse 1 up to 'your people . . .'

Adults: 'There will be a time . . . came into existence.'

Children: 'When that time comes . . . written in the Book.'

Adults: 'Of those who are sleeping . . . shame and everlasting disgrace.'

Children: Verse 3

Prayer of the Faithful

Celebrant
As God's love has drawn us, let us pray.

Reader
That the Church may grow and flourish,
protected from evil within and without;
that in worship and ministry
God's love may be brought into places of darkness
and offer many the light of hope.

Silence

Lord our God:
show us the path of life.

That our shrinking world
may bring about co-operation
and a fresh appreciation of one another's cultures;
that we may encourage one another
in goodness, peace and love.

Silence

Lord our God:
show us the path of life.

That we may take time
to cherish our loved ones in the present moment,
and value the blessings we receive each day.

Silence

Lord our God:
show us the path of life.

That God's healing touch
may bring wholeness and peace
to those who suffer,
and hope to those who are close to despair.

Silence

Lord our God:
show us the path of life.

That God's love may surround those
travelling through death
and bring them safely to heaven.

Silence

Lord our God:
show us the path of life.

We pray now with Mary,
who showed us how to wait
with a quiet heart:
Hail, Mary . . .

As God's stillness fills our hearts,
we make our private petitions.

Silence

Celebrant
Trusting in your promise to hear us, Father,
we offer you these prayers,
through Jesus Christ.
Amen.

TREASURE SEEKERS

Aim: To know that love lasts for ever and heaven is full of it.

Starter

Give out chocolate buttons to suck and see who can make theirs last the longest.

Teaching

Some things only last as long as a chocolate button. They are nice to suck but we know they won't last for ever. Bubbles don't last long either. (Blow a few and enjoy their colours and roundness, until they pop.) Lots of good things are with us for just a little while, so it's a good idea to really enjoy them while we have them.

Some things, like long journeys, or grown-up conversations, seem to go on for ages and ages! But they don't go on for ever. In the end, it's time to get out of the car, or the grown-ups say goodbye and we can carry on walking to the swings.

What will last for ever and ever and ever? To give them a clue, show them a red heart shape. It's *love* that will last for ever, and that's because our God is Love, and God lasts for ever and ever. What kind of loving things do we do? (Share ideas.)

One day, at the end of everything, God will gather up all that goodness and love into his heaven, so it's safe for ever, and not one bit of it will be lost.

Praying

God of love, we thank you
for all the love in our world.
What a good thing that love
lasts for ever and never wears out!

Activities

On the sheet there is the shape of a heart. The children cover this with glue and then sprinkle glitter, sand or tiny off-cuts of shiny paper on to the page. At the moment they can't see what will stay and what won't, but when they shake their sheet, the thing that lasts is the love.

PEARL DIVERS

Aim: To begin to look at what the Bible tells us about the end of time.

Starter

Predicting the weather. Beforehand prepare a large notebook with different types of weather pictures on each page. (The pages need to be thick enough for the pictures not to show through.) Everyone takes a turn in giving the weather forecast for the next day, and then you turn the page to reveal what it really is, and so on.

Teaching

Predicting the weather in some countries is dead simple because it's nearly always the same. In other climate zones, the weather is very changeable, which makes it hard to predict. Like the weather, some things in life are pretty certain, while others are things we have no idea about.

Today we're going to look at something which none of us knows much about at all, except that one day it will happen. It's the end of the world. We hear and read about all kinds of horror stories, where great chunks of meteors crash into the earth, or there's a nuclear war which kills all the people and the environment, or the sun suddenly flares up and swallows up earth. (Place down a few appropriate paperbacks and film fliers.)

Jesus helped his students (and us) to look at what the end of everything might really be like. He explained that there will be all kinds of terrible things going on beforehand, just as we read about in the newspapers and many poor people are having to live through at the moment – things like wars and rumours of wars, famines where many people starve because they have no food, and natural disasters like floods and earthquakes. (Place down appropriate pictures from newspapers and magazines.)

(Place down a cross with a question mark over it.) Do these things mean the end of everything is here? Jesus says they are like the 'birth pains' but they aren't the end (or the 'birth') itself. Jesus warns all his followers that we'll need to be on our guard, in case all the terrible things happening make us lose our faith in the God of love. (Cover the cross completely with the terrible pictures.) The ones who will be saved for ever are those who keep their faith (clear away the pictures so the cross is visible again) and have lived out their lives with love (place your hand on the cross), guiding others along the right pathways, and looking after those who need help. That was Jesus' way, and that is to be our way as his followers.

One thing we are sure about is that nothing which is loving, kind or true is going to ever disappear, because God will gather it all up safely. That means that the people who are kind and loving and honest will be the heroes and heroines at the end of time, whether they are rich or poor, famous or completely unknown in this world. All goodness gets a hero's welcome!

Praying

Lead me, Father, through this life,
along the pathway of your love.
May I keep to it, help others to find it, and,
one day, may it lead me straight into your heaven!

Activities

There is a 'Which lasts longest?' activity on the sheet, and the children will be making a model pathway of love that leads to heaven, following the instructions. They will each need a card base, and some modelling medium – which could be clay or plasticine.

GOLD PANNERS

Aim: To explore how the kingdom of heaven is both in the present and the future.

Starter

Beforehand make a number of inkblot shapes on different pieces of paper, and invite everyone to say what shapes they see in the shapes.

Teaching

In inkblots, clouds and shadows, we can often see pictures. Some people would say that what we see shows our character! Today's readings look into the misty future – to the end of time, and two prophets tell us what they see. One of the prophets is Daniel, and the other is Jesus himself.

First read the passage from Daniel. What pictures does the prophet see? Is it terrifying, hopeful, or a mixture? On a sheet of paper headed 'At that time', write the events in different coloured pens to reflect their mood.

Now look at the Gospel for today. Once again, write the events on the sheet in different coloured pens. Does Jesus seem to be excited about this time, or concerned for his followers? What is it that bothers him? He is wanting to impress on his followers the need to be careful and on our guard, in readiness for these times.

We are left with the sense that it will be a frightening time leading up to the Day of the Lord, with evil multiplying and many being led astray. But there is still the strong certainty that through it all the true followers will be kept safe, and nothing good or loving will be lost. Whatever people are really like will be shown for everyone to see – our motives and secret thoughts, as well as what we choose to let people see normally. It's quite a thought.

Praying

You show me the path of life;
in your presence there is fullness of joy,
and in your right hand are pleasures for evermore.
(From Psalm 15)

Activities

On the sheet they are encouraged to see how the kingdom of heaven is both now and in the future, and there is space for them to try a watercolour painting of the Daniel or the Mark reading.

CHRIST THE KING

Thought for the day

Jesus Christ is the everlasting King whose kingdom is not of this world, but grows in the hearts of his people and lasts for ever.

Reflection on the readings

Daniel 7:13-14
Psalm 92
Apocalypse 1:5-8
John 18:33-37

It is always difficult to describe heavenly things in terms of our human experience, but Daniel tries to give a faithful account of his vision of the one he calls the Ancient of Days, sensing the everness of his wisdom and power, his piercing integrity and all-knowing perception. Daniel witnesses the moment of one like a son of man entering heaven and receiving the authority and dominion which are his for ever.

We who have met Jesus in the Gospels, and heard him refer often to himself as 'Son of Man', recognise the one who enters heaven as the Lord and Saviour who loved us enough to die for us. The Gospel for today refers us to Jesus' conversation with Pilate, just before his crucifixion. Jesus tells the Roman governor, who represents the worldly power and authority of the whole Roman Empire, that his kingdom is not of this world. He is not therefore a threat to the authorities in terms of violent uprising and revolt. The kingdom of God is a lot more powerful, far-reaching and long-lasting than any empire!

In the reading from Apocalypse we are back in the world of vision and prophecy, written for those who had witnessed the crucifixion and resurrection of Christ, the outpouring of God's Spirit in tongues of flame, and the business of living as followers of Christ in an often hostile world. There will come a time when Christ the everlasting King will appear in all his glory, and every eye shall see him.

The Church's year has come full circle. We began last Advent by preparing ourselves for the coming of Jesus, both at his birth into our world and at the second coming. We have walked with Jesus through his life and ministry, led mainly this year by Mark's dynamic Gospel account. We have watched Jesus and listened to him, sorrowed and rejoiced with him. We have seen the gradual understanding of the disciples and their transformation through the gift of the Holy Spirit. And now, as we celebrate Jesus, King of all ages and nations, born for this, living and dying and rising for this, we proclaim the basic Christian belief which will enable us to press forward into our Advent preparations: Jesus Christ is Lord!

Discussion starters

1. How does this faith we celebrate today transform our outlook and enable us to face suffering?

2. What is your vision of heaven?

All-stage talk

Beforehand prepare a long length of lining paper on which the alphabet is written clearly. Fix it up where everyone can see it, or ask people to hold it. (Please don't make them hold it high or their arms will drop off!)

Claim that on this sheet you have the whole of the Bible, the complete works of Shakespeare, every love letter ever written, every postcard and Christmas letter ever sent. You also have the names of every person and every place.

At this point a pre-arranged person walks out to protest. Preachers are supposed to tell the truth and here you are telling porky pies. You can't possibly have all that on this sheet of paper. You've only got a few letters!

Meet the challenge by inviting them to find their own name from the sheet, which they spell out letter by letter, and have to admit that they are on the sheet after all. Get someone else to find 'To be or not to be' and 'Come, Lord Jesus'. These are also found to be there.

Our God is like A to Z – the beginning and the end of everything, all thoughts and ideas, all creation, all love, all hope, all existence. That's why we worship God – God has always been. God is, at this very moment now. (Pause for everyone to become aware of that amazing fact.) And God will always be, for ever. God's kingdom is wherever Jesus reigns as our King. And that means wherever people say, 'Yes!' to Jesus, 'I really want to be in your kingdom!'

And we know what being in Jesus' kingdom is like, don't we? It's full of love and joy and peace, full of forgiveness and patience, full of hope and healing. Today it's as if we've brought out our flags to wave as we celebrate Jesus as our wonderful, everlasting King, who sets our lives dancing!

All-age ideas

- If you have bunting stored away for summer fairs, bring it out today and festoon the entrance to the church.
- Make the flower arrangements reflect the royal dignity and power of Jesus, with gold and scarlet colours, and perhaps including a gold crown.
- Use two voices in the Gospel for the conversation between Jesus and Pilate.

Prayer of the Faithful

Celebrant
As children of the kingdom,
let us make our prayers to the eternal God,
who loves us.

Reader
We pray that the kingdom may come
in the worldwide communities
of those who believe in Jesus Christ –
may our lives enthrone him.

Silence

Spirit of the living God:
may your kingdom come.

We pray that the kingdom may come
in the nations of our world
and in their leadership;
for God's values to take root and grow;
for each person to be respected
as a beloved child of God.

Silence

Spirit of the living God:
may your kingdom come.

We pray that the kingdom may come
in our homes and families,
our neighbourhoods and places of work,
in all thinking, all speaking and all action.

Silence

Spirit of the living God:
may your kingdom come.

We pray that the kingdom may come
in all hospitals and surgeries,
and in every place of pain and sadness.

Silence

Spirit of the living God:
may your kingdom come.

We pray that the kingdom may come
in the final stages of earthly life,
in the journey through death,
and in the awakening to eternal life.

Silence

Spirit of the living God:
may your kingdom come.

We make our prayer with Mary,
Mother of Christ the King:
Hail, Mary . . .

The God of Peace is listening;
in this silence,
we name those we know
who are in any particular need.

Silence

Celebrant
Most merciful and loving Father,
we ask you to hear and answer our prayers
which we offer in the name of Jesus.
Amen.

TREASURE SEEKERS

Aim: To celebrate Jesus as our King.

Starter

Everyone helps decorate the room with paper chains and gold crowns. Then sing and dance to some praise songs, using recorded music such as the Kid's Praise albums.

Teaching

Talk about the dreams we have, and then tell the children the vision of Daniel as a story, like this.

Long, long ago there lived a man called Daniel. Daniel worshipped God and tried his best to live God's way. In the days of King Belshazzar, king of Babylon, Daniel had a dream. It was such an amazing dream that he couldn't get it out of his head. Daniel kept thinking about his dream, and in the end he realised that the dream had been given to him by God. So Daniel thought to himself, 'If God has shown me these amazing things in my dream, I expect he wants me to tell all the others about it.' So Daniel wrote his dream down, and this is it.

'As I looked, I saw a great throne put in its place, and God Almighty sat down on the throne. His clothes were as shining white as snow. His hair was white like sheep's wool. His throne was flaming with fire, blazing and glowing. From the throne there ran a river of fire, pouring out, and burning brightly. Thousands and thousands of people were standing before the throne, as if they were waiting for something. The books were opened.

'Then I saw in front of me what looked like a man. He was coming with the clouds of heaven, closer and closer to Almighty God, and they led him up to the throne. This man was made King over all the people in every place and every time. And as I looked I knew that he would be King for ever and ever and ever.'

That was the dream which Daniel dreamed long, long ago. Long before Jesus had been born. And yet God had shown Daniel a picture of heaven, and he had seen Jesus, coming into heaven and being made King for ever.

Praying

Jesus, you are my King.
Reign in me and my home,
reign in my life for ever.
Amen.

Activities

Together make a large collage picture of Daniel's dream. Have the outline drawn already (based on the picture below) and bring some shiny flames of fire for the children to stick on to the throne and the fiery river. They can stick wool on to the clouds and coloured tissue paper to the rest of the picture. Call the picture: Daniel's dream about heaven.

On the sheet the same picture is there for them to colour or build with collage, and they can find the matching crowns and flames.

PEARL DIVERS

Aim: To look at the kind of king Jesus is.

Starter

Sit in a circle and share some of the dreams we remember.

Teaching

Give each child their sheet on which they can draw Daniel's dream as you read it to them. Can they work out who the 'son of man' is that Daniel saw in his vision? Explain that, as with all dreams, it's picture language. So why a throne? Why fire? They show us God's great power, and fire also purifies gold and silver, brings light into darkness and has to be treated with great respect.

What kind of king is Jesus shown to be in this dream? He's the King of all time and space, not for a little while but for ever.

Just before Jesus was crucified he was taken to

Pilate, the Roman governor, who wanted to ask Jesus about him being accused of being a king. Was it true? Have the Gospel written out as a script, with two people reading it.

Yes, Jesus was a King, but he didn't have earthly power like Pilate, for instance. How was it different? Jesus reigns in people's hearts and souls. Our lives become his kingdom's territory when we invite Jesus into them. You can tell a life where Jesus reigns. The person is gradually growing wiser and more loving, finding it easier to forgive, and they find they are wanting to reach out to others and do good. Perhaps they have already begun to notice some of these things happening in their own lives.

Praying

Our Father, who art in heaven,
hallowed be thy name;
thy kingdom come;
thy will be done on earth
as it is in heaven.
Give us this day our daily bread;
and forgive us our trespasses,
as we forgive those who trespass against us;
and lead us not into temptation,
but deliver us from evil.
Amen.

Activities

They can complete their picture of Daniel's vision, cut it out and mount it on coloured paper beside the decorated Lord's Prayer. There is also an alphabet for them to find the names of some pictures.

GOLD PANNERS

Aim: To recognise Jesus Christ as the everlasting King of all.

Starter

Give everyone a large post-it note on which they write ten sentences beginning with 'I am . . .' Then they stick their note to themselves and go round reading one another's statements.

Teaching

It's not easy to decide on ten 'I am . . .' statements, but taken altogether they do give a little idea of who we are. Today, the last Sunday of the Church's year, we are in a way summing up everything we know about Jesus Christ, both on earth and in heaven, and the shorthand for all of that is that he is Christ the King. We'll try to unpack it a bit.

Begin by reading Daniel's vision. Point out that Daniel was writing long before Jesus had come, yet he 'sees' Jesus entering heaven and being made king.

Now go to the Gospel, reading it with different people taking the different parts. Pilate's job, as Roman governor, is to establish whether this so-called king is likely to pose a threat to the Roman empire. As Jesus says, that would be so if his kingdom were 'of this world'. But it isn't. In what way is the kingdom of heaven not 'of this world'? If the territory of the kingdom of heaven is not geographical, where is it found? (Think back to the parables of the kingdom, and all Jesus' teaching about kingdom living.)

So today we see Jesus at his most weak and vulnerable, humanly speaking, on earth, and entering heaven in glory. All of that is the same Jesus, the Servant King who was obedient even to death on a cross.

Finally look at the reading from Apocalypse, where Jesus Christ is seen as the faithful witness, the firstborn from the dead, and the ruler of the kings of the earth. We are reminded that Jesus is the visible image of the unseen God, totally faithful to speaking out God's words and revealing his love to us. And one day he will come in glory, seen by everybody.

As we look back over the past year, and all we have learnt of Jesus, it makes us want to worship, and proclaim with Christians all over the world and all through history, that Jesus Christ is Lord!

Praying

Jesus is Lord!
Creation's voice proclaims it,
for by his power each tree and flower
was planned and made.
Jesus is Lord!
The universe declares it;
sun, moon and stars in heaven cry:
Jesus is Lord!

(Taken from the song *Jesus is Lord!* by David J. Mansell
© 1982 Springtide/Word Music (UK)/CopyCare)

Activities

In the activities on the sheet they are helped to hold in balance the power and glory of Jesus' kingship with his humility and obedience – the Servant King. They try to catch hold of the image of heaven as described by Daniel, and look at the idea of the words of the Gloria and God's presence in past, present and future.

APPENDIX

Holy, most holy, all holy the Lord
(Second Sunday of Lent, Pearl Divers)

Ho - ly, most ho - ly, all ho - ly the Lord, in

Capo 1   D   G   D

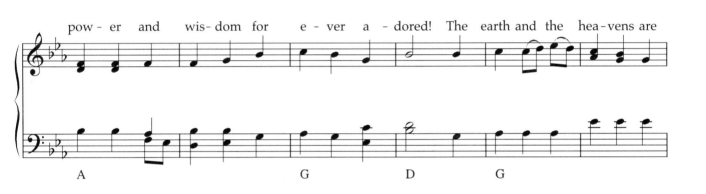

pow - er and wis - dom for e - ver a - dored! The earth and the hea - vens are

A   G   D   G

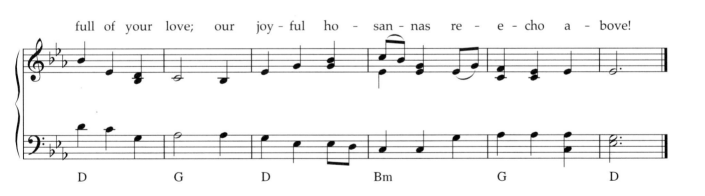

full of your love; our joy - ful ho - san - nas re - e - cho a - bove!

D   G   D   Bm   G   D

Jesus, you love me
(Sixteenth Sunday of the Year)

Je - sus, you love me, you love me ve - ry much;

I love you, Je - sus, I love you ve - ry much!

Theme from Beethoven's *Pastoral Symphony*, arr. Kate Gallaher
This arrangement © Copyright 1999 Kevin Mayhew Ltd